# Transforming America's Military

# Transforming America's Military

*edited by* Hans Binnendijk

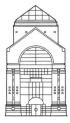

NATIONAL DEFENSE UNIVERSITY PRESS
WASHINGTON, D.C.
2002

Opinions, conclusions, and recommendations expressed or implied within are solely those of the contributors and do not necessarily represent the views of the Defense Department or any other agency of the Federal Government. Cleared for public release; distribution unlimited.

Portions of this book may be quoted or reprinted without permission, provided that a standard source credit line is included. NDU Press would appreciate a courtesy copy of reprints or reviews.

Library of Congress Cataloging-in-Publication Data

Transforming America's military / Hans Binnendijk, editor.
    p.cm.
  ISBN 1–57906–057–9
  1. United States—Armed Forces—Reorganization. I. Binnendijk, Hans.
UA23 .T69 2002
355.3'0973—dc21

2002074294

First Printing, August 2002
Second Printing, February 2003
Third Printing, June 2004

NDU Press publications are sold by the U.S. Government Printing Office. For ordering information, call (202) 512–1800 or write to the Superintendent of Documents, U.S. Government Printing Office, Washington, D.C. 20402. For GPO publications on-line access their Web site at: http://www.access.gpo.gov/su_docs/sale.html.

For current publications of the Institute for National Strategic Studies, consult the National Defense University Web site at: http://www.ndu.edu.

# Contents

# Part III—Coordinating Transformed Military Operations

# Part IV—Broader Aspects of Transformation

# Illustrations

## Tables

## Figures

# Acknowledgments

It has taken a team to produce this volume. First, I thank the authors of each chapter for their willingness to meet with me many times to discuss the evolution of this book and their contributions to it. Second, I thank Richard L. Kugler for his conceptual contributions to the overall structure of the book and to many of its core arguments. Another member of the team was Major John Davis, USAF, who helped orchestrate the authors and managed the draft chapters. Next, a special thanks goes to Teresa J. Lawson, who edited each chapter and provided invaluable advice as the book matured. Thanks also go to Leigh Caraher and Gina Cordero, who helped me proofread the final manuscript.

Finally, thanks are due to the editorial staff of National Defense University Press—General Editor William R. Bode and editors George C. Maerz, Lisa M. Yambrick, and Jeffrey D. Smotherman—who brought this publication to completion under the supervision of Robert A. Silano, Director of Publications.

# Introduction

Hans Binnendijk

M ilitary transformation is the act of creating and harnessing a revolution in military affairs. It requires developing new technologies, operational concepts, and organizational structures to conduct war in dramatically new ways. The United States is undertaking such a transformation to tackle its 21ˢᵗ century missions. A properly transformed military can develop significant advantages over a potential enemy. But the process also introduces risks that, if not properly managed, could dangerously undermine military capability.

This book, therefore, sets out the arguments for a purposeful and measured transformation that relies on sound experimentation as the basis for change, rather than the riskier strategy, proposed by some, of skipping a generation of technology. We argue that change must tie all of the services together in joint transformation efforts. Similarly, we must not neglect our coalition partners. A successful transformation will be one that has been conceived broadly to include homeland defense, space, cyberspace, and, though they may seem mundane, crucial reforms in weapons procurement and logistics.

Historically, revolutions in military affairs have had a powerful impact on both society and the nature of warfare. For example, effective development of the stirrup after the 8ᵗʰ century in Europe allowed mounted warriors to dominate their immediate regions and contributed to the development of the feudal state. Feudalism in its turn was destroyed when improved artillery in the early 15ᵗʰ century meant that castles could be successfully attacked. The development of large sailing ships armed with numerous cannons in the early 16ᵗʰ century facilitated the growth of European colonialism. Napoleon's *levée en masse* and the rise of the large "citizen army" helped create modern nationalism. In the mid-19ᵗʰ century, improvements in rifling, breech loading, and repeating rifles led to mass carnage on the battlefield, which spurred the development of defensive trench warfare. In the 1930s, improvements in armor, sea power, and air power returned the initiative to the offense. Nuclear weapons produced the Cold War: for four decades, the most powerful offensive weapons were dominant but could not be used for fear of massive retaliation.

Three examples illustrate the power that technology and new operational concepts can have on the battlefield. At Crécy in 1346, the English king Edward III deployed his longbowmen, protected by dismounted knights, in a new form of combined arms warfare. Against them, the French army under Philip IV lost more than 1,200 knights. Nearly 70 years later, King Henry V used similar tactics at Agincourt, this time on the offensive. France was again defeated, and England was able to lay claim to large portions of France.

Napoleon standardized his equipment so that broken matériel could be quickly repaired, and he developed new ways to package food. He was thus able to field his large citizen armies with reliable equipment for long periods of time. These innovations, plus his brilliant use of the cannon, let Napoleon dominate Europe militarily, until he overreached.

Germany and France had equivalent equipment at the outset of World War II, but Germany concentrated its armor and combined it with attack aircraft and radios in the new operational concept called blitzkrieg. Meanwhile, France planned to re-fight World War I more effectively; its armor was dispersed throughout its forces, and it relied excessively on the Maginot Line and the Ardennes as buffers. While only a small fraction of the German force was organized for blitzkrieg (10–15 percent), this was enough of a spearhead to let the Germans overwhelm France in a matter of weeks. Eventually, Hitler also overreached.[1]

Not all efforts to combine new technology and operational concepts are successful; not all result in victory. During the 1950s, for example, the United States set out to transform its military with new nuclear capabilities. Tactical nuclear weapons were integrated into many military units; operational concepts envisioned the early use of nuclear weapons on the battlefield. By the mid-1960s, however, it became clear that use of these weapons would be limited, both by deterrence and by world opinion. The nuclear weapons that had been placed at the core of the new force could not be used. The military that had been built in the 1950s around nuclear weapons found itself fighting in Vietnam without them. This lesson must be kept in mind as the United States proceeds with a new military transformation.

## The Basis of Transformation

Today's military transformation is based on many new technologies, and perhaps the most important is information technology. The impact of information on the battlefield was first displayed during Operation *Desert Storm* with new and highly accurate precision strike weapons. Two years later, Alvin and Heidi Toffler pointed out that nations make war the way they create wealth.[2] Just as the agricultural and industrial ages each had their own distinctive style of warfare, now the information age calls for transformation to a new kind of information-based warfare.

Accordingly, in the mid-1990s, the Joint Chiefs of Staff published *Joint Vision 2010* and *Joint Vision 2020* to guide military change in the information age. The underlying theory was that the U.S. military would be able to use a *system of systems* to concentrate long-range firepower, instead of massing battle platforms against key enemy nodes. American firepower would be brought to bear concurrently rather than sequentially to cause the quick collapse of an enemy's resolve. The key concepts involved going beyond mobilization and mass to emphasize speed and information.

The transformation effort was started by the Clinton administration and boosted by the Bush administration. The Quadrennial Defense Review (QDR) 2001 created new goals for transformation: to protect the homeland and our information networks; to project and sustain power in distant theaters and deny our enemies sanctuary there; and to leverage information and space technology. The events of September 11, 2001, refocused elements of military transformation on homeland security. By the end of 2001, a new transformation budget had been earmarked and a "Transformation Czar" was appointed at the Department of Defense (DOD).[3]

Meanwhile, each of the military services has been developing new operational concepts to implement *Joint Vision 2020*. The Navy has focused on *network-centric* warfare, using new information technologies to link the forces together digitally. The Air Force has concentrated on *effects-based operations*, which assess how best to destroy the connections between elements of an enemy's political and economic networks with minimal collateral damage. The Army has focused on *rapid and decisive operations*, that is, reaching the conflict quickly and acting before the enemy can react. Elements of these three strategies are merging together. This book is designed to consider where we should go from here.

## How the Book Is Organized

Part I of this book explores the foundations of today's military transformation: new missions, new technologies, and new operational concepts. Part II assesses the progress that is being made in this effort by each of America's military services. Part III analyzes the coordination and integration of these separate service efforts, while noting the capabilities gap being created with our allies. Part IV reviews broader aspects of military transformation, particularly those arising after the September 11 attacks.

### Part I—Foundations of Transformation

Developing the capability to perform necessary missions more effectively and with fewer casualties is the underlying purpose of military transformation. Chapter 1 by Sam Tangredi argues that decisions on how to transform must follow from a careful consideration of the priorities of these objectives and missions. During the Cold War and for the past decade, priorities were determined by the spectrum-of-conflict model, which placed a premium on high-intensity conflict, despite its low probability of occurrence. As a result, the 1990s witnessed a readiness-versus-engagement debate that deprecated the value of military involvement in operations other than war. Tangredi argues that, especially after September 11, the United States needs to adopt a new hierarchy-of-missions model that identifies survival interests, vital interests, and value interests. Resource allocations should be made based on this hierarchy of missions. The QDR 2001 moves U.S. strategy away from the task of winning two major theater conflicts nearly simultaneously and allows the military new flexibility to deal with a broader array of missions. It thus implicitly moves in the direction of a new hierarchy of missions. Tangredi believes that the National Military Strategy and *Joint Vision 2020* must also be adjusted to account for these new missions because they put too much emphasis on fighting major theater wars against a similarly organized opponent.

Technology is the great enabler of military transformation. Chapter 2 by Thomas Hone and Norman Friedman reminds us that militarily significant technologies have often developed simultaneously in different nations, and it is the side that can use the technology most effectively that gets the edge. The process of transformation, consequently, requires developing a vision of how new technologies might benefit the military, funding the research and development of new technologies into weapons, maintaining an industry that can produce equipment embodying the new technologies, developing service doctrine to use those technologies effectively, and training troops to use the new capabilities. None of these steps can be skipped.

Hone and Friedman demonstrate dramatically how even a wildly imaginative vision could become reality by looking back a century to H.G. Wells' novel *War of the Worlds*. In this novel, the Martian enemy uses space capabilities to support its military campaigns; it fires heat rays and chemical weapons; it dominates the battlefield with armored walking machines; it possesses a global command and control system. One hundred years ago, these ideas were at the furthest reaches of fiction, yet today, the United States possesses each of these capabilities in various forms. Chapter 2 projects the impact of emerging technologies over time and identifies dozens of potentially transformational technologies, many of them, especially in the information area, developed primarily by the commercial sector. Hone and Friedman suggest that DOD needs to rely more on the commercial sector as it develops its concepts of network-centric warfare.

What should be the strategy for transformation that is based on the demands of new missions and the capabilities of new technologies? Chapter 3, which I wrote with Richard Kugler, explores both the evolutionary and the revolutionary approaches that have tended to clash during the past decade, both within DOD and at the national level. Reviewing a century of history, the chapter concludes that neither extreme makes sense by itself. The key lesson from World War II is that getting operational concepts right is as important as possessing new technology. The lesson from the attempts at building a force around nuclear weapons during the first decades of the Cold War is not to base a wholesale transformation on a single design concept or technology. The lesson from the post-Vietnam period is that a pluralism of ideas and organizations, though turbulent, may yield a better outcome than a single plan controlled from the top.

Applying these lessons, the chapter argues for a blend of the evolutionary and revolutionary approaches and notes that the 2001 QDR moves in this direction. Such a purposeful and measured transformation should have certain characteristics. It should:

- rely heavily on vigorous experimentation to test new concepts and technologies before deployment
- maximize joint experiments and operations
- focus as much on the medium term (6–10 years) as on the long-term
- reengineer the current force to get results in the medium term
- blend a high-tech spearhead force (perhaps 10 percent of the overall force) with improved legacy systems
- hedge against possible failure of experimental systems.

The chapter ends with an examination of 10 operational concepts that are being considered by defense analysts to build and employ a transformed force.

## Part II—Transforming the Services

Part II analyzes the transformation now taking place in the services, beginning with chapter 4 on the U.S. Army by Thomas McNaugher and Bruce Nardulli. The Army is considering the most ambitious transformation of any of the Armed Forces. Its post-Cold War missions have shifted dramatically from tank warfare on the plains of Europe to rapid and decisive operations in distant and hard-to-reach theaters. The Army experimented with digitization in the 1990s, inserting computers into armored vehicles and infantry platoons in an effort to provide a common operational picture and lift the fog of war. The focus, however, was still on heavy divisions. Operation *Enduring Freedom* in Afghanistan has demonstrated both the strengths of the Army's Special Operations capabilities and the limits of using existing heavy legacy forces for operations that require agility.

The Army plans to deal with this transition by proceeding on three parallel tracks, developing simultaneously an Objective Force for the long term, a medium-term Interim Force, and a Legacy Force to hedge against the risk of failures or shortcomings with the other two. The key element in the Army's long-term vision is the Future Combat System: small (16–20 ton) vehicles networked together will replace both the 70-ton M–1 Abrams tank and the 32-ton M–2 Bradley fighting vehicle. The Army is betting that dramatic improvements in information technology, sensors, active protection systems, robotics, and weapons technology can replace heavy armor and existing firepower. The authors argue that there is risk in this approach and that if these technologies develop too slowly, evolutionary options remain open. For example, the Army could rely more on prepositioning of equipment, using the Interim Brigade Combat Teams as the Army's rapid early-deployment force, examining more joint force options, and considering a mixed hybrid force rather than the homogenous divisions envisioned for the Objective Force. The authors argue that, with regard to the war on terrorism and homeland security, the entire relationship between Army Special Operations Forces and regular forces must be reexamined and that National Guard and Reserve units may need reorganization to pursue homeland missions. The Army will have the opportunity to hedge its technology bets and consider reorganizing for new missions as its transformation proceeds.

The mission of the naval services—the Navy and Marines—has changed even more fundamentally than that of the Army; the Cold War mission of controlling the high seas has given way to a mission of facilitating intervention on shore. The Navy also has become a prominent air force; in fact, virtually every ship serves as a platform for aircraft and missiles. Chapter 5 by William O'Neil points outs that the Navy has adapted to this new mission and capability by using existing naval platforms in new ways. The Navy must be inherently conservative about change because its platforms take from 10 to 15 years to conceive and build, and they must last for another 35 years. Much of the change required for the Navy to perform new missions better has therefore taken place with information technology, both to link dispersed ships together for a more coordinated network-centric striking capability and to provide greater accuracy for its missiles.

O'Neil assesses issues that will determine the future shape of our naval forces and concludes that the Navy is currently on the right track. He discounts concerns that the Navy will not be able to gain access to a potential enemy's littoral to support land-based operations, arguing that no potential enemy has spent the resources to gain a capability even remotely like that of the former Soviet Union during the Cold War. While it is true that mines, missiles, and small, fast craft are relatively cheap and improving in capability, American counters to these threats have improved even faster. He sees no need, therefore, to reshape U.S. naval strategy to deal with a threat that appears relatively insignificant. He rebuts arguments for smaller carriers and a proposed fleet of smaller, faster boats designed to operate in littoral regions. He sees a clear role for unmanned vehicles both in the air and under the sea but cautions against using these systems for operations such as close-in air support. He argues that, despite the advent of highly accurate missiles, carrier-based aircraft will remain at the core of naval strike capabilities. The Marines, he notes, have adapted doctrine to develop an expeditionary maneuver warfare capability, but he cautions that future plans of the Corps rely heavily on short takeoff and vertical landing aircraft (for example, the Osprey and Joint Strike Fighter) that are vulnerable to technical and budgetary problems. In an appendix to this chapter, Bing West further analyzes the Marine Corps concept of expeditionary maneuver warfare. After September 11, the Navy has taken on yet another new mission: supporting the Coast Guard in efforts to protect our own littoral from terrorist attack.

During the past two decades, notes David Ochmanek in chapter 6, the Air Force has made remarkable strides in dominating air operations, controlling and exploiting space, identifying potential targets in all weather conditions, and attacking both moving and fixed targets with high precision. Whereas during the Vietnam War it took a rough average of 170 bombs to destroy a small fixed target, today it takes just one bomb, which can be delivered by a stealthy B–2 loaded with 16 such weapons. The Air Force has already employed many of the advantages that are flowing from modern technology, and thus its future transformation plans will be evolutionary compared to those of the Army.

The Air Force now operates in three domains at once: air, space, and cyberspace. Ochmanek says that the key question for the future Air Force is whether, in the face of looming new threats and resource constraints, the United States can retain its current degree of dominance. The answer to that question depends on how well the Air Force can meet certain challenges, such as overcoming antiaccess capabilities, destroying small mobile targets, operating despite advance air defenses, destroying deeply buried facilities, assuring continuity of space operations, halting ground invasions from the air, and improving both command and control as well as deployability. Ochmanek assesses three key choices facing the Air Force in its efforts to meet these challenges. First, despite the recent successes of bombers in Kosovo and Afghanistan, Ochmanek argues against dramatically decreasing fighters and increasing bombers (currently at a 9 to 1 ratio) and suggests instead that more needs to be done to assure forward basing and to harden forward aircraft shelters. Second, he argues that the Air Force continues to need both stealthy penetrating platforms and standoff weapons, such as cruise missiles, because many missions require that aircrews get close enough to observe their targets. In the short run, the Air Force needs to replace its depleted inventory of cruise missiles, while, in the longer run, unmanned combat air vehicles may be able to perform many of the more dangerous missions now flown by fighter pilots. Third, Ochmanek argues that, despite the potential advantages of developing a space strike capability, it will be too costly and will remain vulnerable to antisatellite weapons. He concludes that straightforward improvements to the Air Force seem to offer more leverage than wholesale changes in force structure and operational concepts.

## Part III—Coordinating Transformed Military Operations

Part III focuses on how to assess and coordinate transformation programs, how to integrate the efforts of the individual services, and how to bring American allies along. In chapter 7, Paul Davis distinguishes between changes required in the medium term, which need careful management and pragmatic engineering, and those that will be required further out (between about 2010 and 2025). Changes that are further out require exploratory experiments and wide-open research and development. Drawing lessons from business and the history of World War II, Davis presents 10 principles for future transformation. Among them, he urges fully exploiting technology, anticipating the nature of future warfare, securing political and economic support for transformation, organizing around the capability to accomplish particular military operations rather than open-ended functions, and laying the groundwork for later adaptations. Applying these principles to the current era, he expresses concern that there is no broad and systematic DOD effort to understand future warfare, that there may be excessive focus on a particular notion of war, and that a better analytical system is needed to assure that good options are generated. Davis proposes a new mission-system analysis that would allow the Secretary of Defense to use capabilities-based planning to consider a wider array of alternative plans for future force structure. To help implement this approach, Davis suggests establishing rapid-exploitation laboratories that bring together operators, technologists, and analysts to pursue mission-oriented concepts through rapid prototyping and spiral exploration.

To achieve its full impact, military transformation in the information age must be joint, not centered separately in the different services. Indeed, the Joint Staff champions efforts to integrate the capabilities of the individual services, while the Joint Forces Command has overall responsibility for joint experimentation and for forming joint force packages. Chapter 8 by Douglas Macgregor calls for a bolder approach. Supported by two recent defense reviews by David Gompert and James McCarthy, Macgregor argues that the United States must abandon the World War II mode of relatively independent, sequential missions accomplished by service components under a regional warfighting commander in chief. He calls for rapidly deployable standing joint forces made up of units from different services that train and exercise together and use common command and control, intelligence assets, and logistics systems. Echelons would be reduced, and a pool of available land, naval, and air forces would be created on a rotational readiness basis. Joint operational concepts are needed so that all parts of the force see the same scenario. The multitude of single-service component commanders, Macgregor concludes, should be supplanted by joint command and control elements.

Transformation creates issues that affect our allies, as Charles Barry explores in chapter 9. Unless it wishes to become an isolated superpower, the United States will probably fight future battles as part of an international coalition, based in large measure on the North Atlantic Treaty Organization (NATO) allies. But the recent wars in the Persian Gulf, Kosovo, and Afghanistan have demonstrated that a significant gap exists between American and allied capabilities. The problem lies both with constrained European defense budgets (together, only about half the size of the U.S. budget) and with differing visions of the European role in the world. Barry argues that this gap may be smaller than is normally believed and that a concerted program of action can close it without bankrupting European treasuries. Without such an effort, however, the gap will grow to the detriment of the Alliance.

Barry reviews the current status of Europe's militaries and concludes that their armies and navies have modernized many of their legacy forces. The real problem, however, rests with airpower, secure communications, command and control, and logistics. Even airpower may improve as the Eurofighter and Joint Strike Fighter come on-line. One problem is that Europe's energies are focused on equipping the European Rapid Reaction Force, which is designed primarily for peace operations rather than high-intensity conflict. There is no vision in Europe of how to transform its militaries for major combat missions in cooperation with the United States. Barry proposes a set of initiatives aimed at correcting this situation.

### Part IV—Broader Aspects of Transformation

Part IV reviews broader aspects of military transformation. The attacks of September 11 pierced America's sense of invulnerability and made strengthening the homefront the Nation's highest priority. In chapter 10, Michèle Flournoy presents a three-pronged strategy to manage the new risk from terrorism. First, prevention must be carried out in an aggressive and proactive manner, potentially even including offensive action. Key to the success of preventive efforts is engagement abroad and better intelligence. Acknowledging the difficult intelligence problem presented by trying to penetrate small cells in more than 60 countries around the world, she argues that the job can be done better by aiming data collection at the right target, better interagency and international sharing of data, more rapid fusing of data, and more effective red-teaming to predict terrorist moves.

Second, Flournoy calls for a strategy of protection, including missile defenses, massive manhunts when necessary, and day-to-day security measures. These efforts require better coordination among an array of Federal, state, and local offices. The problem is so complex that clear priorities must be set. Third, a response strategy must include training and equipping first responders and improving procedures for continuity of government and for restoring the provision of essential services. A priority should be placed on countering the bioterrorism threat. Flournoy calls for a major public-private initiative on the scale of the Apollo Program to deal with it. She does recommend several other initiatives to be undertaken by the Assistant to the President for Homeland Security but also argues that, in the long run, a more comprehensive office is required. She also recommends establishment of a new commander in chief (CINC) for Homeland Defense and urges efforts to prepare elements of the National Guard for homeland security missions. Many of these suggestions have now been adopted by the Bush administration.

The new focus on homeland security has implications for transformation of U.S. strategic forces. It has reinforced the Bush administration's interest in building missile defenses, and in the process, transforming the nature of nuclear deterrence. The administration has taken three key steps in this effort: deciding to withdraw from the 1972 Anti-Ballistic Missile Treaty, issuing a new Nuclear Posture Review, and agreeing with Russia to dramatic reductions in deployed force. Taken together, these steps suggest an alternative paradigm for strategic stability; though somewhat vague, it appears to be based more on defense than on mutual assured destruction. In chapter 11, Peter Wilson and Richard Sokolsky review both the offensive and defensive elements of the equation and conclude that much of the Cold War theology still governs American strategic planning.

With regard to missile defense, the Bush administration has set aside the ground-based midcourse intercept architecture of the previous administration in favor of an intensified research and development (R&D) program and the prospect of a multilayered architecture that is as yet undefined. Missile defense technology has demonstrated some successes in the hit-to-kill concept and the airborne laser, but there have also been setbacks such as the Navy Area Wide System and the Space-Based Infrared Sensor System. Wilson and Sokolsky argue that the deployment of space-based weapons would constitute crossing a red line that might provoke a dramatic reaction from the Russians and others. On the offensive side, they applaud the agreement with Russia to reduce U.S. operationally deployed warheads from about 6,000 today to a range of 1,700 to 2,200. However, they are concerned that the remaining force will not be taken off alert status and that the eliminated warheads will not be destroyed but placed in a ready reserve. Therefore, the hair trigger remains in place, and the cuts could be too easily reversed.

Space forces have contributed greatly to the acceleration of U.S. military transformation. They have shifted from a nearly exclusive focus on strategic uses and preconflict intelligence to integration with theater forces as part of the operational targeting sequence. In chapter 12, Stephen Randolph argues that, because of resource pressures and competition from less expensive capabilities such as unmanned aerial vehicles (UAVs), American space forces will probably not see a major expansion in mission areas over the next few years. Randolph also points to three reasons why America's near-absolute dominance in military space capabilities during the past decade may be coming to an end: commercial capabilities with military applications that are available to all nations, the growing utility of small and less expensive satellites, and growing efforts by potential adversaries to exploit the vulnerabilities of the U.S. space force. In 2000, the Space Commission examined these trends, and many of its recommendations for organizational change have now been adopted; however, it may be some time before those reforms yield concrete results.

Randolph examines the immediate challenges now facing the space force, including both further integrating space and theater forces as well as maintaining control of space and, if necessary, denying space capabilities to adversaries. He notes that the international legal regime governing the deployment of weapons in space is surprisingly permissive, in part because cost-effectiveness considerations have in the past prevented pursuit of many options. He concludes that development of conventional precision-guided weaponry delivered from space might be the most promising potential mission for space-based weapons. But the costs of deploying weapons in space remain nearly prohibitive, and, moreover, exploitation would require a breakthrough in launch technology. Given resource restraints and the failure of the commercial sector to contribute as much as anticipated to technological development, it will be important for the United States to continue to invest in space R&D, to retain trained personnel, and to support the domestic industrial base.

Military transformation is enabled by new information technologies, and in chapter 13, Jacques Gansler reminds us of the vulnerability of the domain of cyberspace. Computer networks control our Nation's power grids, natural gas pipelines, and transportation systems. "E-government" is booming, and DOD is increasingly dependent on information networks in peace and war. These networks offer high-value, low-risk targets to a broad array of potential attackers with a diverse range of motives. The Internet is most vulnerable, but even Defense networks might be penetrated.

Gansler notes that the Pentagon expects about 40,000 attacks annually, most of which are unsuccessful. But large-scale exercises, such as ELIGIBLE RECEIVER 97, and real-world attacks, like the one that began in 1998 and has apparently been traced to Russia, make it clear that new steps must be taken to protect America's growing dependence on cyberspace. Gansler proposes a public-private sector partnership to provide new protection. The goal of Gansler's proposals is to create an Internet infrastructure that is "highly automated, adaptive, and resilient to all types of attacks." But with at least 20 nations developing information warfare doctrine and with new capabilities available to terrorists, the United States remains extremely vulnerable to these "weapons of mass disruption."

The military transformation process will be successful only if defense research and development and defense procurement processes are tightly coupled. In chapter 14, Mark Montroll examines the defense R&D complex and concludes that both government and commercially run efforts are experiencing serious problems. Government laboratories face the aging of an expert workforce without adequate replenishment, along with a scarcity of infrastructure resources. The consolidation of commercial defense firms during the past decade has increased corporate debt and reduced industry willingness to carry out R&D without financial support from government. Several efforts have been undertaken during the past decade to transition promising technology into the force more quickly. Programs—for example, the Advanced Technology Demonstrations, Advanced Concept Technology Demonstrations, Joint Experimentation Programs, and Future Naval Capabilities program—have yielded successes, such as the Predator UAV, but too many constraints still exist in the acquisition process, and funding is often unavailable even for very promising initiatives. Although useful acquisition reforms have been made, the rate of technological improvement now vastly outpaces Federal ability to incorporate it into the force. To speed the process, DOD is increasingly using prime contractors that are responsible for producing much of the research and development, but industrial constraints on sharing the technology often limit collateral benefits for other defense purposes. Montroll suggests that the Pentagon might learn from the practices of commercial firms that systematically conduct wide searches to identify and acquire the technologies needed from outside.

*Joint Vision 2010* called for the development of "Focused Logistics" in an effort to streamline the support required to project military force. In chapter 15, Paul Needham describes the various initiatives being undertaken by the services to reduce their logistics footprint in-theater by as much as 50 percent. These reforms draw from an array of commercial business practices, such as the anticipation of demand and just-in-time logistics dependent on rapid delivery of orders. Most of these reforms are enabled by information technologies that expedite the ability to reach back to storage areas in the United States. Other reforms include charging the regional CINCs for transportation costs in peacetime as a way to encourage cost-effectiveness. But Needham also points out that many of these new business practices could increase the vulnerability of forward-deployed units in wartime should the just-in-time system break down. These risks must be balanced with the advantages of adopting commercial practices.

## A Note of Caution

The transformation process has already had a profound impact on the way in which America fights, and more improvements can be expected. Resources will remain constrained, even with the $48 billion defense increase requested by the Bush administration in early 2002 (of which less than $10 billion is for new procurement). By 2007, DOD's procurement budet is expected to increase to $100 billion annually, and its R&D budget to $60 billion—big increases in both areas. But resources are not the whole answer; indeed, many ardent military reformers even fear that the budget increases will take pressure off the Pentagon to reform. Sound operational concepts and new organizational structures may be more important than new weapons to the medium-term transformation.

Even if transformation is successful, this same success may raise certain risks. First, if the American military appears able to win victories at low cost, war might become a preferred instrument of diplomacy rather than an instrument of last resort. This situation would lead to an unhealthy militarization of American foreign policy. Second, there are some contingencies for which even a transformed military may be inadequate, and leaders must understand these limits and not be rash. Such contingencies include preventing a terrorist attack on U.S. interests, fighting in certain types of terrain, and sustaining conflict against a large enemy that is unwilling to capitulate despite battlefield losses. Third, America's capability might reduce the military need for allies and lead to an inclination to go it alone. This trend could lead to diplomatic isolation. Fourth, U.S. military dominance could breed resentment abroad and result in the accumulation of more enemies. And fifth, highly autonomous systems inherent in the new force increase the risk of friendly fire casualties. None of these risks is cause enough to slow down efforts to develop the best military possible, but dealing with those risks will require prudence on the part of America's political and diplomatic leadership. America cannot afford to overreach.

A key question is this: Will transformation enable the U.S. military to retain its status as the world's best fighting force? The answer is: Yes, but only if transformation is carried out wisely and effectively, and only if due regard is given to the constraints that will continue to face the exercise of military power. It is with these cautions in mind that we explore the issues of transformation of the U.S. military at the beginning of the 21st century.

## Notes

[1] See H.W. Koch, *History of Warfare* (London: Bison Books Limited, 1987); and Andrew F. Krepinevich, "Cavalry to Computer: The Pattern of Military Revolutions," *The National Interest* 37 (Fall 1994), 30–42.

[2] Alvin and Heidi Toffler, *War and Anti-War: Survival at the Dawn of the Twenty-first Century* (Boston: Little, Brown, 1993).

[3] On November 26, 2001, Secretary of Defense Donald H. Rumsfeld announced the establishment of the Office of Force Transformation within the Office of the Secretary of Defense and the appointment of VADM Arthur K. Cebrowski, USN (Ret.), as its director, reporting directly to the Secretary and Deputy Secretary of Defense.

# Part I

# Foundations of Transformation

# Chapter 1

# Assessing New Missions

Sam J. Tangredi

T he tragedies of September 11, 2001, were transformational events for the American people. Gone is the comfort of post-Cold War common wisdom—the latent belief that globalization had set the stage for a new world order in which economic markets, not force and violence, ruled. Once again, national security issues dominate the American political agenda. As President George W. Bush stated on September 15, "We're at war. There has been an act of war declared upon America by terrorists and we will respond accordingly." This response has included both traditional overseas combat operations—focused initially on the Taliban in Afghanistan—and an emphasis on homeland security at a level not seen since the civil defense effort of the 1950s.

To military planners and defense analysts, the support of the American public for both an immediate military response and sustained preparations to prevent or defeat future threats has been gratifying, even though it came at such a tragic cost. While no one predicted the use of hijacked domestic airliners in kamikaze attacks on civilian targets, warning of the potential for terrorist-style asymmetric attacks on the American homeland has been a prominent theme in defense literature for several years. The U.S. Commission on National Security/21st Century—better known as the Hart-Rudman Commission—bluntly forecast in its initial 1999 report: "America will become increasingly vulnerable to hostile attack on our homeland, and our military superiority will not entirely protect us . . . Americans will likely die on American soil, possibly in large numbers."[1]

Until the recent tragedies, such analysis was largely relegated to the background of an unconvincing defense debate dominated by pressing domestic concerns. But with the addition of detection of letter-borne anthrax to the terrorist attacks, the American public became convinced of the need for a comprehensive and effective military program that includes some element of transformation in capabilities to meet emerging threats.

Yet public support for the military response to terrorist threats—and the transformations that may be necessary—can only be sustained through a clear public understanding of the capabilities and the limitations of American military power. The Bush administration has attempted to set out such an explanation with the release of the Quadrennial Defense Review (QDR) Report on September 30, 2001. While the erratic development of the 2001 review resulted in a report with limited detail concerning force structure and programmatic decisions, it does lay out a series of defense priorities—described as a paradigm shift—with "defense of the U.S. homeland" as "the highest priority for the U.S. military."[2] Other priorities described as elements of a "new force sizing construct" include the capacity to:

- deter aggression and coercion forward in critical regions
- swiftly defeat aggression in overlapping major conflicts while preserving for the President the option to call for a decisive victory in one of those conflicts—including the possibility of regime change or occupation
- conduct a limited number of smaller-scale contingency operations.[3]

This force sizing construct is designed to optimize the military to achieve "four defense policy goals," described in the QDR Report as assuring allies and friends, dissuading future military competition, deterring threats and coercion against U.S. interests, and decisively defeating any adversary if deterrence fails.[4] These defense policy goals are, in turn, identified as supporting a series of enduring "U.S. national interests and objectives" (discussed below).

While the QDR Report addresses priorities, goals, and national interests, it does not lay out a specific listing of anticipated military missions. Yet without identification of expected missions for which to prepare, defense planning cannot sensibly proceed.

## Identifying Future Military Missions

What are the missions that the U.S. military will be called upon to carry out in the 21st century? The answer to this question is the prime determinant of decisions concerning the size, characteristics, and force structure of the U.S. Armed Forces. The events of September 11 have thrust the United States into a protracted conflict against terrorism, but counterterrorism, aerial strike, and special operations are only a small slice of the primary missions for which U.S. forces must be prepared.

Defining missions is one of three initial steps in creating a rational and effective defense policy. First, national security objectives must be identified; second, the security environment in which those objectives will be pursued must be evaluated;[5] and third, the missions must be identified that military forces will be expected to accomplish to achieve these objectives within the context of the current and future security environment.

None of these steps are easy; all require thoughtful, coordinated analysis. Carl von Clausewitz, the Prussian military philosopher who continues to influence modern strategy, wrote that "everything in war is very simple, but the simplest thing is very difficult."[6] This difficulty, exacerbated by the friction of democratic politics, also applies to defense planning; the initial steps are often entangled by leaps of faith.

Such entanglements are apparent in public reactions to the emerging defense policies of the administration of President Bush, as well as throughout the overall debate on the need for military transformation. Indeed, the results of the recent Quadrennial Defense Review—whose process itself took several controversial turns—revealed friction among participants in the defense decisionmaking process as to how to determine the appropriate missions for which U.S. military forces should be shaped.

To some extent, these differences are the natural result of the current administration's attempt to change policies that had been established over the previous 8 years. But they also reflect the fact that although different military missions have been emphasized since the end of the Cold War, there has been little agreement on how to conceptualize the relationship between these emerging missions and the tasks for which the U.S. military has traditionally been prepared. There has been no generally accepted replacement for the spectrum-of-conflict model that characterized the relationship between military missions during the Cold War, despite the fact that significant elements of this model are no longer considered primary or even likely national security threats.

The spectrum-of-conflict model carries with it an implicit prioritization of military missions that arguably no longer applies in the post-Cold War world. It is this implicit prioritization that makes argument over models and taxonomies of military missions more than merely academic. The three initial steps in defense planning described above imply a natural linkage between priority objectives, greatest potential threats, and the prioritization of assigned military missions. Logically, the prioritization of missions should determine the shape and size of military force structure, which, in turn, would drive explicit choices in the expenditure of resources.

The friction of politics aside, it would make little sense to expend the majority of resources on the lowest priority mission or to hedge against the least of all potential threats. Instead, it makes greater sense to focus the most resources on primary objectives, high-priority missions, and the most likely or most deadly of anticipated threats. Decisions to *transform* the military to a new set of capabilities or force structure should be the consequences of reprioritization of objectives, reassessment of anticipated threats, or emergence of differing sets of missions. Making these choices in an organized fashion requires some sort of model or prioritized listing.

The purpose of this chapter is to outline such a model of identification of military missions, linking them to national objectives and anticipated threats.[7] This effort is meant to be illustrative rather than prescriptive. In examining the differences between the traditional spectrum-of-conflict model—and its implicit assumptions and prioritization—and a new model that can be termed a *hierarchy of missions*, the chapter also illustrates part of the analytical rationale for military transformation.

Ultimately, any decision for transformation will, implicitly or explicitly, reflect a new prioritization of missions. The hierarchy-of-missions model attempts to capture this emerging reprioritization, based on defense policy statements, reports concerning the Quadrennial Defense Review, and deductive reasoning.

## Contradictions and Transformation in Context

There are apparent contradictions in what the American people will expect of their military in the 21st century. The end of the Cold War has ushered in a popular perception that a major military conflict requiring the global commitment of vast, powerful forces is highly unlikely. Yet there is also the expectation of an increasing number of smaller but perhaps more direct threats to America's security. This perception received a dramatic and painful public airing through the events of September 11 and subsequent incidents of anthrax contamination.

At the same time, the military success in Operation *Desert Storm*, and in Kosovo as well, has raised expectations of what America's high-technology Armed Forces can achieve with relatively little in the way of casualties or civilian collateral damage. As of mid-October 2001, operations in Afghanistan appear to have reinforced these expectations.

The result of the intersection of these three impressions is that the public (or at least those members of the public who express their concern on defense and security matters) has a mixed view of the type of military in which it wants to invest. They appear to want to maintain an over-whelming military advantage over all possible opponents but not to spend at the levels of the Cold War or even of the *Desert Storm* era. They seem to want their government to do something about the tragedies of the modern world that are broadcast to them on CNN, but they do not want military involvement in quagmires such as Vietnam or Somalia. Political rhetoric and media commentary may have convinced them that they cannot have both an increasingly high-tech warfighting force directed against threats to the homeland *and* forces sufficiently large as to intervene simultaneously in the multitude of lower intensity peacekeeping operations of concern to the international community.[8]

The increasing integration of economies and societies commonly characterized as globalization would seem to foretell a future in which Great Power war becomes obsolete but intervention in smaller-scale contingencies is inevitable. "We are envisioning . . . an era marked by both an increasing integration of societies and a need for greater commitments of military forces. That might seem an inherent contradiction, but it is possible nevertheless."[9]

Globalization also suggests that threats once considered of low military significance, such as nonstate terrorism, international crime, or ecological degradation, will become important factors in national security planning. Indeed, the response to terrorism has already become the primary focus of American security efforts. Creeping proliferation of weapons of mass destruction and longer-range strike systems also may increase the potential for direct threats to the U.S. homeland. Yet until September 11, many defense experts, including many current military leaders, argued that such engagement and interventions (and by implication, extensive homeland defenses) take away from what should be the true focus of the U.S. military: supporting the Nation's most vital interests by being ready to fight and win America's wars. This position—most widely held in the U.S. Army, less so in the U.S. Air Force, and infrequently expressed in the U.S. Navy and Marine Corps—holds that intervention in operations other than war results in a de facto reduction in readiness for actual high-intensity combat. This view may seem to be dormant during the current focus on steps to increase homeland security, but it is reflected in the emphasis on the procurement of new, high-technology power-projection systems reflected in such pre-September 11 planning documents as *Joint Vision (JV) 2020*. As *JV 2020* argues, "If our Armed Forces are to be faster, more lethal, and more precise in 2020 than they are today, we must continue to invest in and develop new military capabilities."[10]

Overlaid on the readiness-versus-engagement debate is the growing call for military transformation in the wake of new emerging threats and continuing technical innovations, particularly in information systems technologies. Proposals for transformation run from vague exhortations for change to advocacy of specific military systems and doctrine.

Some view transformation as a change toward more rapid, lighter, and more lethal forces that effectively and definitively refocuses the U.S. military on new forms of the "high-end" warfighting of major theater war. Such new forms might include information warfare against civilian infrastructure or war between space systems. Part of this warfighting capability would include defenses against direct threats to the homeland, such as a national missile defense. This view implies that ground troops in operations other than war—such as peacekeeping—obtain only marginal benefits from such improved technologies as precision strike systems (and that such operations other than war are of limited utility in forwarding U.S. security interests). High-technology transformation is, therefore, all about maintaining U.S. military superiority over all potential opponents for years to come. As evidenced by the QDR process and Secretary of Defense Donald Rumsfeld's public statements, this approach largely corresponds to the Bush administration view of transformation.

Others view transformation as an enabler that will convert a ponderous, heavy, and largely single-mission warfighting force structure into a more nimble contingency force that would be more effective in smaller-scale contingencies. Technological innovations, such as advances in precision strike, nonlethal weapons, and more rapid means of troop deployment, are touted as giving new capabilities for successful interventions at relatively low cost. An implication of this view is that since high-end warfighting is decreasingly likely, the U.S. military needs to be reoriented toward missions of greater frequency, and technological transformation can be the means to do so. Although the Clinton administration did not emphasize a policy of military transformation, the "new capabilities for successful intervention" approach reflects the general inclination of officials in the Office of the Secretary of Defense during the tenures of William Perry and William Cohen.

The assumptions common to both of these positions are that military transformation is carried out for a purpose and that it is not merely a reaction propelled by technological changes completely beyond anyone's control. An alternative argument could be that what is being called transformation is merely an enlightened approach toward evolutionary changes in technology that are driven by other factors than the purposes for which armed forces might be used. This alternative argument is somewhat inaccurately captured in the shorthand that "technology drives strategy," one side of a debate that was quite popular in the 1970s but that somewhat exhausted itself in more recent decades.[11] However, even that argument would not necessarily eliminate the need for choices in determining which technologies should be adopted by military forces; even so, some sort of mission prioritization is necessary.

## Spectrum-of-Conflict Model

The spectrum-of-conflict model was used in a number of DOD publications and briefings during the Cold War, particularly during the 1980s.[12] Figure 1–1 is a representative version of the spectrum-of-conflict model.

The spectrum is represented by a notional curve created by points on two axes: *level of violence* (x) and *probability of occurrence* (y). Activities at lower levels of violence have a much higher probability of occurrence than activities at the higher end. The conflict activities along the curve are broken into three general subgroupings in order of decreasing probability: *peacetime presence, crisis response,* and *global conventional war.*

The activities viewed as traditional military functions are clustered at the higher end of the level of violence (x) axis. The higher end also represents responses to occurrences that would pose higher levels of more direct threats to the lives and well-being of individual Americans and to the survival of the Nation. At the far right end is strategic nuclear war, which represents the most extreme direct threat to the U.S. homeland. Further down the level of violence, but higher in probability of occurrence, are theater nuclear war and global conventional war (shown both as a subgrouping and as a single point on the curve). Although theater nuclear war is meant to describe conflicts involving nuclear strikes on targets outside the U.S. homeland, the potential for such a nuclearized conflict to escalate into a strategic exchange is presumed to be high, making it the second highest threat. Using the same logic, the curve moves down the level of violence and up the probability of occurrence with limited war, use of force, show of force, surveillance, and peacetime presence.

On the surface, the spectrum-of-conflict model is an understandable, idealized representation of the frequency that military force might be used in differing but related activities. Out of context, it could be swiftly

Figure 1–1. **The Spectrum-of-Conflict Model**

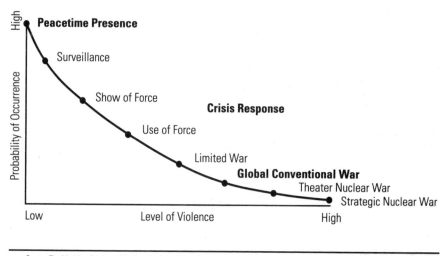

*Source: The Maritime Strategy*, U.S. Naval Institute *Proceedings*, January 1986 supplement, 8.

dismissed as merely academic, a clever illustration. But, in reality, its use to describe U.S. military activities illustrates specific assumptions about how military power should be used, as well as specific sets of priorities for the missions that the military is designed to carry out.

The U.S. military services used the model throughout the Cold War to explain why their activities and force structure differed, though each was logical. The Department of the Navy used the model to illustrate the importance of peacetime forward naval presence, an activity to which naval resources were devoted on a routine, rotational basis. The Navy accepted the logic that most assets should be used for the most common activities, at least while they are not needed for actual combat. But it also argued that each naval unit should be capable, to some degree, of carrying out missions all along the spectrum. This view leads to a specific set of priorities in both operations and design, toward a forward-deployed Navy of high endurance, multimission units.[13] These priorities are also consistent with historical justifications for maintaining a powerful oceangoing Navy.

The Department of the Army interpreted the spectrum somewhat differently. It viewed the level of violence as the dominant axis. Although such missions as peacetime presence, surveillance, and shows of force were necessary, the focus of Army combat units would be on the missions at the higher levels of violence. As a practical matter, the mission of strategic nuclear war had been assigned to the other services; thus, the Army focus remained on theater nuclear war and global conventional war.[14] From this point of view, everything to the left side of the curve was a lesser included case of the missions on the curve itself. This de facto prioritization naturally emphasizes the development of heavy combat units optimized for high-intensity conflict against a similarly endowed foe—a logical emphasis, since the expected opponent was the Soviet Army. From this perspective, it would be illogical to train or optimize front-line units for missions such as limited war or peacetime presence. The abilities to carry out such missions were assumed to be byproducts of preparing for global conventional war.

Under this logic, the Army would theoretically conduct limited wars—such as Vietnam—with less capable units than those positioned against possible Soviet invasion in the Fulda Gap and elsewhere. Although this theory was difficult to implement in practice, officer rotation and assignment policies of the Vietnam era seemed to signal a desire to preserve Army strength for what was perceived as "the real fight." This theory also corresponded with the desire of political leaders to keep the Vietnam intervention a limited war. But even when the Army rebuilt itself after Vietnam, the dominant focus toward preparing for major war was reflected in the perception that involvement in lower intensity conflicts, peacekeeping, or operations other than war detracted from readiness for the primary military mission of global or major regional war. The Clinton administration emphasis on using military forces in operations other than war and in nontraditional roles revealed tensions with the existing focus on the high end of the conflict spectrum.

For much of the Cold War, the Department of the Air Force designed its force structure almost exclusively for missions at the very highest level of violence. Deterring strategic nuclear war was the ultimate mission, represented by the organizational dominance of the Strategic Air Command. Theater nuclear war was seen as a secondary aspect of this mission, with shorter-range attack aircraft and fighter-bombers focused on this task. Preparations for a global conventional war also mandated developing dual-use systems and maintaining considerable strength in tactical air forces and transport squadrons. All missions that fell lower in the violence axis were to be executed by high-intensity systems diverted from what was seen as their primary purpose. (This is the origin of recent debates on the employment of high demand/low density assets, such as airborne warning and control system [AWACS] aircraft.) The concept of the independent use of air power to conduct strategic attacks and interdiction fortified the belief that lower intensity conflict was just more of the same activity to be conducted on a lower priority basis. One example was the use of B–52 bombers, trained for individual penetration of Soviet airspace but used for massed, high-altitude bombing missions in Southeast Asia.[15]

## Shifting Down the Spectrum

The collapse of the Warsaw Pact and the Soviet Union (1989–1991) seemingly reduced the threat of strategic and theater nuclear war, as well as of global conventional war, almost to the point of nonexistence. But no obvious replacement emerged for the spectrum-of-conflict model to illustrate the missions for which the military would be trained and prepared. Operation *Desert Storm*, which could be described as a major theater war or major regional conflict that involved significant portions of U.S. and allied military strength, seemed to represent merely a shift down the spectrum of conflict to a level somewhat lower than global conventional war.

The reconstitution strategy of President George Bush (which was delayed by *Desert Storm*) sought reduction of the U.S. military by almost one-third. However, it was intended as a balanced reduction that would keep a "portfolio of capabilities" that could allow for future shifts of emphasis up or down the conflict spectrum, depending on current or emerging threats. Forces in the strategic triad could be reduced or taken off alert, but the deterrence of strategic nuclear war was still considered an important high-end task. Capabilities required to move conventional forces swiftly to conduct global war were downsized but retained in structure to facilitate responses to lower levels of conflict that might occur anywhere on the globe.[16] In the early Clinton administration, Secretary of Defense Les Aspin adopted an evolutionary "two major regional contingency (MRC)" approach to force sizing, since the possibility of a global war against a single opponent seemed remote. However, the two-MRC strategy and its successor, the two major theater war (MTW) strategy, required similar if smaller forces than the single global conventional war.

The Clinton administration initiated a variety of "lower level of violence" military actions, including punitive strikes, shows of force, other smaller-scale contingencies, and a series of operations other than war. The pace and resource requirements for such activities appeared to critics to threaten the level of readiness actually required to prepare for two overlapping regional wars, thereby calling into question the assumption that those activities were truly lesser included cases. After conducting air operations over Serbia in support of North Atlantic Treaty Organization (NATO) intervention in Kosovo, the Air Force declared itself "operationally broke," having consumed resources at a level previously thought necessary for an MTW. During the 1993 Bottom-Up Review and 1997 QDR, the Navy convinced the Secretary of Defense that its peacetime presence mission required a greater naval force structure than that actually necessary to conduct two major theater wars. An obvious disconnect was developing between the size of forces necessary to conduct such "lower intensity of violence" missions and the implications of the spectrum-of-conflict model. Simply viewing the military as shifting its focus down the spectrum of conflict did not provide a coherent guide to deciding force structure issues, as it had done during the Cold War.

In terms of the post-Cold War missions the Nation's leaders are assigning to U.S. military forces, the prioritization inherent in the spectrum-of-conflict model no longer made sense. For some, the question became: Was the model no longer valid, or were the missions being assigned to military forces somehow not "appropriate"?

## Are Emerging New Missions a Reality?

Those viewing the prioritization in the spectrum-of-conflict model and arguing that lesser-level-of-violence missions are a detriment to military readiness for major conflict often imply that these military missions of the 21st century are new. A common perception is that an ever-increasing number of missions have been added to the responsibilities of the post-Cold War U.S. military. This viewpoint is reinforced by the use of a host of new terms and descriptions about what we expect our Armed Forces to do. *Peacekeeping, peace enforcement, humanitarian assistance, stability operations, military operations other than war, peace operations,* and *engagement* are a few of the terms used with increasing frequency. The involvement of U.S. forces in such missions around the globe has become a significant political issue, with many seeing such involvement as a severe detriment to overall military readiness. As a Presidential candidate and as President early in his term, George W. Bush postulated that U.S. forces have been overextended through their use in such missions and suggested a policy of cutting back on such involvement.

In fact, many such missions—though perhaps not the modern terms that describe them—have been routine peacetime responsibilities of American military forces throughout history; examples abound. Technology aside, intervention in Haiti in 1994 was conceptually similar in form if not in intent to that in 1915. The 1923 Report to Congress of Secretary of the Navy Edwin Denby reveals that naval forces were then involved in patrolling the Yangtse River to "suppress banditry and piracy"; providing disaster relief to Yokohama, Tokyo, and Nagasaki in the wake of a major earthquake and tsunami; conducting a noncombatant evacuation of over 260,000 Greeks and Armenians following the capture of Smyrna by Turkish troops; and fulfilling their role as the primary participant of the International Ice Patrol in the North Atlantic shipping lanes.[17] Naval officers served as governors of Samoa, Guam, and the Virgin Islands. The United States had just made a historic (if not lasting) effort in multilateral arms control, crisis stability, and engagement with the signing of the Washington Naval Treaty. All of these are activities that would make the most modern multilateral interventionist proud.

Such overseas activities may have been primarily a Navy and Marine Corps responsibility, but it should also be recalled that the Army spent a good portion of its history pacifying Native American tribes, conducting "nation building" in the former Confederate States during Reconstruction, training engineers to build railroads, pursuing Mexican revolutionists following raids in the southwest United States, and dispersing potentially unruly groups such as the Bonus Marchers. Such missions are not entirely new.

What is new, however, is the widespread and intense public awareness of these missions and the sense of importance attached to them by policymakers. When viewed only through the prism of the Cold War, these missions represent radical shifts in the purpose and employment of military forces. But the inherent prioritization of the spectrum-of-conflict model would treat these "new" missions simply as lesser included elements of global conventional war. Here is where contradictory expectations, calls for transformation, and biases of the model collide. If the potential for global conventional conflict is very low, interpreting lower-intensity-of-violence missions as lesser included cases makes no sense. Worse, force structure decisions that could optimize the military to deal with the expected lower-intensity-of-violence missions might be deflected by the perceived need to retain or improve readiness for global conventional war.

In fact, the collision (some critics called it an impending "train wreck"[18]) that bedeviled Clinton administration defense policy was between the apparent desires of the policymakers to optimize military force structure for smaller-scale contingencies and operations other than war and the professional military leadership desire to maintain a high level of readiness for the two-MTW construct that replaced global conventional war as the high-intensity mission. This was not insubordination on the part of the professional military leadership; the civilian policymakers also insisted on retaining the two-MTW construct as the primary force-sizing tool. Their insistence resulted in a series of embarrassing Congressional hearings in 1998–1999 in which the Joint Chiefs of Staff first argued that force readiness was acceptable and then reversed themselves and said it was significantly degraded. The reversal was less the result of subterfuge than of confused policy; the two-MTW strategy may have been the force-sizing yardstick, but it was not given full resources and did not reflect administration expectations as to what constituted the real military missions. In the background lay the inherent prioritization of the spectrum-of-conflict model, making the administration's real highest priority missions subordinate to higher intensity missions, which were not expected to take place.

## Bush Administration Priorities

President George W. Bush's campaign statements indicated a strong commitment to the improvement of military readiness and support for significant military transformation.[19] Following his election, some initially interpreted his statements to mean that a significant increase to the defense budget would finance all potential costs for increased readiness, current force structure programs, and robust transformation. Not only was this view unwarranted, but it missed a significant point about the emphasis on transformation, a point made evident by the incoming administration's focus on tax cuts rather than substantial across-the-board increases in defense. Arguably, transformations are not needed when evolutionary improvements are affordable. The need for transformation is most evident when existing plans are no longer considered affordable and are no longer appropriate to changing priorities. The change in priorities itself may well be a result of the recognition of how unaffordable the current defense program had become.

These changed priorities are identified in the QDR 2001 Report and had been previously reflected in the public statements of the President, Secretary of Defense, and Deputy Secretary of Defense, along with the initial QDR Terms of Reference setting out the parameters of the review. First, the administration clearly intends to revoke the previous two-MTW construct as a force sizing tool and replace it with a requirement for outcomes of one "big win" and one "restore order" in the case of two overlapping MTWs. Second, funding for homeland defense will be substantially increased, and a national missile defense (NMD) will be developed and deployed. Prior to September 11, NMD appeared the likely dominant defense priority throughout the administration, but it has been supplanted by the war on terrorism.

Third, the skepticism expressed by defense officials concerning the efficacy of lower intensity military intervention and humanitarian actions, particularly when allied or coalition military forces might be readily available, would have suggested a reduction in American involvement in these activities. However, actions necessitated by the war on terrorism may instead require the Bush administration to become involved in even more smaller-scale contingencies than during President Clinton's tenure, starting with de facto U.S. intervention in the Afghan civil war.

Fourth, current readiness and future transformation of the force will be emphasized. Transformation goals center on homeland defense, precision strike, rapid mobility, and a lighter land force. Finally, any future defense budget increase—in light of homeland security priorities—will be directed to homeland defense, NMD, readiness, and gradual transformation and may not be sufficient to cover the cost of maintaining the current force size. As the QDR Report concedes, however, these objectives were largely developed before September 11 and may be modified based on the outcome of current counterterrorism efforts.[20]

Extrapolating from these observations, a hierarchy of national security interests that appear to guide Bush administration defense planning can be developed. This *hierarchy of missions* would be an effective replacement of the spectrum-of-conflict model for illustrating the priority of missions for which future military forces would be designed.

## Toward a Hierarchy of Missions

The first step in developing an illustrative hierarchy of missions is to categorize national security interests as *survival interests, vital interests* (which could also be considered *world order interests*), and *value interests.* These terms would replace the "vital, important, and humanitarian and other interests" used in the 2000 (and earlier) Clinton administration National Security Strategy.[21] Such a categorization is consistent with the spirit of previous attempts to organize national interests. Table 1–1 illustrates the categories of interests and the politico-military objectives related to each, which can be identified based on analysis of public statements.

Table 1–1. **National Security Interests and Politico-Military Objectives**

| Survival Interests | Vital Interests | Value Interests |
|---|---|---|
| Missions: | Missions: | Missions: |
| Survival of the Nation | Defense of treaty allies | Prevent internal conflict or |
| Territorial integrity | Defense of democratic | peacemaking |
| Economic security | and pivot states | Peace operations |
|  | Deter or win regional conflicts |  |

## Survival Interests

Survival interests include three related but functionally different objectives: survival of the Nation, territorial integrity (homeland security), and economic security.

The functional differences become clearer when the military missions associated with each politico-military objective are identified (table 1–2). For example, the objective of survival of the Nation would depend upon military missions such as nuclear deterrence, national missile defense, and strategic reconnaissance and warning.

Another survival interest is the objective of territorial integrity, dealing with threats that target the American population but not on a scale comparable to nuclear war. Associated military missions would include critical infrastructure protection, counterproliferation, and counterterrorism, often described as *homeland security*. This term is frequently defined to also include NMD and military assistance to civil authorities during natural disasters such as forest fires. However, NMD falls more logically into the category of survival of the Nation. Active-duty military assistance to civil authority in nondefense-related matters is generally conducted on an ad hoc basis or by the National Guard; since such assistance is focused on the well-being of Americans, it is included in the category of economic security.

Associated with the survival-interest objective of economic security would be the military missions of ensuring freedom of the seas and space, access to raw materials and protection of sea lines of communication (SLOC), integrity of financial operations (such as computer network defense [CND] against foreign opponents), and military participation in counterdrug and counter-international crime operations. These missions span the intensity spectrum but can be associated with a particular type of

Table 1–2. **Survival Interests**

| Objective: Survival of the Nation | Objective: Territorial Integrity | Objective: Economic Security |
|---|---|---|
| Missions: | Missions: | Missions: |
| Nuclear deterrence | Critical infrastructure protection | Freedom of seas and space |
| National missile defense | Counterproliferation | Access to raw materials and SLOC protection |
| Strategic reconnaissance | Counterterrorism | Integrity of financial operations (against foreign threat) |
| | | Counterdrug and counter-international crime operations |

interest; they would not necessarily have been considered high-priority missions under the old spectrum-of-conflict model. Table 1–2 lists the military missions of the survival interests category. The difference in prioritization between the hierarchy-of-missions model and the spectrum-of-conflict model can be seen using, as an example, the mission type *integrity of financial operations (against foreign threat)*. In the information age, integrity of financial operations would primarily involve CND operations. This mission's apparent level of violence (or lack of it) would give it a very low priority under the spectrum-of-conflict model; integrity of financial operations would be considered by most to be a nontraditional military mission. However, this view is only accurate based on the Cold War experience; in previous eras, it would have been considered quite traditional. Absent an overwhelming threat to the survival of the Nation or territorial integrity, as was posed by the Soviet Union throughout the Cold War, integrity of financial operations is an important national security mission.[22] Its level of violence does not determine its priority.

## Vital Interests

Many military missions that would likely be considered traditional in terms of the Cold War experience would fall into the interest category of vital or world order interests. Table 1–3 provides an illustrative listing of vital interests—ones critical to the long-term vitality of American democracy but that do not necessarily pose an immediate threat to the lives and domestic property of Americans. Military missions associated with vital interests range along the full spectrum of conflict, but many tend to be associated with a high intensity of conflict. The distinction between vital and survival interests is more than just the location of potential operations. It is also one of immediacy: while the threats to these vital interests are very real, they are not always felt immediately by Americans. The assumptions of mutual deterrence and homeland sanctuary that existed in the latter period of the Cold War no longer seem valid. This raises the question of whether overseas military operations can be successfully conducted against a determined opponent if U.S. survival interests can easily be threatened. Threats in the survival category create a de facto prioritization that relegates vital or world order interests to second place—a close second, but second nevertheless.

Placing national security interests such as the defense of treaty allies in the vital instead of the survival category immediately raises the question of whether such a separation represents an isolationist defense policy. But this criticism betrays a lack of recognition of how profoundly different today's security environment is from that of the Cold War period. Through its ideological hatred toward democracy, the Soviet Union remained an overriding threat to collective Western security. Such a threat does not exist today and is unlikely to reappear in the next 25 years.[23]

Although the possible emergence of a military peer competitor is a top future security concern to the Bush administration, other NATO governments seem less concerned at this prospect. With the wane of hostile ideologies, this threat appears more directed toward the United States in its current position in the international system than toward NATO. Such a view colors both the European reluctance to endorse U.S. adoptions of national missile defense (and renegotiation of the Anti-Ballistic Missile Treaty) and the administration's decision to shift its defense focus to Asia. It also points to the reality that there is a de facto separation between threats to the U.S. homeland and threats to other NATO members.

French President Charles de Gaulle's rhetorical Cold War question was about whether the U.S. Government would ever seriously "trade Washington for Paris." It is now a fair question to ask whether—in the absence of a collective threat on the scale of the Soviet Union—anyone would consider trading Paris for Washington. Whatever the answer, the renewed urgency of the objective of homeland security indicates at least a partial answer to the question of whether the United States could successfully conduct combat operations overseas against an enemy that

Table 1–3. **Vital / World Order Interests**

| Objective: Defense of Treaty Allies | Objective: Defense of Democratic and Pivot States | Objective: Deter or Win Regional Conflict |
|---|---|---|
| **Missions:** | **Missions:** | **Missions:** |
| Overseas and forward presence | Forward presence with limited infrastructure support | Forward presence with limited infrastructure support |
| Power projection and conventional rapid response | Long- and intermediate-range strike | Counter-antiaccess operations including: countermine warfare; suppression of enemy air defenses; suppression of enemy coastal defenses; amphibious and airborne |
| Conventional C⁴ISR (command, control, communications, computers, intelligence, surveillance, and reconnaissance) | Special operations | |
| | Power projection of expeditionary, rapid response capability | |
| | Expeditionary C⁴ISR | Long- and intermediate-range strike |
| | | Special operations |
| | | Power projection of expeditionary, rapid response capability |
| | | Expeditionary C⁴ISR |

could threaten the American homeland. It may be more difficult today than it was during the Cold War, primarily due to uncertainty concerning the efficacy of nuclear or conventional deterrence. Heightening this uncertainty is the fact that military assets that would be needed to support such homeland security functions as domestic consequence management are currently earmarked for overseas deployment in the event of a major theater war. In the absence of a formal prioritization of missions, an ad hoc choice may have to be made between overseas power projection and homeland security in the event of a threat to retaliate against American territory.[24] The result is an emerging de facto prioritization in military missions, placing conventional regional war in the category of vital rather than survival interests.

Within the overall category of vital interests, the objectives can be separated into three categories: defense of treaty allies, defense of democratic and pivot states, and deter or win regional conflict.

Although defense of treaty allies is an objective that has existed at least since the establishment of NATO in 1948, in recent years it has not been seen as an objective separate from the generic requirement of providing a two-MTW capability. Two factors influenced this amalgamation: the assumption that NATO and bilateral U.S. allies Australia and Japan no longer faced plausible direct threats to their security (although South Korea, another bilateral ally, did face such a threat), and the assumption that major theater war would more likely occur in the developing world (again, with South Korea as the exception). The canonical two-MRC/MTW cases—war with Iraq and North Korea—reflect these assumptions. But the reality is that treaty allies are the only states to which the United States is *obliged* to commit its forces to defend. This makes defense of these states a separate and higher priority mission, de facto as well as de jure, than other vital interests.

Because all of the U.S. treaty allies are economically developed states with considerable supporting infrastructure, and most have considerable regional military strength of their own, the objective of defense of treaty allies paradoxically requires relatively few unique military missions. Capabilities for three major military missions are required: overseas/forward presence; power projection and conventional rapid response; and providing advanced C⁴ISR (command, control, communications, computers, intelligence, surveillance, and reconnaissance capability) for major conventional war.

Overseas or forward presence acts as a reassurance to the allies, a potential deterrent to aggressors, and a means of making combat forces immediately available in case of attack on an ally. With its treaty allies, U.S. forces can generally rely on a developed base structure, facilitating the maintenance of ground forces. The presence of U.S. forces reinforces existing national capability and thus is not the sole means available to thwart aggression. Presence reinforces the viability of the treaty alliance; its political effect may actually be greater than the combat effect of the forces themselves.

Power projection of rapid-response forces is an obvious necessity for allied defense. Again, however, the existence of extensive airports, seaports, and infrastructure for debarkation and military support allows for faster, more efficient force projection than in austere theaters. Forces can be tailored, but more importantly, their timing of phased movement in the theater can be mutually agreed upon and prepared in advance.

The provision of advanced C⁴ISR capabilities to treaty allies reflects the dominance of U.S. capabilities in this sector. An example is AWACS aircraft; some are under direct NATO control, but most are under U.S. national control. The extensive U.S. investment in space systems has created another area in which the United States can provide direct support to allies. Treaty allies do not lack national C⁴ISR capabilities; however, U.S. capabilities are global, generally more technologically advanced, and of considerably greater extent. Whereas U.S. combat forces may only be a greater version of existing allied combat capability, U.S. C⁴ISR capabilities often reflect a qualitative, not just quantitative, addition.

The term *pivot state* describes regional powers that make considerable contributions toward maintaining regional peace and thereby support U.S. national interests in free markets, U.S. access to resources, and enlargement of democratic governance.[25] Defense of democratic and pivot states is not merely a lesser priority version of defense of treaty allies; it reflects a need for different types of forces, planning, and power projection. An example of a pivot state is Egypt, a populous nation whose relations with Israel are key to ensuring peace in the Middle East. Egypt receives considerable U.S. financial and military support for its efforts; a significant threat to Egyptian security would also be a threat to U.S. policies in the region.

Not all pivot states are Western-style democracies, but most generally could be considered at least emerging democracies. Defense of other democratic states can also be considered a vital interest of the United States, since democracies tend to support regional peace and world order and to hold interests similar to those of America. In light of terrorist assaults on democratic institutions, an attack on an individual democratic state implies an attack against global democratic institutions.

The objective of defense of democratic and pivot states requires a more extensive combination of the types of military missions that are often associated with preparations for major theater war. As with treaty allies, forward presence provides reassurance of U.S. commitment and initial crisis response. However, the lack of a formal alliance often means that only limited infrastructure exists or is available for forward presence forces. The resulting forward presence with limited infrastructure support is of a less permanent nature than that in allied territory and is, of necessity, primarily naval in nature.

Long- and intermediate-range strike, particularly with precision weapons, is also a critical mission in conducting operations in defense of democratic and pivot states. These capabilities also would be among the military force requirements in defense of treaty allies, but here the probable lack or destruction of supporting air bases is likely to require direct attacks by long-range forces, perhaps even those based in the continental United States (CONUS). Precision strike is aimed at blunting an initial enemy attack and interdicting follow-on enemy forces as well as bringing combat operations to the territory of the aggressor in an effort to destroy "centers of gravity."[26] Precision strike may also allow for "effects-based operations" designed to directly influence the aggressor's decisionmaking process.[27]

Special operations are critical to the success of any military campaign, but even more so in the defense of states with limited infrastructure or in campaigns in which U.S. forces do not have other means of gathering information. Such operations are likely to be conducted within the aggressor state with the purpose of creating direct effects, such as destruction of decisionmaking nodes and war-supporting infrastructure, as well as gathering information. Special operations are a component of the overall power projection of expeditionary and rapid response forces, but they particularly come to the fore in cases where direct power projection of forces from CONUS is difficult or unwarranted.

Power projection of U.S. expeditionary and rapid response capability remains the primary mission of the Armed Forces in all overseas conflicts. Expeditionary forces are those designed to mount attacks within the theater as part of routine deployment and forward presence and that are capable of sustaining themselves for initial operations with only limited assistance from the host nation's infrastructure. Such forces include amphibious Marine expeditionary units, naval forces, expeditionary air forces, and airborne forces. Comparable to expeditionary forces, rapid reaction forces are heavier (although not necessarily as heavy as in the past) and more powerful forces that depend more on local infrastructure such as ports of debarkation but can be transported from CONUS into the theater fast enough to blunt an aggressor's continued forward movement and commence the reversal of the enemy's gains. Advocates of transformation envision most of America's future active-duty forces possessing an increased capacity for rapid reaction.

As in defense of treaty allies, C⁴ISR capability is crucial for effective battle management. In the case of non-treaty allies, such C⁴ISR capability is necessarily expeditionary in nature.

As an objective, deterring and winning regional conflicts require the same or similar missions as the defense of allies and of democracies or pivot states. An additional requirement, however, is the capacity to conduct them in an antiaccess environment in which U.S. forces have no toehold or logistics support in the region. This might occur because potential supporters in the region are reluctant to allow U.S. forces to use their territory, lest their own infrastructure or forces become targets of the aggressor, or it may be the result of the aggressor's success in swiftly defeating regional opponents and ejecting U.S. forces from the region.

Access operations against antiaccess efforts require the capability to fight through layered regional defenses. This might include counter-mine warfare, suppression of enemy air defenses and suppression of enemy coastal defenses, and amphibious and airborne operations. Although all these capabilities may be required under the conditions of less demanding scenarios, the antiaccess or area denial environment would be extremely taxing on the forces assigned to conduct these sub-missions and require specialized and advanced capabilities that are likely to require considerable resource investment to develop.

### Value Interests

Categorizing military missions in terms of *value interests* implies more than simply assigning a priority. Critics could argue that the very use of the term *value* places such interests in the nonvital category and reduces the likelihood that the U.S. Government will take action in their regard. Where *vital* interests are said to be drivers of realpolitik, *value* interests might be thought to reflect a lesser or occasional commitment.

But the reality is that throughout much of America's history, its overseas activities have been in support of values such as the enlargement of democratic governance and the suppression of particularly brutal regimes or activities.[28] The United States—motivated by the universality of its democratic principles—routinely chooses to take actions that cannot be strictly defined under realpolitik as purely national interests. Table 1–4 provides an illustrative list of such internationalist value interests. Historically, these are not necessarily treated as less vital interests. These value interests focus on the reduction of overt violence and maintenance of peace in areas of the world prone to conflict. This emphasis is something more than simply the defense of democratic regimes, allies, or pivot states. Illustrative are the U.S. efforts in Bosnia and Kosovo to stem conflicts in which there were few if any supporters of Western-style multiethnic democracy and no apparent natural resources or issues of direct security to the United States. Efforts to stop genocide or ethnic cleansing clearly represent values.

U.S. military forces have routinely been used to support such value interests long before recent emphasis on humanitarian actions. They acted as the primary humanitarian assistance agency of the United States

Table 1–4. **Value Interests**

| Objective: Prevent Internal Conflict or Peacemaking | Objective: Peace Operations |
|---|---|
| Missions: | Missions: |
| Noncombatant evacuation | Multinational peacekeeping |
| Low-intensity conflict | Peacetime military engagement |
| Special operations | Humanitarian assistance |
| Peace enforcement | Other interagency assistance |
| Psychological operations | |
| Civil-military affairs | |
| Foreign military training | |
| C⁴ISR support | |

throughout much of its history, prior to the creation of such specialized entities as the Agency for International Development and the Peace Corps.

Although the use of military force to support value interests hardly constitutes an emerging mission, the forms of such missions have changed with the complexity of modern culture and the impact of globalization. Value interests can be divided into two objectives: preventing internal conflict/peacemaking, and performing more generalized peace operations.

Preventing internal conflict or peacemaking implies the use of armed force to "make" peace, which may sometimes include conducting limited military operations against a warring faction. Peacemaking, a concept greater than simply peace enforcement, does not assume the existence of a peace agreement. Rather, it implies action to curb lawlessness and violence in order to create conditions in which a peace agreement can be reached. The unsuccessful 1991 attempt to quell clan warfare in Somalia can be considered an example. Peacemaking operations require forces capable of conducting such military missions as noncombatant evacuation, low-intensity conflict, special operations, peace enforcement, psychological operations, civil-military affairs, foreign military training, and C⁴ISR support to foreign military forces. All of these missions are also elements of other objectives, such as deterring or winning regional conflicts. However, they are primary or dominant missions of the peacemaking objective and may require specially trained forces to conduct them successfully in a lower intensity environment.

The term *peace operations* is meant to encompass the day-to-day engagement activities of forward-deployed U.S. forces. Unlike peacemaking, peace operations are not expected to involve the use of force against an enemy. Military missions in this category include multinational peacekeeping under existing peace agreements; peacetime military engagement with foreign military forces; humanitarian assistance under permissive (relatively nonviolent) conditions; and other interagency assistance that does not involve conflict with an armed enemy. Peace operations are assumed to be the primary mission of U.S. Armed Forces when they not engaged in conflict or in peacetime training.

## Comparison to QDR 2001

The Bush administration Quadrennial Defense Review Report identifies a series of "enduring national interests" that the "development of defense posture should take into account."[29] The interests identified include:

- ensuring U.S. security and freedom of actions, including U.S. sovereignty, territorial integrity, and freedom; guarding the safety of U.S. citizens at home and abroad; and protecting critical U.S. infrastructure
- honoring international commitments about the security and well-being of allies and friends; precluding hostile domination of critical areas, particularly Europe, Northeast Asia, the East Asian littoral, the Middle East, and Southwest Asia; and maintaining peace and stability in the Western hemisphere
- contributing to economic well-being, including the vitality and productivity of the global economy; the security of international sea, air and space, and information lines of communication; and access to key markets and strategic resources.

The similarities between these listed interests and the interests, objectives, and missions of the hierarchy-of-missions model described in this chapter are obvious, but there are also differences. The hierarchy model was developed to tie missions directly to interests and therefore draws more detailed distinctions between categories. Although the interests listed in the QDR provide general guidance for defense policy goals, the report does not attempt to translate them into military missions. Its focus is on the "paradigm shift" in force-sizing criteria, away from the two-MTW construct to a capabilities-based approach that supports national interests. No priorities for the various U.S. interests are stated explicitly; however, the body of the report makes it clear that the first priority is U.S. sovereignty and territorial integrity, and with it, protection of citizens and critical infrastructure. This interest category is referred to as "ensuring U.S. security and freedom of action"; this is implicitly consistent with the thesis of this chapter that assuring U.S. homeland security is a prerequisite for effective overseas operations.

## Implications of the Hierarchy-of-Missions Model for Military Transformation

The purpose of this volume is to provide a context for the discussion of technology and military transformation. As a first step toward identifying the need for transformation, this chapter has examined the missions that can be expected to be assigned to the U.S. military in the 21st century in terms of a conceptual model that reprioritizes such missions along lines mirroring Bush administration priorities. This reprioritization reflects the passing of the immediate threats of the Cold War era, whose mission priorities were reflected in the spectrum-of-conflict model.

When such missions are viewed in terms of the resource constraints placed on the defense budget, cynics could charge that the hierarchy of survival, vital, and value missions merely confines the value missions to the "underfunded" category. But a quick look at U.S. foreign policy indicates that this outcome is not inevitable, nor even necessarily likely. Different Presidential administrations have made different choices as to funding priorities among the three categories. Arguably, much of U.S. foreign policy is directed toward the defense of such values as democratic governance and human rights. Globalized media play a considerable role in amplifying public concern for the promotion of these values. A Presidential administration could choose to allocate resources among the three categories based on the degree of risk it is willing to accept in any one mission area.[30] Survival interests are likely to be funded more fully than, but not to the exclusion of, value-interest mission areas. A strong virtue of the hierarchy-of-interests model is that it forces explicit decisions on funding priorities, rather than assuming that missions in the vital or value categories are merely lesser included cases of the survival category missions with lesser included funding profiles.

The hierarchy of missions captures the new priorities based on the emerging contours of the future security environment and the apparent expectations of American policymakers. But it does not correspond with the implications of the current visions of the Joint Staff and services as reflected in the existing National Military Strategy or in *Joint Vision 2010* and *Joint Vision 2020*.[31] All three documents discuss a range of military missions necessary for American security, but the strategic and operational concepts they endorse are based on the spectrum-of-conflict approach to analyzing the relative importance of individual missions. Thus, the potential exists for a lack of consistency between the new missions and how the U.S. military presently expects to prepare itself. This raises questions about the purpose, timing, and extent of military transformation.

It also clouds our understanding of the effects on these new missions of recent and expected advancements in military technology. To reach a better understanding, several questions can be raised:

- Do the emerging missions drive the development of these new technologies, or do the new technologies merely enable a more effective response to traditional missions?
- Does the U.S. military need to transform itself radically to carry out these emerging missions effectively?
- Does significant transformation need to be carried out for the U.S. military to capitalize on the new technologies?

Obviously, none of these questions can be answered in terms of the hierarchy-of-missions model alone. Rather, discussion of such questions in the context of the new model is intended as a gateway to the other chapters of this book.

### Notes

[1] The U.S. Commission on National Security/21st Century, *New World Coming* (Washington, DC: September 15, 1999), 141.

[2] Department of Defense, Quadrennial Defense Review Report (Washington, DC: Department of Defense, 2001), 18 (hereafter QDR 2001 Report).

[3] Ibid., 17.

[4] Ibid., 11.

[5] For a "consensus view" of the future security environment based on a survey of official and unofficial studies since 1996, see Sam J. Tangredi, *All Possible Wars? Toward a Consensus View of the Future Security Environment, 2001–2025*, McNair Paper 63 (Washington, DC: National Defense University Press, 2001).

[6] Carl von Clausewitz, *On War*, trans. Peter Paret and Michael Howard (Princeton, NJ: Princeton University Press, 1976), 119.

[7] The logic of the approach is based on the integrated path method used in Michèle A. Flournoy, ed., *QDR 2001: Strategy-Driven Choices for America's Security* (Washington, DC: National Defense University Press, 2001), 352–372.

[8] For the purposes of this chapter, the term *warfighting* refers exclusively to military capabilities designed for countering the armed forces of a future military peer competitor or an aggressive regional power. It is meant to distinguish between the capabilities, organizational structures, and doctrine needed to defeat relatively modern and well-organized enemy forces involved in cross-border aggression from those optimized for smaller-scale conflicts. Although many of these capabilities are the same, doctrine regarding their use may vary.

[9] Thomas Keaney, "Globalization, National Security and the Role of the Military," *SAISphere*, Winter 2000, accessed at <www.sais-jhu.edu/pubs/saisphere/winter00/indexkk.html>.

[10] Chairman, Joint Chiefs of Staff, *Joint Vision 2020* (Washington, DC: Government Printing Office, June 2000), 2.

[11] For the purposes of the analysis presented in this chapter, the assumption of transformation as purposeful change is adopted, and the simple "reaction to technology" thesis is, at least temporarily, rejected.

[12] It has been used as a planning tool and in war college courses up to the present. See, for example, Mahan Scholars, *Navy 2020: A Strategy of Constriction*, MS 99–02 (Newport, RI: Center for Naval Warfare Studies, U.S. Naval War College, August 2000), 29, 50. The spectrum-of-conflict model is not just an American construct; it has been used by other militaries. See Carol McCann and Ross Pigeau, *The Human in Command: Exploring the Modern Military Experience* (New York: Kluwer Academic/Plenum Publishers, 2000), 2.

[13] There has recently been an internal Navy debate about whether the fleet should be described as "forces for presence, shaped for combat" or "forces for combat, shaping through presence." See explanation of this debate in Sam J. Tangredi, "The Fall and Rise of Naval Forward Presence," *U.S. Naval Institute Proceedings* 126, no. 5 (May 2000), 28–32.

[14] Theater nuclear war was an emphasis in the "Pentomic" Army of the 1950s and early 1960s but was gradually deemphasized as the Cold War went on, since no one could determine how to fight it without triggering a strategic nuclear exchange. The mission of strategic nuclear war fell primarily to the Air Force and the Navy.

[15] John J. Zentner, *The Art of Wing Leadership and Aircrew Morale in Combat*, Cadre Paper No. 11 (Maxwell AFB, AL: Air University Press, June 2001), 82–85.

[16] For a detailed discussion of President Bush's reconstitution strategy, see James J. Tritten and Paul N. Stockton, eds., *Reconstituting America's Defense: The New U.S. National Security Strategy* (New York: Praeger Publishers, 1992).

[17] Although Secretary Denby's report implies that the U.S. Navy alone evacuated this large number of civilians from Smyrna, the Navy most likely participated in a coalition effort to transport the refugees. Other evidence indicates that the U.S. Navy accounted for the transport of only about 11,000 of the overall number of refugees. See Dimitra M. Giannuli, "American Philanthropy in the Near East: Relief to the Ottoman Greek Refugees, 1922–1923," Ph.D. dissertation, Kent State University, 1992, 131. See other examples in Bernard D. Cole, "The Interwar Forward Intervention Force: The Asiatic Fleet, the Banana Fleet, and the European Squadrons," paper prepared for the U.S. Navy Forward Presence Bicentennial Symposium, Center for Naval Analyses, Alexandria, VA, June 21, 2001.

[18] See, for example, Daniel Gouré and Jeffrey M. Ranney, *Averting the Defense Train Wreck in the New Millennium* (Washington, DC: Center for Strategic and International Studies, 1999).

[19] George W. Bush's most notable campaign statement on readiness was made in the "A Period of Consequences" speech delivered at The Citadel, Charleston, SC, September 23, 1999.

[20] QDR 2001 Report, iii–v.

[21] The hierarchy of missions model was developed independently of and prior to the publication of the QDR 2001 Report. For Clinton administration national interest categories, see The White House, *A National Security Strategy for a Global Age*, December 2000, 4.

[22] Involvement of military forces in computer network defense does raise legitimate concerns about potential violations of the prohibitions of *posse comitatus* against the use of U.S. military forces against domestic crime. Such concerns would need to be discussed and resolved. For that reason, and because of the difficulty involved in distinguishing foreign from domestic attacks, agencies other than the Department of Defense might be better for the mission of protecting the integrity of financial operations.

[23] See discussion in Tangredi, *All Possible Wars?*, 42–50.

[24] Flournoy, *QDR 2001*, 229–230.

[25] Robert Chase, Emily Hill, and Paul Kennedy, eds., *The Pivotal States: A New Framework for U.S. Policy in the Developing World* (New York: W.W. Norton, 1999).

[26] Von Clausewitz defined *center of gravity* as "the hub of all power and movement, on which everything depends." Currently, it is used to describe the theoretical target of strategic air power. For discussion on Clausewitz's view, see Ronald P. Richardson, "When Two Centers of Gravity Don't Collide: The Divergence of Clausewitz's Theory and Air Power's Reality in the Strategic Bombing Campaign of World War II," course paper, National Defense University, 1995, accessed at <www.ndu.edu/ndu/library/n1/95-E-36.pdf>. For a discussions of the modern usage, see Mark Anthony, et al., *Developing a Campaign Plan to Target Centers of Gravity Within Economic Systems* (Maxwell AFB, AL: Air University Press, May 1995); and Mark Cancian, "Centers of Gravity Are a Myth," *U.S. Naval Institute Proceedings*, September 1998, 30–34.

[27] *Effects-based operations* are defined by Air Force strategists as "military actions and operations designed to produce distinctive and desired effects through the application of appropriate movement, supply, attack, defense, and maneuvers." One of the most recent discussions of the concept (from which the definition was taken) is Edward Mann, Gary Endersby, and Tom Searle, "Dominant Effects: Effects-Based Joint Operations," *Aerospace Power Journal* (Fall 2001), 92–100.

[28] See argument in Walter A. MacDougall, *Promised Land, Crusader State: The American Encounter With the World Since 1776* (Boston: Houghton Mifflin, 1997).

[29] QDR 2001 Report, 2.

[30] For an outstanding analysis of military risk, see Kenneth F. McKenzie, Jr., "Assessing Risk: Enabling Sound Defense Decisions," in Flournoy, *QDR 2001*, 193–216.

[31] Chairman, Joint Chiefs of Staff, *Joint Vision 2010* (Washington, DC: Government Printing Office, 1996). United States Joint Chiefs of Staff, *National Military Strategy of the United States—Shape, Respond, Prepare Now: A Military Strategy for a New Century* (Washington, DC: Department of Defense, 1997).

# Chapter 2

# Harnessing New Technologies

Thomas C. Hone and Norman Friedman

This chapter describes new technologies and their likely transformational effects on military operations in the near (5–10 years) and far term (20 years out). We focus on the United States because much of the technological development important to military operations is taking place here. At the same time, our crystal ball is no better than that of our readers. Put another way, predicting the future is extremely risky, especially predicting the future of technology. Children in the 1950s, for example, might have expected by the 21ˢᵗ century to see frequent space voyages to planets in our solar system, nuclear fusion power plants producing abundant and cheap electricity, and space planes able to reach Tokyo from New York in 3 hours or less; they would most likely not have foreseen the airbus, global warming, or the personal computer. Despite the difficulty inherent in predicting the future of technology, however, we can develop an appreciation for the ways in which technology has transformed warfare in the past, and we attempt to do this in the first part of this chapter. This appreciation can shed some light on what may happen in the next several decades, which is the subject of the remainder of the chapter.

We must begin by asking, "What is transformation?" The "Transformation Study Report" conducted for the Secretary of Defense and completed on April 27, 2001, defined *transformation* as "changes in the concepts, organization, process, technology application and equipment through which significant gains in operational effectiveness, operating efficiencies and/or cost reductions are achieved."[1] This definition covers not only what is normally thought of as technology, such as the ability of an aircraft to cruise at supersonic speed, but also "organization" and "process." That is, it covers both technology and the social structures and processes by which the technology is made an accepted part of daily life. The definition ties together concepts, equipment, organization, and processes.

This chapter, however, focuses only on technology—the devices and equipment that embody critical scientific concepts. Organization and process issues are left to other chapters. We offer here no definition of technology as our starting point because we all know, at some elementary level, what modern technology is and what it does. What is so extraordinary about current digital technology is the way that it has penetrated our everyday lives, from the personal computer to the wireless phone to the thermostat that regulates the heating and cooling of homes, offices, and factories. This is a repetition of the process that introduced earlier forms of technology, such as the automobile, rotary telephone, and electric typewriter. First a single, everyday device becomes digital, and then, rather soon, many more devices become digital. Why? Because these devices better support essential activities or supplant existing technology. This phenomenon becomes apparent from the answers given by people randomly chosen to explain what technology is. They will point to technologically sophisticated devices: those devices that incorporate today's information technology, and especially those things that have made their work or their everyday lives better. We will do the same. We will describe devices that will change the way war is fought, assuming that scientists and engineers continue working as they have.

## Nine Characteristics of Modern Warfare Technology

First, military organizations that can adopt and promote new technologies clearly have a critical edge in "modern" warfare. This was certainly true when modern warfare was attrition warfare, and it is true even now, when the stated policy of the United States is to avoid attrition warfare like that seen during World Wars I and II. As the military services of the major nations well understood after World War II, adapting the technology developed in the civilian world, such as radios, to military uses was not enough. They had to take the next step and actually foster the development of technology, knowing from experience gained in wartime that this development would be essential.

Second, technology is something that can be deliberately and consciously developed by human beings working within complex organizations. Thomas Edison, for example, is recognized as a gifted inventor, but he is also less frequently recognized for an even greater achievement: developing the first systematic technology research laboratory in the United States. Third, new technology is useless to military organizations unless their members "formulate a doctrine to exploit each innovation in weapons to the utmost." This point, made succinctly nearly half a century ago by Professor (and reserve Major General) I.B. Holley, Jr., in his classic study *Ideas and Weapons*, is now generally accepted. Indeed, we might combine the second and third points into "Holley's Law of Technological Innovation in the Military": The adoption of new technology within a military service requires that the service develop a doctrine for the successful use of this technology in war, and neither the doctrine nor the technology will be developed unless that military service has an organization whose members understand technology and can make binding decisions about its support and application.[2]

Fourth, militarily significant technologies are often developed almost simultaneously in different nations. A classic example of this phenomenon is radar, which was under development as a military technology in eight countries (France, the Netherlands, Italy, the United Kingdom, Germany, the United States, the Soviet Union, and Japan) before World War II. Current versions of this same phenomenon are the ubiquitous personal computer and wireless phone. Given the often rapid spread of new technology, the question then becomes, "Who can best use it as an instrument of war?"

Fifth, there is no guarantee that a new technology, once developed in the laboratory or even in prototype form, will receive adequate funding to become an operational capability. Radar's historical development also illustrates this point. Just before World War II, Adolf Hitler's regime reduced funding for microwave radar development because his war strategy was to rely on quickly defeating his enemies. This neglect of long-term technology development, though consistent with Hitler's strategy, cost his regime dearly once the war became one of attrition. In Japan, the problem had a different cause. There, uncoordinated army and navy programs inhibited the establishment of an efficient electronics industrial base and hence the fielding of adequate numbers of operationally useful radars.[3]

Sixth, the development or refinement of one technology may complement the development of another and lead to results that no one had anticipated. An example is the development of the small, reliable cruise missile in the early 1970s. Cruise missiles were not new in the late 1960s: both tactical and strategic versions had already been fielded, but most were quite large weapons because their engines were heavy. Furthermore, because they consumed a lot of fuel, their necessarily large fuel loads also added to their weight and size, thereby limiting operational utility. The development of a small, lightweight turbine engine by Williams International made possible a much smaller cruise missile, one that could be fired from a torpedo tube, launched by a carrier-based attack aircraft, or fired by a small fast-attack craft. Adding digital processors to radar seekers and radar altimeters gave improved accuracy, stealthiness, and reliability to this new generation of cruise missiles powered by the smaller, more efficient engine. There are many other cases of such synergy in the historical relationship between technology and warfare.[4]

Just having a technology, however, is not enough. Our seventh point about technology is that a military service also needs access to an industry that can produce the equipment embodying that technology in sufficient numbers. The historical development of radar, once again, illustrates this point. In August 1940, a British delegation showed the cavity magnetron to representatives of the American military services. This device generated signals for high-power microwaves and made it practical to develop airborne radars. The British would have needed to produce the new device, along with its receiver and display sets, in quantities sufficient to equip thousands of aircraft. Because British industry apparently lacked the capacity for such production, the American electronics industry, with its greater industrial capacity, served as the foundation for the rapid wartime introduction of this new technology.

Our eighth point is that possessing a technology, even in quantity, is no guarantee that it will be decisive in war. The doctrine, which Holley argued was so essential, has to be implemented through training, and this means that training techniques and technology may be as crucial as production capacity. This is particularly true of sophisticated simulators to give soldiers the "feel" of how best to use a new technology in combat. For example, with night-vision devices—infrared detectors or visual light magnifiers—modern ground forces can fight around the clock. The availability of these devices, however, does not guarantee that they will be used effectively. Both the Iraqi forces and the U.S.-led Gulf Coalition forces had advanced night-vision devices in the 1991 Persian Gulf War. American forces, however, employed superior training technologies and were therefore better prepared to use this technology effectively in battle. Since training is a key factor, the Department of Defense (DOD) spends a great deal of energy and money to advance the technology of training, even though the benefits of this effort are often not apparent until after a conflict.

Our ninth point concerning the relationship of modern technology and warfare is that the military's initial experience with a new technology can reveal problems with making the new capability operational. Over time, as the technology is better understood, the number of systems needed (both experimental and operational) to work out the bugs will decline. This means that a military service may have to invest in a number of prototypes, or even in numbers of different types of operational models, before the technology is proven in operations.

The introduction of jet engines into the Air Force after World War II reveals this tendency. Aircraft powered by these engines can be divided into three categories. The first category consists of experimental aircraft built to test a new design or concept, such as the Bell X–1 series aircraft designed to break the sound barrier. The second category includes aircraft built as part of a development program, such as the XF–88 McDonnell penetration fighter of 1946. Though such aircraft were never produced for actual service use, tests on them helped jet propulsion technology mature. The third category consists of operationally fielded aircraft, such as Republic's F–84.[5]

The result of several decades of experimentation and production can be thought of as a funnel, with many options in the beginning (the mouth of the funnel). Gradually, through tests and the evaluation of actual operations, some technological possibilities are abandoned and others matured. The result is a narrowing of options (the throat of the funnel) and the eventual production of large numbers of standard but sophisticated designs. The F–86 Sabre Jet represents a first-phase production jet interceptor, the F–104 a second-phase type, and the F–15 a third-phase type. All three aircraft shared the same basic mission, but considered sequentially, they showed the evolution of operational jet aircraft. Our point is that the number of experimental and developmental models tends to decrease as the technology is better understood: as it shifts from being a *revolutionary* technology to an *evolutionary* technology. The exception is when new technology requires a new approach. The current example of a new technology that is still in its revolutionary phase is that of vertical take-off and landing. The V–22 acquisition program was based on an assessment that vertical take-off and landing technology had passed through its revolutionary stage and was essentially evolutionary. Recent events have shown that this assessment was erroneous.

These nine characteristics of technology and its effects on warfare reveal that much has been learned about the subject. This is not unknown territory. Defense officials have given a great deal of thought for decades about how to apply technology to modern war. In 1981, for example, William O'Neil (author of chapter 5 in this volume) wrote a classic essay entitled "Technology and Naval War." This effort, undertaken while O'Neil

worked in the Office of the Secretary of Defense, identified the technological trends that were shaping the future of war at sea: stealth, linked surveillance systems, information processing, and stand-off weaponry.[6] In
September 1987, Lt. Gen. Glenn Kent, USAF (Ret.), then working for the
RAND Corporation, presented a paper to the American Association for
the Advancement of Science entitled "Exploiting Technology." He covered
a number of lessons that had been learned about turning a technological
advance into an operational weapon, and he also discussed the larger,
strategic implications of digital technology. For example, he noted the potential of precisely guided conventional munitions to have strategic effects.[7] Officials such as O'Neil and Kent have been instrumental in developing policies and procedures for surveying technology for those elements
that have military implications. They and their successors have kept U.S.
forces armed with the most technologically advanced sensors and weapons
of any military force on earth.

The official interest in, and exploration of, advanced technology is
just as strong now as it was during the Cold War. For example, to improve
the process of moving a technology from an engineering laboratory, such
as Lockheed's Skunk Works,[8] to a developmental program, the Secretary
of Defense has established the Office of Technology Transition.[9] Since
September 2000, the office of the Deputy Under Secretary of Defense
(Science and Technology) has produced a number of plans and
"roadmaps" showing potential paths from demonstrated technologies to
likely future programs.

Although there is no way to predict how specific investments in
basic research will produce technologies of military value, there are ways
to evaluate and compare proposals that purport to show how a certain
technology can add to the military power of the United States. For example, software designer Barry Boehm is a well-known pioneer in the field
of software development and metrics. His work on software standards,
much of it promulgated over a period of two decades by the Institute of
Electrical and Electronics Engineers (IEEE), has helped the defense industry to judge the technological maturity and developmental requirements of new software.[10]

There has also been a great deal of progress in recent years in understanding how technologies develop and how they can be adapted to warfare
at an acceptable cost to the Nation.[11] In July 1999, for instance, the General
Accounting Office published a report entitled "Better Management of
Technology Development Can Improve Weapon System Outcomes." This

report, drawing on the work done by the Air Force and the National Aeronautics and Space Administration, described how certain measures, referred to as technology readiness levels, could be used to gauge a technology's maturity. Put another way, the report argued that there were quantitative means for determining whether a given technology was ready for development in a military acquisition program. Though there is still no consensus within the defense acquisition community that these measures are in fact completely reliable, the work to create and then test them in actual programs is a sign of the progress that has been made in linking new technology to measures of its production (and hence its military) potential.[12]

## Some Recent History

This improved understanding of how technologies develop is useful in comprehending what has happened and why. We can also use it to anticipate future technological developments that may have a major impact on warfare. To show how, table 2–1 presents a set of projections of transformational technologies that could have been compiled in 1920. The 10 listed technologies all became critical in later years.

Some of these projections were actually made following World War I. The Navy's Bureau of Aeronautics, for example, chose to fund the development of larger and more powerful radial piston engines, despite technical concerns in the mid-1920s that such powerful engines would wrench themselves out of the aircraft that they powered. Both the Navy and Army financed the development of gyroscopes for bombsights and analog computers for gunnery fire control. The Naval Research Laboratory was the original home of radar research and development in the United States. Both services financed the development of high-frequency radio, radio direction-finding, and radio intercepts and decryption of coded messages. In 1920, it was clear that the piston-engine aircraft was a rapidly advancing technology. So, too, were electronic devices and analog computers.

But there were some real surprises that a knowledgeable observer could not reasonably have projected in 1920. The one that transformed warfare was the nuclear weapon, especially the plutonium bomb.[13] Nuclear propulsion of submarines and ships was just beyond the 20-year time horizon, but serious thought about naval nuclear power plants followed quickly on the heels of the work done by the Manhattan Project.

Table 2–2 looks not at projections but at transformations. It highlights the spectacular growth in the sophistication and military utility of aviation, from a decidedly auxiliary role in World War I to an essential role in World

Table 2–1. Notional U.S. Projections in 1920 of Transformational U.S. Military Technologies

| Technology | Short Term (5 years, ca. 1925) | Interim (10 years, ca. 1930) | Long Term (20 years, ca. 1940) |
|---|---|---|---|
| Aircraft engines | Development of radial piston engines | 1,000 horsepower (hp) radial engines | 2,000 hp radial engines |
| Bombsights | Fixed bombsight + low-level bombing | Dive bombing; gyroscopic sight | Computing sight |
| Aircraft structures | Wood + fabric | Metal + fabric | All metal |
| Electronics | Vacuum tube amplifiers, active + passive sonar, intercepting and jamming low + medium frequency radio signals | Intercepting high-frequency (HF) signals, effective HF, reliable active sonar | High Frequency Direction Finding (HFDF) Frequency Modulation (FM) radios, radio navigation, radar, and jamming radio signals |
| Nuclear weapons | Reasoned speculation by scientists | Developing particle accelerators | Potential energy measured |
| Jet engines | Laboratory experiments | First design patented | Development |
| Computers | Naval artillery fire control with analog devices well established | Stable elements in bombsights and in naval gunfire computers (all analog) | Routine use of automatic data processing equipment + mechanical calculators |
| Helicopters | Concepts | Lab experiments | Prototypes |
| Amphibious vehicles | Ships, boats, and commercial off-the-shelf technologies | Prototype landing craft | Landing craft + tractors |
| Air defense command and control (C²) | Binoculars and telephones | Binoculars + telephones, sound detection devices | Radar, FM radios, networked control and surveillance |

War II. The funds pumped into aviation in World War I stimulated the technology; that technology, coupled with battlefield radios and new tactical concepts, led to effective combined arms warfare—to blitzkrieg.

Table 2–2 also shows the rapid growth in electronics just before and during World War II. Almost all of the elements of electronic warfare were introduced in some form during World War II, including the essentials of electronic countermeasures (ECM) and counter-countermeasures (ECCM). For electronics, World War II was a period of rapid and intense development that carried over into the Cold War.

*Industry* in table 2–2 refers to *modern* industry, with its planning, financing, and linkage between research and development and production. Modern industrial organizations learn quickly and therefore can adapt to changing situations. They can capitalize on new research, plan and execute major projects, and sustain huge social initiatives, such as modern war. But during World War II, U.S. industry essentially displayed an improvement on the production effort of World War I. Neither World War I nor World War II dramatically altered American industry. The major alteration waited on the creation of a set of organizations linked electronically to produce increasingly sophisticated digital systems; this came about as a consequence of Cold War efforts that produced a software industry that is still transforming warfare.

Several patterns can be observed here. The first is that different technologies have transformed warfare at different speeds. For example, even if some might not agree that aviation turned into a war-transforming technology in World War I, by 1919 the scientific and industrial basis for effective combined arms aviation existed. It needed refinement before the early crude radio-telegraphs could be turned into effective voice radios on aircraft, and the military aircraft flying in 1920 were limited in terms of range and bomb load. However, better, lighter radios and heavier, more powerful piston engines were simply projections of existing technology. In other words, predictable improvements could be expected, eventually and inevitably, to lead to a military transformation if only military organizations continued investing in them. The required technological revolution had already taken place.

In contrast, the technological revolution required to underpin electronics had not taken place by 1920, but by 1930, it had. Following considerable investment in the technology as war approached, all forms of warfare employed electronic technologies in World War II. Electronics, however, did not *transform* warfare in this global contest. War remained a

Table 2–2. **Transformational Technologies: World War I, World War II, Cold War**

| Technology | World War I | World War II | Cold War |
|---|---|---|---|
| Electronics | Mainly strategic role (for example, diplomatic communications, as with the Zimmerman telegram) but tactical role at sea. Low and medium radio frequencies. Encryption + decryption are important but not critical. Field telephones in armies | Robust tactical and strategic telephone and radio communications. Encryption and decryption and intercepts essential. HF radio. HFDF, radar, sonar and widespread electronic countermeasures (ECM). Also radio navigation | More radar frequencies. Aerial radar. Radar linked to display technology. Digital processing of signals. Phased array radar. Advanced ECM and electronic countermeasures (ECCM). Integrated avionics. Over-the-horizon radar. Stealth. Exploitation of much more of electronic spectrum |
| Aviation | Scouting + patrolling, mostly conceptual beginning of close air support (CAS). British develop aircraft carriers. Much use of lighter-than-air craft for range and endurance | Mass production of advanced aircraft. CAS, strategic bombing, air transport, effective carrier aviation. Jet aircraft. Radar bombing + bombing by radio navigation | Nuclear weapons-equipped long-range bombers. Mid-air refueling. Stealth. Supersonic cruise. Cruise missiles. Precision guided munitions. Unmanned aerial vehicles |
| Industry | Mass production. Mechanization of agriculture begins. Integrated industrial production of some products such as automobiles. Mass consumer markets for industrially produced items. Industrial mobilization not successful in World War I | Industry becomes a prime target. Total social and economic mobilization. Beginning of the "industrialization" of research and development (R&D). Basic industrial model = same as during World War I. Industrial mobilization is a success | Industry and research centers are *the* prime target. Industrialization of computer hardware development and manufacturing. "Lean" manufacturing possible. Shift away from mobilization model of World War II. R&D begins as a government-provided good, then, with post-Cold War information revolution, becomes a privately provided good subject to market forces |

destructive struggle of attrition, exhausting the mobilized national resources of all of the participants except the United States. Electronics truly transformed warfare only in the digital age, when electronics enabled, for example, area bombing to be replaced by true precision targeting.

Table 2–2 also reveals the logic behind the industrial bombing campaigns of World War II and the survival of that targeting strategy into the Cold War. It shows why a blanket attack upon an enemy's industry does not make sense in the post-Cold War world. Today, the American military can hit what it can see with precision. Conventional forces with precision weapons can now, it is said, produce strategic effects. War, or at least some of its forms, has been *transformed*.

But some technologies are missing from table 2–2, and these missing elements suggest how difficult it is to look beyond imminently expected technological developments. Nuclear weapons and space are absent; they were not anticipated or developed until midcentury or later. Yet if any technology transformed war, it was that of nuclear weapons. Will any technology similarly transform war in the next 25 years? Micromachines and hybrid organic-electronic computers are candidates for that role. Some have suggested that space technology, currently providing reconnaissance and communications support to military operations, is in the same relative position that aviation technology was in 1919. The high cost of producing and orbiting satellites may, however, prevent such a pervasive transformation. Instead, the new technologies of advanced software, "intelligent" devices, and digital telecommunications are more consistent with the transformational patterns displayed in table 2–2.

In World Wars I and II, emerging technologies were infused with lots of money and pushed by demand for new devices. Thus, these emerging technologies advanced quickly, laying the foundation to change future combat. The Cold War was no exception to this pattern. One particular emerging technology funded by the Cold War—the personal computer—joined to another—the Internet—to transform not only warfare in Western industrialized nations but also much of society and culture. Investments in software and related hardware have continued at wartime levels since the end of the Cold War, resulting in predictably rapid growth in software and software-related technologies. However, since private-sector sources are largely responsible for maintaining these high investment levels, public agencies such as the Department of Defense have not been able to control or direct the rapidly emerging capabilities resulting from this growth. Thus, the future, when

DOD will depend on private sector investment in information technology for advances, may be very different than the Cold War, when it was DOD that financed so much basic research with military implications.

## Impact of Technology on Military Tasks

This section matches technologies against 12 military tasks likely to be required in 3 future time periods—within the Future Years Defense Program (FYDP [a 5-year period]), out to 10 or 12 years, and what would be needed in 2020 to support the expectations expressed by the Chairman of the Joint Chiefs of Staff in *Joint Vision 2020*[14] (see table 2–3). The "military tasks" are drawn primarily from the "Final Report" of the Conventional Forces Study (otherwise known as the Gompert Study) done recently for the Secretary of Defense, augmented to transcend the Gompert Study's focus on conventional forces.[15] We drew on our own experience and knowledge for the technologies. Note that legacy systems embodying accepted technologies would persist across each of these time horizons. For example, the B–2, listed as a FYDP system under the "Long Range Strike" military task, should also be performing this task in 2020. There is even a chance that the Air Force will still be flying B–52s in combat roles at that time.

Table 2–3 shows that there will be a shift from chemical explosives in warheads to directed energy weapons. However, chemical explosives and propellants will still be manufactured and used; unguided, chemically explosive small arms and other weapons will have roles for many years to come. For example, chemical explosives can generate electromagnetic pulses to overload many existing digital circuits, thereby giving chemical explosives a new lease on life even in a network-centric battlefield. Such technological developments do not stand out in table 2–3 but are examples of how certain existing technologies will have, at least for a while, important roles to play in warfare.

Table 2–3 also indicates that future weapons (although not necessarily their platforms) will zero in on targets faster. The potential to acquire and share real-time data will grow, and weapons will be able to act on this data to strike mobile targets. Deployment of hypersonic missiles can be expected by 2020, if not sooner. We should, by then, also see missiles that can loiter above a battlefield at subsonic speeds yet are capable of suddenly attacking at *hyper*sonic speeds.

Even now, sensors, digital communications signals, and weapons increasingly are being netted together, and systems designed for such networking (such as the Joint Tactical Radio System) will first supplement and then replace current systems. The Tomahawk land attack cruise missile, for example, survives as a legacy system because it can be linked to the signals broadcast by global positioning system (GPS) satellites. Although designing a new composite missile with stealth characteristics that could operate in a netted environment might be better in terms of cost, that approach would be too expensive right now, so this transition will occur only when future modifications to the Tomahawk cease to be cost-effective.

Successfully implementing *Joint Vision 2020* in a fiscally constrained environment will require a choice between much improved networks, on the one hand, and new systems, such as directed energy weapons, on the other, because the country cannot afford both. The network choice would seem to be an easy and obvious one, except that directed energy weapons promise to reduce ammunition requirements so dramatically that it may be difficult for DOD to avoid investing in them. One of the goals of *Joint Vision 2020* is "focused logistics," and one big step toward this goal would be to eliminate numbers of conventional munitions. Moreover, directed energy weapons may be the only effective counter to certain forms of missile attack.

One way out of the dilemma created by the high cost of both systems and the links among them would be for the military services to rely on private industry to construct netted or networked systems. This approach would not be without precedent: military forces in World War I relied on industrial telephone capabilities, and in World War II they relied on radio equipment built to commercial electronic standards. The military risks that are associated with such commercial off-the-shelf command and control are great, however. They include the risks of interception of digital signals and invasion, disruption, or even destruction of the network. But if U.S. industry has any advantage in this area, it is in software development; American commercial developers are currently pioneering developments for advanced digital communications.

## Likely Future Technological Developments

Table 2–4 lists potentially transforming technologies and their development across time. This list of technologies is compiled from current unclassified periodicals, such as the IEEE *Computer*, augmented by our own additions.

Several points about table 2–4 are worth noting. First, very few of the table's boxes are blank; many technological areas are likely to produce militarily useful capabilities. All of the areas listed are being monitored by

Table 2–3. **Transformational Technologies (by Military Tasks)**

| Military Task (from Gompert Study) | In Current FYDP | Interim Force | Supporting *JV 2020* |
|---|---|---|---|
| Air Combat | Stealth supersonic cruise, AIM–9X, AIM–120, AIM–7F | Directional explosive fuze, helmet-directed targeting, active electronically scanned array | Dual-role missile, miniature air-launched decoy |
| Missile Defense | National Missile Defense (NMD), modified Aegis missile defense system, airborne laser (ABL) prototype | Mature NMD (kinetic kill), mature ABL, ground-based laser, space-based infrared sensors (SBIRS) | Space-based laser |
| Naval Strike | Air-launched PGMs (JDAM [joint direct attack munition], SLAM–ER, JSOW [joint standoff weapon]), Tomahawk Land Attack Missile, advanced digital guidance systems for missiles and projectiles | Land attack standard missile, advanced gun system | Stealthy cruise missile, hypersonic cruise missile, laser, rail gun |
| Ground Combat | Hypersonic antitank missile, Longbow Hellfire, guided ATACMS (Army tactical missile system), Javelin, V–22 tilt-rotor aircraft, Comanche networked with other Army systems | Light armored vehicle, lightweight ATACMS (High Mobility Artillery Rocket System—truck-mounted ATACMS), tactical laser, digital battlefield | Netted support to reduce the force "footprint" |
| Long-Range Strike | B–2, Tomahawk, Terrain Contour Matching, Digital Scene Matching Area Correlation, Global Positioning System (GPS) | Advanced (stealthy) cruise missile | Hypersonic weapons to reduce response time |

| | | | |
|---|---|---|---|
| Air Strike | Laser-guided bombs, sensor fuzed weapon, long-range precision strike weapons with digital guidance, control, and submunition fuzing | Small Diameter Bomb, autonomous air-launched weapon (for example, Low Cost Autonomous Attack System), Brilliant Anti-Tank Submunition | Directed energy (lasers) |
| Amphibious Combat | V–22, advanced assault amphibian, mine neutralization | Netted fire support, urban warfare sensors | Quad-rotor vertical/short takeoff and landing aircraft |
| Space Operations | Communications and reconnaissance only | Low Earth orbit antisatellite (ASAT) capabilities | ASAT against geosynchronous satellites |
| Information War | Organized hacking to gain intelligence or to shut down enemy systems; limited deception | Emphasis on deception to counter netted warfare | Effective information assurance |
| Command and Control | Link 11, Link 16, and other tactical digital links, plus satellites and digital decision support tools | Direct satellite phones, advanced digital links among large networks of users and sensors, and joint radio | New frequency range for greater bandwidth |
| Sensors and Reconnaissance | Joint Surveillance Target Attack Radar System, NAVSTAR navigation satellite, GPS, PROPHET (Common platform for Army signals intelligence and electronic attack systems), advanced deployable sonar arrays | SBIRS, Discover II | Space-based air-control radar |
| Strategic Mobility | Maritime Prepositioning Ships, C–17 transports | High-speed ships | Heavy-lift aircraft, mobile offshore base |

DOD, and many are being funded directly. Second, this comprehensiveness contrasts with the many blank boxes in the historical snapshot presented in table 2–1. In 1920, there were many areas not being funded or studied by the military departments. Even the development of 2,000-horsepower radial piston engines for aircraft was judged high risk, while nuclear weapons, jet aircraft, helicopters, and amphibious tractors were not even under consideration. Today, DOD has processes and procedures for monitoring and encouraging wide-ranging technological developments. This institutionalization of the link between technology and the Nation's military organizations, which was brought to fruition during the Cold War, is itself an important—even *transformational*—innovation and should be treated as such. The issue today is how to maintain this link.

Table 2–4 also indicates some technical obstacles that inhibit the military from developing sought-after capabilities. For example, there is no entry under "Supporting *JV 2020*" for "High-Speed Surface Ships," despite the fact that such ships would be extremely important militarily if they could be produced and operated at a reasonable cost. The basic obstacle to high-speed, high-capacity surface ships is the resistance of water to any ship moving on and through it. Similarly, economically feasible use of space depends on having a cheap way to loft satellites into orbit. Right now, there is no cheap way to do so, certainly not for the large satellites that meet the requirements of DOD. In both cases—ships and space—certain unavoidable physical obstacles have to be surmounted, and table 2–4 highlights these barriers. However, the services continue to examine and invest in space and high-speed ships because the potential payoffs are so great.

Improved communication, command, and sensor technologies are listed in table 2–4, which shows how critical these digital, software-driven technologies are to advances in a number of areas. Admiral William Owens, USN (Ret.), former vice chairman of the Joint Chiefs of Staff, has been saying for years that the critical "revolution" is informational. In *Lifting the Fog of War*, Owens argues that microprocessors were the key element in unmanned aerial vehicle (UAV) development. He defines the *ongoing revolution in military affairs* as "the ability to achieve *integrated sight*—the stage where the raw data gathered from a network of sensors of different types is successfully melded into information."[16] Table 2–4 supports these arguments, although Owens might expect battlefield leaders to be able to draw information from netted raw data earlier than this table projects.

Table 2–4 also shows how many complex technologies there are with military implications. It is not enough for agencies within DOD to watch a limited number of critical technologies; a great number have to be tracked and assessed. For example, technology number 6 in the table is "Avionics Miniaturization." Miniaturization is possible because computer chips have gotten not only smaller but also more capable and reliable. What technologies have improved so that the chips could get better and smaller and cheaper? Photolithography is one; another is the manufacturing of reliable silicon substrates. Indeed, what we have seen in this particular field is the application of quantum physics to industrial processes, but the details of how this is done are beyond the understanding of even well educated officials. In other words, understanding technology so as to direct it is harder than it was just a few decades ago, and many of the people who understand new technology are not working for the Department of Defense. How can their expertise be used to DOD advantage?

One answer is that DOD can purchase much new technology "off the shelf" from commercial vendors and thereby stay up with the best technology that private firms can field. But commercial vendors are not particularly interested in the problems of distinguishing decoys from an actual warhead in space or of identifying a shallow trajectory ballistic missile's likely target once it is launched. What private firms can offer commercially may not *ever* meet DOD needs.

How, then, are DOD leaders to know which specific technologies to watch and which to invest heavily in? A very interesting recent paper on the military potential of lasers illustrates this dilemma. The author, Mark Rogers, claims, "Laser technology has matured so substantially in recent decades that the United States now has the capability to use lasers from space-based platforms to change radically the conduct of war." Yet he also admits that semiconductor lasers, which are most efficient in converting "input energy into laser light," are not suitable as weapons. Moreover, he acknowledges that "it is difficult to point laser beams with great precision," and therefore it is not easy to keep the focused beam on the target long enough to destroy it. In consequence, Rogers admits that a space-based laser weapon would be expensive, vulnerable to antisatellite weapons, and face "significant engineering challenges."[17] So what are DOD leaders to do? Invest heavily? Or wait, while investing in limited advanced research projects?

There is no easy answer to these questions because we cannot see the future clearly. One or more nascent technologies may turn out to be

## Table 2–4. Transformational Technologies across Time

| Technologies | In Current FYDP | Interim Force | Support *JV2020* |
|---|---|---|---|
| Robust, high-capacity digital communications | JTRS (Joint Tactical Radio System), CEC (Cooperative Engagement Capability), Link 16, DCGS (Distributed Common Ground Station), Prophet | These will mature and be joined by National EHF and Laser SATCOM | Polar MilSatCom for constant coverage |
| Long-range precision navigation | GPS, DSMAC, TERCOM | Anti-jam GPS | Higher precision GPS |
| Spaced-based sensors | Optical and infrared imaging, ELINT (electronic intelligence) | Discover II (near real-time GMTI [Ground Moving Target Indicator]) | Real-time coverage of airspace by space-based radar |
| STOL/VSTOL | V–22 | JSF (Joint Strike Fighter), V–22 | STOL C–130 Quad-rotor |
| Blended wing, or advanced airframes | B–2 | Boeing's near-supersonic commercial airliner | Heavy-lift aircraft SST |
| Avionics miniaturization | MIDS (Multifunctional Information Distribution System) | AESA and Link 16 | UAV (unmanned aerial vehicle) packages for autonomous operations |
| High-speed surface ships | Hydrofoils, Landing Craft Air Cushion (LCAC) Vehicles | SLICE (hybrid SWATH and hydrofoil) | |
| UAVs | Global Hawk | Armed UAVs (UCAVs [unmanned combat aerial vehicles]) | Micro, netted UAVs |

| | | | |
|---|---|---|---|
| UUVs (unmanned underwater vehicles) | Mine detection | Fast UUVs | MANTA (lethal UUV with a data link) |
| Cheap lift to orbit | Commercial off-the-shelf (COTS) rocket | Reusable rocket | Aerospace vehicle |
| Laser-tactical | Target designator | Tactical high energy laser, Tuned lasers | Small portable tactical weapon |
| Laser-strategic | Airborne laser (ABL) | ASAT/ballistic missile defense (BMD) | Space-based laser |
| High-energy propulsion | Ducted rocket | SCRAMJET | Cruise-and-then-accelerate motor |
| Air-breathing cruise missile propulsion | Fanjet | Advanced propeller design for very long range | High density fuel will lower fuel weight or increase range |
| Radar | Passive phased arrays, digital processing | AESA for aircraft | Multistatic systems using available energy |
| Digital decision support tools | Tools for using networked tactical picture on ships | Extension of MTS (mobile terminal system) technology to mobile ground forces (the digital battlefield) | Extension to tactical aircraft (the pilot's associate) |
| Energy storage | Batteries | | Advanced capacitors for pulses of power |
| Energy generation | Turbo-generators, diesel generators | Fuel cells | Solar collectors |
| Robotics | In manufacturing | Mobile battlefield sensors | Combat robots |

Table 2–4. **Transformational Technologies across Time**—*continued*

| Technologies | In Current FYDP | Interim Force | Support JV2020 |
|---|---|---|---|
| Nonlethal devices | Irritants | Chemicals and other means to incapacitate personnel | Materials which degrade or break down substances |
| Digital networks | Internet and equivalents | Broadband nets (DSL+ [Domain Specific Languages]) | Intelligent net (self-policing) |
| Display technology | 2-dimensional with limited interaction | Interoperable operating pictures, 3-dimensional display | Virtual reality |
| Digital memory | Megabytes of RAM, gigabytes of hard memory | Gigabytes of RAM, terabytes of hard memory | Distinction between RAM and hard memory vanishes |
| Software | Intelligent Agents, Training Simulators | Interconnected universal small devices, appliances | Self-writing and self-testing software |
| Sensors (detection level) | Link 11 (netted at vector level) | CEC, unattended sensors, Advanced Deployable Sonar Arrays (netted at detection level) | (netted at raw data level) |
| New materials | Carbon neon tubes for high strength fibers | High-temperature super-conductivity, "super explosives" | Organic electronics |
| Super cruise | F–22 | Hypersonic cruise | Space plane |
| Stealth | B–2 | Reduction of secondary signatures | Stealth independent of shape (broadband ECM) |

| | | | |
|---|---|---|---|
| Micro-machines | Ring-laser gyros | "Smart" fuzes, small sensors | Massive reduction in the size and weight of many devices |
| Medical | Design-to-order drugs | Artificial blood, remote treatment, rapid antidotes to "designer" biological | Artificial and nonhuman organs, nerve regeneration, organ regeneration |

"sleepers," apparently useless initially, but very important once developed. For example, there are DOD officials who believe that exotic nonlethal weapons might have a bright military future. There are chemicals that cause metal to turn brittle, for example, and other chemicals that put a stop to combustion in vehicle and aircraft engines, and even sticky foams that could immobilize soldiers without otherwise harming them.[18] It is not possible to predict what new and militarily useful technologies will come out of basic scientific research labs. It is not possible to eliminate technological surprises or to prevent key developing technologies from drawing scarce resources away from investigating exotic but promising new technologies. The balance between pursuing exotic, risky technologies and pragmatic, well-understood technological developments is the subject of the final section of this chapter.

## Conclusion

The future of science and technology is often thought of and described in fantastic terms, even while revolutionary changes are taking place right before our eyes but are not necessarily recognized as such. A classic example is the affordable automobile. Henry Ford developed it in order to revolutionize American society, which it did. But who, 50 years ago, would have described the affordable automobile as a revolutionary technology? In the 1950s, revolutionary technology was space travel, intelligent robots, and the means to eliminate dreaded afflictions such as polio, heart disease, and cancer. But the really revolutionary technology was sitting in the garage.

This tendency to miss the revolutionary implications of what most of us think of as not-so-revolutionary technology is not new. In 1898, in his novel *War of the Worlds*, H.G. Wells posited some highly advanced but not—from today's perspective—impossible technology. The Martian vehicles traveled through space and survived the descent through the earth's atmosphere. The Martians used a "heat ray" or laser with devastating but short-range effects on unprotected living things or combustible material. The Martians also employed chemical weapons against British units who tried to attack them from outside the range of their laser weapon. This deadly gas, released from rocket-propelled canisters, killed human beings but decomposed, after a time, into a substance that was benign and easy to dispose of.

Mobile machines were the fourth advanced technology possessed by the Martians: they assembled a flying machine from component parts and moved over the ground with three-legged walking machines that could outpace a horse. Although Wells did not describe a technologically advanced Martian command and control system, the Martians obviously possessed one since the movement of their invading forces was deliberate and coordinated, even though these forces were dispersed across the industrialized nations of the earth.

These advanced technologies are not considered fantastic today. Our military forces have lasers, are trained to fight and survive in a chemical warfare environment, send reconnaissance and communication satellites into space to support military campaigns, and are extremely mobile. But our capabilities are more than a century beyond the world of H.G. Wells. His contemporaries—even his scientific contemporaries—did not expect that his visions *could* become reality. Wells the science fiction writer was too far ahead of them. The science required by his advanced technologies, such as relativity and quantum mechanics, had yet to be understood.

By looking into their own recent past, however, H.G. Wells' late-19th-century contemporaries might have gained a greater understanding of an ongoing revolution that was transforming the way in which they would wage war. During the 19th century, the sources of new technologies changed dramatically. New technologies had traditionally not resulted from purely experimental efforts, like Faraday's invention of the dynamo; he demonstrated it about 1830, when there was no practical use for it. By the end of the century, however, technological advances built upon known scientific principles. For example, in the mid-1860s, James Clark Maxwell codified electromagnetic phenomena in a series of equations that implied the existence of electromagnetic waves. Maxwell's work apparently led Heinrich Hertz to experiment with this radiation, now called radio waves. Once Hertz demonstrated the existence of radio waves, Guglielmo Marconi and others exploited them by inventing a practical device, the radio.

This transition was a considerable break from the past. It was the beginning of the modern link between science and everyday technology. Yet this link was not the key to the revolution in warfare that took place as the 19th century rolled over into the 20th. Thermodynamics, for example, explained how steam engines worked. It was eventually employed to increase the efficiency of engines, most notably the diesel, but the railroads that revolutionized the movement of troops to the battlefield did not depend for their development on an understanding of thermodynamics.

Wells' contemporaries could have identified three technologies that were revolutionizing and transforming warfare: railroads (in transportation), mass production (in manufacturing), and mechanization (in agriculture). The agricultural revolution made it possible for a limited part of a population to feed the whole country, freeing the remaining population for service in mass armies or industry. This revolution thereby eased the impact of mass conscription on a nation's food supply. The transportation revolution made it possible to transport large armies quickly; the manufacturing revolution made it possible to arm them. Although railroads greatly improved an army's strategic mobility, this did not extend to its operational mobility; once dismounted at a railhead, troops could not move very quickly or very far. A relatively well-equipped mass army therefore could be transported and fed best close to railheads.

This combination of railroads and improved agricultural productivity created the possibility that mass armies could be shifted from front to front quickly. Massive, rapid mobilization became a real possibility. The contrast between rail-borne mobility and road-bound mobility made it almost impossible for these mass armies to make decisive gains, since a defender could generally bring troops to the front faster than an attacking army could pour them through gaps in the front lines. Breakthroughs were sometimes realized, as in the Franco-Prussian War of 1870, but World War I showed that mass plus railroads plus industrial production could result in a stalemate.

Tactical-level factors inhibiting maneuver, such as machineguns, intensified this stalemate, but its strategic roots were based upon the three technological revolutions. Since national economies, not militaries, produced these revolutions, the source of stalemate was beyond the reach of front line armies. As a result, 20th-century airpower advocates began to argue for striking civilian industries directly.

Important lessons about the relationship of technology to war were thus apparent as long ago as Wells' time. The first lesson was that science had begun to stimulate technology. The second was that developments *outside* the military—developments stimulated by technological change— could have a profound influence on how war was fought and could even influence the circumstances under which war would begin. The third lesson was that technological investments for nonmilitary purposes (as in the railroads) could provide major military payoffs.

Projecting the technological future runs the risk of creating visions unconstrained by cost considerations or by the limits of the physical world and the sciences. Such visions are, like the conflict depicted so vividly in *War of the Worlds*, a form of fiction. At the same time, there is also the equally dangerous risk of *not* investing in promising technologies. And there is a third risk, too—that of ignoring changes because they seem so *ordinary*.

What really are the essential military implications of the so-called information revolution, for example? On September 11, 2001, terrorists attacked the United States from within. They financed their preparations with funds that had been transferred electronically from banks in the Middle East to banks in America. With those funds, they bypassed the forward-deployed, highly trained, technologically sophisticated forces of the United States. In effect, an apparently "ordinary" electronic funds transfer was a key element in a larger strategy of terror. Is this sort of information age routine act like the automobile—a common technology with long-term implications that are truly revolutionary but nonetheless not perceived as such by most people?

## Notes

[1] Office of the Secretary of Defense, "Transformation Study Report: Transforming Military Operational Capabilities" (Washington, DC: Government Printing Office, April 27, 2001), chart 5.

[2] Holley put it in a negative form: "the failure to emphasize better weapons rather than more weapons and the failure to attach sufficient importance to the formulations of doctrine [issue] directly from inadequate organization." I.B. Holley, *Ideas and Weapons* (New Haven: Yale University Press, 1953), 176.

[3] See the entry for *radar* in I.C.B. Dear and M.R.D. Foot, eds., *The Oxford Companion to the Second World War* (Oxford: Oxford University Press, 1995), 918–923.

[4] See, for example, Thomas Heppenheimer, "The Navaho Program and the Main Line of American Liquid Rocketry," *Air Power History* (Summer 1997), 4–17.

[5] For the actual data on these aircraft, see M.S. Knaack, *Encyclopedia of U.S. Air Force Aircraft and Missile Systems* I, Post-World War II Fighters, 1945–1973 (Washington, DC: Office of Air Force History, 1978).

[6] W.D. O'Neil, "Technology and Naval War" (Office of the Under Secretary of Defense, Research and Engineering, Department of Defense, 1981).

[7] Glenn A. Kent, "Exploiting Technology," presentation to the American Association for the Advancement of Science on September 29, 1987, and published for distribution in January 1988 (RAND Corporation, P–7403).

[8] For Lockheed's own explanation of the Skunk Works (the designers of the winning Joint Strike Fighter prototype), see "The Skunk Works Approach to Aircraft Development, Production and Support," Lockheed Advanced Development Company (August 1992).

[9] Section 2515 of Title 10, USC, established the Office of Technology Transition with the Office of the Secretary of Defense.

[10] See Boehm's "Software Engineering" in the *IEEE Transactions on Computers*, C25, no. 12 (December 1976), 1226–1241. See also the publications of the IEEE Standards Board and editions of the *IBM Systems Journal* of the 1980s.

[11] See, for example, Andrew Hargadon and Robert Sutton, "Building an Innovation Factory," *Harvard Business Review* (May-June 2000), 157–166. Also see the office of the Deputy Under Secretary of Defense (Science and Technology), "Defense Science and Technology Strategy," May 2000.

[12] General Accounting Office, "Report to the Chairman and Ranking Minority Member, Subcommittee on Readiness and Management Support, Committee on Armed Services, U.S. Senate," GAO/NSIAD–99–162, "Better Management of Technology Development Can Improve Weapon System Outcomes" (July 1999).

[13] The coupling of the jet engine and nuclear weapons drove the development of digital computers. To defend the Nation and continent, the North American Air Defense Command (NORAD) needed an effective, rapid response command and control ($C^2$) system that stressed automated computational capabilities. The digital computer, however, was beyond the time horizon of table 2. In discussing it, we are getting ahead of ourselves.

[14] Chairman, Joint Chiefs of Staff, *Joint Vision 2020* (Washington, DC: Government Printing Office, June 2000).

[15] "Conventional Forces Study, Final Report: Exploiting Untapped Potential to Meet Emerging Challenges" (The Gompert Study).

[16] William A. Owens with Edward Offley, *Lifting the Fog of War* (New York: Farrar, Straus and Giroux, 2000), 133. Emphasis in the original.

[17] See Mark E. Rogers, "Lasers in Space," in William C. Martel, ed., *The Technological Arsenal* (Washington, DC: Smithsonian Institution Press, 2001), 3–19.

[18] Joseph W. Siniscalchi, "Nonlethal Technologies and Military Strategy," in Martel 129–152.

# Chapter 3

# Choosing a Strategy

Richard L. Kugler and Hans Binnendijk

What strategy should guide the transformation of U.S. military forces in the years ahead? What basic philosophy, goals, and actions should animate the process of changing U.S. forces so that they are prepared for the future? These weighty questions require answers. Transformation is too important to be left to chance or to the vagaries of politics. It is a dynamic that can be pursued in more ways than one and that can succeed or fail. It definitely requires a guiding hand. To help shed light on this issue, we begin by exploring the nature of transformation and the U.S. historical experience with it. With the stage thus set, we then analyze key strategies for pursuing transformation and present a set of new operational concepts for carrying it out.

The Department of Defense (DOD) intends to pursue transformation in meaningful ways, but a debate is raging over the best strategy for doing so. The debate is polarized between two quite different strategies: one evolutionary, the other revolutionary. Focused mostly on the coming decade, the evolutionary "steady as you go" strategy proposes to transform in ways that, although important, are small in scope, slow-paced, and limited in vision. While this strategy seeks to acquire weapons now emerging from the research and development pipeline, it does not invest heavily in futurist technologies, and it proposes mostly modest changes to legacy force structures, platforms, and operations. By contrast, the revolutionary "leap ahead" strategy proposes to move in faster, bolder, and riskier ways. Focused mainly on 10 to 20 years from now and beyond, it wants to skip emerging weapons in favor of exotic technologies, while carrying out radical changes in U.S. forces and doctrines. A responsible case can be made for each strategy, but the tensions between them must be resolved if transformation is to unfold smoothly and not be ripped apart by two incompatible visions at war with one another. Embracing one strategy at the expense of the other could leave the Armed Forces shortchanged in the future—either by not changing them enough or by changing them too much in the wrong ways.

Instead, this chapter suggests that the United States should pursue a sensible blend of both strategies: a *purposeful and measured transformation*. This strategy aspires to keep U.S. forces highly ready and capable in the near term, to enhance their flexibility and adaptability in the mid-term, and to guide their acquisition of new systems prudently in the long term. While this strategy relies on emerging weapons to modernize U.S. forces, it urges vigorous experimentation with new technologies as they become available. It seeks ways to reorganize and reengineer traditional force structures so that they can perform joint operations more effectively in the information age. It also employs new operational concepts to guide the creation of future combat capabilities that meet the challenges ahead.

The transformation strategy that we urge is neither a slow crawl ahead nor a blind leap into the distant future but instead a deliberate and well-planned march into the 21st century. It offers a way to balance continuity and change so that American forces remain superior in the coming years, while they gain the new capabilities needed to handle a widening spectrum of contingencies, missions in new geographic locations, and growing asymmetric threats. Above all, this strategy reflects awareness that transformation should be neither taken for granted nor pursued in simplistic ways. Because it is so vital, it demands careful analysis and wise judgment.

Modern military forces are complex institutions that can be thrown off kilter by imprudent meddling. Worse, they can be badly damaged if they are reshaped to fit some new, single-minded design that does not turn out as hoped. In transforming U.S. forces, the goal is to strengthen them for dealing with a complex and dangerous world, not simply to take chances in the mistaken belief that radical approaches are necessarily better than tried-and-true practices. New ideas should always be subjected to careful appraisals of their consequences—both good and bad—before they are adopted. If the dilemma is deciding whether to mimic a timid ostrich or an aggressive hawk, the answer is to behave like an owl, wisely seeking an intelligent blend of continuity and change, at a pace that is fast enough to be meaningful yet slow enough to be managed effectively. A purposeful and measured transformation is a strategy for an owl.

## Bringing Transformation into Focus

The difficult challenge facing DOD is to pursue transformation while also attending to the rest of its agenda, which includes keeping the Armed Forces ready for near-term crises and balancing its investment priorities. Transformation clearly is important, but what exactly does it mean? Transformation often is used as a rallying cry to promote one particular theory of defense reform, but this is a misleading use of the term. Official DOD documents use the term in a generic sense rather than as an endorsement of any particular approach. The dictionary does likewise; it defines *transformation* as a "substantial change in appearance, nature, or character." Changes of this sort can occur in more ways than one, but for a true transformation of a military to occur, it must be guided by coherent rules or concepts, and it must produce alterations in structures and functions that are major, not minor.

Normally, transformation occurs in response to new strategic conditions abroad or to changes bubbling up from within the military, or—as is the case today—to a combination of both. It involves a process of change that is more profound than normal, steady-state modernization, which occurs as new weapons and capabilities evolve in the natural course of events, with mostly incremental consequences. Rather than business as usual, transformation represents an effort to prepare military forces to be different than in the past and to wage war differently as well. Almost always, military forces are trying to improve themselves, but they seek to transform themselves only at widely spaced intervals when new technologies and requirements make the step desirable, necessary, or unavoidable.

Some proponents interpret transformation mainly as a process of acquiring new weapons platforms to replace the tank, fighter plane, or aircraft carrier. While some traditional platforms may need replacing or modification, this interpretation of transformation is too restrictive and serves one particular reform agenda. A military establishment might, in fact, retain its legacy platforms while changing in so many other areas (for example, doctrine, organization, and operations) that it emerges as heavily transformed. Indeed, this has been the common approach to transformation pursued by the U.S. military, which has undergone several waves of major changes in the past 60 years without switching platforms. A good example is the U.S. Navy. Two decades ago, it rejected calls for converting to small carriers or even replacing carriers with land-based aircraft for maritime missions. It was widely accused of a hidebound unwillingness to break free from the past, but it changed in so many other ways, including technology and doctrine, that it became transformed in warfighting capabilities.

In today's setting, transformation is aptly portrayed as a wide-ranging process of adjusting to the imperatives and opportunities of the information age. Such a transformation often begins with the arrival of new technologies, such as modern computers and information warfare systems, but it does not end there. Depending upon how far it is pursued, it can lead to changes throughout a military establishment; it might or might not involve new platforms, but it is often carried out in multiple different ways. To a degree, the process is driven by its own momentum, but military establishments have a wide range of choice in determining the breadth and pace of transformation. This discretion should be guided by a transformation strategy: it is important to how the process unfolds and critical to whether it is carried out effectively.

Transformation does not boil down to a choice between doing nothing and changing everything or between crawling ahead slowly and leaping forward at blinding speed. Transformation can be partial yet meaningful. For example, it might fully alter only 10 to 20 percent of the posture, while modestly changing most of the remainder, and still produce a big improvement in combat capabilities. It could also be phased to unfold gradually as a choreographed sequence of events and to build on its achievements steadily as it unfolds. We argue for a purposeful and measured transformation anchored in such a vision of a careful, well-planned process. It starts with partial but pivotal changes and then expands to pursue broader departures as they prove their worth.

As table 3–1 suggests, transformation can take place within three categories of "inputs" (that is, the combat forces and their assets) and a fourth category of "outputs" (the military capabilities and combat performance of the forces). Each has multiple important subcategories. Transformation might have a significant impact on only some of these categories and subcategories, or most of them, or all of them. The critical relationship is that between inputs and outputs: between force characteristics and battlefield performance. A big change in one force characteristic, but not others, might produce little impact on battlefield performance. This transformation would be ranked as minor. By contrast, a large number of modest changes in multiple force characteristics could produce big changes in battlefield performance. This would be a truly major transformation, even though its surface manifestations might appear minor.

A partial, limited transformation could occur if a military force acquires new technologies (such as new command, control, communications, computers, intelligence, surveillance, and reconnaissance [C⁴ISR] systems and smart munitions) but does not change in other significant ways. A more ambitious transformation might replace old weapons with new weapons but not acquire different platforms. An example is buying new artillery tubes or jet fighters whose capabilities permit different tactical uses than before.

## Table 3–1. Components of Defense Transformation

| Inputs: Transformation of Force Characteristics | Outputs: Transformation of Capabilities and Battlefield Performance |
| --- | --- |
| **Transformation of Technologies and Weapons**<br>Information systems and grids<br>Technologies and subcomponents<br>Legacy weapon systems<br>New platforms<br>Smart munitions | Improved capacity for swift deployment<br><br>Improved firepower, maneuverability, survivability, sustainability |
| **Transformation of Force Structures**<br>Combat force structures and organizations<br>Logistic support and mobility<br>Command structures and command, control, communications, computers, intelligence, surveillance, and reconnaissance systems<br>Domestic infrastructure and bases<br>Overseas presence, bases, and facilities assets | Better capacity to perform missions and operations, old and new<br><br>Capacity to support wider spectrum of strategies and contingencies<br><br>Improved adaptability: Capacity to perform strategic U-turns adeptly |
| **Transformation of Force Operations**<br>Networking of forces<br>Joint doctrines<br>Service doctrines<br>Regional commander in chief's operation plan and campaign plans<br>Interoperability with allies | |

The combination of new technologies and weapons might lead to new operational doctrines for employing forces on the battlefield but not produce major alterations in force structures and organizations, such as the mix of divisions and air wings. Alternatively, a military might alter its structures and doctrines but not its weapons. As a result of such changes, a military force might improve greatly in combat power and versatility, enough to "transform" what counts: its operational style, battlefield performance, and ability to win wars. Yet to the casual observer, its outward appearance might not be much different from its predecessor.

A more profound transformation occurs when a military force employs new technologies and weapons to make major changes in platforms, such as replacing manned fighters with robot-piloted aircraft or heavy tanks with lightweight, wheeled vehicles; in force structures, such as replacing carrier battlegroups with patrol boats and submarines or armored divisions with brigades that operate only deep-strike missiles and attack helicopters; or in operations. Such changes would greatly alter the force posture's internal characteristics, including its physical structure and outward appearances, as well as its battlefield performance. Sweeping changes of this sort, which occur infrequently, involve radically different technologies, forces, and approaches to warfighting, and exemplify defense transformation at its most dramatic. But they are not the only type of transformation to occur or to be sought. The limited, partial transformations occur more often, but when they elevate military capabilities or alter the face of war, they are portentous developments in themselves.

Because any ambitious transformation, either partial or whole, cannot be carried out overnight, its timelines are important. A partial transformation is normally pursued in the near term and mid-term, over a period of 5 to 10 years or so. This tends to be the case if it employs technologies and weapons that already exist or will be procured during this period, and if it does not undertake significant alterations in force structures and platforms. It may set the stage for a bigger transformation later, but it might instead be self-contained. A wholesale transformation typically takes longer to carry out—15 to 20 years or more—and produces radically different forces that meet new strategic needs in the long haul. A key feature of a radical transformation is that it may deliberately bypass improvements in the near term and mid-term in order to pursue long-term goals. Especially if resources are limited, partial changes in the mid-term might not be a transition step but instead a barrier to achieving bigger changes in the distant future.

The specific features of both partial and wholesale approaches are crucial in determining how the future is to unfold. Because these two approaches have different timelines, in theory they can interlock together in supportive ways, with a partial transformation laying the foundation for bigger changes later as new technologies emerge. Such complementarity is not, however, automatic or easily achieved. Indeed, partial and whole transformations can be competitive, with each consuming so many resources and energies that it stymies the other. This presents defense planners with hard choices. Complementarity must be deliberately sought by designing these two approaches to work together.

Regardless of whether transformation is partial or whole, it is a means to an end, not an end in itself. Its success is measured by its capacity to produce better forces, greater capabilities, and higher performance, not by the extent to which it overturns past practices. As a result, it must be pursued with strategic goals and coordinated plans foremost in mind. No military establishment can expect to remain current with modern warfare by sticking its head in the sand like an ostrich, denying change in the hope that it will go away. But a full-scale hawkish transformation should be pursued only when it makes strategic sense, not in response to a mystical faith that radical change always begets big progress.

## Historical Legacy: Transformation Strategies in the Industrial Era

The strategic challenges facing the U.S. military today can be illuminated by surveying the historical record of transformations during the 20th century. While today's information era is different from the industrial era, the rich experiences of the past century provide useful guidelines for thinking about how to act now. History is said to be rife with examples of militaries that transformed themselves wholly and quickly and then triumphed in war against opponents who failed to do so and suffered calamitous defeat afterward. Closer examination of the historical record, however, suggests a more complicated reality. Some successful transformations were less complete and one-sided than is often supposed. Others brought unanticipated troubles rather than spectacular benefits. Still others succeeded as a result of multiple activities carried out in partial ways at moderate pace, rather than a single design pursued wholly at breakneck speed. The bottom line is that both a strategy of changing slowly and one of leaping ahead boldly often fail. The successful transformations, as this historical review reminds us, were those that unfolded in purposeful and measured ways.

### Transformation in World War II

Napoleon often is credited as the creator of modern armies and warfare, but transformation in the industrial era has its main origins in the last few decades of the 19th century. The Prussian Army used modern artillery and other new weapons to win a series of wars, especially the clash with France in 1870 that unified Germany, making it Europe's dominant military power. Afterward, armies everywhere viewed newly emerging technologies—the telegraph, railroads, mobile artillery and infantry, the machinegun, airplane, and naval dreadnought—as heralding the domination of fast-paced offensive campaigns as key to winning wars quickly. Virtually all European forces prepared accordingly, but when World War I erupted in 1914, it surprised them by turning into a lengthy defensive stalemate of trench warfare and bloody attrition. The German Army was ultimately defeated in 1918 by an imposing coalition of Britain, France, and the United States, but it collapsed from exhaustion rather than being defeated by bold strikes and maneuver. The experience taught the lesson that wholesale military transformations sometimes produce results quite different from the visions of their designers.

World War II proved to be the opposite of stalemate; new technologies and military doctrines combined to restore offensive warfare to dominance on land and at sea. The paradigm case of successful transformation is often said to be the Battle of France in May 1940, when the German Wehrmacht overpowered French and British forces in only 6 weeks. A popular interpretation holds that the Germans won because, in the interwar years, they wholly transformed their forces by adding large numbers of tanks and airplanes to their inventories. By contrast, it is said, the French and British clung to old forces and a defensive mentality that was manifested in the outdated Maginot Line. Closer inspection shows, however, that the forces of both sides were more similar than is commonly realized. The Germans attacked with 136 divisions, mostly infantry units with horse-drawn artillery. They fielded about 3,000 combat aircraft and 3,000 tanks, but these assets provided only 20 to 25 aircraft and tanks per division: small numbers compared to today. Their tanks, moreover, were mostly light models, not the feared medium and heavy tanks used later in the war. The allies defended with 142 divisions (104 French) aided by 2,700 tanks and 2,000 combat aircraft. Thus the modern technology of the two forces was similar in size, quality, and composition. In essence, this was a parity fight; contrary to popular lore, it was not a contest in which the allies were grossly outnumbered and outclassed because they had turned a blind eye to transformation.

The outcome turned not on big differences in forces and technology but instead on operational doctrines and the manner in which battlefield maneuvers were conducted. Sensing an opportunity to win quickly with a bold offensive, the Germans pursued a battlefield strategy of blitzkrieg. Rather than distributing their tanks across the entire posture, they concentrated them into a few units, and they learned how to blend their armor and airpower together in combined arms operations. They concentrated large forces in the Ardennes forest, employed them to penetrate thin allied defenses there, and then advanced rapidly into the rear areas, where they maneuvered speedily to unravel allied defenses. The French and British were vulnerable to this attack not because they were hunkered down in the Maginot Line. It covered only southern France, not the northern battle-field where the main fighting occurred. The primary reason was that as they advanced most of their northern forces into Belgium along the Dyle River on their left flank, they withheld few operational reserves at their center, especially tanks and aircraft, thereby exposing themselves to the German thrust through the weakly defended Ardennes.

The effect of the Ardennes breakthrough was to fracture the allied defense posture in half, allowing the Germans first to trap the northern component at Dunkirk and then to destroy the southern component in the aftermath. Sensing their danger early in the battle, the allies tried to maneuver forces to block the penetration but failed. Had they withheld more reserves and been able to use them well, they might well have stopped the German advance. The main lesson is that while the Germans had transformed only partly, they had done so wisely. They not only acquired enough new weapons to wage an offensive campaign but also created a new operational doctrine for using them decisively. While the British and French were not blind to the new era of warfare, they had pursued their own partial transformation unwisely. They acquired enough new weapons and technologies but failed to use them effectively.

The Germans also used blitzkrieg warfare to drive deeply into Russia when they launched Operation *Barbarossa* in mid-1941. In the process, they surrounded, cut off, and defeated in detail huge portions of Russia's unprepared army. But by 1942, Germany's main enemies—Russia, Britain, and the United States—were learning how to cope with blitzkrieg warfare. Over the next 3 years, they used their modern weapons to craft mobile offensive campaigns that allowed them to overpower and ultimately defeat the outnumbered Wehrmacht. While tanks and aircraft played big roles in their counterattacks, such traditional weapons as infantry and artillery, plus potent logistic support and industrial production, carried a great deal of the load as well. World War II in Europe was fought with a mixture of old and new technologies. Radar was one new technology that greatly changed warfare, and there were many others as well. In the end, nonetheless, the outcome was driven by sheer numbers and mastery of modern doctrine, not by technological supremacy or different levels of physical transformation. Indeed, the Germans fielded the best-quality hardware and lost anyway because they had bitten off more than they could chew.

Combat in the Pacific theater also reflected a blend of the old and new. Japan initially gained the upper hand, but the United States ultimately rallied to win. Popular lore holds that the Pacific war ushered in the era of aircraft carriers and long-range airpower and brought the fading era of battleships to an end. It is true that aircraft carriers were hugely important in such key battles as Pearl Harbor, Midway, the Marianas, and others. But battleships and other surface combatants dominated the critical Solomon Islands naval battles of 1942, and they greatly influenced the decisive naval battle of Leyte Gulf in 1945. Along with carriers, their firepower support was vital in allowing the U.S. Army and Marine Corps to carry out their island-hopping campaign throughout the war. From Guadalcanal and Tarawa to Iwo Jima and Okinawa, the many bitter island battles were fought primarily with infantry soldiers and artillery. As in Europe, the Pacific war was waged by the Americans and Japanese, nearly until the end, with parallel technologies and weapons, and with partly transformed forces.

## Nuclear Transformation: The First Two Decades of the Cold War

Shortly after World War II ended, the Cold War broke out. Because the conflict with the Soviet Union initially was political, the United States disarmed and also slowed the process of transforming its military forces with new technologies and doctrines. When the Korean War erupted in 1950, jet aircraft were used for the first time in large numbers, but otherwise that conflict was waged with weapons, forces, and doctrines inherited from World War II. The big change came after the Korean armistice was signed, when the Eisenhower administration decided to nuclearize the American defense strategy. This effort was driven by three goals that reinforced each other: strengthening U.S. forces by equipping them with nuclear firepower; deterring Soviet aggression in Europe at a time when North Atlantic Treaty Organization (NATO) conventional forces were too weak to halt a major attack; and buying security on the cheap because nuclear weapons were less expensive than conventional forces. The result was to propel the Armed Forces into a wholesale transformation driven by a single-minded design anchored in exciting new technologies and weapons systems. This ambitious effort was carried out in just a few years: never before have U.S. forces been changed so totally and quickly under a single organizing principle. This design concept proved short-lived, however; it produced the wrong forces for the new strategic circumstances that were to unfold in the 1960s.

To carry out its strategy of massive retaliation, the Eisenhower administration procured a large force of over 2,000 nuclear-armed strategic bombers, with emphasis on the B–52. Later it also started to deploy intercontinental ballistic missiles (ICBMs) and submarine-launched ballistic missiles (SLBMs), which were intended to supplement the bombers, not replace them. It authorized deployment of 7,000 tactical nuclear weapons to Europe to permit NATO to use rapid escalation to halt aggression. As a logical byproduct of this effort, it worked with the military services to reconfigure their conventional combat forces for nuclear war. The Air Force was especially nuclearized. Its new fighters of the 1950s were designed mostly to shoot down enemy nuclear bombers and to conduct tactical nuclear strikes in the enemy's rear areas. The Army was also affected; its new Pentomic divisions were so tailored for nuclear operations that they could not mount much of a conventional defense. The Navy was similarly influenced, as its carriers, aircraft, and other combatants were redesigned for nuclear strike operations at sea or on land. The consequence was a gleaming new U.S. military posture, primed for nuclear war, but incapable of fighting serious conventional wars. The same was true for European forces in NATO.

Almost overnight, however, massive retaliation was invalidated as an all-purpose strategy when the Soviet Union surprised the West by making fast progress nuclearizing its own strategy and forces. By the early 1960s, it was poised to begin procuring large numbers of ICBMs and SLBMs; it had already begun to deploy several hundred medium- and intermediate-range ballistic missiles targeted on Western Europe and to distribute 6,000 tactical nuclear warheads to its ground and air forces. The effect was to cast a bright spotlight on the Warsaw Pact's imposing superiority in the conventional war arena. The Soviet nuclear buildup meant that the United States and its allies became less able to deter conventional aggression by threatening nuclear escalation. This step now became too risky because the Soviets were capable of retaliating with devastating nuclear counterblows. The Berlin crises and Cuban missile crisis exposed the dangers inherent in this situation. Alarmed, the Kennedy administration felt compelled to pursue a major rebuilding of U.S. conventional forces to deter nonnuclear attack and to broaden its options. All four services were suddenly instructed to reverse course by retailoring their forces, weapons, and doctrines for traditional warfare. In addition, the Kennedy administration had to initiate a bruising debate with the European allies to persuade them to abandon massive retaliation in favor of a new strategy of flexible response, one that mandated an expensive buildup of their own conventional forces. For both the United States and NATO, the 1960s were largely spent trying to recover from the setbacks of their nuclear transformation during the previous decade.

Because the reform process was far from complete by the mid-1960s, the United States fought the Vietnam War with forces that were halfway between a design for nuclear war and one for conventional war. For the most part, U.S. forces were well equipped and enjoyed major technological advantages over the enemy, yet they suffered from some liabilities of the past. For example, U.S. air forces were not well designed for conventional bombardment missions, and ground forces lacked special logistic assets for expeditionary operations. Smart munitions did not appear until late in the conflict. Many innovations had to be made as the war unfolded, in use of helicopters, forward air controllers, and sensors, for example. More important, forces from the four services were not well prepared for joint operations and often encountered trouble working together. Beyond this, overall U.S. military strategy was flawed. Victory could not be achieved through gradual escalation and sustained attrition warfare against a stubborn North Vietnamese enemy that refused to be driven from the battlefield. U.S. forces returned from Vietnam frustrated by their inability to translate sophisticated technology into decisive victory, but in the agonized political climate of the early 1970s, little was done to recover from the damage, much less to prepare for the future.

### Building Modern Transformed Forces: The Past Quarter-Century

In the mid- to late 1970s, heightened Cold War tensions helped propel U.S. military forces back along the path of rehabilitation and progress. Several factors combined together to accelerate the process. Key was the worried atmosphere that permeated DOD, which translated into a desire to improve U.S. forces in big ways. Senior civilians helped set the stage by urging innovation, and senior military officers, determined to recover from Vietnam, shared the sentiment. The Carter administration began to set strategic priorities by focusing on NATO and later the Persian Gulf. The Reagan defense buildup of the 1980s provided the funds needed to fuel an ambitious effort to enlarge U.S. forces, improve their training and readiness, and procure new weapons. New technologies emerging from the research and development process enabled the U.S. military to modernize with an entirely new generation of weapon systems that were significantly better than their predecessors. The services began developing vigorous new doctrines for battlefield operations that promised to take full advantage of the weapons being procured. The result was a process of fast modernization and enhanced readiness that, by the late 1980s, had strengthened U.S. forces significantly. Although force structures and platforms did not change a great deal, major improvements were made in munitions and sensors, command and control systems, missiles and other technologies, doctrine, and operations.

Where the nuclear transformation of the 1950s had been driven by a single design, this transformation was quite different. Its guiding theme was better conventional forces, but its varied and broad-based efforts were driven by multiple different designs and theories, not all of them initially well coordinated with each other. A number of innovative ideas came from outside the services and even outside the Department of Defense. The four services were highly influential; each often marched to the beat of its own drummers, competing with the others while fighting off unwelcome challenges to its traditional structures yet responding to new technologies and doctrines emerging from within its ranks and elsewhere. Meanwhile, the defense industries produced new technologies and weapons at often bewildering speed in ways that steadily broadened the range of operational choices available to the services, sometimes pushing them in unanticipated directions. A good example is the cruise missile, which appeared as new technology bubbled upward, rather than resulting from a new strategy imposed from the top down. By contrast, the new fighters and tanks were products of a strategic design, but when their capabilities became apparent, they were employed to create fresh, unanticipated doctrines.

Strong efforts were made in the Planning, Programming, and Budgeting System and the joint planning arena—by many authorities in the Office of Secretary of Defense, the Joint Staff, the services, and the regional military commands—to discipline this transformation and guide it in sound directions. But even so, its chief characteristic was pluralism in its ideas and organizations, reflecting the dynamics of economic markets and democratic politics, rather than control from atop by any single plan. While this process was turbulent and confusing, it worked. It produced the best military forces in world history: transformed forces that were well aligned with new directions in defense strategy for the 1990s, not out of phase with them.

This process worked effectively, despite its lack of central control, because it was guided by a set of new operational concepts developed by the Pentagon and the armed services as transformation was getting under way. These new concepts not only provided direction to each service but also imparted a sense of direction to joint planning and overall U.S. military strategy:

- "power projection and rapid reinforcement" called for a better capacity to deploy U.S. forces swiftly to Europe, Asia, and the Persian Gulf
- "maritime supremacy" called for the Navy to switch from defensive missions to offensive operations aimed at sweeping the seas of enemy blue-water navies
- "expeditionary operations" encouraged the Marine Corps to evolve beyond amphibious assault to become a more flexible, multipurpose force
- "multimission air operations" led the Air Force to broaden beyond air defense to pursue interdiction, close air support, and other contributions to the land battle
- "operational art" led the Army to move away from linear defense toward mobile reserves, maneuver, and powerful counterattacks
- "AirLand battle" provided a concept for coordinating ground and air missions in attacking enemy forces.

It is noteworthy that the successful transformation orchestrated by these concepts was carried out in the face of a determined Soviet buildup of its "antiaccess" and "area-denial" capabilities, aimed at preserving the Warsaw Pact predominance in Europe. The Soviet navy acquired a blue-water capacity with Backfire bombers, attack submarines, and missile-carrying surface combatants to challenge NATO for control of the North Atlantic. On the European continent, the Soviets created a huge force of theater missiles and tactical nuclear systems, 500 medium bombers, 4,200 combat aircraft, and nearly 100 heavily armed divisions capable of a blitzkrieg offensive. Rather than respond to this threat by resorting to a standoff defense strategy from the sea, the United States and its European allies asserted their strategic interests by pursuing a stalwart forward defense of NATO borders. The result was a sustained peacetime competition between the two military alliances that saw NATO strengthen its position, ultimately checkmating the growing threat and establishing a robust defense posture. Had war erupted in the early 1970s, the Warsaw Pact would have been expected to win, but if it had occurred in the late 1980s, NATO would have acquitted itself far better and perhaps won the contest. This dramatic change in the force balance may well have played a major role in the Soviet Union's decision to throw in the towel in 1990. By any measure, the U.S. and NATO military buildup accomplished its political and strategic purposes.

Because U.S. defense strategy in the Cold War's final stages became increasingly global, a key strategic innovation was better strategic-mobility assets for rapid reinforcement. Heavily a product of civilian leadership, the acquisition of better airlift, sealift, and prepositioning permitted faster power projection and overseas deployment from the United States, thereby contributing greatly to improved force balances in Europe and the Persian Gulf. The U.S. Navy, shaking off challenges to its traditional force structures, built new carriers, F–14 and F–18 fighters, Aegis defenses, cruise missiles, surface combatants, and submarines. As a result, it rebuffed the Soviet threat and emerged as dominating the North Atlantic and other seas as well. Meanwhile, the Marine Corps broadened beyond traditional amphibious assault missions to perform a wide variety of other ground and air operations. The Air Force acquisition of new F–15 and F–16 combat aircraft, the A–10 tank-buster, airborne warning and control systems (AWACs) and joint surveillance and target attack radar systems (JSTARS) $C^2$ capabilities, improved avionics, smart munitions, and cruise missiles greatly enhanced its capacity to win the air battle, perform strategic bombardment against enemy rear areas, and contribute close air support to the ground battle. The Army's goal was to transform its infantry-heavy forces from the Vietnam era into a modern force of armored and mechanized units. Patriot missile batteries, which replaced the I-Hawk system, provided greatly improved air defense; improved artillery systems and better munitions significantly enhanced its ability to generate large volumes of accurate, lethal fires; Abrams tanks and Bradley infantry fighting vehicles provided the enhanced tactical mobility, survivability, and firepower to permit it to transition away from stationary linear defense to mobile maneuvers and mastery of the operational art. The combination of stronger air forces and ground forces greatly enhanced the capacity of the U.S. military not only to defend against strong attacks but also to pursue offensive operations against them.

The transformation of U.S. forces was accompanied by efforts to upgrade allied forces in Europe and to strengthen alliance-wide interoperability. The acquisition of new combat aircraft and naval combatants contributed to the growing combat power of NATO more than is commonly realized. U.S. improvements led the way by blending together continuity and change to create stronger forces with a growing capacity for joint operations. The extent of these gains in modern warfare was put on display in the Persian Gulf War of early 1991, when U.S. forces led a large, multinational coalition to inflict decisive defeat on a well-armed

Iraqi adversary. The *Desert Storm* success was massive, but it was no accident, and 10 to 15 years earlier, it would not have been possible to such a decisive degree. The same was true of the many other successful American crisis operations that occurred in the 1990s, including in Kosovo where U.S. airpower won a war virtually on its own.

This U.S. military transformation was heavily influenced by new technologies and weapons, but it was anchored in efforts to make effective use of traditional force structures and platforms and in concerted attention to training, readiness, and skilled personnel. It focused on acquiring capabilities that were linked to well understood operational concepts that reflected a clear understanding of modern war's political and military dynamics. Overall, it was not an impulsive effort, but instead the culmination of a long, well conceived, well funded transformation lasting over a decade. Its positive impact on U.S. defense preparedness is the central military lesson of the Cold War's final climactic years.

## Managing Change: Transformation for the Information Era

Today, the U.S. military stands on the brink of another transformation of special importance. In the early 21st century, warfare is in transition from the industrial age to the information age. Managing this transition effectively is vital to preserving American military superiority. The historical lessons of the past can be drawn upon to help illuminate the path ahead. Nonetheless, the transformation strategy chosen for the coming period must make sense for reasons of its own.

The imperatives of transformation are clearest when a military finds itself lacking modern weapons and facing strong enemies capable of defeating it in battle. The opposite situation exists today. The U.S. military is easily the world's strongest, armed with weapons and capabilities that far overshadow those of any potential rival. The challenge facing it therefore is not one of scrambling its way to the top, but of staying there. The absence of a clearly identified threat against which to counterbalance, or some other clear strategic guidepost to follow, means that the United States will need to set its own relative standard regarding how its forces should change. Setting such standards is difficult because the future of defense technology and warfare is so cloudy. Nobody doubts that major changes are in the wind. Several decades from now, U.S. forces will be very different from those of today. But in the coming 10 to 20 years, the proper mix will be hard to determine and will shift over time. For these reasons, crafting a sound transformation strategy requires making tough judgments about how the process of change should unfold.

### Strategic Framework for Transformation in the Quadrennial Defense Review

A principal motive for transforming U.S. forces is to take advantage of the changes unfolding in military technology, doctrine, and weapon systems. Equally important, global security affairs are changing in ways that are rapidly altering future U.S. military requirements. Globalization is making the democratic community more prosperous and secure, especially in Europe, but also in Northeast Asia, the two geographic focal points of U.S. defense strategy during the Cold War. As the Pentagon's Quadrennial Defense Review (QDR) Report 2001 points out, however, globalization and other dynamics are creating a vast southern belt of instability that stretches from the Balkans and Middle East to the East Asian littoral. There and elsewhere, the danger does not derive from any single threat, such as a new superpower rival, but rather from troubled economic conditions and chaotic security affairs, which combine to produce a diverse set of threats. One threat comes from regional rogues, such as Iraq, that are willing to pursue aggression against their neighbors. Another threat comes from terrorists, their sponsors, and the anti-Western ideologies motivating them. A third threat comes from the ongoing proliferation of weapons of mass destruction (WMD) and lethal conventional weapons. A fourth comes from struggles over energy supplies and other natural resources, including water. A fifth comes from the upsurge of ethnic warfare in troubled states. A sixth threat might come from China, should it pursue geopolitical aims in ways that menace U.S. interests and regional stability.[1]

According to the QDR Report 2001, this multiplicity of dangers and threats means that the spectrum of operations facing U.S. forces is steadily widening. While being prepared for major theater wars (MTWs) will remain important, contingencies at the lower end of the spectrum have been steadily increasing in recent years. These include ethnic wars, counterterrorist conflicts, limited crisis interventions, and peacekeeping. The future may also witness wars at the higher end of the spectrum, including against WMD-armed opponents, coalitions of countries opposed to the United States, or perhaps even China. The prospect of a widening spectrum of conflict, better-armed enemies, and operations in new, unfamiliar geographic locations promises to confront U.S. forces with stressful demands and requirements unlike those faced since the Cold War ended. Whereas U.S. force operations during the Cold War were mostly positional and continental, they seem destined to become more mobile and littoral. Indeed, the U.S. overseas presence is likely to see its mission shift from local border defense of allies to serving as regional hubs of power projection in ways that interlock with forces deploying from the continental United States.

As the QDR Report 2001 reveals, the old preoccupation with being prepared to wage two concurrent MTWs is giving way to a more flexible construct. The new emphasis will be on maintaining multiple capabilities, not on dealing with single threats or contingencies. A new force-sizing standard apparently will call upon U.S. forces to be capable of conquering enemy territory in a single big MTW, while mounting a stalwart defense in a second regional conflict and carrying out multiple smaller-scale contingencies (SSCs). This standard and related calculations likely will generate requirements for forces similar in size to those of today, but with the capacity to operate successfully in a wider set of circumstances than regional wars in the Persian Gulf and Korea. Regional commanders in chief (CINCs) will be called upon to design a diverse set of operation plans (OPLANs), campaign plans, and strike packages so that they can handle the widening array of new challenges in their areas of operations. Forces stationed in the United States will need to become capable of deploying responsively to support these CINCs and their missions. Whereas earlier CINC force operations tended to be small or large, they will increasingly require medium-size packages whose mix of ground, naval, and air forces is tailored to the situation at hand.

The new U.S. defense strategy articulated by the QDR Report 2001 mandates that forces remain highly capable in the near term and beyond. U.S. forces will need to be well trained, highly ready, well equipped, sustainable, and able to carry out modern joint doctrine. To retain a sizable margin of superiority over adversaries, they will need to improve their capabilities in these areas as the future unfolds. They probably will not require a breakneck qualitative buildup akin to the Reagan era, but they will require the steady improvements that accompany robust modernization and preparedness efforts. The amount of increase needed in any single year might not be large, but over the course of a decade or so, the total increase could be substantial, forces that are perhaps 25–50 percent stronger than now. Meeting this goal will require persistent efforts by DOD, adequate funding, and innovation.

As the QDR Report 2001 says, the future will require more than the steady amassing of greater combat capabilities in a technical and mechanical sense. It also will require that U.S. forces become highly adaptable, flexible, and agile. This especially will be the case in the mid-term and beyond, when current global conditions could mutate in major ways. Rather than being rigidly fixed for a narrow set of contingencies and response patterns, U.S. forces will need to be able to operate in a wide set of crises and to respond in diverse ways that change greatly from case to case. They will need to be able to react adroitly to surprising events, to shift gears abruptly, and to perform strategic U-turns gracefully. These characteristics necessitate that U.S. forces provide a flexible portfolio of assets and modular building-blocks that can be combined and recombined to meet fluctuating situations and operational needs.

These emerging requirements, and the strategic conditions that generate them, mean that transformation cannot be single-dimensional in its thinking. Only a few years ago, transformation was seen in mostly linear terms, as an exercise in balancing readiness, modernization, and futurist technological innovation. This agenda will remain important, but emerging global security conditions necessitate that transformation also be carried out in ways that respond to new strategic challenges, missions, and international imperatives. The act of designing U.S. forces to handle changes that both bubble up from below and emerge from abroad greatly complicates how transformation must be planned. Transformation, moreover, cannot focus on only one time frame or strategic goal; it must ensure that U.S. forces become steadily more capable from the near term onward, acquire greater flexibility and adaptability for the mid-term, and absorb the exotic new technologies, weapons, and doctrines that will become available in the long term. Achieving all three of these goals necessitates a transformation strategy that is sophisticated, balanced, and multifaceted. The looming challenge will be to carry out this complex transformation with the resources that will be available, to set priorities in sensible ways, and to distribute shortfalls so that the risks in any single period, and in any functional area, are properly balanced.

### "Steady As You Go" Strategy

A "steady as you go" transformation strategy would aim to achieve a slow, evolutionary march into the future. Inspired by the time-honored slogan, "If it ain't broke, don't fix it," it is anchored in the premise that because U.S. forces are already the world's best by a wide margin, they do not need a major face-lift or overhaul. Instead, this strategy is based on the assumption that U.S. forces require only a gradual increase in capabilities that comes from steady-state modernization without big, hasty changes in platforms, structures, and operational concepts. Under this strategy, transformation will remain an element of DOD planning, but not the most important venture. Barring a major upsurge of new funds for acquisition, its pace will be similar to that of recent years. A decade or so from now, U.S. forces will be better armed than today, but their core features are likely to be mostly similar to now.

While this strategy may not inspire visionaries, it has several advantages. It is manageable because it does not overburden DOD. It allows U.S. forces to maintain their high readiness and to modernize gradually without subjecting them to an avalanche of difficult changes. It is prudent because it does not bet the future on risky, unproven ideas that could have negative unintended consequences. This strategy also is feasible because it can be carried out with the resources that realistically can be expected to be available. It will command the support of the military services and CINCs. It will allow the services to purchase significant numbers of new weapons now emerging from the research and development (R&D) pipeline, thereby recapitalizing their rapidly aging inventory. This strategy provides room to adopt new ideas and technologies as the services verify their merits. It can be safely relied upon to deliver its goods. Provided future defense budgets are big enough to support both readiness and accelerated modernization, it will produce the steady but meaningful increases in capabilities that it offers.

The drawbacks of this strategy are equally obvious. By preserving U.S. forces mostly as they exist today, this strategy may suffice for the near term, but its suitability for the mid-term and long term is suspect. While it will elevate U.S. force capabilities in a technical and mechanical sense, it might not produce the gains in flexibility, adaptability, and agility that are needed for the mid-term and beyond. It might not improve U.S. forces in the specific ways that will be mandated by growing adversary threats. For example, it might not adequately enhance their capacity to overpower antiaccess/area-denial threats. It runs the risk of perpetuating problems that are already evident with existing force structures, such as the Army's ponderous, slowly deploying formations. It might not robustly pursue joint operations, information-era networking, and new doctrines. It might overlook opportunities to strengthen U.S. forces through innovative programs and faster pursuit of exotic new technologies, weapons, and platforms that could become available in the long term.

Those who support this strategy assert that DOD and the services already have transformation well in hand and do not need to accelerate or greatly alter it. Critics deride this strategy as too stodgy, perpetuating industrial-era forces in the information era. Perhaps they are too harsh; this strategy can be pursued faster and more aggressively than a turtle-like crawl into the future. But transformation does require a powerful strategic vision and a coherent plan for making defense changes that are not only desirable but also necessary. U.S. forces cannot afford to stand pat or to act as though the coming era will reward business as usual. The steady as you go strategy suffers from the risk that it will neglect the future, not master it.

### "Leap Ahead" Strategy

The "leap ahead" strategy is the polar opposite of "steady as you go." Leap ahead embodies revolutionary goals, bold agendas, fast progress, and big changes. Rather than focusing on the near term or mid-term, it is occupied with radically transforming U.S. forces for the long term. Some of its proponents argue that U.S. forces should focus intently on just one or two new operational concepts; examples are standoff targeting and Asian littoral operations. Others go considerably further. They calculate that the coming 10 to 15 years will provide a strategic pause, a period of lessened international dangers that will enable U.S. strategy to focus on preparing to meet greatly enhanced threats in the distant future, including China's potential emergence as a military power and WMD proliferation to several regional rogues. Accordingly, they are willing to accept smaller forces and less modernization in the coming decade to fund new technologies and forces that can defeat future threats. An extreme version of this strategy calls for DOD to skip virtually the entire generation of weapons now emerging from the R&D pipeline in order to release funds for speeding the march into the distant future. Such Pentagon perennials as the F–22, the Joint Strike Fighter, Crusader, Osprey, DD–21, and the new CVNX carrier could fall victim wholly or partly to this reprioritizing.

A centerpiece of leap ahead is a bigger R&D effort in such areas as ballistic missile defenses, information systems, space assets, and a host of exotic technologies. The strategy argues that traditional platforms are dinosaurs that will be extinct 2 or 3 decades from now. Accordingly, it calls for vigorous development of new platforms and force structures. For the Air Force, it would replace today's fighters with strategic bombers, unmanned combat aerial vehicles (UCAVs), and cruise missiles. For the Navy, it would replace today's big carriers and associated battlegroups with smaller carriers, arsenal ships and submarines that fire many cruise missiles, mobile off-shore bases, high-tech surface combatants, littoral ships, and fast patrol boats (such as those proposed as part of the Streetfighter concept). For the Army, it would bypass the Interim Force's mix of heavy, intermediate, and light units to accelerate conversion to a mobile, high-tech force based on ultra-light forces and deep fires: an advanced version of the Objective Force now being pursued.

A main attraction of the leap ahead strategy is its innovativeness, creativity, and forward-looking mentality. It shakes off preoccupation with the near term to focus attention on the distant future, its new technologies, and its new forms of warfare. This strategy's attitude of being willing to upset applecarts and to accept high risks in pursuit of big payoffs is commonly portrayed as a healthy antidote to bureaucratic conservatism. By opening the door to an exciting new era of high-tech forces, leap ahead offers a path for the U.S. military to break away from the traditional practices of the past. Its emphasis on a few bold operational concepts offers a way to design future forces to wage war differently than now and to channel the acquisition of new technologies so that they combine together to produce integrated doctrines.

The drawbacks of this strategy become evident when its details are subjected to scrutiny. A main liability is that it may mortgage the near term and the mid-term in order to invest in the distant future. What will happen to U.S. security if the future produces major conflicts and wars in the next 10 to 15 years, not a strategic pause of relative peace? Will U.S. forces possess the necessary capability and flexibility if the world remains dangerous in this period? If not, this strategy has potentially fatal flaws. This strategy also risks tearing the U.S. military apart in order to pursue ideas that may prove to be poorly conceived or simply infeasible. Some of its operational concepts may make sense but only as contributions to a larger enterprise. As single-minded designs, they could leave the U.S. military less flexible and adaptable than today. This strategy's emphasis on exotic new technologies sounds appealing in principle, but many of them are unproven and untested. Indeed, a number are little more than glimmers in the eyes of scientists; they may prove to be infeasible or ineffective even if they are fully funded. This strategy could also leave the U.S. military in trouble in the distant future. How are the services to gauge technological directions if they do not acquire the weapons now emerging from the R&D pipeline, learn from their features, and make informed judgments about follow-on efforts? In addition, this strategy also suffers from imposing political problems. It is not likely to elicit the enthusiastic support of the services, which will be the institutions responsible for bringing it to fruition. If added atop the existing defense budget, its high costs could break the bank. If it is funded by imposing draconian cuts elsewhere, it could produce an unbalanced defense program, resulting in big losses of valuable capabilities in exchange for pursuing distant visions that could prove ephemeral.

Proponents praise this strategy for its daring vision. Critics regard it as an uncharted leap into the unknown, and perhaps into a bottomless void. The truth of the matter is hard to know without embracing the strategy in order to see if it works. But there are ample reasons for being skeptical of its sweeping formulations and alluring promises. Today's U.S. forces became the world's best not because they lurched ahead or embraced single-minded designs but because their improvements were carefully planned, tested, and evaluated as they became available. Nor did DOD lose sight of its multiple goals, its need for balanced forces, and its responsibility to protect national security across all time periods, not just the distant future. To the extent that these lessons apply in the future, the leap ahead strategy suffers by comparison. Parts of this strategy may make sense, but wholly buying into it is a different matter.

### Purposeful and Measured Transformation

Our preferred strategy aims for a sensible blend of "steady as you go" and "leap ahead" because this is the best way to pursue transformation safely and effectively. If carried out wisely, this strategy is capable of eliciting the support of the services, achieving success with the budgets likely to be available, and accelerating effective reforms while keeping U.S. military strength intact. In balanced ways, this strategy strives to achieve all three key goals of keeping U.S. forces ready in the near term of 5 years, enhancing their flexibility and adaptability in the mid-term of 6 to 15 years, and acquiring exotic new technologies especially for the long term. This strategy's key feature is its explicit focus on the mid-term, which becomes not only a core planning concept in its own right but also a bridge for linking the near term with the long term.

By focusing on the mid-term, this strategy provides targets and milestones for gauging how improvements in the near term and beyond can be orchestrated for steady improvement of U.S. military capabilities, flexibility, and adaptability. It provides a solid framework for gauging how long-term changes and new technologies can be pursued with firm standards and concrete goals. Under its guidance, long-term planning no longer involves a great leap from near-term capabilities into a hazy future. Rather it becomes a well-focused exercise for determining how to build upon mid-term achievements to pursue the further improvements needed afterward.

In essence, this strategy helps provide binoculars for seeing the future with enough clarity to know how to prepare.

Joint operations will be key to future defense strategy and missions, and thus one of this strategy's principal aims is to develop better forces and assets for this purpose. In modern warfare, each service requires contributions from the others in order to carry out its missions. Naval and marine amphibious forces are critical to securing access to littoral areas so as to allow ground and air forces to deploy safely. They also provide fully one-third of U.S. tactical air power and deep-strike assets for intense combat once deployment is complete. Ground forces require help from air power to degrade enemy maneuver forces and logistic support, while air forces benefit when ground forces compel the enemy to mass its forces, thereby exposing them to air attack.

Equally important, joint operations generate greater combat power and battlefield effectiveness. They permit integrated campaigns that create maximum leverage and firepower through coordinated missions. Modern warfare places a high premium on swift, simultaneous missions carried out by multiple components, rather than the slower-unfolding, sequential missions of the past. Speed and simultaneity by jointly operating forces are used to fracture the cohesion of enemy forces, disrupt their battlefield strategy, and leave them vulnerable to the effects of maneuver, fire, and shock action. They have become vital to winning quickly and decisively, with few losses to American and allied forces. Creating a better capacity for joint operations can be pursued through such steps as acquiring new C$^4$ISR systems, developing information networks, pursuing joint doctrines, and perhaps establishing joint task forces at key commands.

In its efforts to develop a better capability and adaptability for joint operations, this transformation strategy does not tear apart existing force structures on the premise that because they worked effectively in the past, they cannot work in the future. But neither does it stand still in this arena. Instead, it seeks to pursue a responsible, well planned effort to reorganize and reengineer current structures in order to make them better attuned to the information age. It uses as a model the ways in which many U.S. business corporations have pursued reengineering of their structures and functions in order to compete more effectively. They have stripped away redundant management layers, abandoned unproductive enterprises, created interlocking information networks rather than hierarchical organizations, and focused organizational functions on profitable business outputs. Reengineering must be handled carefully in order to enhance existing practices rather than destroy them, but if carried out wisely, it can produce constructive innovations. U.S. military forces can profit from similar reorganization and reengineering to enhance their combat power, even in the years before new weapons and exotic technologies arrive on the scene.

Critics often say that the Army is the service that is most in need of such changes in order to replace its big, ponderous forces with streamlined combat and support units that can deploy swiftly and strike lethally in a joint setting. One idea, for example, is to replace the Army's existing corps of three divisions (105,000 soldiers) with a smaller corps of 5 to 6 brigade-sized combat groups totaling 65,000 troops. As other chapters of this volume suggest, similar thinking can also be applied to the Air Force, Navy, and Marines, and to the DOD domestic infrastructure. In the Navy, for example, reengineering might involve stationing Marine infantry units on carriers and configuring amphibious assault ships to operate as small aircraft carriers. Efforts to develop new ideas and experiment with them already are under way by the Joint Forces Command and the services. The issue is whether, and in what ways, these efforts should be accelerated or changed. A general guiding principle stands out. The services should not be hostile to change and innovation, but instead welcome it as the best way to prepare for the 21st century of warfare. Clearly, they should not embrace new ideas for their own sake because new ideas are not necessarily good ideas. But they should experiment vigorously with attractive ideas and, when these ideas show merit, adopt them in a careful manner.

A purposeful and measured transformation also means that the U.S. military will need to modernize its weapon systems soon, not in the distant future. Many current weapons are still the world's best, but most were bought years ago and are anchored in technology developed in the 1970s. Many will soon be approaching the end of their useful lives, and some will shortly become either obsolete or too costly to maintain. Others will lose their competitive status on the battlefield as enemy forces acquire new technologies capable of shooting down U.S. aircraft, destroying U.S. tanks, and sinking U.S. ships. Critics who argue that the coming generation of technologies should be skipped in order to pursue future exotic systems often fail to remember that the armed services *already* have skipped a generation because they procured few new weapons in the late 1980s and 1990s. The extended "procurement holiday" of that period forecloses another lengthy holiday in order to energize the R&D process for distant achievements. If such a holiday were taken, U.S. forces would find their capabilities increasingly eroding in the dangerous period ahead as they wait for exotic weapons that will become available only in the far distant future.

Air modernization is the highest priority and most expensive program, but the ground and naval forces will need modernization as well. Critics often deride the new aircraft and other weapons now emerging from the R&D pipeline as merely "legacy" systems rather than as transformational platforms. But their capabilities are often so significantly advanced over existing models that they make the term *legacy* seem suspect. As past experience shows, there is nothing wrong with perpetuating legacy platforms if the result is to acquire new technologies and subcomponents that produce impressive capabilities that meet future requirements. The real issue is not whether these new aircraft and other weapons should be procured but instead whether enough of them can be bought with the funds likely to be available. Fiscal realities may conspire to slow the purchase of these new weapons, but this does not erode their military worthiness for the coming era.

In the view of this transformation strategy, the need to acquire new weapons emerging from the R&D pipeline does not negate the powerful reasons to consider alternative platforms and to pursue exotic technologies. Such new platforms as UCAVs, lightweight armored vehicles, and new naval combatants offer the potential to enhance U.S. combat capabilities, not as substitutes for legacy platforms but as complements to them. The same applies to such new technologies as robotics, new computer systems, ultra-smart munitions, hypervelocity missiles, electromagnetic rail guns, directed energy weapons, and nanotechnology. This transformation strategy calls for relevant new platforms and technologies to be funded, developed, tested, procured, and deployed as they mature, but they should not be acquired wholesale simply for their own sake. As they become available, they can be subjected to cost-effectiveness evaluation and integrated into the evolving force posture accordingly.

What kind of force posture will a purposeful and measured transformation likely produce in the mid-term and somewhat beyond? In addition to being more capable and adaptable, the posture will be aligned with new U.S. defense strategy and future missions. It is likely to deploy similar manpower levels and combat formations as today, but it will have different internal characteristics. Perhaps 10 to 20 percent of the posture will be radically transformed in order to carry out demanding new operations in special areas (discussed below). It will possess ultra-high-tech weapons, brand-new structures, sophisticated information systems and networks, and specialized capabilities. The remainder of the posture may be labeled legacy forces, but they will be different from current forces in key ways. They will have reengineered structures, they will be equipped with new weapons and support assets, and they will be better tailored for joint operations. This, of course, is a snapshot of the posture at one point in time. The posture will be evolving continuously as the future unfolds, gradually incorporating more changes in structures, technologies, and weapons. But if this snapshot accurately portrays the mid-term, it offers promise that U.S. forces will be significantly improved, still superior over opponents, able to win their wars, and transformed in the ways that count.

## New Operational Goals to Guide Transformation

If a purposeful and measured transformation is to succeed, it must be guided by sound operational concepts that specify how U.S. forces should be prepared, deployed, and employed for combat missions and warfighting. A critical task is to evaluate new concepts to determine whether they fit sensibly into overall defense strategy and transformation goals, will actually produce their advertised capabilities in cost-effective ways, and can be blended together to provide wise guidance for building forces and allocating resources.

*Joint Vision 2020* (*JV 2020*), a document produced by the Joint Staff in 2000, currently provides the main intellectual leadership for defense planning. Focused on joint forces for full-spectrum dominance, its core strategic concepts call for decisive force, power projection, overseas presence, and strategic agility. Based on this strategic architecture, *JV 2020*'s key operational concepts include information superiority, dominant maneuver, precision engagement, full-dimensional protection, and focused logistics. Within the military services, such concepts as rapid decisive operations and effects-based operations have gained prominence as ways to help supplement *JV 2020*.[2]

While *JV 2020* remains valid, recent defense reviews have produced a new set of operational concepts that are potential candidates for inclusion. Each of them is significant individually, but seen collectively, their importance grows. Many offer potent ideas for guiding transformation, acquiring new technologies, and creating new force structures. Virtually all of these concepts focus on keeping U.S. forces superior to future adversaries, mostly through acquiring new technologies and systems. They reflect presumptions that future adversaries will be stronger than now; will have access to information era systems; and will employ asymmetric strategies to help foil U.S.

---

Table 3–2. Ten New Operational Concepts for Building and Employing Transformed Forces

---

**Operational Concepts for Building Transformed Forces**
Joint response strike forces for early entry operations
Enhanced information systems and space-based assets for force networking
Accelerated deployment of theater missile defenses for force protection
Realigned overseas presence and better mobility for swift power projection
Interoperable allied forces for multilateral operations

---

**Operational Concepts for Employing Transformed Forces**
Maritime littoral operations for projecting power ashore
Standoff targeting and forcible entry for antiaccess/area-denial threats
Enhanced tactical deep strikes for effective use of joint air assets
Decisive close combat operations and deep maneuver for ground assets
Deliberate and sustained operations

---

operations. In particular, they presume that future enemy forces will launch swiftly unfolding strikes in order to win quickly before U.S. forces can arrive on the scene. As a result, these concepts call upon U.S. forces to deploy swiftly and to win decisively, with minimum American and allied casualties. They thus seek to dominate future wars by controlling them, defeating enemy forces operationally and destroying them, occupying key territory, and producing favorable political outcomes.

The new operational concepts can be grouped into two categories (see table 3–2). The first category provides concepts primarily for building transformed forces through new technologies and reengineering of structures. Owing to their general characteristics, such forces could be employed in combat in a variety of different ways. The second category provides guidance on more specific ways to employ these forces in crises and wars. All 10 concepts can be considered goals of transformation. See the appendix to this chapter for a detailed discussion of each concept.[3]

These new operational concepts are key to forging a purposeful and measured transformation because they provide a concrete sense of how future forces should operate and of the capabilities that will be needed. Their main thrust is to prepare high-tech combat forces, with advanced information networks and space assets, backed by strong mobility forces and lean logistic supply units. Their offensive measures will create jointly operated forces from all services that can strike lethally at long range while dominating close engagements on the battlefield itself. Their defensive measures will help protect U.S. forces against new-era threats, especially weapons of mass destruction and antiaccess/area-denial threats. Their emphasis on developing a wider network of bases and facilities, including along the Asian littoral, will help enable U.S. forces to operate in new geographic locations. The effect will be not only to create better capabilities in a technical sense but also to enhance adaptability, especially in contingencies at the medium-to-high end of the spectrum.

Nevertheless, these and other new operational concepts must be evaluated carefully to ensure that they make strategic sense, will produce new capabilities required by the armed services, and fit together to provide a coherent approach to warfighting. If they prove out, these concepts offer a new strategic vision for building and employing future U.S. forces, strengthened in multiple ways to carry out demanding missions through new-era joint operations. They will need appropriate weapons, technologies, and other assets for these new missions and operations, and therefore the transformation process must be accelerated. But this vision does not require a frantic leap into an uncharted future. It can be accomplished through a purposeful and measured transformation focused on the midterm that embodies a mixture of continuity and change through a combination of upgraded legacy forces and some ultra-sophisticated forces.

This appealing vision of enhanced American technological prowess should not lose sight of equally important strategic judgments: that the Armed Forces must remain well trained and well led, that wars will remain contests of willpower, and that U.S. combat operations will always need to be guided by well conceived political and military goals. Moreover, this vision has important global political implications that need to be recognized and handled wisely. The idea that the United States is assembling swift, high-tech strike forces backed by missile defenses will be welcomed by some countries, but it already is triggering apprehension in others, including allies and adversaries. Diplomacy will be needed to underscore that the United States is behaving responsibly, not like a rogue hyperpower with a unilateral agenda. Embedding American defense preparations in multilateral security ties, interoperability with allied forces, and partnership relations can help reduce apprehension. The larger point, of course, is that strongly transformed forces will help enhance the credibility of the United States abroad, strengthen its capacity to mold peacetime security affairs in ways that safeguard its interests, and defeat enemies that threaten the safety of the American people.

Notwithstanding their many attractive features, these concepts should not be viewed as a cure-all or as offering a stand-alone defense strategy. While they mainly focus on wars at the high end of the spectrum, most do not pay comparable attention to the lower end, where force improvements may also be needed. Their preoccupation with new technologies for strike operations, if carried too far, might risk overlooking the many other types of warfighting and the need for well prepared forces that are ready in many ways. These concepts will need to be accompanied by measures in such mundane and often-neglected areas as logistic support, maintenance, and war reserves. Otherwise, they could create forces that possess glittering new technologies but lack the overall wherewithal to fight effectively.

These concepts and related transformation endeavors must be accompanied by a sound resource strategy and balanced investments. Adequate defense budgets will be needed: sustained increases that permit new ventures. Absent major reductions in other areas, nonetheless, fiscal constraints will be tight for many years, and priorities therefore must be set. None of these concepts offers a free lunch; all of them require investments in new capabilities. Fortunately, several of them are not very expensive. They can be carried out adequately with funding support that is consistent with foreseeable budgets. The exceptions are missile defense, space assets, and air modernization, all of which carry big price tags if pursued fully. In these and other costly programs, investment decisions will need to be made with a balanced focus on high-leverage payoffs and cost-effectiveness. Otherwise, spending on a few big-ticket concepts could leave the others starved for funds.

If savings must be found, the answer is not necessarily neglecting these concepts or slashing combat forces, which consume only one-third of the DOD budget. Equal or greater savings likely can be found by controlling the spiraling operations and maintenance (O&M) budget, trimming manpower across DOD, and reengineering domestic support structures. A great menace to affording transformation is the rising cost of the defense budget in other areas. DOD operating costs today (per capita spending for O&M and military manpower) are about 25 percent higher than a decade ago in constant dollars. Per capita spending on O&M today is fully 50 percent higher than a decade ago. Today, the annual O&M budget of about $125 billion is fully double the procurement budget, which stood at only about $62 billion for fiscal year 2002. In the 1980s, procurement spending was the same size as O&M budgets, not far smaller. Today's procurement budgets are far short of the amount needed to fund a major acquisition effort for transformation. Bigger procurement as well as research, development, test, and evaluation budgets are expected in the coming years. Unless ways can be found to stem the rising tide of operating costs and the domestic defense infrastructure, a successful transformation will be difficult to achieve regardless of how many new concepts are created.

Even if adequate funds are available for transformation, the need for a coherent plan and program will not go away. The strength of these 10 operational concepts lies not in their individual features, but in their capacity to work together to create a composite theory of force preparedness and employment doctrines. Any effort to pursue only a few concepts, while neglecting the others, could produce an unbalanced force incapable of the full-spectrum operations required by future strategic challenges. For example, preoccupation with missile defenses, standoff targeting, and littoral maritime operations could result in inadequate forces for direct crisis interventions. Likewise, an emphasis on forcible entry and deep strike, to the exclusion of close combat capabilities, could result in a lack of strong ground forces.

The armed services will be best served by investing wisely in a full set of valid new concepts in affordable, well planned ways, while attending to the other aspects of defense preparedness. In the final analysis, a strong military posture will be marked by the capacity to perform many missions and operations effectively, rather than a few superbly and others poorly. This is a central lesson of the past decades, during which the United States struggled hard to build its superior forces of today. It likely will prove to be the guiding beacon for building and using transformed forces for the 21st century.

## Appendix: Key Features of New Operational Concepts

This appendix provides additional information on the characteristics, attractions, and potential drawbacks of 10 proposed new operational concepts.

### Joint Response Strike Forces for Early Entry Operations

The concept of joint response strike forces for early entry is anchored in the premise that U.S. forces must become better at deploying to a crisis in the early stages, during the critical initial days and weeks. It calls for configuring a portion of the military posture for rapid deployment followed by the demanding defensive and offensive operations that take place in the early stages, often in the face of enemy surprise attacks aimed at winning before large U.S. reinforcements arrive. Some proponents argue that this concept could result in creation of standing joint task forces in the major theater commands and the continental United States (CONUS), charged with deploying rapidly and fighting aggressively. Irrespective of command arrangements, this concept calls for joint forces configured for early entry, capable of halting the attack, seizing the initiative by degrading enemy forces, striking such initial targets as WMD systems, and securing rear areas for later-arriving reinforcements. In the view of its proponents, the strength of this concept is that it could focus defense planning on "tip-of-the-spear" forces, with the remaining forces providing multiple powerful shafts. Its drawback is that it could result in insufficient attention to follow-on reinforcements that could also be critical to winning.

Forces that will begin arriving within 2 to 4 days and complete their deployment within 30 days must be highly ready, capable of moving rapidly, and unencumbered by ponderous logistics. Limited in size and often outnumbered, these forces must be equipped with advanced information systems, modernized weapons, and ultra-high-tech systems that provide high lethality, survivability, and tactical flexibility. Air forces would require stealthy interceptors and fighter bombers, supported by AWACs and JSTARS, and ample stocks of ultra-smart munitions. Perhaps three to six fighter wing equivalents, backed by strategic bombers, could be needed for a single operation. Naval forces must be capable of potent littoral capabilities for initially defending zones of joint operations, supporting troop movements ashore, and bombarding enemy forces from long distances. A carrier battlegroup, an amphibious ready group, and other specialized combatants usually will be needed. Ground forces must be capable of protecting air bases and seaports, conducting active reconnaissance of enemy forces, and engaging in blocking actions and limited meeting engagements when necessary. These will be light mechanized forces—lean enough to deploy swiftly but strong enough for intense combat—or lean armored units, coupled with air assault and deep fires assets: at least a division and preferably a corps for a single operation.

## Enhanced Information Systems and Space-Based Assets for Force Networking

While information operations are already a staple of *JV 2020*, the proposed new guiding concept calls for accelerated efforts to develop new systems that could further enhance combat operations. Its ultimate goal is to network all joint forces fully so that they can work together in conducting high-speed, simultaneous, and decisive operations. This network would bring all forces—across all services and missions, from top to bottom of the command structure—into close contact in ways providing high coordination even if the forces themselves are widely distributed. This concept calls for a network of interlocking information grids that provide dominant battlespace awareness: an intelligence grid, a communications grid, an engagement grid, and a logistic support grid. It also calls for strong information warfare assets: the capacity to defend U.S. networks against enemy attacks and to degrade enemy networks.

This concept, moreover, envisions greater use of space-based assets. Modernized satellites for communications, navigation, and intelligence surveillance will be needed, with systems capable of operating in all weather conditions and linked directly to the deployed forces. Also envisioned is a global satellite system that provides near-real-time targeting data: a JSTARS in space. If weapons in space are deployed, they are likely to be limited initially to missile defense systems, but in the distant future, other strike assets and transport systems might be deployed there. Greater reliance on space will necessitate defensive systems for protecting against enemy interference, coupled with capabilities to degrade the enemy's use of space. Overall, the strength of this concept lies in its capacity to move U.S. forces more boldly into the information age with technologies that enemies will be hard-pressed to match any time soon. But preoccupation with information systems and space should not come at the expense of neglecting combat forces and weapons. Seeing the battlefield better than the enemy does will not, itself, guarantee victory.

## Accelerated Deployment of Theater Missile Defenses for Force Protection

The recent effort to accelerate deployment of missile defenses is a major departure in U.S. defense strategy and an important part of transformation. Currently, public attention is focused on national missile defenses (NMD) and other homeland defense measures. However, the deployment of theater air and missile defenses (TAMD) may be more important for facilitating overseas military operations. Whereas NMD will protect U.S. territory, TAMD will protect the Armed Forces in war zones from attack by theater ballistic missiles and cruise missiles armed with WMD or conventional warheads. TAMD also will help protect allied countries and their forces. Currently, several systems are being developed. Lower-tier systems would provide defense against short-range missiles: the primary system is Patriot Advanced Capability (PAC–3). Upper-tier systems would defend large areas against medium-range and intermediate-range missiles: included are Theater High Altitude Area Defense (THAAD), the Navy Theater Wide System, and airborne lasers.

Decisions have not yet been made on the exact mix of systems, but deployment likely will unfold faster than for NMD. The combination of NMD and TAMD defenses will enhance the capacity of U.S. forces to operate safely in an era of accelerating WMD proliferation. The risks are threefold: missile defenses will not be foolproof even against limited threats; they will complicate political relations with allies and other countries; and costly options could result in funding shortfalls for other combat forces. A consideration for future force operations is that missile defense deployments will not take place in a strategic vacuum. During the Cold War, American strategy relied on several key concepts to integrate its use of conventional and nuclear forces, such as extended deterrence, forward defense, flexible response, graduated escalation, and massive retaliation. Over the past decade, conventional wars have been waged outside the shadow of nuclear escalation. In the future, conventional wars likely will be waged against enemies possessing WMD systems. A new set of integrated concepts for determining how to handle escalation will be needed, but unlike the Cold War, missile defenses will be a factor in the equation.

## Realigned Overseas Presence and Better Mobility for Swift Power Projection

The concept of realigned overseas presence and better mobility for swift power projection calls for switching overseas presence away from lingering Cold War missions toward the new missions and strategic geography of the future. It would focus the U.S. presence in Europe (109,000 troops today) away from NATO border defense and toward becoming a hub for power projection into distant areas, not only on Europe's periphery but in the greater Middle East and Persian Gulf as well. It also would use a reengineered U.S. presence to help guide allied forces into their own transformation. While it will continue defending on the Korean peninsula until a peaceful resolution is achieved there, this concept would launch similar changes in the American posture in Asia of nearly 100,000 troops, to focus on new power-projection missions along the Asian littoral and in South Asia. The result might be fewer troops in Europe and more in Asia; more important, the forces would be reengineered for swift deployments to distant areas, and they would be equipped with information-era structures and assets for new missions, which often will be mobile and littoral, not stationary and continental. Along with these changes to forces would come efforts to develop better access to bases, facilities, and infrastructure along the unstable southern belt.

This concept also calls for stronger strategic-mobility assets to speed the deployment of CONUS-stationed forces and logistic support assets to crisis zones. It would invest in more prepositioning of equipment and stocks afloat and ashore, bigger and faster transport ships, improvements to existing heavy air transports, better offshore logistic support, and faster offloading abroad in places where access to big ports and airfields is limited. As new technology becomes available, super-heavy air transports and ships might also be acquired. Overall, the combination of a realigned overseas presence and better mobility for swift power projection offers promise in the mid-term, and this concept can be mostly carried out with existing or emerging technologies. But altering overseas presence can alarm countries losing U.S. forces as well as those gaining them. In addition, while modest increases to strategic mobility forces are affordable, major improvements could be expensive.

### Interoperable Allied Forces for Multilateral Operations

The concept of interoperable allied forces for multilateral operations recognizes that most U.S. combat operations will be multilateral, often involving major participation by allies and partners. Accordingly, it calls for efforts to reengineer and improve their forces so that they can operate with American forces that are undergoing transformation. This concept emphasizes the need for allied information systems and networks that can interoperate with U.S. networks. In the coming era, interoperability will mostly be a product of establishing connectivity between

American and allied information nets, rather than acquiring identical weapons and munitions. This concept also envisions allied improvements to provide better expeditionary forces, power projection assets, long-distance logistic support, modern weapons, and smart munitions. It aims not for mirror images of the Armed Forces, but instead for allied forces that can participate as team players, often carrying out niche missions of their own.

In Europe, this would involve a follow-on to the NATO Defense Capability Initiative (DCI). Adopted in 1999 as a multiyear plan, DCI was broadly cast and is now stalling. A new initiative would focus more narrowly on configuring modern allied forces for networked operations and for new expeditionary and projection missions. Such a plan could be integrated with European Union efforts to create multilateral forces of its own. In the Persian Gulf, this concept takes advantage of improving Saudi and Kuwaiti forces, and those of other friendly countries, to provide better niche assets in such critical areas as initial defense, suppression of enemy antiaccess efforts, and support of U.S. reinforcements. In Asia, it envisions the forces of Japan, South Korea, Australia, and other countries gradually becoming better at power projection, new missions, and interoperability with the Armed Forces. Overall, the idea of better and more interoperable allied and partner forces makes strategic sense and is vitally necessary if future U.S. military strategy is to succeed and burdens are to be shared fairly. But this concept faces political constraints. Convincing these countries to respond with bigger defense budgets and improved forces is easier said than done. Even when allied and partner forces are militarily capable, multilateral combat operations can be difficult to carry out. When allied forces fall short in their missions, American forces must pick up the slack or risk damaging battlefield setbacks.

## Maritime Littoral Operations for Projecting Power Ashore

Ever since the Cold War ended and the Soviet naval threat disappeared, the U.S. Navy has increasingly focused on littoral operations. In the past decade, the Navy has played important littoral roles in *Desert Storm*, Kosovo, the Balkans, peacekeeping, enforcing no-fly zones in the Persian Gulf, and helping deter MTW aggression by Iraq and North Korea. Such missions will continue, but new maritime littoral operations will be different and more demanding. These operations increasingly will focus not just on controlling littoral waters but also on using the littoral to project naval and marine power ashore in support of joint campaigns. In the coming years, these naval missions will be conducted against enemies that may possess missiles, mines, and submarines capable of threatening American ships. Naval forces, supported by joint assets, will be operating along the vast Asian littoral for the strategic purpose of reassuring allies and friends, protecting critical sea lines and commerce zones, and dissuading China from pursuing excess geopolitical ambitions.

The combination of heightened threats and new emphasis on Asian littoral missions has given rise to a mounting debate over the Navy's future. One issue is its size: whether it should stay level at about 300 ships, grow, or decline as a result of slow shipbuilding. Another issue is the nature of the Navy's future ships: whether big carriers and traditional combatants should dominate or, instead, the Navy should procure different platforms. A third issue is political: determining how to employ Asian littoral operations in a manner that advances American interests and regional stability rather than inflaming tense situations. Resolving these issues wisely will be key not only to charting the Navy's course but also to carrying out U.S. defense strategy and foreign policy in an era of accelerating globalization.

### Standoff Targeting and Forcible Entry for Antiaccess/Area-Denial Threats

The operational concept of standoff targeting and forcible entry is focused on overpowering antiaccess or area-denial threats so that the Armed Forces can gain decisive entry into hot crisis zones. Its two components are intended to work together on behalf of the same strategic purposes. Whereas standoff targeting helps suppress enemy defenses, forcible entry operations complete the job and establish U.S. forces at forward locations in the crisis zone. The challenge is to integrate these two components with their relative contributions in mind.

Standoff targeting involves using strategic bombers, cruise missiles, and future exotic systems to bombard enemy targets from long distances. The use of strategic bombers to support theater campaigns is hardly new; the United States employed B–52s in Vietnam and made significant use of bombers and cruise missiles in *Desert Storm* and Kosovo. The idea has gained added prominence recently for two reasons. Some analysts fear that in future conflicts, American forces either will lack access to forward bases and infrastructure or will be unable to operate safely against enemy antiaccess/area-denial threats. In addition, the existing forces of nearly 200 bombers and ships with cruise missiles can generate up to one-fourth of the military's air-delivered firepower. The growing accuracy of smart munitions is giving them the capacity to carry out lethal bombardment campaigns on their own, from rear bases and outside enemy threat envelopes.

A key effect can be to help suppress enemy defenses, thereby allowing other U.S. forces to converge. The time has arrived to make full use of these increasingly effective assets in American plans for future theater war.

Standoff targeting clearly has a contributing role to play in future defense strategy. At issue is whether it should be supplementary to or a replacement for traditional forward-deployed forces. Arguments against relying too heavily on this concept are severalfold. The act of abandoning forward commitments in favor of rearward stationing could unnerve allies and friends that rely on American security guarantees, while suggesting to adversaries that the United States is losing the willpower to resist them. Some analysts dispute the notion that forward bases will often be lacking, and they assert that future enemy threats can be readily overcome. They note that the act of relying heavily on standoff targeting could necessitate a big increase in associated forces, perhaps requiring more B–2 bombers and cruise missile ships in numbers that divert major funds from other combat forces.

Forcible entry asserts that U.S. military strategy should remain anchored in forward operations but acknowledges that future antiaccess/area-denial threats will necessitate a concerted effort to become better at directly inserting combat forces in the face of opposition. Supporting this concept is historical legacy. The Armed Forces have been operating successfully against such threats since World War II. The threat posed by Soviet forces during the Cold War was considerably more potent than that likely to be mounted by future rivals any time soon. Nonetheless, the combination of enemy ballistic missiles and cruise missiles, submarines and mines, and WMD systems means that future crisis interventions in many places will be more difficult than those of the past decade, when little opposition to U.S. deployments was encountered.

Forcible entry will require a joint, coordinated effort by all services. The challenge will be to improve the forces in ways that are effective, balanced, and affordable. Better standoff targeting and other strike assets will be needed to help suppress enemy defenses. The Navy will require better networked defenses against cruise missiles, ballistic missile defenses, and other threats. The Air Force and Army will need to become proficient at swiftly deploying stealthy air interceptors and Patriot batteries. The Army and Marines will need to be able to deploy light, dispersible forces in the early stages. Airfields, ports, and other infrastructure will require hardening. Improved capabilities will be needed for offshore logistics and force projection into unprepared areas. Often lost in the clamor for expensive programs in this arena is recognition that better allied forces potentially can carry much of the early defense load, thereby easing the forcible entry challenge for American forces.

### Enhanced Tactical Deep Strikes for Effective Use of Joint Air Assets

The concept of enhanced tactical deep strikes aims at upgrading the capacity of forward-committed U.S. forces to conduct lethal air bombardment of enemy formations in their rear areas. While strategic bombers and cruise missiles can help, a deep strike campaign would be carried out primarily by tactical air forces, multiple launch rocket systems (MLRS) with Army tactical missile systems (ATACMs), attack helicopters, and long-range artillery. Major progress has been made recently in strengthening the Armed Forces in this arena but further gains are possible. JSTARS and navigational satellites permit near-real-time targeting, including targeting against mobile ground forces. Such munitions as the joint air-to-surface standoff missile (JASSM), the joint direct attack munition (JDAM), the joint standoff weapon (JSOW), sensor-fused weapons (SFW/Skeet), and the brilliant anti-tack munition (BAT) permit highly accurate, lethal strikes against a wide spectrum of targets, including armored vehicles. The F–22, Joint Strike Fighter (JSF), and F/A–18 E/F provide stealthy aircraft for suppressing enemy air defenses and carrying out major bombardment using the full spectrum of modern munitions. As UAVs and UCAVs mature, they can complement these combat aircraft in useful ways.

As these systems are acquired, deep strike campaigns will become an increasingly important part of operational strategy for keeping enemy forces at bay, destroying them rapidly, and winning wars decisively. Effects-based targeting can help determine optimal ways for allocating strikes against enemy forces, infrastructure, and industry, thereby further enhancing the effectiveness of deep strikes. Yet deep strike campaigns cannot win wars on their own. Especially in conditions where the weather is bad, the terrain is difficult, the enemy must be overpowered in a few days, or territory must be occupied, strong ground combat forces will be needed. For deep strike campaigns to succeed, smart munitions must be available in adequate quantities, and air forces must have the support assets and spares needed to generate high sortie rates. Because shortfalls already exist, buying sufficient stocks of smart munitions is a critical priority. Modernization with new combat aircraft is important, but the high cost of buying several thousand new models will necessitate a resource strategy of phased procurements to ensure affordability.

### Decisive Close Combat Operations and Deep Maneuver for Ground Assets

The concept of decisive close combat operations and deep maneuver focuses on ways to strengthen Army and Marine forces for close combat and deep counterthrusts so that they will continue to enjoy superiority over enemy forces in situations where crushing, fast-paced ground campaigns are needed, accompanied perhaps by war-termination efforts that occupy enemy territory. Currently, active Army forces provide four light divisions (infantry, airborne, and air assault) and six heavy divisions (armored and mechanized). In its Interim Force plan, the Army intends to reconfigure six brigades with light armored vehicles so that they can deploy rapidly, including aboard tactical air transports. In pursuing its Objective Force over the long term, the Army plans to create new fighting vehicles that will replace heavy tanks and artillery tubes with weapons that weigh far less but have comparable firepower and survivability. This vision depends heavily on major progress in exploratory research and development programs that will take years to develop, and even then could encounter serious trouble in creating new ground weapons that are light but survivable, powerful, and embedded in protective systems. Until then, the Army may be well served by anchoring its plans on Interim Forces, keeping its tanks and other weapons, and making better use of prepositioning to be able to deploy faster than now. Heavy forces with prepositioned equipment often can deploy faster than light forces, with no prepositioning, from CONUS.

Some critics argue that today's focus on technology should be accompanied by continuing efforts to reorganize and reengineer Army force structures. Progress in this area could help reduce the Army's multiple command layers and large logistic support assets, while creating new combat formations for swift maneuvers and decisive strikes in joint operations. The Army and Marines are not pursuing near-term modernization with full suites of new weapons, but they are seeking new helicopters and artillery tubes plus upgraded tanks and infantry fighting vehicles. Progress in these programs will be needed as part of any effort to pursue this operational concept.

### Deliberate and Sustained Operations

The previous nine concepts assume that the Armed Forces will swiftly deploy to a crisis and then launch aggressive operations aimed at rapidly overpowering the enemy and attaining decisive victory within a few days or weeks. Afterward, American forces presumably would withdraw from the scene as soon as possible. Such short, explosive, high-tech wars may be common in the future most of the time, but U.S. defense strategy should also plan for other types of wars. Some conflicts may be marked by deliberate operations aimed at controlling a crisis over a lengthy period, rather than overwhelming enemy forces immediately. An American presence may remain for a long time in order to exert control over political aftermath.

Deliberate operations may not be the preferred norm of American military strategy, but they can be made necessary by a host of considerations: crises that build slowly, allies that balk, physical constraints that prevent U.S. forces from deploying fast, enemies that refuse to be beaten, or wars interspersed with periods of diplomacy. Sustained operations can occur not only as a result of wars dragging on without a conclusion but also as a result of political decisions to occupy the territory of a defeated enemy as part of war-termination policies. Today's no-fly zones in Iraq are an example of compelled political settlements that require an enduring postwar presence on friendly soil. Peacekeeping, of course, is a hallmark of deliberate sustained operations. This concept calls attention to the need for the Armed Forces to remain prepared for these operations, even as they acquire greater capabilities for winning rapidly and decisively. Remaining prepared for such operations requires a focus on traditional combat forces (for example, infantry), logistic support units, and war reserve stocks that otherwise might lose favor in a defense strategy focused on winning rapidly and decisively. It also necessitates remaining aware that modern war may not always take the form that American plans, forces, and technology want or expect.

## Notes

[1] See Department of Defense, Quadrennial Defense Review Report (Washington, DC: Department of Defense, 2001).

[2] See Joint Staff, *Joint Vision 2020* (Washington, DC: Government Printing Office, June 2000).

[3] For more analysis, see Hans Binnendijk and Richard L. Kugler, *Adapting Forces to a New Era: Ten Transforming Concepts,* Defense Horizons 5 (Washington, DC: Center for Technology and National Security Policy, National Defense University, October 2001).

**Part II**

# Transforming the Services

# Chapter 4

# The Army: Toward the Objective Force

Bruce R. Nardulli and Thomas L. McNaugher

The Army faces the clear challenge of becoming more rapidly deployable without sacrificing survivability and lethality. The transformed organization must retain the survivability, lethality, and tactical mobility of heavy forces and the agility and deployability of light forces.[1]

The Army has launched a major effort to transform itself and the way it conducts land operations. Officials regard the endeavor as the "most significant and comprehensive effort to change this Army in a century," one that will "revolutionize land-power capabilities."[2] The goal is a ground force that is more rapidly deployable and tactically agile than, but as survivable and lethal as, today's heavy forces. It will be a "full spectrum" force, dominant not only in war but also, with minimal modification, in peacekeeping, humanitarian intervention, and disaster assistance operations. The centerpiece of the fully transformed Army would be the Objective Force, a ground force that would bear little physical or operational resemblance to today's Army. But long before the Objective Force takes shape, the Army will begin to incorporate interim brigade combat teams (IBCTs) equipped with light armored vehicles and adapted to new tactics. Army transformation thus aims to make change very rapidly, even while establishing the basis for more dramatic change over the longer term.

Post-Cold War strategic realities, notably the emergence of a broad array of missions in unpredictable locales, make transformation necessary. Change is made possible by new technologies, especially information technologies that promise to allow greater situation awareness, more precise fires, and more distributed, nonlinear operations. The new technologies were producing change even in the Cold War Army. The demands of the new strategic setting add new dimensions to the transformation in areas such as mobility and agility.

Like any other ambitious endeavor, transformation faces sizable risks. These perils usually are defined largely in technological terms, many of which are inherent in the Army vision of its future. Moreover, almost every risk has a technological dimension to it. But the risks here run well beyond those associated with technology. Can the Army find and train people—followers as well as leaders—able to fight the distributed, nonlinear, all-arms warfare it envisions? An even larger risk stems from the steady elimination of a margin for error, ambiguity, or uncertainty. Paring away armor to reduce weight shifts the burden of force protection increasingly to information. Given what is available today in the way of light antiarmor weaponry, the need for situation awareness is dauntingly high.

Another risk is that the strategic factors driving Army transformation will evolve unfavorably over the years in which the Army hopes to implement transformation. What if a Cold War-like set of strategic circumstances—a more geographically focused, heavily armored threat—were to reemerge over the next 20 years? Further compounding the complexity are the uncertainties surrounding the unfolding war on terrorism and the Army role in it, both in waging offensive operations against terrorists and their sponsors and in the evolving area of homeland defense.

These risks compel the Army to move cautiously, relying on extensive experimentation and employing significant hedges against full or partial failure. If transformation is carried forward properly, however, even a partial failure—measured against the Army's very high standards of success—is likely to yield more effective ground forces. With this perspective in mind, this chapter will examine the proposed Army transformation and the opportunities and hurdles that lie ahead.

The chapter begins by outlining why transformation is necessary. It then touches upon key enabling technologies, most notably the array of information systems and networks underpinning the envisioned transformation. We next describe the Army's three-pronged approach to transformation, which provides for an Interim Force on the way to the futuristic Objective Force, while maintaining and modernizing the present Legacy Force. Issues crucial to the Army transformation—its organization and doctrine as well as its technology—are explored, as are options for transformation if conditions differ from present-day projections. These options include both evolutionary and "leap-ahead" alternatives. Finally, we outline the implications of the war on terrorism for U.S. military missions and hence for demands on the Army.

## Why Transform the U.S. Army?

Even before the Cold War ended, the Army was realizing that the information revolution promised potentially radical improvements in the effectiveness of ground forces, as well as significant changes in their organization. The Soviet Union first called attention to this issue in the 1970s with discussion in military journals of what it called the *military technical revolution*. By the 1980s, the label had been altered in the United States to the *revolution in military affairs*, but the core theme remained the same: given what the information revolution was doing to commercial firms, surely it could work radical change in military forces. The air services saw ways to exploit the new technology to produce greater precision in air-to-air and air-to-ground firepower while managing more complex air operations. Army officers also sought advances in precision. In addition, watching commercial firms eliminate layers of management, the Army also had cause to wonder whether information technologies might not portend significant alterations in the traditional combat hierarchy as well.[3]

In this sense, the strands of today's Army transformation reach well back into the Cold War. The artillery branch, for example, exploits satellites and electronics to use the global positioning system to lay in its artillery pieces and to add speed and precision to aiming artillery tubes (this was the role of the Tactical Artillery Fire Control [TACFIRE] system). Information technologies have been used to improve the accuracy and rate of fire of the M–1 tank. In the early 1990s, the Army inaugurated Force XXI, an effort to use communication technologies to create a more distributed, networked ground force armed not only with more precise fires, but also with much better intelligence on the position of its own as well as enemy forces. The 4th Infantry Division (Mechanized) at Fort Hood, Texas, has served as an experimental testbed for these new technologies and concepts, which are also referred to as digitization. The 4th Division became the Army's first fully digitized division in 2001.[4]

While one stimulus for transformation arose from technological trends rooted in the Cold War era, a second set of forces rose out of the Army's post-Cold War experience. The stable paradigm of large-scale, high-intensity conflict with the Soviet Union gave way in the 1990s to a series of diverse operations in disparate locations. These ranged from heavy armor operations in the Persian Gulf War to rapid lighter interventions in Haiti and Panama, to humanitarian intervention and urban warfare in Somalia, and then to peace enforcement in the Balkans. War remained a possibility;

indeed, throughout the 1990s, the Nation asked all of the services to be ready to fight two major theater wars simultaneously. But most deployments the Army experienced in the 1990s were smaller-scale contingencies.[5]

This new and broader menu of missions called, first, for a full-spectrum force, one as capable of performing operations other than war (OOTW) as of fighting war itself. The difference in force requirements is not trivial. While there are technologies, operational concepts, and organizational functions that span both domains, there are also substantial differences, as the Army has discovered in trying to accommodate a steady diet of OOTW while retaining the strength and skill for major high-intensity combat. In particular, it has discovered that while it is already a full-spectrum force in terms of having the capabilities needed for a diverse array of OOTW located somewhere in the warfighting structure, these capabilities do not readily emerge from that structure, and their use in OOTW can impose a heavy burden on the warfighting force.[6] Conversely, the Army has discovered that forces well designed and prepared for wartime operations can find themselves deficient in OOTW.[7]

The Army's experience in the 1990s also revealed a need for much improved strategic responsiveness. In sharp contrast to the geographic focus of the Cold War experience, which allowed for massive prepositioning of units, equipment, and supplies in Europe and Northeast Asia, the post-Cold War Army must be able to deploy rapidly around the world. This requirement favors a lighter force, hence the goal of an Objective Force featuring a family of vehicles all considerably lighter than the M–1 tank (65–70 tons) or the M–2 Bradley Fighting Vehicle (roughly 32 tons).[8] Given that so much of what the Army takes on an operation consists of fuel, ammunition, and spare parts, however, strategic responsiveness also demands reduced logistics requirements for future Army forces. The stated goal of Army transformation, achievable or not, is the ability to deliver a brigade anywhere in the world 96 hours after "wheels up," a division within 120 hours, and a full corps within 30 days.

Responsiveness is, however, more than a matter of delivering forces to a theater rapidly. It includes the ability to move about the region once there. In regions with very poor infrastructure, M–1 tanks may become nothing more than expensive bunkers. Thus, even if the Army were able to preposition equipment and supplies for its heavy forces in key locations around the world, it would still need a lighter, more mobile force in many tactical situations.

A final component of strategic responsiveness has to do with the organization itself. Armies geared to fight big wars generally tend to be organized around relatively large components. Combined with the Nation's seeming aversion to casualties and the Army's own post-Vietnam desire to mass forces for decisive operations, this organizational feature has often seemed to prevent the Army from offering the President and the Secretary of Defense a wide range of ground options in contingencies. When advising senior military and civilian leadership on possible ground options during the 1999 Kosovo conflict, for example, Army leaders appeared to offer only very large ground force alternatives involving multiple divisions and requiring months of preparation. Whatever the military merit of these alternatives, they were not palatable politically. The Army risked being viewed, rightly or wrongly, as unwieldy and inflexible, and thus irrelevant.

The need for greater strategic responsiveness was recognized during the Clinton administration and has also been adopted by the Bush administration. The terms of reference of Secretary of Defense Donald Rumsfeld's Quadrennial Defense Review (QDR) 2001 note the importance of broadening the range of military options available to the President.[9] They call for enhancing the employability and deployability of U.S. forces, extending their reach, and minimizing their deployed footprint. They identify a need for forces that are "lighter, more lethal and maneuverable, survivable, and more readily deployed and employed in an integrated fashion."[10] Although these phrases apply to all U.S. military forces, they have obvious significance to the Nation's ground forces.

The demands for change emanating from the Army's 1990s experience mesh with the technological impetus for change. A heavy tank force is also able to exploit the information revolution to achieve greater effectiveness; such is the case with the 4th Infantry Division. But as the Army seeks lighter vehicles, the premium on good information rises sharply. Armor is, in effect, an insurance policy against ignorance of the enemy's location and weaponry. Short of truly miraculous improvements in the stopping power of light armor, future Army vehicles will lack that insurance policy as they advance into enemy forces likely to be armed with a growing assortment of readily available antiarmor munitions. They will have to know where the enemy is to a degree that heavy forces would like but do not require. It will be even more crucial for them to be able to take the enemy on at a distance and with lethal precision.

## Getting There from Here: Key Enabling Technologies

General Eric Shinseki's "transformation speech" on October 12, 1999, focused attention mainly on medium-weight vehicles. Since then, a major competition among off-the-shelf candidates for the Army's interim armored vehicle has reinforced this focus while drawing attention to the underlying wheeled-versus-tracked debate that is roughly as old as motorized vehicles. Yet clearly at the core of the Army's transformation are information technologies, with which the Army had begun to experiment well before October 1999, notably in Force XXI and the digitization program. Presumably the fruits of that effort can be transferred, in whole or in part, to the Interim and Objective Forces of the future. Army transformation will stand or fall mainly on its success in exploiting information technologies.

The technological challenges in this area are daunting. The ground environment has always been less forgiving to complicated devices than the air or sea. Hence the Army has found it more difficult than its sister services to pack electronic components into its platforms. Nonetheless, the effort continues to equip future Army forces with new and better capabilities, including greatly improved situation awareness, enhanced command, control, communications, computers, intelligence, surveillance, and reconnaissance (C⁴ISR), and expanded use of robotics.

The objective of greatly improved situation awareness is to have ready access to a wide scope of information relevant to ongoing Army operations, from initial deployment to reception in the theater to engagement and sustainment of the deployed forces. In particular, the ability to have real-time information and shared displays on the disposition of friendly and enemy forces—the common operational picture—should allow the Army to engage enemy units more effectively. This in turn holds out the prospect that physically lighter Army forces can retain high lethality and survivability against heavier enemy forces, and thus it directly contributes to the Army's strategic responsiveness.[11] This information is also essential to driving down logistics requirements, which for many heavy units make up about 80 percent of the Army's strategic lift requirement.[12]

C⁴ISR must be enhanced. Fundamental to future force survivability and lethality is the ability to see and hit enemy forces before they can engage lighter U.S. units. The Army concept for doing so calls for a highly networked system of sensors and communications permitting rapid direct and indirect fires. Improving the speed, quality, and reliability of sensor-to-shooter links is essential to minimizing the time between target identification and engagement by direct or indirect fires, using Army or other joint service assets. Likewise, networked fires allow strikes in quicker succession, over increasingly wide areas, and against more dispersed targets. All these capabilities should contribute to the combat effectiveness of a much lighter U.S. Army against a heavier and perhaps larger enemy ground force.

Army officials envision a significantly expanded role for robotics at various levels of sophistication to reduce both casualties and the need for extensive logistics support. On the high end in this realm are largely autonomous unmanned ground vehicles that can locate and engage targets.[13] Less futuristic are robotic vehicles that can be directed by manned command vehicles to perform various tasks.

How far the Army can exploit information technologies—and in particular, whether it can achieve the extremely high levels of situation awareness some senior officers expect—remains an item for speculation. The key hedge against failure in the information realm is improved armor or better active protection systems, such as sensors that see an antiarmor munition in flight toward the vehicle and activate some mechanism to kill it before it hits (ideally, without also endangering friendly soldiers nearby). Improved armor includes an array of composite and self-repairing, self-strengthening "smart" armors now in laboratory development. Some combination of enhanced situation awareness and enhanced vehicular protection presumably can yield an acceptable overall level of protection.

Reducing the logistics footprint of deployed Army forces calls for advances in a range of technological areas. The Army speaks of "ultra-reliability" in its machinery, for example. Success in this area would involve not only the development of new technologies but also a willingness—rarely seen in Cold War-era weapon development projects—to sacrifice performance goals for greater reliability. Developing munitions of smaller caliber could cut the physical size of ammunition deliveries substantially, while greater accuracy could reduce the numbers required for success. New engine technologies could reduce fuel consumption or, in the more distant future, totally change the kind of fuel required. One promising technology is fuel cells producing water as a byproduct, allowing the Army to reduce water supplies to its deployed units.

Given that so much of the Army emphasis is on rapid deployment, the future of long-distance transportation technology is relevant as well. The service emphasis on exploiting technology to reduce the weight of any deploying force is partly driven by the limits of technology in making advances in long-distance transportation, especially in airlift. There is little indication of any pending revolution over the next few decades in the ability to move great weights long distances rapidly by air. While some promising uses of technology are in the works for improving airlift capacity, such as heavy-lift dirigibles, the mainstay of long-distance deployment by air will remain traditional fixed-wing transport aircraft. Substantial improvements undoubtedly will be made in avionics, durability, engine efficiencies, and overall supportability, but the strategic and tactical airlift fleet of 2025, in terms of raw lift per aircraft, will not be significantly different from today's.[14]

Fast sealift technologies continue to demonstrate prospects for incremental increases in speed. Far less sensitive to weight and dimensional restrictions than aircraft (barring a truly revolutionary breakthrough in airlift), sealift will remain the principal mode of strategic deployment for most Army units, whether they be Legacy, Interim, or Objective Forces.

The risks here are obvious. Ground forces are not well adapted for rapid and dramatic technological advances; ground warfare is too complex and unfolds in too unforgiving an environment to permit leaps into the technological unknown. Yet the proposed Army transformation depends on significant advances in a staggeringly wide array of technological realms. To be sure, advances across the whole array are not essential for progress. But the reduction in armored protection and the need for strategic responsiveness nonetheless create huge demands for significant improvements in today's accepted performance.

## The Plan for Transformation

The Army's specific roadmap for transformation is captured in the trident chart (figure 4–1) that has become familiar since Chief of Staff General Shinseki launched formal transformation in October 1999. The three prongs on this chart—Legacy Force, Interim Force, and Objective Force—seem redundant unless the risks inherent in achieving the Objective Force are appreciated. Backups and hedges are essential, and if they are pursued properly, a variety of transformation outcomes could yield improved ground forces.

The three prongs serve different purposes and offer different backups. The Interim Force is a near-term effort to produce lighter and more mobile brigades and divisions. It is meant above all to solve an operational shortfall that was exposed when the 82[d] Airborne Division deployed to Saudi Arabia in 1990, days after Iraqi heavy forces invaded Kuwait. The inability of these airborne units to do much against the heavier Iraqi armored forces highlighted the Army's lack of a force that was both rapidly deployable and

Figure 4–1. **The Army Transformation**

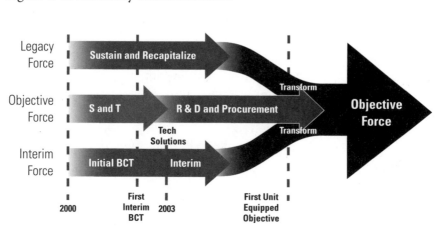

*Source:* Army Transformation Briefings, Association of the U.S. Army (AUSA) Transformation Panel, Institute for Land Warfare, October 2000, available at <www.ausa.org>.

sufficiently survivable and lethal to engage heavier opposing forces success-fully. Creation of the Interim Force also gives the Army a vehicle for exper-imenting with lighter and more networked capabilities. These new units could, if successful operationally, also help create a constituency within the Army for medium-weight units.

The Objective Force is the force of the distant future, the end prod-uct of long-term research and development efforts meant to culminate in radically improved Army effectiveness and responsiveness. As such, it is the most dependent of the three forces upon advances in science and tech-nology and the ability to incorporate these new technologies into the force. The Objective Force is to be based on a class of completely new plat-forms, collectively known as the Future Combat Systems, which are to weigh 20 tons or less. Initial elements of the Objective Force are currently scheduled to enter the force by 2010, with the entire Army converted by about 2032.

The Legacy Force consists primarily of the Army's current heavy ar-mored and mechanized divisions, modernized at some level to retain their effectiveness. This part of the transforming Army will remain essential for missions where heavy forces can dominate. It will also serve to ensure against an uncertain future in which threats may materialize that require the range and depth of capabilities contained in the heavy forces. Like the

IBCTs, elements of the heavy force can be used to test various advanced technologies and concepts in support of the longer term transformation, most notably digitization. The Legacy Force also serves as a hedge against setbacks in aggressive Army transformation efforts; maintaining this force is a way to mitigate the many risks the push toward the Objective Force entails.

In sum, the Army transformation plan pursues all three prongs as the means to balance current and near-term risks against future risks. The risks to be balanced are multidimensional: risks due to uncertainty about the future strategic environment, technology risks associated with the transformation, and institutional risks of pushing the Army too fast or in too many directions during the transformation process. The Army transformation does not fall neatly into either of the two dominant schools described in chapter 3 about transformation strategies. The Objective Force and the envisioned end-state of the full transformation embody truly revolutionary military change, but the overall process is much more evolutionary in nature. By adopting the three-pronged approach to transformation, the Army has in fact embraced a mixed strategy.

What follows is a detailed examination of the three forces to reveal the relative scale of the technologies and risks involved, their implications for long-term risk management and force tradeoffs, and how the Army intends to straddle the evolutionary/revolutionary transformation divide.

## The Interim Force

The Interim Force is intended to be a full-spectrum combat force consisting of medium-weight brigades, known as Interim Brigade Combat Teams (IBCTs). Embedded within division structures, the teams are designed to complement the capabilities of existing light and mechanized forces. Although optimized for small-scale contingencies, these brigades are expected to be employed across a range of military operations, from conducting stability and support operations to participating in major theater war as a subordinate maneuver element of heavier forces. The force's principal operational attribute is its high operational and tactical mobility.[15]

The IBCTs are designed to have several core qualities. In addition to being C–130-transportable and full-spectrum-capable, they must also be able to operate in environments with very limited infrastructure. The IBCTs should not require major air/sea ports of debarkation and are not intended to need much time and resources for reception, staging, onward movement, and integration.[16] They are designed to be ready for operations, including combat, almost immediately after arriving. These highly mobile forces must also be capable of moving long distances rapidly. The intent is to have them organized to deploy with a minimal logistics footprint, carrying enough supplies for 3 days of operations without outside support.[17] To keep the IBCT footprint small, they are to rely on division and higher echelons for additional capabilities from outside the operational area, such as intelligence and indirect fire support. Robust, advanced C[4]ISR systems are therefore needed to ensure that they have the full range of necessary capabilities.

The interim armored vehicle (IAV) is a light wheeled vehicle that will come in two variants, a mobile gun system and an infantry carrier, and is intended to be the Interim Force's primary combat platform. The IAV is based on existing light armored vehicles modified with advanced digital communications and information enhancements, many of which will be upgrades based on relatively mature technologies. The Army is currently planning to fund six to eight IBCTs; the first is being organized at Fort Lewis, Washington.[18] The first IBCT is scheduled to be fully fielded in spring 2003 and to reach full operational capability in 2005.[19] Between 2,131 and 2,791 IAVs will be needed to equip the IBCTs (depending upon the number of teams actually fielded).[20]

As currently organized, the IBCT is infantry-heavy and will have a combined arms capability at the battalion and company level. This structure is intended to give the teams a greater range of operational capabilities at the brigade level. The IBCTs also will reduce the need to pull together a task force from different units on short notice, which can slow deployment, add time to achieving full operational capability in the field, increase the size of the deploying force, and reduce force effectiveness by losing unit cohesion. Integrating a combined arms capability at these lower echelons is also meant to provide the IBCT with enhanced combat power. The team's heavy infantry orientation is best suited for military activities, whether peacekeeping or combat operations, in terrain where dismounted infantry will be in especially high demand.

Three motorized combined arms infantry battalions are the major IBCT fighting components. Other elements include the reconnaissance, surveillance, and target acquisition (RSTA) squadron, an anti-tank company, an artillery battalion, a brigade support battalion, engineering, military intelligence and signal companies, and the brigade headquarters and headquarters company.[21]

IBCTs will rely greatly on situational understanding, provided by the RSTA squadron, to compensate for their lack of heavy armor protection. For example, the organic artillery battalion of the IBCT would be expected to conduct counterbattery fire before the enemy shoots, based on RSTA squadron targeting information. Thus, its information flows will be essential to survivability of the medium-weight brigades.

The RSTA squadron is responsible for the traditional roles of reconnaissance, surveillance, and target acquisition, with a much greater emphasis on precision and speed in conducting these roles. It is also intended to provide a much broader situational understanding of the overall operational environment, including not just military but also political, cultural, economic, and other information relevant to the operation. With information and mobility, augmented by RSTA and intelligence, surveillance, and reconnaissance assets, the IBCT will be able to conduct dispersed, nonlinear operations with its units, even though individual tactical engagements may be widely separated geographically (a typical IBCT area of operations will be 50 square kilometers).[22]

Operating in the smaller-scale contingencies for which they are optimized, the IBCTs are expected to require little or no augmentation from higher echelons. Augmentations will likely be required for other roles, especially for major theater war-like high-intensity combat, in which the IBCT may require additional nonorganic assets such as lift and attack helicopter assets, more artillery, and air defense. Any significant augmentation would increase the amount of time a team would need to deploy. Although IBCTs are designed principally to fill the near-term light-heavy gap, they will also help explore innovative doctrine and organization employing medium-weight forces. As such, the IBCTs are envisioned as "the vanguard of the future Objective Force."[23]

## The Objective Force

The Objective Force is built around the Future Combat Systems (FCS), a family of vehicles that will weigh 16 to 20 tons and will be sized to be transportable within the C–130 or similar aircraft. If fully realized, the Objective Force is meant to provide the Army with the ability to deploy a combat-capable brigade anywhere in the world in 96 hours, a division in 120 hours, and 5 divisions in 30 days. As they are characterized by senior Army leadership, "Forces equipped with FCS will network fires and maneuver in direct combat, deliver direct and indirect fires, perform intelligence, surveillance, and reconnaissance functions, and transport soldiers and material."[24]

The FCS is envisioned as a system of systems in which manned command and control vehicles are networked with many unmanned reconnaissance assets and platforms delivering weapons. This networked group of systems is intended to perform as a combined arms team. Manned vehicles would perform many combat operations from concealed positions, reducing their exposure to enemy fires and direct engagements and helping these light FCS platforms survive on the modern battlefield. Superior sensors and networks would provide the means to locate and track targets from these more concealed positions. Robotic vehicles operating as necessary in more exposed areas could fill requirements for line-of-sight capability.[25] Advanced composite armor and active protection systems, including a variety of sensors to detect and rapidly engage incoming weapons, enhance vehicle and crew survivability, as do a variety of low-observable (stealth) characteristics built into the platforms.[26] The Army's investment in science and technology for the Objective Force aims to resolve several challenges posed by the FCS concept:

- balancing sustained lethality, survivability, and deployability
- reducing strategic lift requirements to move and sustain the force
- providing battlefield awareness at all levels of command through secure, digitized communications.

Overcoming these challenges depends heavily on solving the networking of all the system elements and ensuring that the network has the capacity, security, and versatility to provide necessary linkages throughout the area of operations. FCS network capabilities go beyond those envisaged for the current Army Battle Command System. The network must be capable of integrating numerous remote ground and aerial sensors, maneuvering robotic systems, and controlling and directing both direct fire and beyond-line-of-sight weapon systems, and it must be able to do so on a highly mobile battlefield. The architecture and protocols for such a system are presently underdeveloped. In addition, there are challenging issues involving the availability and management of the necessary bandwidth for the network. This networking has been identified as one of the major technical hurdles in implementing the FCS concept.[27]

The FCS concept also envisions direct and indirect fires coming from the same platform, using modular ammunition. One design concept is for missiles to be vertically launched from boxes carried onboard robotic indirect-fire platforms and capable of using different types of munitions. Current operational concepts rely heavily on networked fires to destroy targets from beyond line of sight as a means to combine high lethality with the concealment that improves survivability. But line-of-sight fires will still be needed for close engagements. Advanced cannon designs are being explored for the FCS that would have the lethality of the Abrams 120-millimeter gun but use a smaller gun to fit on the 20-ton platform. By incorporating both indirect and direct fires into the FCS, the platforms should be capable of delivering ordnance up to 50 kilometers.[28]

According to Army plans, the initial FCS will incorporate the most advanced capabilities feasible, and later upgrades will incorporate additional assets as technologies mature.[29]

### The Legacy Force

The Legacy Force plays a central role in Army transformation, that of insurance while the major changes of the Interim and Objective Force take hold and mature. Regardless of its experimentation with new technologies, doctrine, and force mixes, the Army is required to maintain its warfighting readiness throughout the 30-year transformation period. Currently, that means being able to conduct major high-intensity warfare in the foreseeable future, a role that will fall primarily to the Legacy Force, supplemented by Interim and Objective Force capabilities as they become available and demonstrate their effectiveness.

The Legacy Force is a hedge against risk at three levels. First, it is a hedge against an uncertain strategic future in which threats and contingencies might materialize in unanticipated ways. Conditions may emerge in which significant numbers of U.S. land forces must intervene against unexpectedly lethal adversaries, under very adverse circumstances, and on high-intensity battlefields. U.S. forces may be tasked to occupy a hostile country and bring down the existing regime. A force in being is needed to achieve such missions under these demanding conditions at acceptable loss rates. Second, the Legacy Force offers insurance against clever adversaries seeking to find a "silver bullet" solution to thwart technically advanced (and therefore technically dependent) U.S. ground forces, especially while those forces are still transforming. Such an adversary will still have to confront a traditional force that, whatever its other limitations, would not present the same types of vulnerabilities. In this sense, the Legacy Force precludes an adversary from finding an easy solution and thereby enhances deterrence in the process.[30] Third, the Legacy Force is a hedge against the technical risks confronting the Interim and Objective Forces. In many instances, the Army is pushing the limits of technology, either in specific technological areas or in integrating technologies in complex ways, particularly for the Objective Force. Failures and setbacks are inevitable, even though the concept itself may prove out in the end.

As part of the Legacy Force transformation, the future of the Army light forces is another important area of change. Some light brigades will become IBCTs, but to date plans for the 82$^d$ Airborne and 101$^{st}$ Air Assault Divisions remain uncertain. These units may remain fixtures of the Army Legacy and future forces. Even with advanced technology, the light forces will not become a substitute for heavy- and medium-weight forces, in terms of combat power. But considerable opportunity exists for improving the capabilities of the light forces even against heavier enemy forces. Such enhanced light forces could complement other transforming forces and add important dimensions to improvements to the range and mix of force options the Army can provide national decisionmakers.

Many of the same information technologies being used to enhance heavier Legacy and Interim forces would be applicable to light forces as well. Improved situational awareness could increase the ability of light forces to avoid engagements in which they are seriously outmatched, while illuminating opportunities where their lighter assets could inflict significant damage on opposing heavier forces. Advanced RSTA, combined with modified operational concepts, could give light forces a much greater indirect fire capability, permitting lethal attacks from safer distances. A more dramatic change could give light forces enhanced mobility and maneuver capability by equipping them with light vehicles. In this case, the price paid in speed of deployment would have to be weighed against potentially significant improvements in the range of threats and operating environments in which light forces could make major contributions.[31]

Simply maintaining today's Legacy Force involves a major resource investment for the Army. Furthermore, a central tenet of transformation is the need both to modernize elements of the Legacy Force—develop and procure new systems—and to recapitalize it—rebuild and selectively upgrade currently fielded systems. As Secretary of the Army Thomas White and General Shinseki have repeatedly noted in testimony before Congress, this entails substantial costs. With 75 percent of major combat systems currently exceeding their engineered design half-life and expected to exceed their full design life by 2010, the cost of operating and supporting these aging systems is on the rise.[32] Consequently, the Army maintains that recapitalization is needed both to enhance force capabilities and to reduce costs, themselves important goals in the overall transformation. These investments create the tension identified in chapter 3 between allocating resources to near- and mid-term improvements versus long-term, more radical changes in the force. New engines for Abrams tanks, Army aviation upgrades, and the introduction of new systems such as the Comanche helicopter into the Legacy

Force, for example, compete with resources that the Army needs to realize the Interim and Objective Forces.

## Transformation Issues

Observers sometimes tend to reduce much of the Army's transformation to its technological dimension. Will information technologies yield the kind of situation awareness and networking required to support the operation of medium-weight distributed forces? Will new engines and guns reduce logistics requirements? Will new armors offer markedly higher protection per ton than the armor available today? Given the pace at which the Army hopes to transform itself, each of these technological questions comes with the appended question: How quickly can we convert what we barely see today on the horizon into serious capability?

Yet ground forces consist of complex combined arms teams in which the role of technology per se is complemented by the role of organization and doctrine. Thus the major obstacles to any ground force transformation have less to do with achieving miraculous advances in technology than with finding the best doctrine to exploit the technologies available at any given time. One can, of course, identify transformational ground force technologies: the stirrup, the breechloading rifle, the tank. Yet in each of these cases, combat success went not to the side with the best technology but to the side having the best combination of technology and doctrine. As is frequently pointed out, France had the superior tank in 1939, but Germany had great doctrine as well as good tanks.

An army develops new organizational concepts and doctrine exploiting the technologies available to it through field experimentation. The U.S. Army experimentation within its Force XXI program highlights how expensive, complicated, and often highly politicized the experimentation process can become. The pressures of cost and politics can result in stylized experiments that validate preconceived tactical notions rather than fostering innovation. Thus, the first issue confronting Army transformation has to do with whether it can develop a level of field experimentation that actually produces optimal new combinations of tactics and technology.

The search for optimal organizations and doctrine applies to the Army's logistics as well as to its combat forces. The tendency again is to seek technological solutions to bigger organizational problems by, for example, designing ultrareliable components, fuel cells that produce water as a byproduct, highly accurate and lethal small-caliber munitions, and so forth. All these technological improvements are desirable, and some may even be achievable, if in markedly different timeframes. Chances are very small, however, that there is a magic technical solution that would significantly reduce the Army's logistics footprint in the combat zone. Achieving that goal will instead require the development of new logistics concepts, comparable to but much grander in scope than the "velocity management" paradigm that has significantly reduced order and ship times in today's Army.[33] This, too, will require a willingness to experiment with innovative ways of doing business.

Experimentation must be linked to the outside world as well as to the Army's own view of its future. Just as the current transformation was prompted by the post-Cold War shift in the strategic situation and the missions the service was asked to perform, so will the course of its transformation, extending over two or three decades, be shaped by further change in the world and in its likely missions. Thus a major issue for Army transformation is whether the strategic environment does actually change enough in the years ahead to require substantially altered capabilities. At one extreme, the reemergence of a heavily armored Russian threat to Eastern Europe could suddenly give the Army's Legacy Force a new lease on life. At the other extreme, light forces may begin to look more attractive in a world of lightly armed guerrillas who present very few targets to airborne sensors yet nonetheless pack lethal punch against both light armor and low-flying aircraft. In all cases, some portion of Army transformation will no doubt pay dividends. But the specific current direction of transformation may take a sharp turn.

Another issue for Army transformation has to do with the availability of financing for it over the long haul. Given the Army's size and the number of platforms it supports, it faces particularly challenging fiscal constraints when it comes to funding the transformation. The continuing peacekeeping demands levied on ground forces in overseas operations exacerbate the resource constraints.

The House Appropriations Committee recently estimated that over the next 12 to 15 years, the Army's transformation costs alone could exceed $70 billion.[34] The unpredictability of successes and failures in key enabling technologies will certainly affect these numbers. If historical experience is any guide, the cost of realizing the necessary technologies is likely to be on the high end of current estimates. The Army faces a daunting long-term challenge in allocating resources in the coming decades among each of the three forces so as to maintain transformation's momentum without jeopardizing essential forces and capabilities in being.[35] The Army has already taken several actions to adjust its transformation to budget realities. The scheduled introduction of the IBCTs has been lengthened from two per year to one per year; several major legacy programs have been cancelled. Although the September 11 attacks will lead to additional resources for DOD, both scale and allocation priorities are yet to be determined. Regardless of funding increases, more hard choices likely await.

## Transformation Options

Technical risks in Army transformation combined with the broader issues discussed above suggest the need for flexibility as the service moves ahead. The Army must continue to transform itself, but it may have to change emphasis and direction as future funding, missions, and technological and doctrinal options become clearer. The three-pronged approach to transformation that the organization is now taking hedges significantly against risks at many levels and thus yields the kind of flexibility the Army is likely to need.

One option that would be forced on the Army if development of needed technologies is slower than expected would be to focus on near- to mid-term evolutionary advances, deferring more revolutionary change until the technologies to support it have matured. This would mean emphasizing selective modernization of the Legacy Force and elements of the Interim Force using the more advanced technologies that emerge from development. Although less mature technologies would be left in development or perhaps dropped, this approach could still produce substantial improvements in strategic responsiveness and other capabilities.

Over the last several years, the Army has undertaken a major effort to preposition equipment sets overseas, both afloat and ashore, to reduce the amount of time necessary to get a force to the area of operations and have it ready for battle. As a result, significant improvements have been realized in the ability of Army forces to arrive in many theaters. While the timelines are not as fast as those proposed for the Objective Force, major force elements can be moved fairly quickly. Efforts may be made to reduce the size and weight of the force packages further by exploiting certain technologies. Much greater precision and availability of indirect fires, along with greater reliance on resources that do not physically go with the units (for example, relying on intelligence capabilities located in the United States) could reduce the size of the forces deployed, including the logistics support required. Using the IBCTs as a base for experimentation, the Army could further explore various brigade structures to enhance responsiveness.

The brigade combat teams could serve as experimental as well as operational elements for a considerably longer period than currently envisioned. The road to the Objective Force would be a gradual, iterative path in which exotic technologies are introduced sequentially and only after much testing and experimentation with the medium-weight Interim Force.

Progress would also draw heavily on experience with the digitized forces at Fort Hood. At every step, new doctrine would be developed and tested. The first FCS might be little more than an IAV with the digitization appliqués from Fort Hood overlaid on it. The first Objective Force thus might be little more than an IBCT with significantly enhanced C⁴ISR. All the while, the heavy forces at Fort Hood would continue to focus on evolutionary advances.

Throughout this process, the IBCTs could also serve as the Army's rapid early-deployment medium-weight force, considerably expanding the range of options the Army can provide. A brigade with substantial combat power could be delivered very quickly using a combination of airlift and fast sealift, with additional follow-on forces (IBCTs or heavier elements of the First Digitized Corps) closing rapidly by exploiting prepositioning ashore and afloat, perhaps with a network of intermediate support bases. An entire medium-weight brigade could be transported by two large, medium-speed roll-on/roll-off ships, each ship having a capacity of 18,000 tons and about 250,000 square feet of usable space.[36] Depending on the location of the IBCT and plausible constraints on airlift availability, it could move more quickly by sea than by air.[37] The Army could allocate some portion of its prepositioned stocks afloat to this role instead of moving heavier maneuver force elements, as is currently the plan. This would allow the Army to become more responsive—lighter and more mobile—fairly soon. Significant increases in the combat power and mobility of the Army's light forces could be another contributing element.

When all are combined with evolutionary technical advances that significantly improve the weight/survivability/lethality tradeoffs (and logistics load), the result could be a much more strategically responsive force of the type envisioned by General Shinseki, even well short of the Objective Force ideal. Such an approach would represent an essentially evolutionary path but could result in dramatic increases in the Army's ability to bring combat power quickly to bear in many contingencies. It would not foreclose pursuing more revolutionary force concepts but would instead permit much more time to develop them.

Another option would be to embrace a "leap-ahead" approach. While the Legacy Force still would function as insurance, investments in its modernization would be substantially reduced, along with reductions in the size of the Legacy Forces themselves, to shift more resources into science and technology accounts. The primary focus would be on pushing digitized, networked elements of the Legacy Force to the fullest extent possible to serve as a testbed to derive the most experience possible for leap-ahead applications for the Objective Force. Investment in the Interim Force likewise would contract, with fewer IBCTs fielded, and again with greater emphasis on their role in experimentation in support of the futuristic leap-ahead force. This tradeoff would assume much more near- to mid-term risk by reducing the capabilities of the Legacy and Interim Forces. Advocates of this approach might argue that the existence of a "strategic pause" makes such risks acceptable and that risks are outweighed by the benefits of more quickly developing a far more advanced and capable force.

A more technically and fiscally constrained Army transformation would also heighten the need for examining more joint force options that could alleviate some of the Army burden and provide synergies that might make better use of Army resources. Major advances in integrating joint forces and realizing the full potential of joint force synergies could potentially constitute if not a military revolution, then a vast increase in the effectiveness of U.S. forces and of individual service elements. In this sense, technological advances that can magnify the power of joint force integration could yield large dividends in terms of combat power. As a service highly attuned to the importance of and need for joint forces, the Army would have to determine what investments it should make in the joint domain as a means to enhance its own land-force capabilities. For example, as the number, sophistication, and responsiveness of indirect fires from naval and air platforms increase, the Army might invest more heavily in C$^4$ISR architectures that will allow ground commanders to reliably call in these fires and less heavily in retaining a full complement of organic land-based indirect fires. Among the benefits would be reductions in the size and weight of rapidly deploying early-entry land forces. Weightier questions would concern future trades between close and deep battle and between maneuver and deep fires and would examine how much the Army should rely on other joint forces to perform the deeper, indirect fire missions. In making such calculations, the Army must evaluate how far joint integration can be relied upon to progress, both technically and operationally, as a complement to its own service improvements, and thereby offer potential savings and tradeoffs. The joint aspect is clearly an element of the Army's transformation equation that has important investment implications.

Finally, even if much of the enabling technology is realized, the question remains whether the entire Army force should be transformed into a homogenous FCS-centric force, or whether a more mixed future force is preferable, with some significant portion containing FCS-like platforms and capabilities, complemented by other force capabilities and attributes. Other blends of Legacy, Interim, and Objective force elements might be devised and must be assessed. For example, if major limits remain to how quickly even advanced medium-weight forces can be strategically deployed by air, and if many heavier digitized forces, using fast sealift along with prepositioned assets, can arrive in theaters on comparable timelines, a blended light/medium/heavy force might represent a more strategically responsive and capable force than a medium-weight force alone. Many important comparisons and force combinations remain to be explored before a definitive decision is made on the makeup of Objective Force units.

## Possible Implications of the War on Terrorism

Army transformation clearly needs to be reexamined in light of the events of September 11 and the announced war on terrorism, which raise two major issues for the Army. First, what will it be called upon to do as part of the campaign against terrorism outside the continental United States, and are its current and future planned forces well designed for these missions? Second, what will the Army's revised role in homeland defense be, and how might that role affect the organization of the total Army, specifically the Army National Guard and Reserve? In addressing these two major issues, the Army will face a period of considerable uncertainty as real-world events and U.S. policy evolve to define the parameters of the war and the scale and type of military missions it requires. As part of any overall reassessment of the trajectory of the transformation, the Army will also have to receive guidance on how the new war on terrorism will affect existing commitments and responsibilities around the globe.

Still, as of late 2001, certain realities were emerging. Both President Bush and Secretary Rumsfeld have stated that the United States will wage an aggressive and sustained offensive campaign against global terrorism abroad. While much of this may take nonmilitary forms, several elements will require military—and specifically Army—forces. Raids of various types undoubtedly will be required to take down camps, seize or kill terrorist elements, neutralize dangerous facilities and weapons, and rescue kidnapped Americans. For many of these contingencies, Army Special Operations Forces (ARSOF) will be the instrument of choice. But as in Afghanistan, U.S. forces are likely to confront not only terrorist forces but also elements of the militaries of states that harbor them. The capabilities of the opposing forces and the scale and duration of the counterterrorism missions may mean that ARSOF will have to be supplemented by regular Army or other joint forces. Furthermore, given the global nature of the terrorist network and the likely prospect that U.S. military forces will be required to respond simultaneously to terrorist events abroad as well as at home, ARSOF assets could find themselves spread thin.

One obvious option is for the Army to expand its ARSOF capabilities. Given the specialization and training requirements of such forces, any significant expansion will take considerable time. In the interim, the Army may want to consider ways in which the institution can better support and perhaps supplement ARSOF by taking on certain missions. The transformation must certainly reexamine the entire relationship between ARSOF and regular Army forces and how these two elements can best complement each other in the future. The traditional separation of the two may have to change to account for the expanded counterterrorism dimension of Army operations and the need for much closer coordination of activities.

A more substantial shift would entail elements of the regular Army becoming more like Special Operations Forces in their ability to deploy rapidly and conduct complex counterterrorism operations. In the near term, the role of the IBCTs in this context might have to be reevaluated. What do they bring to this type of contingency? How might they best be configured for these types of operations, including the need for close cooperation with ARSOF and other (joint) special operations forces? Furthermore, the war on terrorism might further stress the deployability of the Army medium-weight force. While the IBCTs and the Objective Force are clearly designed with rapid deployability in mind, the constraints of deploying these forces exclusively by air have already been noted. So too have the clear advantages of moving the force by fast sealift, especially if one assumes that many operations will be conducted relatively close to the littoral. Yet the need to eliminate terrorist sanctuaries suggests that U.S. Army forces might have to be prepared to operate in more remote, austere, and landlocked areas falling outside of traditional U.S. national interests. These conditions would compound the challenges of both rapid deployment (which might require air) and sustainment. New types of units combining light- and medium-weight forces should be considered. A strike force hybrid that is considerably more lethal than light forces alone, but more rapidly deployable by air than the full IBCT, is one possibility.

The many surveillance and targeting technologies embedded in the IBCTs and anticipated for the Objective Force have applicability for the counterterrorism war, but they too are likely to require modifications. How, for example, might future unmanned aerial vehicles be better designed and employed to monitor, track, and rapidly attack a range of targets associated with terrorist training camps and facilities? What types of ground sensors hold promise for related missions? How might these capabilities best be integrated and tied to rapid strike assets, be they Army or joint? The most demanding technology issues are, however, still likely to rest on the Army's ability to deploy rapidly and to sustain and command the right types of forces in the area of operations.

The war on terrorism could easily come to challenge Army command and control. Ground operations could be relatively brief yet extremely complex and geographically dispersed. Such operations might have to be undertaken quickly to take advantage of fleeting targets or to minimize warning to sponsoring states. If the operations are of a scale and type beyond the capabilities of traditional Special Operations Forces, the Army must be prepared for rapid deployment of headquarters that can provide the necessary joint (and perhaps combined) command and control for such operations. The emphasis could well be on standing headquarters at lower echelons, particularly the brigade level. The alternative of drawing on division and corps headquarters assets would likely prove too cumbersome and time-consuming for such rapidly unfolding scenarios. The enhanced command and control embedded in the IBCTs is a step in the right direction.

The aftermath of September 11 added to the command burden of working operationally with allies and coalition partners. A sustained effort against global terrorist networks will increasingly require Army involvement with a wide range of partners, including some nontraditional ones. Transformation's counterterrorism component must allow for ease of operation with very disparate militaries, local police, and other security services.

While counterterrorism operations will generally involve lighter Army forces, President Bush has also made it clear that countries and regimes that harbor terrorists will be held accountable. This includes the possibility of occupying particular countries or otherwise bringing down their regimes by direct U.S. use of force. Even against lesser opponents, this would require a serious land combat capability. There is also the prospect that offensive counterproliferation aimed at nuclear, chemical, and biological threats will become a key element of the larger war on terrorism. This opens up a number of complex and demanding missions for the Army, whether countering state or subnational opponents. In assessing future requirements to fight the war on terrorism, the Army must also include the forces necessary to conduct these types of demanding operations.

The Army also will have additional responsibilities in homeland security, at least in the near term. Its traditional support functions to state and local authorities, primarily through National Guard units, are likely to be expanded to deal with terrorist threats to the homeland. The Army may have both growing near-term responsibilities (pending the buildup of civilian alternatives in particular areas) and additional longer term and enduring roles and missions for which the Army is best suited. These could include greater emphasis on consequence management, especially in terms of chemical, biological, radiological, nuclear, and high-explosive attacks and protection of key infrastructure, both military and civilian.

Most Army assets for homeland defense reside in the Army National Guard and Reserve units. The Nation must decide whether these components will require significant reorganization in light of the new mission. Arguably, for example, many homeland defense missions could be handled by civilians, as has been the case in federalizing airport security guards since September 11, 2001. Critical infrastructure security might be handled in substantial part by detection technology, minimizing personnel requirements of any kind. Army personnel, whether from the active or Reserve components, might still serve as early responders, surging to fill near-term needs. But civilians might fill in quickly thereafter in most cases.

To the extent that the Reserve components are asked to handle homeland defense, they will require modification in training and equipment.[38] But the effects on the total Army are likely to run well beyond the immediate need to train and equip specialized units for these tasks. Because so much of the total Army's combat support and service support capabilities lies in the Reserve components, Reserve soldiers and units have come to play a significant role in peacekeeping and stability operations, which call for these capabilities. In this capacity they also have helped reduce operational tempo problems in the active force associated with repetitive deployments to Bosnia and Kosovo. If substantial numbers of reservists are now pulled over to homeland defense, the active force may have to consider a new mix of skills as well as new policies to calm its tempo problems.

It is fitting to end a chapter on Army transformation with an assessment of the Nation's war on terrorism, since that war highlights the need for, but also the risks facing, the Army's transformation. What better way to highlight the expeditionary, unpredictable nature of the Nation's global military engagement, after all, than through military action in the rugged, landlocked terrain of distant Afghanistan? What better illustration of the potential of information technologies than the "air-land battle" fought by small special forces teams linked to high-flying bombers with their precision-guided munitions? And what better example of the phrase "full-spectrum" than a war that would seem to portend a little—perhaps a lot—of almost every mission, from combat raids to peacekeeping and humanitarian relief? Against the backdrop of a decade in which the Army engaged in heavy armored warfare on the Arabian Peninsula, a humanitarian relief mission in Somalia, the stabilization of politics in Haiti, and peace enforcement in Bosnia and Kosovo, the war on terrorism embodies the unpredictable missions and theaters for which the Army must now prepare. The contrast with the Cold War's predictable stability, its mature theaters, stable allies, and established enemies could not be sharper. Nor could the need for transformation be much clearer.

Yet the risks, too, are evident and lie well beyond the realm of pure technology. Post-Cold War missions have tested the Army's diversity. They have called for armor, but also for special forces; for infantry, but also for military police and civil affairs experts. They have called for large deployments with massive backup, but also for very small deployments that benefit from leaner logistics and support. The Army has met these challenges because, somewhere in its structure, it has these capabilities. In theory, it makes sense to "collapse the difference between heavy and light forces" to produce a coherent, generally uniform Army called the Objective Force. But it remains to be seen whether this can be done. The Army needs to move down this path carefully, testing at every step.

Above all, the Army needs to remain wary of the information revolution even as it exploits it aggressively. There is no more demanding environment for information technologies than that encountered on the ground in land warfare. Whether those technologies can operate at the exquisitely high performance levels that transformation seems to require, much less do so reliably, remains to be seen. Even if those performance requirements can be met, however, it should never be forgotten that potential enemies have choices in the years ahead as well. As the Army (like the other services) transforms, adversaries surely will adapt as well; only time will tell whether they can find weaknesses in the realm of information more easily than they could poke holes in or avoid the Army's traditional heavy formations.

The Army does not represent its transformation as a three-pronged undertaking without reason. Those prongs are, among other things, hedges against the risks that attend the effort. The Interim Force prong, with its IBCTs already being formed, allows for considerable experimentation and operational experience in advance of the more ambitious FCS project. And the Legacy prong provides the Army with armored backup until it is sure that the far more information-intensive Objective Force will work as intended. Future experience and experimentation will determine when and how those prongs come together.

## Notes

[1] Department of the Army, United States Army Field Manual (FM) 1, *The Army* (Washington, DC: Government Printing Office, June 14, 2001).

[2] Army Chief of Staff General Eric K. Shinseki, in testimony before the U.S. Senate, Subcommittee of the Committee on Appropriations, Department of Defense Appropriations for Fiscal 2001, April 25, 2000, 397; and Joint Statement before the House Armed Services Committee by the Honorable Thomas E. White, Secretary of the Army, and General Eric K. Shinseki, Chief of Staff, United States Army, On the Fiscal Year 2002 Army Budget Request, July 18, 2001 (hereafter Joint White/Shinseki Statement of July 18, 2001).

[3] See, for example, Douglas A. Macgregor, *Breaking the Phalanx: A New Design for Landpower in the 21st Century* (Westport, CT: Praeger Publishers, 1997).

[4] For background see Dennis Steele, "The Hooah Guide to Army Digitization," *Army Magazine*, September 2001, 19–40; and "Battlefield Digitization: A Special Report," *Army Magazine*, August 2000, 16–35.

[5] While smaller-scale contingencies represent one broad category of operations, in the case of ground operations, this category alone encompasses a great diversity of Army missions and activities.

[6] For an assessment of how even relatively small noncombat operations can have substantial impacts on Army forces well beyond the deploying units, see J. Michael Polich, Bruce R. Orvis, and Michael Hix, *Small Deployments, Big Problems*, Issue Paper IP–197 (Santa Monica, CA: RAND, 2000).

[7] For example, command and control problems arose in Somalia when the 10th Mountain Division, normally expected to cover a 30-kilometer front in wartime, had elements deployed out to over 100 kilometers. Line-of-sight FM communications well suited for traditional combat frontages proved inadequate over these much greater distances.

[8] An earlier Army effort to close the gap between deployment speed and combat capability was the High-Technology Light Division of the 1980s. For a description of its history and fate, see Richard J. Dunn III, "Transformation: Let's Get it Right this Time," *Parameters*, Spring 2001, 22–28. The 1990 Gulf experience highlighted the deficiency more dramatically and heightened the sense of urgency.

[9] Donald H. Rumsfeld, Secretary of Defense, *Guidance and Terms of Reference for the 2001 Quadrennial Defense Review*, June 22, 2001.

[10] Ibid.

[11] It can also reduce the quantities of forces required and their density. As Army FM 1 notes, "The common operational picture provided through integration of real-time intelligence and accurate targeting reduces the need to fill space with forces and direct fire weapons."

[12] Joint Statement before the Senate Armed Services Committee by the Honorable Thomas E. White, Secretary of the Army; and General Eric K. Shinseki, Chief of Staff, U.S. Army, On the Fiscal Year 2002 Defense Budget, Committee on Armed Services, U.S. Senate, July 10, 2001, 18 (hereafter Joint White/Shinseki Statement of July 10, 2001).

[13] In its June 2000 overall "Technology Assessment" of technologies required for the Army transformation, the Army Science Board concluded that autonomous robotics were unlikely to be available until after 2015.

[14] Indeed, much of that force is already programmed with the future C–17 purchases.

[15] The IBCTs can be moved within the theater quickly by C–130s to enhance flexibility and commanders' options for using the force. Still, a single 20-ton light armored vehicle would consume the entire lift capacity of a C–130.

[16] Reception, staging, onward movement, and integration (RSOI) is the last step of the strategic deployment process that reunites personnel and equipment in the theater as coherent units, moves the units to the operational area, and prepares them for employment. The Army's emphasis on strategic responsiveness, along with mounting concerns over enemy efforts to deny or disrupt deploying forces, places a premium of minimizing RSOI requirements and timelines.

[17] Steele, "The Hooah Guide to Army Transformation," 26.

[18] On July 12, 2001, the Army announced that the next four brigades to be transformed to IBCTs would be the 172[d] Infantry Brigade, Forts Richardson and Wainwright, Alaska; the 2[d] Armored Cavalry Regiment (Light), Fort Polk, Louisiana; the 2[d] Brigade, 25th Infantry Division (Light), Schofield Barracks, Hawaii; and the 56th Brigade of the 28th Infantry Division (Mechanized) of the Pennsylvania Army National Guard. See Joint White/Shinseki Statement of July 18, 2001.

[19] Frank Wolfe, "Shinseki: Earliest Full Fielding of First IBCT Projected In Spring 2003," *Defense Daily*, June 14, 20001, 9; and Joint White/Shinseki Statement of July 18, 2001.

[20] U.S. General Accounting Office, *Defense Acquisition: Army Transformation Faces Weapon Systems Challenges*, GAO–01–311, May 2001, 8.

[21] U.S. Army, "The Interim Brigade Combat Team, Organizational and Operational Concept," draft, June 30, 2000.

[22] Ibid.

[23] Prepared Statement of General Eric K. Shinseki, Department of Defense Appropriations for Fiscal Year 2001, Hearings before a Subcommittee of the Committee on Appropriations, U.S. Senate, April 25, 2000, 402.

[24] Joint White/Shinseki Statement of July 18, 2001.

[25] U.S. General Accounting Office, *Defense Acquisition: Army Transformation Faces Weapon Systems Challenges*, GAO–01–311, May 2001, 6. The U.S. Army and the Defense Advanced Research Projects Agency entered into a 6-year collaborative program to develop and demonstrate the Future Combat Systems concept.

[26] In terms of technical maturity, passive protection of lightweight ground vehicles with ceramic and composite-based lightweight armors capable of surviving a first-round hit from a medium-caliber weapon have been developed. Outstanding research issues in active protection systems and stealth technology indicate that these capabilities will not be available before the end of the decade.

[27] Glenn W. Goodman, Jr., "Futuristic Army Vision," *Armed Forces Journal International*, May 2001, 26–34.

[28] Army Transformation Briefings, Association of the U.S. Army (AUSA) Transformation Panel, Institute for Land Warfare, October 2000, accessed at <www.ausa.org>; and Glenn W. Goodman, Jr., "Futuristic Army Vision," *Armed Forces Journal International*, May 2001, 26–34.

[29] See Army Transformation Briefings. For details of the Army's science and technology strategy and key objectives in support of the transformation, see *2001 Army Science and Technology Master Plan,* U.S. Army, Office of the Deputy Assistant Secretary of Defense for Research and Technology.

[30] An adversary could, of course, prove wrong in believing it had found a chink in the Objective Force armor; when engaged by that force, it could instead suffer a devastating defeat. But even so, one would want to compel an adversary to confront the Legacy Force challenge as well. The more roadblocks there are to a perceived "win on the cheap," the stronger deterrence will be.

[31] These and other future options for U.S. Army light forces are covered in detail in John Matsumura, et al., *Lightning Over Water: Sharpening America's Light Forces for Rapid Reaction Missions,* MR–1196–A/OSD (Santa Monica, CA: RAND Arroyo Center/National Defense Research Institute, 2000).

[32] Joint White/Shinseki Statement of July 10, 2001.

[33] In 1995, the Army implemented a logistics Velocity Management initiative focused on improving the speed and accuracy of material and information flows from providers to users. Emphasis was on replacing the traditional reliance on mass with velocity. For a discussion of the initiative and its various elements, see John Dumond, et al., *Velocity Management, The Business Paradigm That Has Transformed U.S. Army Logistics,* MR–1108–A (Santa Monica, CA: RAND, 2001).

[34] U.S. General Accounting Office, *Defense Acquisition: Army Transformation Faces Weapon Systems Challenges,* GAO–01–311, May 2001, 1.

[35] In the fiscal year 2002 Army budget, for example, Secretary White testified that science and technology for the transformation was fully funded, but with a shortfall in the modernization and recapitalization of the Legacy Force. Testimony before the Senate Armed Services Committee, Hearing on Defense Authorization Request for FY 2002, July 10, 2001.

[36] An IBCT would weigh somewhere between 16,000 and 20,000 tons, depending upon the level of augmentation, while a "pure" IBCT would likely require more than 250,000 square feet of deck space.

[37] Positioning more Army assets forward, DOD recently decided to have an IBCT stationed in Europe by 2007 and directed that the Army explore additional options for enhancing ground capabilities in the Gulf region. See Department of Defense, Quadrennial Defense Review Report (Washington, DC: Department of Defense, September 30, 2001), 27.

[38] On suggested adjustments to the Army National Guard for homeland security see, for example, *Reserve Component Employment Study 2005* (Washington, DC: Department of Defense, June 1999).

# Chapter 5

# The Naval Services:
# Network-Centric Warfare

William D. O'Neil

T he U.S. Navy and Marine Corps are organizationally and legally distinct armed services under the Department of the Navy, a single military department of the Department of Defense (DOD). Often referred to as the naval services, the two have grown up and worked closely together over the entire history of the Republic. Any satisfactory account of transformation must consider both their separate identities and their interconnections.[1]

The U.S. Marine Corps (USMC) is a ground force structured to move ashore from the sea, against strong opposition if necessary. At sea, Marine strike fighter squadrons serve in aircraft carrier air wings. Marine air-ground task forces (MAGTFs) deploy aboard Navy amphibious ready groups. The two services work closely in getting Marine forces to the scene of entry and safely ashore, and the Navy provides a substantial portion of the heavy firepower to support marines operating ashore in the littorals, as well as certain support functions.

We begin with an overview of missions and some of the technology enablers that seem most applicable in the naval context. Next comes an outline of potential visions for naval forces transformation. The bulk of the chapter examines a variety of issues that are broadly relevant to transformation. In keeping with the theme of the present volume, technological issues receive emphasis. Finally, brief sections tie the arguments together and summarize.[2]

## Naval Missions

Over the past three millennia and more, navies arose out of the desire of nations to prosecute overseas expeditions and to prevent enemy raids on their own coasts. Gaining control of the sea—by defeating the enemy navy or by confining it to harbor out of fear of defeat—served for both protection and expedition. For states and circumstances that did not need or contemplate expeditions, sea control or denial became the preeminent naval mission, at least in principle. For the American naval services, however, sea control has never been a primary issue in practice, at least not since the War of 1812. Their original role was, instead, primarily the promotion and protection of overseas commerce and influence. In the 20th century, the U.S. rise to world power created demands for the naval services to facilitate major overseas expeditions and to conduct lesser ones on their own. In the 1950s, the Navy added a nuclear strategic strike mission and, in the 1980s, a significant conventional strategic strike mission.

Navy control of the seas is now all but unchallenged, as it has been except on local scales since 1945. The naval services maintain overseas presence in support of American interests more vigorously and visibly than ever. Both the Navy and Marines devote major efforts to assuring that their forces can "kick in the door" to insert U.S. power wherever it may be needed in littoral regions and that they can mount heavy conventional strikes. The Navy ballistic missile submarine force is a cornerstone of American strategic deterrence.

The end of the Cold War prompted a searching reassessment of mission needs by the naval services. The collapse of the bipolar superpower balance increased demands for overseas expeditions on a moderate scale and for lesser interventions to promote and protect commercial and political interests. This required capability for small expeditions, conventional strategic strikes, and visible presence. Although the importance of the strategic strike mission and the resources allocated to it were declining, changing technologies prompted increased attention to advances in this area. The 1990s brought further adjustments in detail. For example, the Navy has moved to position itself for the homeland defense mission, to improve protection of the U.S. metropolitan territory from threats of attack with weapons of mass destruction by rogue states or nonstate groups—a development in evidence even prior to the terrorist attacks of September 11, 2001. In general, however, there have been no major revisions of the vision of naval missions in recent years.

## Technology Enablers

The development of aircraft in the 20th century entirely transformed naval warfare; virtually every ship today serves to a significant extent as a platform for aircraft, manned or unmanned (including missiles), while Marine Corps doctrine completely integrates ground and air forces.

Technological progress in aviation was most rapid from about 1930 to 1960. Since then it has slowed noticeably, despite continued strong demand. The constraint has been, and continues to be, that the realization of ideas for technological advancement requires major investment, while promise of returns is often uncertain. Thus, advances will continue to be incremental. However, defense remains a large factor in the aviation market, and focused development investment by DOD might have a significant effect in particular areas, such as those discussed below.

Of no less importance, particularly at sea, has been the advent of electronic systems for sensing and communication. While the pace of information technology (IT) development has slackened due to economic factors, on the whole it appears that the economic and technological makings are in place for further substantial progress.

Although progress in aeronautical and electronic technologies continues to provide the principal potential technology enablers for the naval services, other prospects for transforming the U.S. naval services are also frequently mentioned, including biotechnology, nanotechnology, fuel cells, and artificial intelligence (AI). Biotechnology is widely expected to be the next major field of technological advance, notwithstanding the controversies and difficulties surrounding it. So far, however, it appears that the markets for biotechnology will principally be in nondefense areas. The basic technologies may eventually prove valuable to defense in ways difficult to foresee, but the specific commercial technologies for the most part will not be.

Nanotechnology involves making materials and devices whose structures are closely controlled at intermolecular scales, much smaller than those accessible to conventional manufacturing technologies. These are the scales at which many of nature's most important effects are obtained, and nanotechnology could well have many significant impacts. Current microelectronic fabrication techniques are an example, but their applicability is limited; self-organizing and self-assembling nanometer-scale systems seem to hold more promise. Present scientific knowledge does not yet appear adequate to support sustained commercial development.

The fuel cell has been heralded as the great power technology of the future ever since its invention in 1839. It picks apart the ionic and electronic flows in oxidation-reduction reactions and captures the electrons to do useful work on their way to completing the reaction. Much progress has been made, but major obstacles remain to doing this efficiently and reliably, especially the fuel cell's need for costly platinum catalysts and its needs for novel fuels. Nevertheless, fuel cells seem likely to find major military application as sources of portable power in cases where suitable fuels can be tolerated and reduced fuel consumption is worth a premium. They will be particularly attractive as substitutes for batteries in long-life applications.

Artificial intelligence must be included on the grounds of popular expectation, not demonstrated potential. Expectations of AI machines whose "intelligence" matches or exceeds that of humans have largely been formed by radically oversimplified models of human neurological functioning. Nevertheless, computerized systems will be capable of increasingly complex repertoires of programmed behaviors.

Aviation remains a particularly promising field for new dual-use technologies: those with military as well as civilian commercial applications. Historical dual-use examples include radial spark-ignition engines used in both military and commercial aircraft (1920s–1930s) and diesel engines for submarines and locomotives (1930s). Examples with potential for the future include advanced performance gas turbine cores, new structural materials and systems, and subsonic/transonic airflow control for improved ratios of lift to drag or controllability, all of which present significant but costly opportunities. The payoff for these would be in improved range-payload performance, which would benefit both long-range civil aircraft and long-range military attack and transport aircraft. More speculative is the possibility of hypersonic aircraft capable of hurtling halfway around the world in 4 or 5 hours; they might carry civil passengers, weapon loads, or military troops and cargo.

The civil economy will not lead in some transformational technologies. After all, nuclear weapons, radar, sonar, gas turbines, radar stealth, and missile guidance systems were all first developed by the military, and all have had significant transformational impacts. Security concerns tend to obscure the prospects for unique technologies of these sorts.

The Navy has sometimes had significant impact on U.S. manufacturing by working with contractors to innovate improvements in technology and modes of organization, as well as facilitating the acquisition of more and better capital equipment to improve productivity. In cases such as aircraft and electronics, progress requires joint efforts on the part of all or most of the four services, while in other areas, such as shipbuilding, the naval services have a natural lead. These efforts are a major focus for the naval systems commands. However, the close, hands-on relations with suppliers that most readily foster efforts to improve manufacturing are subject to economic and political demands for arms-length competition in defense procurement.

## Service Visions of Future Missions and Capabilities

The visions of the naval services of their missions and capabilities emphasize vigorous change and growth within a context of continuity. Following the major shift toward expeditionary roles early in the 1990s, missions came to be seen predominantly in evolutionary terms. As rapidly as economic and technological resources allow, both services are moving to improve and extend their capabilities for overseas expeditionary warfare in support of American policy and interests. The Navy also focuses on capabilities for strike warfare to the same ends. Both the Navy and Marines emphasize maintaining and exercising overseas presence as an instrument of American international influence and to facilitate rapid response to fast-developing crises. Efforts include:

- exploiting the inherent mission flexibility of aircraft carriers by equipping them with more advanced aircraft and weapons and improving training
- increasing the ability of marines to move rapidly and decisively to their objectives by introducing new troop aircraft and landing vehicles
- strengthening surface ship capabilities to deliver fire ashore, both for independent strike missions and to support ground forces, by providing more and more diverse fire systems
- replacing Marine Corps AV–8 Harrier light attack aircraft with modern, multimission short takeoff/vertical landing (STOVL) fighter-attack aircraft to provide expanded capabilities for air-to-air combat as well as ground attack
- supplementing and partly replacing slow-responding dedicated mine-countermeasure assets with organic capabilities that travel with and are integrated into rotationally deploying naval strike/amphibious forces
- freeing USMC ground forces from cumbersome and vulnerable logistics "tail" to permit more rapid and effective maneuver, by emphasizing precision over mass and improving logistics and transport technologies
- deploying advanced antimissile systems aboard surface ships to protect both the fleet and expeditionary units and the theater assets necessary for force insertion
- developing defensive technologies against future missile and undersea threats

■ equipping and training Marine forces to serve a variety of short-of-war needs, such as protection and evacuation of American personnel threatened by foreign unrest or terrorism—especially in techniques and with systems that can reduce the likelihood of casualties among civilians.

## Transforming Assets, Structures, and Operations

The most central strategic factor in U.S. defense for the naval services is that the potential theaters for military action all lie overseas. Since ships remain the only practical means of transporting heavy military equipment and supplies to these places, the naval services have a special responsibility not only for transport but also for assuring that forces can be put into action from the sea. The rest of this section therefore examines potential transformation of naval assets, followed by shorter discussions of transformation of structures and operations.

### Transforming Assets

Navies are particularly dependent on capital equipment: ships, weapons, aircraft, and the shore infrastructure to support them. Viewed strictly as a ground force, the Marine Corps is relatively "light" and correspondingly less rich in ground-combat capital equipment. But getting marines to the scenes of amphibious or expeditionary operations and into the fight involves a great deal of specialized equipment. Moreover, the Corps has its own integral specialized air and logistics components. All USMC aircraft and most of the systems for landing are on Navy books and accommodated aboard Navy shipping. Thus, from an investment standpoint, the naval services are generally best viewed as a single entity, sharing use of a great pool of common capital.

Under current policies and budget realities, the capital turnover or replenishment cycle is a matter of several decades. Because the naval services, like other services, need to turn over some investments much more rapidly—for instance, their IT equipment—other matériel must last longer than the nominal average lifetime (say 35 years for the sake of argument, although in reality it might be somewhat less or more). From a top-level management perspective, there are two major challenges: long life and slow change. The Department of the Navy knows how to make its critical equipment last a long time, but it is difficult to be sure how to make it productive and effective for 35 years and more. This is especially true because major commitments often must be made 10 to 15 years or so before new equipment enters the force in large quantity, sometimes stretching the need for foresight out to half a century or more. Moreover, with less than 3 percent of the naval service capital turning over each year, it takes a long time to make a major change in the service capital structure. Thus, the naval services need to exercise a lot of foresight in deciding on the right thing to buy and to prepare to buy, in this year and this Program Objective Memorandum (POM) cycle. Put another way, in deciding what to buy now, Navy leaders need to look far beyond the POM period. If they buy a lot of equipment that will not still be productive in 35 years, they could leave future leaders with a force that has serious deficiencies. However, a few missteps will not be fatal because things change slowly.

Several categories of missions and associated assets are of particular importance to naval transformation: access denial; information technology; unmanned vehicles; standoff; short takeoff and landing and vertical takeoff and landing aircraft; proposals for so-called super-platforms; and stealth.

### Littoral Warfare and Denial of Access

Naval forces have been intervening in land wars time out of mind. By the 17th century, nations had begun to invest heavily in coastal defenses to prevent this. Fortifications, seacoast artillery, and physical barriers were built. Ever since then, the impossibility of breaching seacoast defenses has repeatedly been asserted and repeatedly been proven wrong. Defenses certainly have posed dangers to seaborne forces and compelled them to modify their technology and operations but have not made it impossible to attack from the sea.

With the United States in possession of overwhelming seaborne power, those disposed to hostility and intending mischief naturally have a keen interest in potential means to deflect it. The term often used for this is *antiaccess* because naval officers (among others) often talk about their forces as providing access to littoral regions.

The anti-ship antiaccess threats that currently receive the most attention are long-range missiles, mines, submarines, and aircraft armed with standoff weapons. Small craft and physical obstacles also need to be considered. None of these are new threats: long-range missiles have been around for more than half a century, anti-ship aircraft for eight decades, the others for a century or more. But new technologies breathe new life into them, even as they strengthen "access" forces.

In objective terms, it is by no means clear that antiaccess is gaining on access; indeed, it is not even clear that it is a serious race. Despite the arguments of those who would have the United States "transform" itself out of even seeking to use its naval power to permit access to overseas theaters, this is not the intention of the naval services.

Three points form the basis of most ideas of antiaccess: finding ships, hitting and killing ships, and anti-ship weapons such as mines and submarines.

- *Finding ships.* It is argued that modern technology makes it easy to see ships wherever they may be; soon this will be possible with commercial space sensors.
- *Hitting and killing ships.* It is argued that modern technology makes it possible, once ships are found, to hit them swiftly and surely with long-range ballistic or cruise missiles.
- *Modern anti-ship weapons.* It is argued that ships are highly vulnerable to modern weapon warheads.

Apart from references to specific systems, such as space sensors and missiles, all of these things have been said in essentially the same terms since the 1920s. They are truer now than they were then, but not by much. The technological advances that enable antiaccess capabilities also help naval forces to counter them. In addition, the United States devotes much greater resources to naval forces than any of our adversaries have available to mount antiaccess threats.

First, consider the issue of finding ships. Most people recognize that submarines are difficult to detect and are likely to remain so. Aircraft carriers seem to lie at the opposite extreme: huge and exposed. Serious engineering studies have explored concepts for "stealthy" carriers, but close analysis has made such measures seem neither necessary nor fruitful. It is difficult to hide an airbase altogether, even a mobile floating one. However, carriers gain quite a bit of invisibility from the immensity of the sea and clutter of other things on its surface. The Persian Gulf, for example, is the smallest body of water in which major surface naval forces operate. Yet a computerized picture of its surface, at a scale just sufficient to allow someone peering closely to distinguish a carrier reasonably well from the thousands of other large objects on the surface, would take about 3,000 large 19-inch computer monitor screens. If smaller ships are to be distinguished, the number must go up further. Moreover, the sensor systems to generate this picture quickly and to refresh it frequently are not available. It would cost immense amounts to build them, and they would be vulnerable to a variety of countermeasures that obscure real ships and generate false targets.

Second, consider the issue of hitting and killing ships. Despite the difficulties, ships will sometimes be found. But any attack on ships over long distances, even by fast weapons such as ballistic missiles, is complicated a great deal by mobility. At a modest distance of 500 kilometers (270 nautical miles) from the weapon launch site, a naval force may move more than 5 kilometers in the interval between ballistic missile launch and reentry. Any non-nuclear missile attacking a ship must have an elaborate system to find the ship and home in on it. This increases the complexity and cost of anti-ship missiles a great deal and exposes them to countermeasures that confuse their elaborate guidance systems.

Moreover, the attacking missiles must get through the fleet's own missile shield, consisting of two or more layers of sophisticated and effective anti-missile systems. The Aegis missile system is able to attack incoming missiles at long ranges and is being upgraded to deal with both endoatmospheric and exoatmospheric ballistic threats. Various versions of the Sea Sparrow missile system offer effective defense at intermediate ranges, and the Rolling Airframe Missile is highly effective at short ranges. Missiles are complemented by an array of countermeasures designed to reduce the probability that an attacking missile's guidance will work properly.

Finally, warships are designed to withstand hits. Today's aircraft carriers are probably the most damage-resistant ships overall that have ever sailed. It is reasonable to liken them to hardened aircraft shelters ashore. They are not proof against all attacks, but it would take an accurate hit by an especially powerful and specialized weapon to have a good chance of putting a carrier out of action. Smaller ships cannot be made as resistant but are nonetheless remarkably tough.

While submarines have received less attention recently, historically they have posed threats to heavy ships just as serious as those posed by aircraft and missiles. Apart from Britain and France, only Russia and China operate nuclear submarines. The nuclear submarine force of the former Soviet Union was recognized as a serious threat to American carriers approaching Soviet maritime frontiers and to a lesser extent in places where the Soviets maintained forward patrols. The threat that they posed was exacerbated by their weapons: 65-centimeter (25.6 inch) torpedoes and large anti-ship missiles, many with nuclear warheads. Today, the two dozen nuclear anti-ship submarines remaining from this fleet are operated by the Russian Federation Navy and seem unlikely to come into play against the U.S. Navy. Meanwhile, Russia's economic and political troubles have adversely affected fleet readiness.

China's naval forces have a handful of nuclear subs of rather dated design, lacking weapons that pose special threats to carriers. China and other states might build newer and more advanced nuclear submarines, but it is doubtful that any of these nations would be better able to bear the economic burdens of such costly armaments than the Soviet Union proved to be.

Only the quietest of submarines can escape being hunted down quickly by forces guided by modern U.S. detection systems. Not only must the submarine be designed and constructed to exacting standards, but it also must frequently be checked by sensitive equipment and adjusted to eliminate emerging noise sources as they develop.

Assuming that our naval forces are pitted against a first-rate modern non-nuclear submarine with a competent crew, the first defense is still the

## DD(X) Update

On April 29, 2002, the U.S. Navy awarded the design contract for a new family of ships, the DD(X) destroyer, to a team headed by Northrop Grumman Corporation and the Raytheon Corporation. This family of ships is designed to incorporate the most advanced information technologies and fire control systems so that it can network with other combat systems and with surveillance and reconnaissance systems. Moreover, the Navy plan represents as much a transformation in acquisition strategy as it does in advanced ship technology. Based upon the same Operational Requirements Document as the cancelled DD 21 solicitation, the DD(X) introduces a spiral development for this family of ships based on a common hull design with new technology introduced over time instead of as a single step procurement. In this fashion, the next-generation cruiser, the CG(X), will be scalable from a common hull and propulsion plant architecture. In addition, the DD(X) will incorporate more land-based and at-sea testing than was planned for the DD 21. Also, the procurement award down-selects only to the design agent with procurement to be recompeted in fiscal year 2005. This contrasts with the DD 21 procurement strategy of initial selection of a full-service contractor.

The DD 21 program had already introduced significant change to the Navy acquisition process. In the past, the Navy specified the hull, mechanical, and electrical systems of a ship and then contracted out the engineering design. For the DD 21 and the DD(X), the Navy specified the operational requirements and the cost and manning goals. The preliminary design of the ship and the technologies to meet these operational requirements were left to two competing industrial teams, both of which developed unique innovative designs. This resulted in a very close competition.

The primary missions of the DD(X), precision strike and volume fires for assured access and support of the Marine Corps forces ashore, require survivability in the littorals. The topside of the vastness of the sea. Modern surface warships, while not as quiet as submarines, have been quieted to an extent that limits the range at which submarines can detect them. Moreover, because the non-nuclear submarine has limited underwater speed and endurance, it may be unable to reach a fast-moving warship even though it does detect it.

Present-day non-nuclear submarines rely on diesel engines for surface and snorkel operation and on lead-acid storage batteries while submerged. There is much interest in what are termed air-independent propulsion (AIP) systems, which are alternative ways to power the submarine while submerged. But AIP schemes now in prospect would all be low-speed systems, good for long submerged patrol but giving little advantage in attacks on warships.

DD(X) will look very different from the current generation of destroyers because of the significant signature reduction built into the design. In addition to the strike and naval ship fire support, the DD(X) will have advanced air and missile defense capability, giving it a multimission capability. The Northrop design, with two helicopter pads and a ramp to launch 30-foot boats, can also support special operations missions.

Significant new technologies as well as physical changes are incorporated into the DD(X). Most prominent is an integrated power system with electric drive propulsion. This will allow the rerouting of power in the event of damage and thereby will remove the single-point vulnerability of critical ship systems. In addition, much of the damage control network will be automated, leading to enhanced survivability and reduced crew size.

The ship will incorporate an advanced gun system for surface fires with a goal of firing guided 155-millimeter rounds 60 to 100 miles. The air defense system will be built around a multifunction radar and a volume search radar for detection and fire control against stealthy targets imbedded in background clutter from either the sea or land. An advanced vertical launch system will support the next generation of missiles.

Reduced crew size is a key feature of the DD(X) design. This element represents a deliberate effort by the Navy to include the cost of the personnel who will operate the ship explicitly in the design selection. Both designs reduce the crew size to one-third that of the current destroyer. This feature, coupled with the utilization of a common hull form for a family of its next generation of surface combatants, is part of the Navy strategy to ensure that it can afford a shipbuilding and operations program to maintain adequate fleet strength into the future.

—Elihu Zimet

Should a submarine succeed in finding a surface naval force and closing to engage, it must reckon with the anti-submarine warfare (ASW) forces. Recognizing that some submarines will be undetectable by passive listening, the Navy has developed a variety of systems that employ advanced technology to detect and locate submarines without depending on their noise. Generally, the actions that submarines must take to attack surface ships will tend to expose them more to detection.

Except for Russia, no submarine force today has weapons that would be particularly effective at attacking large, survivable ships like aircraft carriers. Even if a submarine overcomes all the odds against it to reach a firing position against a carrier, there is a substantial chance that the carrier will suffer only limited damage because of the limits of the submarine's weapons. Other ships are generally more vulnerable.

Mines deserve particular discussion. No innovation has had a more dramatic impact on naval "access" concepts than mines. By far the greatest users of mines have been Britain and the United States, whose mining campaigns in the two world wars accounted for thousands of enemy ships. These two great sea powers (and air powers) had the means to deliver mines in massive numbers—about half a million of them in the two conflicts. It was offensive mining (that is, planting mines in enemy waters) that did most of the execution.

This illustrates the trouble with using mines as antiaccess weapons; in most cases, those who seek to deny access do not have the means to lay enough mines to make a major difference. This is not to say that our naval forces would not find mines difficult to deal with, but it is a difficulty fundamentally different from the one the United States inflicted on the Japanese late in World War II.

It is possible, of course, to get more effect from small numbers by using more sophisticated mines that can go after their targets instead of merely waiting for them. But these are more costly, more vulnerable to countermeasures, and more difficult to employ effectively.

In addition, mine countermeasures (MCM) is an area in which the Navy has been most inventive and vigorous in transformation. It has sought an "organic" MCM capability to deploy as part of its battlegroups rather than solely as a separate auxiliary service. Major efforts include unmanned semisubmerged MCM vehicles that can be deployed aboard surface combatant ships, including destroyers and smaller warships, and compact airborne systems that can be deployed with normal shipboard helicopters. These will not be sufficient to substitute entirely for dedicated separate mine countermeasures forces but should improve the fleet's ability to operate with acceptable risk in the face of mine threats. Naturally, the success of these efforts will depend not only on the degree of technical success in equipment development but also on the development of effective doctrine for employment and on training fleet forces.

In sum, then, although many nations may have adopted antiaccess strategies, having the means to put such a strategy into effective operation is another matter. Notwithstanding advances in technology and commercial space capabilities, naval forces at sea will remain invisible most of the time, particularly when they are most concerned to stay undetected and employ detection countermeasures. Without the ability to keep continuous track of our naval forces, those who would deny access will find their options severely limited. They will have to shoot as the opportunity presents itself, rather than waiting to mass their forces in favorable circumstances, and their weapons are unlikely to be numerous enough or good enough to overwhelm strong naval defenses. By the time our forces are close enough to permit more frequent detection, those who would deny access will find themselves under heavy attack. American surface naval forces are by no means invulnerable, but the odds favor them quite strongly.

This is not to say that all is well. Unless they are well hardened, fixed facilities needed as part of U.S. access to a theater, such as ports and airfields, could be at risk from much simpler and cheaper missiles than those needed to hit moving ships. Ships lying at anchor or constrained to move slowly for long periods could find themselves in similar straits. Amphibious forces assaulting defended beaches could be exposed to a wide variety of particularly difficult threats. All of this makes it more difficult to be sure of moving from the sea to the land—the final key step.

It is for reasons such as these that the naval services have been moving to free themselves from dependence on ports for offloading and on airfields for air power and to introduce sea-based capabilities for area and even theater-wide defense against tactical ballistic and cruise missiles.

If antiaccess forces had economic and technical resources on the scale of those that the United States devotes to naval forces, access could be seriously at risk. In the days when the Soviet Union was spending itself into insolvency to keep up with the United States, the ability of our naval services to conduct offensive surface operations in Soviet waters was open to grave doubt. But our capabilities have advanced greatly since then, and none of our potential adversaries of today even approach the Soviets in technical or economic resources for antiaccess. To a large extent, those who worry greatly today about naval force vulnerability are falling into the trap of Cold War thinking.

### Information Technology and Naval Transformation

Information has always been a dominant factor in naval warfare because finding the enemy has always been the first problem of action at sea. New technologies for communications, sensing, and information processing have always been taken up eagerly by naval forces, and they have always been especially interested in technologies to deny information to enemies. It is surprisingly difficult to point to a truly fundamental advance in physics or technical principles that has affected IT over the past several decades; instead, IT seems to have had most of its effect in doing better and faster what has long been done. Nevertheless, recent rapid increases in microelectronics densities have spurred the search for truly new and revolutionary uses. In the Navy, this has been summed up in the phrase *network-centric warfare* (or *operations*). This term implies a geographic and organizational decentralization and dispersion of functions and the use of communications and sensor systems to achieve distant action with minimal need to mass physical forces. While the Marine Corps is less prone to employ the network-centric label, it too is vigorously exploring concepts of this sort.

How much the two naval services actually spend on things that might be classed as IT is unclear in their accounting systems, but the amount undoubtedly is substantial. There seems reason to believe that, much like U.S. industry, the services have realized gains in productivity as a result. In specific instances, they can point to quite striking improvements, but few would claim that they have experienced broad transformational changes as yet.

Predictions of omnipotence for naval information technology rest principally on expectations that better, more timely information about both enemy and friendly forces will enable far more rapid, decisive action. However, the gains may be less dramatic than sometimes portrayed and may depend on investments in other areas beside information technology.

Major advantages in information are not new to war. In World War II, for instance, allied superiority in signals intelligence frequently provided allied forces with dazzling information advantages over German and Japanese opponents. The communications technology and other aspects of IT that American forces used to coordinate activities were crude and slow by today's standards, but they were generally faster and better than those of enemies. Close examination of the history, however, shows clearly that this superiority in information rarely was decisive in itself. Superiority also required forces of decisive mass that could be moved swiftly in response to the information and that could exert dominating combat power at the point of contact. For another example, the Royal Air Force (RAF) successfully defended England against attack by Hitler's Luftwaffe in 1940, after France had fallen to the Nazi blitzkrieg. It was the first operational use of radar, and the RAF probably could not have prevailed without it. Even with radar accurately reporting virtually every German raid, however, the RAF would have been helpless if it had not already invested in a fighter force commensurate with what the Luftwaffe threw against it.

### Warring Automatons

The IT revolution brought about unmanned and smart automatic weapons and systems. As with IT, this trend can seem more recent and dramatic than in fact it is. Sophisticated, entirely autonomous weapons have been widely used in naval warfare for more than half a century, and autonomous systems for reconnaissance and information collection at sea have almost as long a history. Security restrictions associated with their advanced technologies have often tended to keep these systems out of the public eye.

Rapid progress in many fields of electronic technology has allowed autonomous systems to carry far more sophisticated computers as well as much better sensors and communications links. But the gap between computer and human capabilities remains so immense that no one has offered any scientifically defensible idea of how, when, or even whether it may eventually be bridged. There are scientific reasons for caution about prospects for replacing fighter pilots or riflemen with machines. Advantages from "dis-manning" platforms might outweigh many drawbacks, but it is tricky to draw valid generalizations.

Human capabilities probably will be easiest to replace in areas that do not depend greatly on visual perception or visual reasoning, hence the caution concerning replacement of humans in matters such as close-in air-to-air and infantry combat. Prospects for automation are brighter in many warfare tasks at sea for which visual faculties are of limited importance. It is no accident that highly automated weapons and systems first appeared and came to be significant in sea operations, starting with mines and torpedoes in the 19th century and going on to homing weapons and unmanned underwater vehicles (UUVs) in the 20th century.

Many warfare automata have been undone through failures of systems that have little to do, at first sight, with the "human-like" functions of the system.[3] Much of this is the result of poorly conceived engineering economies, resulting in employment of low-reliability systems for critical functions such as propulsion or control. Also, with no humans aboard, engineers must foresee and prepare for all possible situations with a thoroughness that is not essential when there is a crew to take up the slack. The relatively low cost of unmanned systems has to be balanced against the costs of frequent replacement of crashed or lost systems. Moreover, the need to do so much from the base has often meant that small, light unmanned aerial vehicles (UAVs) have trailed massive logistic and support systems. Such problems may yield to better engineering, but thoroughly engineering such systems will be quite expensive.

Progress is being made in the technical and economic problems of unmanned systems, if not so rapidly as often imagined or claimed. The incentives to do so are greatest in applications for which conventional manned systems are least satisfactory. Principal potential advantages include:

- freedom from risk of loss or capture of pilots or crewmembers
- endurance that is not limited by human capacities
- lack of human life-support demands, especially important for operations in harsh environments
- minimum size not constrained by human dimensions and mass.

Sensor carrying is a major function for unmanned vehicles and can be especially well served by these attributes. For the most part, this has so far largely involved adaptation of existing classes of sensors for UUVs, UAVs, and other unmanned systems. In principle, however, unmanned vehicles could lend themselves to novel strategies of sensor design. This may offer avenues for significant extensions in surveillance and reconnaissance capabilities if the sensor system and vehicles can be designed into an integrated total system architecture.

Almost unnoticed in the debate about unmanned systems has been the progressive decrease in the "manning" requirements of many kinds of naval systems. The number of crewmembers required to fly and fight one aircraft, for example, has generally shrunk to one, or sometimes two where circumstances demand redundancy; other crew members are carried strictly to operate special mission systems. The proposed new DD(X) class of land-attack destroyers is planned for a crew of only 95 on a ship whose size and functions are comparable to a World War II cruiser with a crew of 900 and whose effectiveness is vastly greater.

## Strike Systems and Platforms

Closely related, both technically and conceptually, to war by automata is war by strike (that is, destroying or neutralizing some particular set of things). Modern concepts of strike warfare trace their origins to the 1890s and the beginnings of powered flight. The United States was a latecomer to the notion, taking it up only in the 1920s, but it has since become distinctively American.

Roughly speaking, there are two great branches of strike-war thought, which are often represented (somewhat misleadingly) by the shorthand terms *strategic strike* (or *pure strike*) and *tactical strike*. The theory of strategic strike is that war can be altogether reduced to actions of strike and that scarcely any other kinds of military operations are necessary or desirable. In tactical strike, the theory is that war can be made more effective and less costly by combining strike and other operations.

Outside of the nuclear arena, naval thought has always tended to be skeptical of pure strategic strike theories, but the Navy has nevertheless built a considerable array of strike capabilities that can to some extent serve strategic as well as tactical aims. Fires from naval guns represented an early form of strike that, much modified and extended, still persists. The introduction of aircraft into the fleet brought a major change in naval strike capabilities, and carrier-based aircraft continue to provide the bulk of multipurpose naval strike capability.

The past 15 years have seen the introduction of ship-launched non-nuclear strike missiles, notably the Tomahawk cruise missile. The Tomahawk has transformed strike capabilities in ways that policymakers have frequently found attractive. Its ability to hit chosen geographic coordinate points up to 1,000 nautical miles inland with good accuracy and high reliability and assurance—and no exposure of crews to death or capture—has brought widespread use despite a cost-per-delivered-warhead that is usually higher than for comparable air-delivered precision weapons. This has led to interest in ways to mass larger numbers of Tomahawks (and possible follow-on missiles) in the theater. One proposal called for an arsenal ship, which is essentially a cargo vessel equipped not only to carry missiles to the scene but also to "offload" them by firing them. However, eschewing the combination of highly concentrated military value and high vulnerability, the Navy elected instead to combine expanded strike missile capacities with warship survivability and a broader range of mission capabilities in its new DD(X) class destroyers. These are designed to provide what amounts to heavy artillery support for Marine Corps and Army troops ashore, up to scores of miles inland. Consideration is being given to supplementing Tomahawk cruise missiles with ship-launched precision short-range ballistic missiles for hitting time-sensitive tactical targets.

The Tomahawk is also carried by submarines, and its ability to reach firing points undetected has proven attractive in some circumstances. This has led to interest in submarines with much larger strike-missile capacities, generally referred to as nuclear-powered cruise missile attack submarines (SSGNs). Present plans are to convert four of the existing Trident ballistic missile submarines (SSBNs) to SSGNs. For a given number of missiles, it will be somewhat more expensive to carry them in submarines than in surface warships, but SSGNs offer very valuable advantages of stealth and surprise.

Carrier-based aircraft remain at the core of naval strike capabilities, in terms of the volume and diversity of the ordnance that they can deliver economically. New generations of aerial strike weapons are for the most part being built to common DOD-wide specifications that will permit their use by naval aircraft. Also, the naval services are procuring at least small quantities of most new weapons, as well as the on-board systems necessary to target and deliver them. Navy strike fighter squadrons are now being equipped with the F/A–18E/F Super Hornet, which offers some significantly improved strike capabilities over its predecessors. The naval services also participate in and support the Joint Strike Fighter (JSF) program. Even though threats to manned strike aircraft generally are relatively manageable today and for the foreseeable future, the additional increment of stealth offered by the JSF will be welcomed for the added flexibility it brings, and it will substantially improve the flexibility of Marine air capabilities.

### *Aircraft and Smaller Carriers*

A mile or more of runway is needed for conventional landing and takeoff—a nuisance ashore and a virtual impossibility at sea. With a few specialized exceptions, the Navy gave up on seaplanes and amphibious aircraft in the 1960s and has since met its air needs through two expedients: launching and recovering more or less conventional aircraft using specialized catapulting and arresting equipment aboard aircraft carriers, and employing special kinds of aircraft with vertical flight capabilities so that they can land and take off in restricted spaces. These latter are termed *VSTOL* (vertical and short takeoff and landing) or *STOVL* (short takeoff and vertical landing) aircraft. From the 1940s to the 1960s, helicopters were the only vertical-landing aircraft to see practical success, but they have since been joined by AV–8 Harrier jet-lift light attack aircraft. The tilt-rotor

MV–22 Osprey is nearing readiness for full production, and the JSF is about to begin development.

The Marines Corps is particularly committed to STOVL aircraft. It is the only U.S. user of the Harrier, the only U.S. service that has definitely committed to the STOVL JSF, and the principal prospective user of the Osprey. While awaiting the Osprey, it operates a large fleet of helicopters. The Harriers and most of its helicopters are quite old, contributing to Marine Corps impatience to see their successors into service. More significantly, both new aircraft are substantially more capable than those they are slated to supplant. The Osprey will materially improve the distance over which Marine ground units can be lifted and the speed with which they get there. Analysis suggests that this will allow Marine forces to engage and defeat opponents in a broader range of circumstances than heretofore possible, at lower cost in casualties. Naturally, it is difficult to be precise about how often these circumstances will arise, and the Osprey probably will not usually make a large difference in how strong an enemy force the Marine units can defeat, but Corps commanders eagerly look forward to gaining the greater flexibility and assurance that it will bring.

The JSF offers an even more striking improvement over Marine AV–8s (Harriers). It will be the first STOVL aircraft with a serious air-to-air combat capability, and it will be able to deliver a much wider and heavier range of precision weapons than the Harrier. Some Marine squadrons today operate F/A–18C/D Hornet strike fighters that offer a measure of these capabilities, but the Hornets are conventional carrier-based aircraft that are less flexible in shore basing and cannot operate from the amphibious ships that carry Marine units.

Both the Osprey and JSF programs have been proposed as possible candidates for a generation of new systems to be "skipped."[4] The consequences for Marine Corps capabilities would depend on what might be acquired in their places. It is difficult to see how either the existing helicopter fleet or the Harriers could be kept in service long enough to meet an entirely new generation of systems that would be unavailable for, perhaps, another two decades. If the existing helicopter fleet were replaced with more modern helicopters, there would be losses in force capabilities and flexibility, as indicated above, at perhaps some marginal savings in procurement costs. In the absence of the JSF, it would seem that Harriers could only be replaced with F/A–18s, again with a significant decline in flexibility. Any other course would involve substantial change in Marine concepts and doctrine and would seem inevitably to involve serious sacrifice in capabilities.

At present, an aircraft carrier must employ both catapults to accelerate aircraft to flying speed and arresting gear to bring landing aircraft to a safe stop on limited deck spaces. In the earliest days of carrier aviation, by contrast, such expedients were unnecessary. Just as at an airfield, the slower, smaller aircraft of the day could launch and recover on a carrier's deck, aided only by the wind of its passage. It has always been clear that a return to this situation would bring some benefits, and the Navy has accordingly been a strong and consistent supporter of research into STOVL technology.

The STOVL issue should not be conflated with that of smaller carriers. It is possible to build carriers that are less than half the displacement (mass) of present models without sacrificing the capability to launch and recover conventional aircraft, essentially by putting a smaller hull under a deck that is nearly as large. The problem with doing so is that a small carrier carries fewer aircraft and less fuel, ordnance, and parts to support them. Indeed, such capacities shrink somewhat faster than overall size, while costs diminish much less rapidly.[5] Analyses of operational experience indicate that smaller air wings would be unable to meet many needs. For the most part, the advances offered by aircraft and weapons technologies pay off in greater capability for the air wing, not in reductions in the numbers of aircraft needed to fulfill its functions.

If the number of aircraft in the air wing is held fixed and if STOVL aircraft are the same size as conventional carrier aircraft of similar capabilities, then an all-STOVL carrier might be modestly smaller and cheaper because catapults and arresting gear would not be needed. The savings would be at most a few percent. Some operational advantages might be significant and might permit some small reduction in air wing size without sacrificing capability. But this would depend on the actual characteristics of the STOVL aircraft. Studies indicate that it would probably be possible to build a quite attractive STOVL aircraft for strike fighter functions by retaining catapult launch capabilities, but the other missions for carrier-based aircraft—especially those relating to surveillance—do not lend themselves so well to STOVL with current or immediately foreseeable technology. Of course, there could well be advantages to operating STOVL aircraft from carriers that were equipped also for catapult launch and arrested recovery of other types of aircraft.

### A Navy without a Top

For 60 years, aircraft carriers and their air wings have been the Navy's dominant force component and greatest expense, making them a natural focus of attention in any debate about transformation. Aircraft carriers and carrier-based aircraft have often been pronounced "obsolete" since the first carriers went to sea just after World War I. It is an issue that must continually be reassessed.

Many of the concerns about carriers do not bear much scrutiny. The ships are not notably vulnerable to either current or reasonably projected weapons. The Navy does not buy other major forces primarily to "protect" carriers; rather, naval forces inherently operate as a combined, integrated whole, and carriers both protect and are protected by the other forces they operate with. The argument has been made for more than 80 years that developments in long-range land-based aircraft make carrier basing an expensive anachronism. However, there remain many important situations in which other forms of air power cannot effectively substitute for carriers. It is notable that rushing carriers to the scene continues to be a chief response of American Presidents to crises.

Nonetheless, it is possible that a decision will be taken to abandon aircraft carrier forces. The consequences of such a decision depend on the details of how the phaseout occurs and what is done to strengthen forces in other respects. It will matter most in situations where only a floating airbase can provide a platform for U.S. tactical air power. How important this may be depends in part on one's perspective on American strategic needs. If U.S. intervention overseas is seen as occurring solely in the context of coalition or alliance efforts to help friendly and cooperative nations defend against external aggression, then it is reasonable to insist that those to whose aid we rush will provide basing for our forces, as well as protection for the bases. In these circumstances, carriers are supplementary rather than primary, and the need for them might logically diminish. On the other hand, we could envision a United States that wished to be able to pursue its own national and alliance interests freely in regions where local support was constrained by political and cultural factors. In this way, basing might be limited or unavailable. One region that has fit this description at least at some times in the recent past is the Persian Gulf, source of nearly 30 percent of world oil production and seat of more than 40 percent of world oil reserves. Another example is afforded by the operations against Afghanistan following the September 11 terrorist attacks, in which carrier decks were initially the only available bases and continued to provide a major asset even once bases in the region had been secured.

In such circumstances, carriers must provide most of the tactical air power for defensive counter air, offensive counter air, suppression of enemy air defenses, and close air support. Additionally, they will normally provide a substantial fraction of strike capability, even with full commitment of long-range land-based air forces and sea-launched missiles. In particular, they will provide a major part of the capacity for rapid and repeated strikes against time-sensitive targets to meet tactical needs. In places such as the Persian Gulf, carrier aircraft remain the most economical means to meet these needs if local land bases are unavailable or restricted. Thus, the absence of carrier forces would leave a hole that could not be filled on an equal-cost basis by other means. Without defensive counter air, committing any other forces except highly survivable long-range strike assets normally would be too risky. Unless the latter can be expected to accomplish all major U.S. objectives, lack of carriers could force the United States to forego military options in theaters where it lacks secure tactical basing.

As a logical principle, other forces whose utility would be sharply curtailed by lack of carrier aviation should be put on the chopping block before or along with carriers. As this includes much of the Nation's surface and amphibious naval forces, it explains Navy insistence that carrier forces are essential.

### Littoral combatants

The Navy faces a serious dilemma in designing small warships: nature favors big ones. An aircraft carrier ten times the displacement of a destroyer needs only about three times the power for equal speed, carries more than ten times the warload, has far better seakeeping, and costs only about five times as much. And the destroyer enjoys similar advantages over a ship that is one-tenth its own size. Recent innovations in hull-forms, materials, and propulsion systems have opened new options for small warships for littoral warfare. Some come from the fast ferry industry and others from foreign navies which emphasize small ships.

To meet its current operational concepts, the Navy needs deployable, self-sufficient, survivable, multicapability ships. In the past, ships much smaller than 3,500 tons displacement have proven unsatisfactory and were retired early. Today, size reductions of as much as one-third can be achieved by building in aluminum or new plastic composite materials (although little if any cost savings are in prospect in the near term). Size and cost reductions may be gained through diesel-electric propulsion or perhaps by applying the emergent technology of the fuel cells to propulsion needs. Further savings may be possible if the Navy finds it can accept lesser capabilities than have been needed to date.

Hullform options for small warships now include twin-hull ships (catamarans) and ships with very narrow central hulls flanked by two or four stabilizing hulls on outriggers (trimarans or pentamarans). Their hull shapes may be tailored to improve seakeeping and speed perform- ance and these hullforms can offer greater space for warloads, superior aviation facilities, and better stability for carrying topweight. These ad- vantages come at some cost in other respects, however, making careful tradeoffs necessary.

*Stealth at Sea*

In practice, stealth means mostly low radar signature. Radar signature is not closely associated with physical dimensions in the way that visual de- tectability is. The B–2 bomber, for example, has a radar signature far smaller than that of much more compact aircraft. In principle, the radar signatures of large ships could also be reduced, and this has been verified by tests of a relatively large demonstrator. Submarines, however, represent the ultimate in radar stealth simply because they operate below the surface of the sea, making them virtually undetectable by radar. On the whole, therefore, it has appeared better to rely on submarines for needs requiring great stealth rather than to develop highly stealthy surface ships. However, in many cases the radar signatures of surface ships have been cut substantially to more eas- ily confuse missile seekers by means of countermeasures.

## Transforming Structures

In principle, the naval services are not independent operational enti- ties. The forces that they build are, for operational purposes, under joint command and control. In practice, however, many significant units of "joint" force are composed entirely of naval services elements, and the naval services generally have considerable latitude to optimize the compo- sition and organization of these units. Thus, their structural concepts have operational as well as administrative implications.

The naval services pioneered flexible mixed-force task-oriented or- ganization for operational purposes in the 1930s and 1940s. These con- cepts have continued to evolve but generally have served well. The services have found effective solutions to the logistical issues involved in flexible mixed forces. This allows them, for instance, to deploy mixed air wings and even small mixed air components (as in a MAGTF) with little penalty in logistical efficiency. Essentially, naval services plans for structural transfor- mation envision continuing to exploit the flexibility inherent in their task organization concepts to meet evolving needs.

## Transforming Operations

The opportunities for transforming existing naval operations are significant. Unspectacular and incremental transformation involves little dramatic new technology and instead builds on training and tactics, as well as improved modes of support.

### Training and Tactics

While technology can enhance precision and effectiveness, the performance of different units, crews, and individuals using the same technology varies greatly. Gains from excellence in tactics and training may be greater than those that can be achieved by introducing a new generation of technology—and may be much more cheaply and quickly obtained.

The secret to transforming training and tactics lies in exact information about operational results as a function of all possible variations. The intuition or feel of operators is a starting point but is usually not nearly adequate as a basis for optimizing the performance of complex systems and forces employing advanced technology. Systematic controlled experimentation, precise and highly specific information about the results of operations in exercises and combat, and detailed analytical modeling and simulation all are key.

For more than half a century, the Navy has been a pioneer in such approaches and has gained greatly in effectiveness as a result. In part, this reflects the conditions of war at sea, which lent themselves to analysis and improvement of tactics and training because of the relatively small numbers of units involved and the fairly consistent environment in which they operated. With improved measurement and analysis technologies, it is now more feasible to extend this work to more complex cases, as the Marine Corps is doing. There is a great scope for wider application and vast benefit to be gained.

### Support Operations

A great deal of the activity of the naval services is support: operations not intrinsically warlike and not inherently military. Even leaving aside the support operations that must be performed in places especially exposed to hostile fire, a huge amount remains. The diversity and dispersion of support operations make them difficult to manage well. Those at the top of the naval services cannot possibly fully understand all of their many operations and must focus on those that are most directly central to naval missions. It is difficult for them to know how efficient each support operation is or how much more efficient it could be.

An effective way to improve the efficiency of these activities is to throw them open to competition. Studies of competitive procurement of support have shown an average 30 percent reduction in costs for constant quality and quantity of output.[6] These gains are achieved even when government teams win the competitions. It is free and open competition, not privatization as such, that brings the benefits. If allowed to compete on an equal basis, "outside" and "inside" organizations have each tended to win roughly half of competitions.

The key to effective use of competition lies in full and exact information about the operations involved. The services must know and be able to measure or assess exactly what output they need from the support activity, and they must communicate this fully and precisely to the competitors. This requires an intensive and disciplined analysis effort, but the rewards are worthwhile.

## Key Choices

The logic of naval services transformation efforts seems difficult to dispute in the context of national strategic needs and priorities. Nevertheless, the naval services, like the others, face a serious affordability problem. Such large parts of their budgets are needed to support current operations that not enough is left over to replace aging equipment and modernize capabilities. In essence, the Nation is borrowing from the future to pay for its current naval capabilities. The hole that this leaves is not so apparent for the naval services as it would be for organizations that replaced their capital at a more rapid rate, but it is no less deep and will be no easier to fill.

This survey of naval transformation has failed to uncover any significant opportunities for economizing through application of new technology. Nor are there obvious opportunities for greatly extending the already long lives of major naval capital equipment. As this suggests, the balance between present and future must be restored largely through some reduction of current operating expenses relative to investment. In principle, this could happen by raising investment while holding operating funding steady, or raising it more slowly than investment. But given the Nation's present financial and strategic circumstances, it seems in practice that the total for defense will not rise sufficiently to obviate the necessity to cut operating expenses to permit more investment. Since operating expenses are primarily driven by military manpower, this suggests a need for cuts in the numbers of personnel.

It may be possible to offset the effects of personnel cuts to some extent by equipping those who remain with superior and more extensive technology; this is the defense analogy to capital deepening in the civil economy. In the Navy, for instance, longstanding efforts to design or refit ships for operation by smaller crews have met with considerable success, and ships today are in many cases more lightly manned than predecessors of similar size and lesser capabilities. Still, the opportunities for naval capital deepening do not appear nearly sufficient to balance the books. This is particularly so for the Marine Corps, whose leaders see little potential for cutting manpower without serious effects on capabilities.

## Conclusion

The naval services are in the process of transforming themselves from forces whose primary capacities facilitated control of the seas into forces increasingly able to use control of the sea as a basis for facilitating intervention ashore. This sweeping change, involving nearly the full range of modern military capabilities, has not lent itself to particular, narrowly defined technological solutions. A great deal of the transformational effort has focused on doctrinal development and change; analysis of actual operational results has demonstrated consistently over many decades that changes in training, tactics, and procedures can often have more effect than changes in technology. Such doctrinal changes tend to be less dramatic and often misunderstood.

The Marine Corps has been particularly active in developing a solid empirical basis for doctrinal changes through a carefully structured program of conceptualization, experimentation, and analysis of results. Much of this has been devoted to extending the spectrum of Marine Corps capabilities so that national decisionmakers will have a broader range of options at various levels of force in many different circumstances. While continuing to expand capabilities to fight and win against numerically superior conventional forces, the Marines have also been developing capabilities for meeting a variety of unconventional demands. Technological elements of this include improved mobility on the ground and in the air, agile logistics, information-gathering systems effective in a variety of environments, and systems that will permit control of hostile noncombatants with minimal casualties.

The Navy has devoted much of its attention to expanding its range of strike options for organic tactical support of naval operations both ashore and at sea, as well as options for employment of the naval strike forces by joint and national commanders. This has meant not only the introduction of new weapons and new strike platforms but also the development of systems and doctrine for their employment. The result has been a quiet but large ongoing change in the volume of strike weapons and in the precision, assurance, and flexibility with which they can be delivered. The Navy's other major focus has been on assuring that naval forces can operate effectively in littoral regions in the face of current and potential threats. Because the Navy exercises such overwhelming superiority over all other navies, this has primarily taken the form of efforts to remedy particular deficiencies or shortfalls in defense against mines and certain specific weapons.

The quest for transformation in the naval services—as elsewhere in defense and indeed throughout government—has primarily been directed toward seeking means to do more and do it better. The officers and officials of the naval services have been imbued with the spirit of excellence, and most of them pursue it with remarkable energy and imagination.

But the need today is not really for the naval services to do more and better, or not simply to do this. Rather, they need to find ways to better balance present and future within a budget level that is essentially constant. That is, the need is not for transformation to do more and better but transformation to do well with less. From the perspective of officers and officials, the bureaucratic incentives to pursue this are mixed at best. Unless and until these incentives are transformed, the measures to accomplish transformation are unlikely to benefit broadly from the enthusiasm and knowledge of those most closely involved with the naval services.

## Appendix: The U.S. Marine Corps: Transforming Expeditionary Maneuver Warfare

By Bing West

For over a decade, the Marines have articulated a warfighting doctrine that emphasizes high-tempo operations and rapid maneuver intended to shatter enemy cohesion. This has encouraged a generation of marines to look for operational opportunities, be willing to exploit openings quickly, and articulate orders in terms of the mission to be accomplished. This doctrine has influenced decisions about equipment and force structure.

For decades, marines have deployed in amphibious-based warfighting units that are self-sustaining and reasonably robust. They have served in sustained land campaigns, as in Vietnam, but what they provide to the Secretary of Defense, day in and day out, year after year, are sea-based warfighting packages that can be moved, landed, employed, and extracted without relying upon any external resources.

Afghanistan might at first have seemed an exception: a landlocked country that would show the limits of sea-based expeditionary power. In fact, a Marine expeditionary unit (MEU) moved inland hundreds of miles across desert and mountains. The action in Afghanistan also illustrated the operational scenario underlying the Marines' dogged determination to get the V–22 Osprey tilt-rotor helicopter and other new equipment, such as the joint strike fighter and the autonomous amphibious assault vehicle.[7]

### Information Technology

Afghanistan also demonstrated advances in U.S. ability to monitor the battlefield and send continuous information, including live imagery, to air, space, and ground weapon systems. This enormous and costly increase in bandwidth among airborne and satellite platforms has not, however, been extended to Marine (or Army) infantry at the company level. The digital IT networks do not include them. This is partially a result of Marine Corps priorities; the bulk of IT spending has gone to staffs above the battalion level and to garrison functions. Also, over the next year, the Navy Marine Corps Intranet will extend to every Marine Corps desktop computer. The goal is to increase productivity. Marines, however, do not fight wars at their desks.

It is not clear what the vision is for extending new IT to Marine rifle squads. Uncharacteristically, the Marines have spent much more time and money upgrading garrison information technology. As the Marines continue to transform their force, IT priorities deserve a careful look.

## Close Air Support

A second area of the Marine doctrine that is ripe for further transformation is the application of close air support. While fire traditionally supports maneuver, the Afghanistan experience opened a new dimension. Air strikes shattered enemy cohesion. Airpower was not a supporting fire; it was the decisive weapon. Maneuver followed airpower.

Certainly the favorable circumstances of that particular battlefield will not always be the case. Nonetheless, U.S. air power above 10,000 feet is now nearly invulnerable and, when linked to GPS coordinates or laser guidance, is highly accurate. Air directed by ground forces has emerged as a devastating offensive weapon.

The Marine Corps pioneered close air support; it is the only service with fire support teams that integrate aviators, artillery, and mortar observers. In Afghanistan, however, the air support was called in by Army sergeants in special forces teams, not by marines.

In an MEU that can place over 600 marines on the ground, current doctrine allows only two or three forward air controllers to call in air strikes. Only an aviator officer who has gone to the proper schools is permitted to call in air support. This skill level may be appropriate for the linear battlefield, where many units are close to one another on a crowded battlefield and where artillery, helicopter gunships, and fixed-wing air must be precisely coordinated in close proximity to ground units. But to train only for that battlefield restricts the maneuver doctrine that the Marines advocate. With lasers and GPS, on a dispersed battlefield, it does not take an aviator to direct air. It is likely the Marines will learn from the experience of the Special Operations Command in Afghanistan and modify their doctrine. However, obtaining the proper equipment to direct air is a separate and harder matter. Marine battalions simply do not have the communications, GPS, and laser sets needed to employ air more flexibly. The infantry does not benefit from the advocacy of the military-industrial lobbyists because it does not have a single big-ticket item around which lobbyists can coalesce to generate political support.[8]

For the Marines to add another arrow to the quiver of expeditionary warfare, they need to adapt their doctrine, and they also need to obtain modern equipment to take full advantage of airpower. There is no doubt that Marine doctrine will change, but securing resources will be the tougher fight because the Pentagon instinct is to associate information technologies, "transformation," and monies with large, inanimate systems. Marine rifle squads—the same size as the teams that performed so well in Afghanistan—must also be brought into the digital age.

## Notes

¹ The U.S. Navy, Marine Corps, and Coast Guard are sometimes treated collectively as *the sea services.* The Coast Guard falls under the Department of Transportation rather than DOD and will not be addressed in this chapter.

² Issues specific to the Marine Corps are outlined in the appendix to this chapter.

³ Bruce Rolfsen in "Predator Problems," *Air Force Times,* April 30, 2001, 8, says that five Predator UAVs were lost in 8 months, none due to enemy action. This is not an isolated occurrence.

⁴ Both the Osprey and the JSF, as well as the USMC new Advanced Amphibious Assault Vehicle, represent the results of previous generation-skipping; the Marine Corps deliberately passed over less ambitious and more conventional technologies that would have been available much earlier to go for the capabilities that it believed suited its needs.

⁵ David A. Perin, "Are Big Decks Still the Answer?" *U.S. Naval Institute Proceedings,* June 2001, 30–33. This article gives a summary relating to issues of carrier size.

⁶ R.D. Trunkey, R.P. Trost, C.M. Snyder, *Analysis of DOD's Commercial Activities Program* (Alexandria, VA: Center for Naval Analyses, December 1996), 2. See also William Brent Boning, et al., *Evidence on Savings from DOD A–76 Competitions,* Center for Naval Analyses Research Memorandum 98–125 (Alexandria, VA: Center for Naval Analyses, November 1998).

⁷ Marine ability to penetrate deeply from a sea base and to fly into hotspots rather than taking beaches will be greatly strengthened by the availability of the V–22 Osprey tilt-rotor helicopter (to get them to the fight) and the vertical take-off version of the joint strike fighter (to provide adequate air support from a distance).

⁸ For example, it was the special forces teams directing the air—not unmanned aerial vehicles (UAVs)—that were the key to the swift dissolution of the Taliban, but the first "plus-up" was $250 million for UAVs: money for hardware, not humans.

# Chapter 6

# The Air Force:
# The Next Round

David A. Ochmanek

A ir forces and space-based assets are playing increasingly important roles in U.S. military operations, due in part to the fairly
rapid evolution of their capabilities. As the technologies, systems,
and procedures associated with air and space operations have developed
and matured, so has their ability to support the needs of combatant commanders. But there seems as well to be an increasingly good fit between
the characteristics and capabilities of air and space forces on the one hand
and the demands of U.S. military strategy and operations on the other.

Operation *Desert Storm* awakened many to the fact that modern air
forces, properly employed, can quickly and dramatically transform the operational situation in many theater conflicts by stripping the enemy of its
air defenses, dismantling key elements of national infrastructure, and isolating, immobilizing, and attriting fielded forces. Since then, U.S. leaders
have relied on airpower to carry most of the burden of combat operations
in the Balkans, the Gulf region, and Afghanistan, while contributing in numerous other ways to U.S. national security. The question facing the U.S.
Air Force (USAF) and the U.S. Department of Defense (DOD) more
broadly is whether, in the face of looming new threats and persistent resource constraints, airpower will be able to retain and perhaps even expand the degree of dominance it currently enjoys over adversaries.

This chapter begins by outlining the basic demands of U.S. military
strategy: the missions that U.S. forces, especially air forces, must be prepared
to accomplish, and the sorts of conditions and constraints that often apply
to those missions. The chapter then briefly reviews capabilities provided by
the U.S. Air Force (and the air arms of the other services) that have undergone particularly rapid evolution over the past two decades or so, identifying some key technological developments that enabled these changes. The
chapter then looks ahead to the types of operational capabilities that the

leaders of today's Air Force seek to provide in the future, and the systems and operational concepts they envisage as necessary for providing these capabilities. Finally, several fundamental choices that the Air Force may face in shaping its capabilities and concepts for the future are considered.

## Joint Missions

As the leading economic and military power in the world and the guarantor of many other states' security, the United States has adopted an ambitious national security strategy that seeks to defend and advance important U.S. interests and to shape the international security environment in positive directions. This strategy calls for the active involvement of U.S. military forces in multiple regions and directs that they must be prepared to conduct a wide range of missions in peacetime, crisis, and wartime. Chapter 1 of this volume describes the missions of the Armed Forces of the United States. They can be summarized as follows:

- *Projecting stability and influence abroad in peacetime,* which calls for stationing and deploying military forces overseas, conducting training with allied and friendly forces, and providing security assistance. Such activities are the glue that binds alliances together, underwriting deterrence and enhancing interoperability among friendly forces.

- *Deterring and defeating large-scale aggression,* which calls for rapid projection of military power over long distances—a demanding task, particularly because the United States has important interests in multiple regions and must guard against the possibility that military challenges to those interests could arise concurrently in more than one location.

- *Protecting and advancing U.S. interests through smaller-scale operations,* which include providing humanitarian assistance, conducting peacekeeping operations and disaster relief, enforcing exclusion zones, reinforcing allies, and conducting limited strikes and interventions.

- *Deterring and defeating the use of weapons of mass destruction (WMD)* against the U.S. homeland, against U.S. forces abroad, and against the territory and assets of allies.

- *Deterring and defeating terrorist attacks* by neutralizing terrorist groups abroad (through capture or destruction) and by dissuading governments from harboring or supporting terrorists.

The Air Force contributes important capabilities to the accomplishment of each of these missions. These capabilities include essential supporting activities, such as airlift, surveillance, and communications, as well as forces for conducting combat. But the centerpiece of the Air Force planning is and should remain preparation to prevail in large-scale power-projection operations, which entail the deployment of sizable numbers of forces over long distances, and the conduct of high-tempo operations against a capable foe. Only the United States has the capability to project large-scale military power today, and it is this capability that sustains favorable balances of power in key regions of the world. As such, it is also essential to the viability of the strategic alliances that form the heart of the Nation's security strategy. Because forces provided by the Air Force constitute a large and growing portion of the combat power available to joint force commanders in the critical opening phases of most conflicts, it is especially important that the United States sustain the ability of those forces to dominate combat operations against the forces of potential adversaries around the world. That will be a demanding task in a world of evolving threats and challenges.

The U.S. Armed Forces also serve purposes that go beyond these specific missions. Perhaps chief among these broader purposes is what DOD calls *dissuasion*: discouraging potential competitors or adversaries from seeking the military capabilities that would be required to challenge the United States successfully. The Air Force plays a particularly important role in this regard because of the superiority that the Armed Forces enjoy in air- and space-based capabilities and because of the important roles played by those forces in U.S. military operations. In Operations *Desert Storm*, *Deliberate Force* (which helped to bring peace to Bosnia), *Allied Force* (the effort to dislodge Serbian forces from Kosovo), and *Enduring Freedom* (which led to the overthrow of the Taliban in Afghanistan), the United States showed that its air forces can destroy selected elements of the power bases of enemy regimes with precision and with virtual impunity. If this capability can be maintained, it should help convince those opposed to U.S. interests that aggressive policies backed by military threats are likely to prove costly and futile if they lead to overt conflict with the United States.

## Constraints and Conditions

As important as an enumeration of missions is an understanding of the conditions under which those missions are likely to be carried out and the constraints that may be placed upon forces during operations. For conflicts involving all but the most important of national interests, U.S. military operations will be constrained by the need to hold down the number of casualties to U.S. and allied forces, to minimize the suffering of innocent civilians, and to act in concert with allies. U.S. threats to employ military power—be they implicit or explicit—can only be effective to the extent that potential adversaries believe they will be carried out. Adversaries understand the constraints on U.S. military actions and are more likely to view military threats as credible if the United States fields forces that can achieve national objectives despite these constraints. For defense planners, these considerations mean that they must continue to offer the Nation's leaders military options that can be exercised with confidence that the risk of friendly and civilian casualties can be held to a level consistent with the interests the Nation has at stake.

Planners should also anticipate that future U.S. military operations would most often be coalition affairs rather than unilateral campaigns. By sustaining a network of security partnerships in key regions, U.S. forces can have some confidence of access to airspace, ports, airbases, and other assets near regions of conflict when they need them. By the end of Operation *Allied Force*, for example, U.S. aircraft were able to operate from bases in eight countries, effectively surrounding Serbia. U.S. forces will also have the opportunity (and the obligation) to operate in concert with allies. Although operating within a coalition can add friction and inefficiencies to the planning and execution of an operation, political leaders almost always will prefer to have partners when they go to war. Thus U.S. forces and operational concepts should incorporate features that enhance interoperability across national lines.

Other conditions are especially pertinent to large power-projection operations. If an enemy is going to challenge U.S. interests through overt aggression (such as the Iraqi invasion of Kuwait in 1990 or a hypothetical North Korean invasion of the South), prudence demands that we assume that the attack will be undertaken so as to maximize the attacker's inherent advantages. Thus, U.S. defense planners must expect to be surprised. Our opponents are not eager for a fight with U.S. military forces; they would prefer to achieve their objectives without having to resort to force at all or, failing that, by a coup de main that succeeds before large-scale U.S. forces can be brought to the theater. Advanced surveillance systems, including sensors on board satellites and airborne platforms, make it harder for enemy forces to prepare for an attack without being noticed, but these systems do not, by themselves, guarantee that U.S. forces will be deployed promptly. Some adversaries, such as the North Koreans, can routinely posture their forces in such a way that little further overt preparation is needed before attacking. Information about a possible attack is, moreover, a necessary but not sufficient condition for reinforcement. Decisions to act must be made in Washington and in other capitals before forces can move, and this takes time.

Therefore, U.S. forces must be postured to respond rapidly to aggression that occurs with little warning. They do this in two ways: first, by having some of the most critical components of a defensive force (forces themselves, munitions, other supplies) stationed or routinely deployed abroad close to potential regions of conflict; and second, by being able to deploy rapidly over long distances.

Related to this is the need for what might be called high leverage early in a conflict. U.S. forces arriving in a theater in the opening days of a major conflict are likely to be greatly outnumbered. Yet if they are to prevent the enemy from achieving its objectives, they must be able to wrest the initiative away from the enemy and defeat its attack quickly. This means that those early-arriving U.S. forces must have great qualitative superiority over the forces they are confronting if they are to succeed in their mission.[1]

Given the inherently demanding nature of power-projection operations and the potential for challenges to arise in many regions, it becomes clearer why the United States today spends so much more on military forces than any other nation: its forces are called upon to perform a uniquely demanding set of missions.

## Roles of Air and Space Forces

The missions outlined above apply to all elements of the U.S. military establishment. Their implications for air and space forces turn on what those forces are likely to be called upon to do within joint campaigns.

Since the earliest days of military aviation, commanders have relied on aircraft to conduct reconnaissance to gain information about the location and disposition of enemy forces. Early in World War I, as aircraft became more capable in this role, they began to be used to contest control of operations in the air. Soon thereafter, military air forces were also being called upon to haul cargo and to attack enemy land and naval forces and other assets on the surface. They were also brought to bear against other elements of national power, such as military-related industries, lines of communication, national infrastructure, and the means of political control, both to reduce enemy ability to conduct military operations and to attempt to coerce enemy leadership into surrendering. As the technologies associated with powered flight matured, so did the capabilities of military aircraft.

Over the last two decades or so, the capabilities of U.S. military aviation in most of these areas—reconnaissance, dominating operations in the air, engaging and destroying forces on the surface, and attacking fixed installations—have grown dramatically, both in absolute terms and relative to those of their adversaries. Indeed, if transformation is defined in terms of a profound change in the character or capabilities of a force, over this period we have witnessed a transformation in certain portions of the military capabilities wielded by the Armed Forces.

### Reconnaissance and Surveillance

New types of sensors, including moving target indicator (MTI) radars and synthetic aperture radars (SAR), enable airborne platforms today to locate and often identify targets, day or night and in all types of weather. The Air Force is also fielding new platforms that increase the utility of these and other sensors to joint force commanders. For example, the Predator and Global Hawk unmanned aerial vehicles (UAVs) permit U.S. forces to observe closely parts of the battlefield for an extended time without fear of losing aircrews to ground fire. Today, with the sensors carried aboard such aircraft as the Joint Surveillance Target Attack Radar System (JSTARS), a division-sized or larger mechanized force could hardly hope to move undetected, assuming that U.S. reconnaissance assets are deployed to the region and that they are free to operate. As sensors and platforms improve and proliferate, U.S. forces will be able to detect and, in some cases, identify smaller formations of surface forces, even in mountainous or densely foliated terrain.

### Dominating Air Operations

Americans have come to expect heavily lopsided results from air combat involving U.S. forces. In historical terms, this is a fairly new development. North Atlantic Treaty Organization (NATO) air forces in Operation *Allied Force* experienced a loss rate of just one aircraft shot down for every 10,000 sorties flown.[2] This compares favorably with the U.S. experience in Operation *Desert Storm*, when four to five aircraft were lost for every 10,000 combat sorties. The loss rates in *Desert Storm* were, in turn, approximately one-tenth those experienced in Vietnam (3.5 losses in

10,000 sorties) and less than one-hundredth those of World War II (51 losses in 10,000 sorties).

These improvements were achieved in the face of capable adversaries. Both the Iraqi and Yugoslav air defense systems consisted, at the beginning of each conflict, of sizable numbers of modern interceptor aircraft; capable radar, surface-to-air missile (SAM), and antiaircraft artillery systems; hardened and redundant command and control facilities; and trained operators. The SAMs employed by both countries were of 1970s-era design, but they were not used sparingly: Coalition aircrews were subjected to more than 700 SAM launches in Operation *Desert Storm* and more than 650 SAM launches in Operation *Allied Force*. Yet the combination of stealth, standoff, dominant fighters, dedicated SAM-suppression aircraft, jamming, information operations, adaptive tactics, and skilled orchestration of air operations effectively neutralized these defenses.

The ability of U.S. forces to suppress enemy air defenses so comprehensively has had important implications for U.S. military strategy. Although the persistence of SAM threats can still restrict U.S. air operations to some degree (for example, compelling aircrews to operate at medium altitudes or higher and for non-stealthy aircraft to avoid certain areas), the ability to dominate air operations provides the basis for unparalleled leverage over enemy forces and nations. Air campaigns involving U.S. forces have become increasingly one-sided. Enemy inability to inflict losses on attacking aircraft can have a profoundly demoralizing effect on enemy forces, populations, and leaders.[3] Dominance of operations in the air also has granted U.S. ground and naval forces sanctuary from enemy air attacks. The effective immunity from air attack of rear-area ports, airfields, logistics bases, and transportation and command and control infrastructures used by U.S. forces has greatly facilitated successful operations.

Attacking light infantry or insurgent forces presents a qualitatively different set of challenges, as shown by the opening weeks of the operations against Taliban forces in Afghanistan. Such forces are not highly dependent on large-scale, easily targeted logistic trains, and they can disperse and take cover underground or in residential areas. Even so, when accurate information regarding the location of such forces can be provided to attacking aircraft and a nearly constant air presence can be maintained, air attacks can make vitally important contributions to friendly ground forces seeking to engage and defeat light infantry.

## Delaying, Damaging, and Destroying Moving Ground Forces

Over the past 50 years, U.S. air forces have improved by a factor of 8 or more their lethality against moving armored columns (see figure 6–1). From the earliest days of military aviation, destroying a single armored vehicle required multiple sorties. However, with the fielding of the sensor fuzed weapon in the 1990s, air forces became capable of destroying multiple armored vehicles with a single sortie.[4] Like the sensors that guide sorties to their targets, these weapons remain effective at night and in conditions of overcast, fog, and precipitation.

The implications for joint operations are profound. Airpower has long been valued as a means of disrupting and delaying the movement of mechanized forces. For example, massive numbers of fighter-bombers flying "armed reconnaissance" missions were instrumental in isolating the beachheads at Normandy from German divisions in the surrounding regions during World War II. However, the job of actually destroying enemy armored forces traditionally has been left to armor. This is changing: today, airpower not only can delay and disrupt moving armored forces; in many conditions, it also can damage or destroy their vehicles at such a rate as to render continued operations difficult if not impossible.

## Destroying Critical Infrastructures

Even greater improvements have been realized in capabilities to destroy fixed targets. With today's laser-guided bombs, a single fighter-bomber sortie is highly likely to be able to destroy a fixed target such as a bridge span, an aircraft shelter, or a small building. Destroying a similar target using unguided weapons required, on average, 50 times as many bombs in Vietnam and 60 times as many in World War II.[5] With the advent of weapons such as the joint direct attack munition (JDAM) guided by signals from the global positioning system (GPS), such accurate attacks are now possible in all types of weather. Because each weapon need not be steered all the way to its target by the aircrew, individual aircraft using JDAM weapons can attack several targets simultaneously. Of course, no weapon always performs perfectly, and countermeasures to precision, such as GPS jamming, must be anticipated. But U.S. air forces' capabilities to attack fixed targets with precision have increased dramatically and have become more robust.

The implications for joint operations are profound. Accurate, large-scale attacks on enemy infrastructure contribute to victory in many ways.

Figure 6–1. **Improvements in Airpower Ability to Destroy Moving Armor**

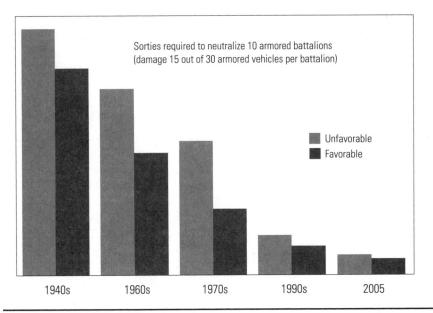

Sorties required to neutralize 10 armored battalions
(damage 15 out of 30 armored vehicles per battalion)

Unfavorable
Favorable

1940s    1960s    1970s    1990s    2005

*Note:* "Unfavorable conditions" include situations in which enemy vehicles are widely dispersed, air defenses preclude optimal delivery profiles, or weather conditions partially obscure targets.
*Source:* David Ochmanek, et al., *To Find and Not to Yield,* MR–958–AF (Santa Monica, CA: RAND, 1998).

They can:

- disrupt the ability of enemy leaders to plan, control, and carry out military operations
- interrupt the production and distribution within a country of such vital war matériel as munitions; petroleum, oil, and lubricants; spare parts; and replacement weapons
- interdict the flow of crucial matériel from outside the country
- put coercive pressure on the enemy leadership by raising the cost of aggression and by eroding morale and support for the regime within the enemy country's population.

As these improved capabilities have been fielded, U.S. military operations and planning have gradually adapted. U.S. air forces demonstrated in Operation *Desert Storm* that, in favorable terrain, they could dominate operations not only in the air but also on the surface. While airpower was not by itself able to compel the withdrawal of Iraqi ground forces from Kuwait, 38 days of nearly incessant air attacks shattered the fighting abilities of a large, combat-tested mechanized army.[6] Eight years later, in Operation *Allied Force*, airpower was unable to curtail the operations of the Serbian forces in Kosovo. However, it did provide the force needed to coerce Serbian leader Slobodan Milosevic to accede to NATO demands that Serbian forces evacuate Kosovo and allow a NATO-led force to secure the province.[7]

U.S. political leaders and combatant commanders have come to rely heavily on the ability of the Nation's air forces to gain information about enemy military forces, to dominate operations in the air while incurring few losses, and to destroy enemy forces and infrastructure targets on the surface. The overwhelmingly favorable outcomes achieved by airpower in Operations *Desert Storm* and *Allied Force* simply would not have been possible with the airpower capabilities of a generation ago.

## Enablers of Transformation

The transformation in the capabilities of modern airpower springs from several related developments. The most obvious are new technologies and systems that enable new operational concepts. Broadly defined, the technology aggregates most responsible for the breakthroughs already described (and, presumably, those to come in the near future) are precision guidance, information management and communications, and stealth.

### Precision Guidance

More than anything else, the ability to hit what one is aiming at is transforming military operations. The quantum increases in accuracy experienced by air-delivered weapons are due primarily to the application of miniaturized electronic components to the tasks of positioning, target location, and guidance (steering weapons to their desired aimpoints). The GPS satellite constellation, which is playing growing roles in nearly every dimension of precision attack, relies on accurate timekeeping so that minute differences in the arrival time of signals from the constellation's satellites can be measured. By comparing these differences, a GPS receiver can locate itself in terms of latitude, longitude, and altitude within 10 meters or so.

### Sensors

Applying accurate firepower effectively depends on the identification of targets. Major advances in sensor technology have helped U.S. forces keep pace with advances in lethality by enabling them to locate and identify large numbers of targets quickly; increasingly they can do so under all sorts of atmospheric conditions. Currently fielded reconnaissance systems employ sensors that can collect electronic signals, passively detect electro-optical and infrared signatures, and develop images of targets using active radar signals.

### Information Management, Decision Aids, Communications

If commanders are to make the best use of the forces available to them, they must have a clear and accurate picture of the status of not only enemy forces but also their own forces. Bringing together massive amounts of perishable information, synthesizing it, and displaying it for commanders and their staffs pose an enormous challenge that has to date been only partially met. The next step is to help commanders use this enhanced information to make better decisions faster. DOD has invested heavily in the capacity to analyze and understand target complexes in potentially hostile countries. Tools are being developed to help future commanders more accurately anticipate the results of alternative courses of action. Similarly, passing information among many users and communicating decisions in a timely fashion has led to an explosion in the demand for communications bandwidth. "Assured connectivity" among large numbers of agents, including individual aircrews, will be essential if future operations are to be dynamically controlled.

### Stealth

Each of the services in the Department of Defense has pursued technologies that reduce the detectability of their platforms, particularly from radars, but the Air Force has made the most progress in fielding operational forces exploiting stealth. Its F–117 and B–2 aircraft, in particular, have played important roles in attacking the most threatening elements of enemy integrated air defenses, allowing the rest of the force to operate more effectively and with less risk. A growing portion of the Air Force fleet of combat aircraft will be stealthy.

### Doctrine, Training, and Other Intangibles

Military capabilities are not simply the product of hardware. They also depend heavily on the training, doctrine, and personal qualities of the people who wield the hardware and command operations. While no single initiative can account for the superb performance of USAF units over the past 20 years, investments in training at all levels have clearly paid off. The Air Force Red Flag series of exercises, begun in the mid-1970s, are the best known example of efforts to give aircrews exposure to the stresses of combat prior to engaging in the real thing.[8] Operational Air Force units train to high standards in their normal daily training as well. Large-scale instrumented ranges and realistic cockpit simulators are available to most USAF fighter and bomber units. With approximately 20 hours of flight training per month, the average USAF fighter pilot gets 2 to 10 times as much time in the cockpit as his or her counterpart in most adversary air forces. The Air Force has also paid increasing attention to the importance of training senior and mid-level officers in the skills required to command and control complex air operations. Continued innovation in the areas of sensors, platforms, weapons, and munitions will likely result in an acceleration of the trend of the past two decades in which air operations have increased in complexity and accelerated in tempo. This will require commensurate increases in the training of operators as well as command staffs.

## The Air Force Vision of the Future

The Air Force has sought to guide its development in part by articulating a vision of its future roles and capabilities, in a document entitled *America's Air Force, Vision 2020*.[9] That vision calls on the Air Force of the future to be able to conduct and integrate operations in three domains—air, space, and cyberspace. It also proposes that future USAF forces should be able to:

- *monitor military situations worldwide and support the ability to act on this information.* The vision sets as an explicit goal the ability to "find, fix, assess, track, target, and engage anything of military significance anywhere."
- *deploy rapidly and sustain forces* by modernizing the airlift fleet, reducing the logistics footprint—the mass and volume of equipment and supplies—associated with deploying units, and pursuing novel support concepts such as "reach-back" to command and control facilities in the United States and "just-in-time" delivery of supplies.
- *achieve strategic and operational effects.* Primary objectives for USAF forces in combat operations are to provide friendly forces with freedom from attack, freedom to maneuver, and freedom to attack, while denying these to the enemy. Achieving these goals will require capabilities to defeat enemy attacks on rear areas and to observe and strike enemy forces and facilities "wherever and whenever necessary." Precision weapons, nonlethal weapons, and directed energy weapons are all mentioned as part of the future Air Force arsenal.

The Air Force vision statement takes note of the need to cope with emerging threats, including advanced aircraft, SAMs, ballistic and cruise missiles, and threats to spacecraft. It mentions the potential need for capabilities to "control space," that is, to ensure that the United States can operate military and civilian-owned assets in space and, perhaps, to deny enemies the same access. It also calls for enhanced capabilities for command and control of air and space operations.

The *Vision 2020* document is intended for public information and as such is not a definitive guide to force development or planning, but rather a set of general aspirations, informed by a broad appreciation of future operational needs and technical possibilities. The document does not provide a sense of how Air Force leadership might address choices and trade-offs that will arise in light of resource constraints. Nor does it grapple seriously with the problems posed by emerging threats such as advanced air defenses, ballistic and cruise missiles, or WMD.

For all of the ambition inherent in the goals articulated in the *Vision 2020* document, the overall impression it gives of the leadership's approach is of an essentially evolutionary path to the future, rather than a break with established ways of doing things. On the other hand, the Air Force is committed to an extensive modernization of its platforms for air combat, airlift, surveillance, and other key functions. As such, the service's approach to transformation, like that advocated in chapter 3, falls between a "leap ahead" program and a "steady-as-you-go" approach.

The *Vision 2020* document shows no evidence that the leadership of the Air Force envisages the abandonment of any of its traditional product lines such as fighter aircraft, bomber aircraft, transport aircraft, intercontinental ballistic missiles, space launch capabilities, or satellites. Since demand for these items has been robust, this is a reasonable position. Fielding new capabilities, then, will involve either adapting existing product lines or adding new ones. For example, the airborne laser or new units dedicated to conducting information operations would be added to existing capabilities. Fighters deployed for more traditional combat missions could be fitted with missiles that could shoot down satellites in low Earth orbit. This approach has the advantage of not giving up proven capabilities until new ones are well in hand. It can also be expensive, however, as the cost to operate and maintain large existing forces consumes the bulk of the service's resources.

## Looming Challenges and Potential New Concepts

To add specificity to the broad content of *Vision 2020*, the operational challenges that U.S. joint forces might face in the coming 20 years or more must be considered, with a particular focus on those challenges that air forces might be best suited to meeting. We can also identify new operational concepts and associated systems that may allow future air forces to deal with these challenges. The focus is primarily on challenges that might arise in the context of combat operations against the forces of regional adversaries.

### Overcoming Antiaccess Capabilities

The first challenge is to maintain the freedom to operate forces (land, maritime, and air) in the presence of attacks by enemy ballistic missiles, cruise missiles, and aircraft, including those delivering chemical or biological agents. Overcoming counteraccess capabilities constitutes one of the most important challenges facing U.S. military forces in the coming years. For land-based forces—aircraft as well as ground forces—the threats posed by ballistic missiles and air attacks constitute the most acute challenge.

The Air Force is taking several complementary approaches to this set of challenges. First, it is developing the airborne laser (ABL), which has the potential to contribute to the defense of joint and combined forces throughout a theater. The ABL will be the first operational system capable of intercepting ballistic missiles in their boost phase.[10] An advantage of this technique is that remnants of successfully intercepted missiles and their payloads are more likely to fall on enemy than friendly territory. Concepts for boost-phase intercept also help to provide defense-in-depth, complementing other theater missile defense programs, which generally operate in the terminal or mid-course phases. Another feature of the ABL is its ability (like ship-borne systems) to deploy to theater without consuming large amounts of airlift or tanker capacity.

The Air Force is also cognizant of the need to make its forces on the ground less vulnerable to attacks by enemy air and missile forces. In Operation *Desert Storm* and subsequent conflicts, U.S. land-based air forces have been able to operate from bases in theater without much concern about survivability. Images of large numbers of aircraft parked in the open attest to the permissive threat environment that these forces have enjoyed since the end of the Cold War. That environment is changing: aircraft in open areas will be lucrative targets for regional adversaries equipped with increasingly accurate ballistic and cruise missiles. Thus, it will be essential that the United States take steps to prepare for conflicts in certain theaters by ensuring that hardened facilities are available for deploying fighters and by enhancing the capabilities and versatility of its fleet of long-range bombers and support aircraft.

Finally, an examination of the forces of potential future adversaries suggests that U.S. expeditionary forces could find themselves struggling to deal with enemy air attacks, at least in certain scenarios. China, in particular, has the potential to field combat aircraft as well as air-to-air missiles of high quality and in large enough numbers that U.S. air forces trying to defend against concerted air attacks on an allied country could suffer substantial losses. If U.S. and allied air defenses are unable to handle the fighters that might escort Chinese bombers, and if those bombers deliver precision guided weapons against their targets, serious damage could result. The key to defeating such attacks is to ensure that future U.S. forces are equipped with highly capable fighters in sizable numbers. The F–22 and the Joint Strike Fighter, both of which will be stealthy and therefore difficult to engage from long range, provide a substantial qualitative edge over projected enemy fighters. Other important enhancements to U.S. air defenses include upgrades to the E–3/airborne warning and control system (AWACS) aircraft and other sensor platforms that can provide warning of impending attacks by aircraft and cruise missiles.

### Destroying Small Mobile Targets

A second challenge is to be able to rapidly locate, identify, and neutralize small mobile targets, including ballistic or cruise missiles on transporter/erector/launchers (TELs), SAM batteries, and small ground force units. Hiders have always had inherent advantages over seekers, and adversaries such as Iraq and Serbia have exploited this to preserve important elements of their military power in the presence of U.S. air superiority. The importance of destroying ballistic missiles before they are launched (as opposed to killing the TEL after launch) and of damaging SAM batteries, even when they are not emitting electromagnetic radiation, makes this set of tasks particularly important. As adversary forces gain access to ever more capable missiles and other weapons, it will become increasingly important that U.S. air forces find better ways to find and engage small mobile targets.

No single new system or concept is on the horizon that will yield a major breakthrough in U.S. capabilities for this demanding task. But a number of promising developments can, in concert, yield substantial improvements. Chief among these are the ability to correlate rapidly among data from electronic intelligence and imagery sensors; sensors that operate in multiple spectrums and that can penetrate foliage; automated imagery processing and change analysis software; procedures to facilitate the exchange of information among analysts, controllers, and shooters; all-weather engagement systems on attack aircraft; and weapons that can search autonomously for particular targets.

### Operating Despite Advanced Air Defenses

A third challenge is to maintain the ability to operate in the presence of advanced and integrated air defenses, especially advanced SAMs. Hunting down SAM batteries is only one of the required elements of the ability to operate in the air against adversaries equipped with advanced air defense systems. Stealthy platforms, concepts for standoff reconnaissance and attack, capable jammers, decoys that resemble attacking aircraft on enemy radars, and dedicated SAM-suppression aircraft are also important. As capable SAM systems such as the SA–10 and SA–20 proliferate, virtually every element of the U.S. SAM-suppression kit will have to be modernized. Given the importance to U.S. strategy of being able to establish dominance in air operations quickly and managing the risk of casualties, these are among the highest priority investments DOD can make.

### Destroying Deeply Buried Facilities

A fourth challenge is to locate and destroy deeply buried facilities and their contents, including command posts and production and storage facilities for WMD, with minimal collateral damage. U.S. adversaries are increasingly protecting their most valued strategic assets from air attack. Following the example set by the North Koreans, they are using dirt, rock, and reinforced concrete to complement their investments in active air defenses. For U.S. forces to hold at risk the full range of an enemy's military assets, they must have better capabilities to neutralize and, if possible, destroy deeply buried facilities.

Methods are being sought to boost the useful kinetic energy available to precision guided conventional munitions so that they can dig deeper. There has also been discussion of the desirability of developing very low-yield nuclear weapons optimized for destroying deeply buried facilities and their contents. The potential importance of destroying the WMD of a rogue state or a terrorist group could well warrant such a development.

### Assuring Continuity of Space Operations

A fifth challenge is to ensure that U.S. military forces and civilian users can conduct uninterrupted operations in space in the face of enemy attacks on U.S. military and commercial satellites and associated infrastructure. The prospect of threats to U.S. military and commercial space assets has already been mentioned, as have some of the possible Air Force responses. (See chapter 12 in this volume.) Besides pursuing antisatellite (ASAT) capabilities, the Air Force can hedge against the consequences of possible attacks on satellites by investing in readily deployable replacement satellites and in responsive launch capabilities. Of course, developing the capability to launch satellites within days, let alone hours, of a decision to do so would require substantial investments by a community that is accustomed to thinking in terms of months and years when scheduling launches. The capability to attack fixed targets deep in defended airspace will also help address this challenge, since much of the infrastructure associated with enemy ASAT operations (for example, launch complexes and ground-based directed energy weapons) will be vulnerable to such attacks.

### Halting Invasions

A sixth challenge is to halt invasions by mechanized ground forces rapidly. Modern air forces have made great strides in their ability to locate, engage, damage, and destroy moving mechanized forces. Improved capabilities to halt invasions rapidly, however, merit continued emphasis for three reasons. First, U.S. defense planners have postured their forces in ways that depend on the ability of early-arriving air forces to destroy enemy armored forces quickly. In Southwest Asia in particular, U.S. joint forces could deploy upwards of 700 combat aircraft but only two or three brigades of ground forces in the opening phases of a future conflict. Therefore, much depends on the antiarmor capability of U.S. air forces, so the capability had better be robust.

This leads to the second rationale: while highly effective systems and concepts for finding and destroying moving armor are being fielded—such as JSTARS, the sensor fuzed weapon, the joint standoff weapon, and the Army tactical missile system (ATACMS) Block II—resource constraints have prevented the services, including the Air Force, from investing aggressively in these systems to obtain them in great numbers. Actual inventories of the most capable antiarmor weapons remain very limited, and for the most part, because of their small numbers, such weapons are not forward deployed where they would be most needed.

Finally, highly robust antiarmor capabilities are one important means of offsetting the threat posed by enemy antiaccess capabilities. Enemies seek to keep U.S. expeditionary forces at arm's length in order to create a window of opportunity within which to achieve other goals, such as overrunning adjacent territories. If every U.S. sortie that gets to the theater of a conflict is very effective, it reduces the chance that the enemy's overall campaign plan will succeed.

## Command and Control

A seventh challenge is to improve capabilities to command and control joint air operations. In addition to the threat-driven challenges addressed above, the leadership of the Air Force has recognized the importance of improving its mode of operations in several key dimensions. First among these are command—determining the best strategy of employment for air forces in a joint operation—and control—providing direction to forces. The prospects for substantial improvements in these areas are good. New computer-based computational tools are being developed that can allow commanders leading an operation to examine numerous alternative strategies and their probable outcomes before deciding how to employ available air assets. Computer-based tools are also helping to automate the laborious process of turning the commander's guidance into concrete directions to participating units via the air tasking order.

The Air Force also aspires to improve the execution of air operations against fleeting targets, such as mobile missiles and small groups of enemy combatants. A key element of future concepts for this will be the creation of capabilities for dynamic control of air-to-surface engagements. Specifically, the Air Force is working out how to pass targeting information directly to aircraft that are conducting interdiction attacks in the minutes prior to their engagements. To be most useful, such information should feed digitally into the engagement and bombing systems on board the aircraft. In pursuing these and other improvements, the Air Force recognizes the importance of the human dimension of command and control. Perhaps the single most important lesson the Air Force learned from Operation *Allied Force* in Serbia was that the United States should not rely on ad-hoc "pick-up teams" to man air operations centers. Accordingly, efforts are under way within the Air Force to create standing teams that train together in peacetime to perform all of the essential functions of wartime air operations centers. The success enjoyed by U.S. fighter and bomber aircraft in engaging fleeting targets in Afghanistan shows that substantial progress has been made in dynamic control since Operation *Allied Force*.

## Deployability

A final challenge is to improve the deployability of USAF units. Aircraft that can self-deploy to distant theaters have long been the fastest means of sending reinforcements abroad. However, the Air Force is seeking further improvements in its ability to reinforce theaters rapidly and to sustain operations from deployed locations. First, it is modernizing its fleet of strategic airlift and tanker aircraft; it is replacing its fleet of C–141s, which first entered service in 1965, with C–17s, and it is upgrading its fleet of KC–135 tankers. Second, the Air Force is working to reduce the logistical footprint that its deploying units take with them. Such measures include expanded prepositioning of munitions, ground support equipment, and other items in theaters of potential conflict, and the use of intermediate support bases for maintenance that cannot be performed at main operating bases. The newest generation of USAF combat aircraft is also being designed for improved deployability. Built-in test equipment, on-board oxygen generators, and other features will allow F–22 squadrons, for example, to deploy and sustain operations with far less ground-support equipment than units with current-generation fighters.

## Key Choices

As the Air Force develops new concepts for meeting the sorts of challenges outlined above, it will find itself repeatedly confronting the need to choose among competing approaches. How it decides these issues will do much to shape the Air Force of the future. Among these basic choices are whether to:

- emphasize combat platforms that are theater-based over those that are longer range
- continue to field platforms intended to penetrate contested airspace, or rather to rely much more heavily on standoff operations and weapons, such as cruise missiles
- emphasize airborne platforms, or instead to press much more aggressively to move more operations into space.

### Theater Basing versus Long-Range Operations

Today, the Air Force's mix of combat platforms is weighted heavily toward aircraft that must be based forward in-theater in order to reach their targets efficiently. For every heavy bomber in the Air Force inventory of combat-coded aircraft, there are more than nine fighters.[11] This strikes some observers as contrary to logic. In a world where adversaries are fielding greater numbers of ballistic missiles of longer range and greater accuracy, and where permission to use bases in forward theaters may not always be assured, the advantages of platforms that can strike from long range seem self-evident. Should, therefore, the Air Force invest more heavily in heavy bombers?

The answer is not straightforward. It is true that heavy bombers carry substantial payloads and can attack targets from great range, allowing them to be based beyond the range of the enemy's most numerous attack means. During Operation *Allied Force*, for example, B–2 bombers flew repeated, nonstop round-trip missions between Missouri and Yugoslavia, delivering up to 16 GPS-guided 2,000-pound bombs per sortie. And because political sensitivities precluded the basing of most combat aircraft in countries around Afghanistan, bombers delivered most USAF ordnance during the crucial opening weeks of the conflict there. Long-range strike capabilities such as these could be invaluable in future conflicts should the risks of deploying forces at forward bases within the theater of conflict be judged too great. But is it reasonable to imagine that future adversaries will actually be able to prevent fighter aircraft from operating in their theaters? And if they could, would it be possible to achieve U.S. objectives using longer-range aircraft and other sources of standoff firepower alone?[12]

Without question, assuming that U.S. expeditionary air forces will be able to operate safely from forward bases that lack hardened aircraft shelters and other facilities is increasingly risky. As U.S. adversaries field ballistic and cruise missiles with GPS-like accuracy and conventional submunitions, aircraft parked in the open, as well as tent cities and lightly constructed living quarters and work centers, will become fairly easy targets.[13] Missile defenses will not be a panacea for such threats, since several defensive layers would be required for highly effective defenses, and deploying these defenses can be time-consuming and place heavy demands on scarce strategic airlift capacity. However, extensive hardening of bases undertaken in advance of hostilities appears to be an effective and affordable countermeasure, in conjunction with active defenses and other steps. Only highly accurate missiles can effectively attack hardened facilities. Though it may be possible for ballistic and cruise missiles to crater runways and other operating surfaces, redundancy and rapid repair capabilities, coupled with some modest active defenses, can overcome the effects of such attacks under most circumstances.

Furthermore, whether or how a force made up purely of long-range assets could accomplish all of the tasks assigned to air forces today is unclear.

First, U.S. forces engaged in large-scale conflicts may have to destroy thousands of targets, including large elements of fielded enemy forces. Doing so within a reasonable time span would necessitate a much larger fleet of heavy bombers than the United States now has. Second, even the most stealthy of bombers can, under some circumstances, be vulnerable to interception by fighter aircraft. Therefore, unless the bombers are to employ long-range standoff weapons exclusively (see below), they may need to be escorted or otherwise supported by fighters that can defeat the enemy's fighters. Likewise, the platforms used to observe the enemy and to orchestrate air operations—AWACS, JSTARS, RC–135s, and others—must get fairly close to enemy airspace to function effectively. These aircraft require protection from enemy fighters and long-range SAMs as well. This synergy between high performance fighters and longer-range aircraft is an enduring reality of air operations that should not be overlooked.

Finally, it must be recognized that long-range bombers can also be vulnerable to airbase attacks. The Kosovo example notwithstanding, operations from the United States to Eurasia are extremely inefficient. To make best use of the heavy bombers, they should be forward-based in places such as Guam for operations in East Asia and southern Europe or Diego Garcia for operations in the Middle East. But as enemies acquire longer-range missiles, even these bases will fall within range of their threat, and it has proven impractical thus far to build hardened shelters for fleets of large aircraft such as bombers.

In short, large-scale air operations against capable adversaries should not be reduced to an either/or proposition. The questions to be addressed are: What is the right mix of longer-range and theater-based aircraft? What can be done to prepare potential theaters of operation in advance so as to mitigate threats to the full mix of platforms? Preliminary analysis suggests that fairly straightforward measures, such as hardening airbases in advance, will be satisfactory responses to most emerging threats to regional airbases. Forward-based forces also play invaluable roles in peacetime and crisis, forging links with regional allies and unambiguously signaling U.S. intentions to resist aggression. Even if accomplishing all the warfighting tasks assigned to air forces using long-range aircraft alone were economically and operationally feasible, it is far from clear that one would want a force comprised primarily of such aircraft. That said, heavy bombers with suitable munitions can make unique and valuable contributions to joint operations; they should be modernized and equipped accordingly.

## Penetrating Platforms versus Standoff Weapons

Since the end of the Vietnam War, the Air Force has been stunningly successful in developing manned platforms and operational concepts for defeating enemy air defenses. The F–117 and the B–2 have shown that, with modest support, they can operate over even dense and integrated air defenses that would pose unacceptable risks to nonstealthy aircraft. Specialized aircraft and weapons, such as the F–16CJ with high-speed antiradiation missiles and the EA–6 standoff jammer, have effectively suppressed SAMs in combat over Iraq and Yugoslavia, allowing nonstealthy aircraft to operate over portions of enemy territory with acceptable risks. Concepts of operation that feature penetrating aircraft are attractive because they allow aircrews aboard attack aircraft to get close enough to their targets to observe them, evaluate the situation, and engage the target with fairly inexpensive weapons, such as laser-guided bombs and short-range missiles, such as the television-guided Maverick, that arrive on target within one minute of release.

However, air defense threats are evolving, and systems and concepts that have proven satisfactory in recent conflicts may not produce similar results as more capable air defenses are fielded. The latest generation of Russian-made, radar-guided surface-to-air missiles presents the most serious new challenges to U.S. and allied air operations. These SAM systems, including the SA–10 and SA–20, feature powerful phased-array radars that can be difficult to jam effectively. The missiles associated with these systems can engage aircraft at ranges of 100 kilometers or more. The entire system can be mobile, so that clever operators, by moving frequently between engagements, can complicate their location and targeting. Because of the long reach of these modern SAM systems, F–16CJs and other nonstealthy aircraft cannot safely get close enough to engage them with currently available antiradiation missiles. New concepts will therefore be needed to retain the ability to observe and attack the full range of targets even in territories defended by modern SAM systems.

One option is to rely more on standoff weapons, such as cruise missiles, that can allow manned platforms to engage targets from beyond the range of the most modern SAMs. Whether launched from aircraft, ships, or submarines, cruise missiles are the one way to strike targets with absolute assurance that no aircrews will be killed or captured by the enemy. Thus, they are ideally suited to small-scale strikes, such as the attack on terrorist training camps in Afghanistan in 1998, in which losses of aircrews would be unacceptable. In larger-scale operations, cruise missiles can be used to strike the best-defended targets and to open the way for manned aircraft by destroying key parts of the enemy's air defenses. Of course, cruise missiles are not invulnerable to enemy air defenses. But they can be used in sizable numbers to overwhelm defenses, and they can be made stealthy as well. In any case, the consequences of losing a cruise missile are of far less magnitude than those associated with losing aircrews.

So why not simply abandon the effort to operate manned aircraft inside the range of enemy air defenses? If the Air Force reduced investments in stealthy aircraft, SAM suppression weapons, and jammers, it could apply those resources to building many thousands of cruise missiles and hauling them to their launch points using existing heavy bombers or new and fairly inexpensive aircraft, such as a variant of the Boeing 767. There are, however, several difficulties with this approach. First, cruise missiles with the range required to neutralize the most capable enemy SAMs are expensive. Arguably, this is true partly because we procure them in small numbers. But it is inherently costly—in terms of both dollars and aircraft payload—to put a turbofan engine, one or more guidance systems, and other devices on a weapon that will be used only once. The cost to deliver 1,000 pounds of high explosive to an aimpoint with a cruise missile will probably always be several times greater than the cost of getting it there via gravity. Even fairly small conflicts may call for attacks on many thousands of aimpoints.

One also pays a price for standoff in terms of time. Today's cruise missiles operate at subsonic speeds; the time to target from an aircraft beyond the range of enemy air defenses might be 30 minutes or more. Such timelines often are not compatible with the need to provide fire support to troops in contact with an enemy. Equally significant is the fact that, thus far, concepts have not been devised to permit effective standoff attacks against all types of targets. Small, fleeting targets, such as missile TELs, isolated armored units, artillery pieces, and infantry, pose particularly hard problems for standoff weapons. Unless a person is in the loop to guide the weapon to its desired target, the target can easily move between the time of sensor observation and the arrival of a standoff weapon. Putting a terminal seeker on the cruise missile to locate the target adds to the cost of the weapon without greatly ameliorating the targeting problem because of the susceptibility of robotic sensors and automated target-recognition algorithms to countermeasures and the comparatively limited field of view of some seekers. Concepts that abandon efforts to operate within range of enemy air defenses raise questions about how the shooters are to find their targets. Most of the sensors used today to locate moving targets are on airborne platforms that must either fly into enemy airspace (such as the Predator UAV) or operate within a certain distance of it (for example, JSTARS and the U–2). Without the ability to suppress long-range air defenses, new ways would have to be found to conduct surveillance of enemy activities.

Of course, the man in the loop does not also have to be on the scene of the engagement. In most operations, the shooter—the aircrew—must also acquire and engage the target. But as sensors on dedicated reconnaissance and surveillance platforms proliferate, people on the ground (or even on a ship or in a large aircraft) with access to data from multiple sensors may well have a better picture of the tactical situation than aircrews in shooter aircraft. This will enable aerial vehicles—manned or unmanned—to haul payloads of guided weapons to target areas and deliver them against individual aimpoints as directed by a controller in a remote location.

One intriguing development that could help standoff weapons engage mobile targets effectively is the possibility of flying large numbers of autonomous munitions over the battlefield. If equipped with an appropriate sensor and the ability to sort out and identify potential targets, a munition that can loiter over a target area can compensate for uncertainty in the target's location. The first generation of such large footprint weapons is the brilliant antiarmor munition developed by the Army for its ATACMS II missile. The Air Force also has been exploring a concept for a powered munition that would cover up to 100 miles while searching for any of several possible types of targets.[14] The most daunting technical challenge for such weapons is the need for sensors and automatic target recognition capabilities that are inexpensive yet highly reliable so as to prevent attacks on civilian vehicles and remain robust against potential countermeasures.

One way to capitalize on some of the key advantages of cruise missiles while reducing the costs associated with one-way missions is to field unmanned combat air vehicles (UCAVs). Like the cruise missile, these vehicles take the aircrew out of the aircraft but allow the aircraft to release its weapons close to the target, then return to base, land, and be reused. This is an attractive concept for many reasons, and the Air Force is pursuing it.[15] Among the major challenges is how best to assure the ability of operators to control the aircraft during demanding maneuvers. If UCAVs prove feasible, they may enable air forces to attack even fleeting mobile targets affordably without risking aircrews to loss or capture.

For the near- to mid-term, the right answer for the penetration-versus-standoff question is one of finding the proper mix. The Air Force needs an inventory of munitions characterized by a graduated mix of direct attack and standoff weapons, covering long range (1,000 kilometers or more), medium range (several hundred kilometers), and short range (up to 100 kilometers). Given the state of current technologies relevant to stand-off attack and the rate at which air defenses are evolving, the Air Force today (like the air arms of its sister services) has almost certainly underinvested in stocks of cruise missiles and other standoff weapons. Its fleets of B–1 and B–52 bombers are particularly dependent on standoff missiles if they are to play important roles in the critical early phases of most future conflicts. Adequately supplying just these platforms with cruise missiles for the first two weeks of two major theater wars would require doubling or tripling the currently programmed buys of the long-range conventional air-launched cruise missile and its successors, and of the medium-range joint air-to-surface standoff missile. Operation *Allied Force* and the efforts to enforce no-fly zones over Iraq have shown that stocks of shorter-range standoff missiles, such as the AGM–130 and the joint standoff weapon, are also in chronically short supply. Research and development efforts relating to concepts for standoff attack probably should focus on improving the affordability of expendable missiles (by developing less expensive propulsion systems, production enhancements, and the like), on munitions capable of seeking and identifying targets autonomously, and on the maturation of recoverable unmanned aerial vehicles.

For now, concepts for locating, identifying, and attacking mobile targets from standoff range are far from being mature enough that the Air Force could responsibly stop maintaining its ability to operate manned combat aircraft in defended airspace. The Air Force should continue to field stealthy high-performance aircraft, modernized defense-suppression assets (including a replacement for the EA–6 jamming aircraft), and accurate direct-attack munitions.

### Airborne versus Space-Based Platforms

Some of the operational conundrums mentioned could be resolved by expanding the capabilities of assets that operate in space. For example, satellites could be used as platforms for SAR and MTI radars designed to detect vehicles on the surface of the earth. If this proved practical, a large constellation of satellites could substitute for JSTARS and other airborne platforms that provide this function today, reducing concerns about the need to deploy and sustain these platforms in theater and obviating the threat posed to them by SAMs and interceptors. Advocates of more ambitious military operations in space have also proposed that strike operations could be conducted from platforms in space. An enduring concept from the Reagan administration's Strategic Defense Initiative is the space-based laser, which would intercept missiles during boost phase. Others propose the possibility of striking targets on the surface from space. One approach would place in orbit satellites that carry guided projectiles. When needed, these weapons could be de-orbited and directed at tremendous velocity to a target such as a fixed installation on the earth. Another concept envisages the development of a space plane, manned or unmanned, that would launch from the United States, enter partial orbit, descend into the upper atmosphere at high speed to dispense several guided weapons, and then return to earth. Either concept could permit national leaders to strike targets anywhere with impunity within several hours of a decision to do so.

A major challenge facing all such concepts today is cost, the most daunting being that associated with placing objects in space. Today, it costs roughly $10,000 per pound to boost a payload into low Earth orbit. This means that even a very accurate weapon weighing 500 pounds would cost $5 million, or 5 times as much as the most expensive cruise missiles, just to be placed in orbit. The expense of developing and building the system would have to be included, and given the difficulties associated with surviving reentry, those costs would not be minor. Objects in low Earth orbit also do not stay over one spot on the earth's surface, which poses a problem for sensors whose purpose is to monitor a particular installation or area, track vehicles, or otherwise develop detailed information about a theater of operations. Some types of sensors can be effective from higher geostationary orbits, but pending improvements in several areas of technology, the types of phenomena of greatest interest to military operations will remain best observed from low Earth orbit. This means that moving many military-related surveillance functions to space would demand large and very costly constellations of satellites.[16] Nevertheless, if this move made it possible to monitor and track all of the militarily significant targets in a hostile nation (or in several nations), it might well be worth the investment.

Finally, satellites—especially those in low Earth orbit—can be attacked, either from the Earth or by other satellites. As the United States grows increasingly reliant on space-based assets to support its military operations, adversaries will perceive growing incentives to develop ways of attacking them, extending into space the competition between measure, countermeasure, and counter-countermeasure ad infinitum. For the foreseeable future, then, we should expect satellites mainly to perform a growing share of such key functions as surveillance, positioning, and communications. Someday, weapons delivered from space may prove practical for attacking selected high-value targets in limited numbers. But even with dramatic reductions in launch costs, weapons from space will not substitute for more prosaic means of delivering firepower in large or smaller-scale conflicts.

## Directions for the Future

The Air Force's vision of its future—and, by extension, its approach to modernizing or transforming—envisages an evolutionary path toward new capabilities. Some will involve new product lines or force elements such as information squadrons, and even new physical principles such as the airborne laser, while others will involve reequipping existing force elements with new platforms, munitions, or other systems. This approach seems consistent with the "purposeful and measured" strategy recommended in chapter 3 for transforming U.S. military capabilities. It features a gradual introduction of new concepts, systems, and capabilities, at a pace driven both by a determination to hold onto most of today's force structure and by constraints on new resources for modernization. The Air Force's planned approach to modernization recognizes the potential leverage inherent in more and better information, and so it emphasizes investments in new airborne and space-based sensors, as well as a host of new battle management capabilities. The Air Force plan also emphasizes forces that are highly adaptable. Both the F–22 and the joint strike fighter, for example, will be multimission aircraft.

This middle way seems appropriate for the Air Force for two major reasons. First, contrary to the views of those who regard the current period as one of strategic pause for the United States, the U.S. Armed Forces in general, and the Air Force in particular, have a full menu of strategically important tasks to accomplish. USAF assets form the backbone of the U.S. capability to deter and defeat large-scale aggression and would provide the bulk of the combat capabilities deployed by joint forces in the critical opening phase of most conflicts. These same assets have been called upon repeatedly to impose the will of the United States on recalcitrant leaders in smaller-scale operations in such places as the Balkans, Iraq, and Afghanistan since the end of the Gulf War. The prospect that these and other demands will continue to be levied upon the Air Force militates against a strategy that would divest the service of substantial capabilities in the interests of accelerating the development of a host of new systems and concepts. Second, analysis of future challenges and operational concepts suggests that radical new approaches to conducting air operations are not warranted in the foreseeable future. While much has been made of the problems and risks that future enemies with antiaccess capabilities may pose for land-based air forces, the fact is that a wide range of countermeasures to these threats are available, and many are already programmed. Some adjustments to current resource allocation plans might well enhance the robustness of future forces in the face of antiaccess challenges. But for the most part, fairly straightforward improvements to the force—purchasing more standoff weapons or better gear for countering chemical weapons—or to theater infrastructures, such as hardening facilities at more airbases, probably offer more leverage than wholesale changes in force structure and operational concepts.

None of this should be taken to mean that complacency is appropriate. The U.S. strategy for advancing its interests in the world is ambitious and will continue to place great demands on the Nation's military forces. Continued and, indeed, accelerated modernization of the Air Force is essential, focused on the challenges outlined in this chapter. As individual programs and initiatives are implemented, the broad outlines of the Air Force of the 21st century will emerge. The most likely trends over the coming two decades can be foreseen now. First, combat aircraft that lack sharply reduced signatures (stealth) will begin to disappear from the inventory, at least from that portion of the inventory intended to operate in or near airspace controlled by the enemy. Second, sensors will increasingly be borne by satellites and UAVs rather than manned aircraft. Satellites are especially attractive as platforms for sensors, such as radars, that emit signals, because it is difficult to hide these from enemy sensors. Stealthy, long-enduring UAVs may be best suited to carrying passive sensors, such as visual and infrared cameras. Survivability might also be achieved by proliferating sensors on large numbers of very small and inexpensive expendable UAVs.

Third, high-performance fighter aircraft will continue to play essential roles in air combat operations, but their roles will focus increasingly on enabling attacks by other means. Fighters operating from hardened forward bases will be responsible for defeating enemy air attacks and air defenses and for "blinding" the enemy by destroying airborne and possible space-based sensor platforms. Fourth, heavy bombers, based at some remove from the theater of conflict, will carry a growing share of the strike role. When confronting enemy forces that are reasonably well equipped and trained, U.S. forces will increasingly rely on long-range standoff weapons to attack most fixed targets; guided direct-attack and shorter-range standoff munitions will continue to bear the burden against fielded forces and other mobile targets. Fifth, aircraft equipped with high-powered electronic jammers will operate from distant bases and loiter outside the range of enemy SAMs. Finally, command and control and supporting analytical and staff functions will be provided by personnel located both within and outside of the theater, working from distributed "virtual facilities" connected by broadband secure communications.

Of course, realizing these trends will take time, talent, and money, three factors essential to any transformation. If the requisite resources are not forthcoming to pursue concepts relevant to the full range of challenges looming in the future, innumerable painful trades will be necessary, inevitably delaying the availability of some important capabilities and threatening the long-term health of the institution. How might the Air Force adapt to prolonged and severe budget shortfalls? The institution's strong inclination will be to make future warfighting capability its top priority. Today, this means primarily modernizing fighter platforms, at least in terms of budgetary demands. With F–15s approaching 30 years of age, investments in new fighters cannot be further postponed. The threat posed by today's air defenses is reason enough to buy stealthy aircraft. When one considers that the next generation of fighters, like this one, will be in the inventory for many decades, it makes no sense to buy nonstealthy ones.

Without sizable and sustained increases in budget authority, however, the Air Force will have to maintain dangerously low levels of spending on a range of readiness accounts in order to free the funds needed to begin modernizing its fighter forces and other critical capabilities. It will also have to stretch out or forego investments in a number of promising areas, such as advanced airborne and space-based sensors, standoff and guided munitions, upgrades to avionics and data links, and airborne jammers that, individually and collectively, could greatly increase operational capabilities. Even at that, the rate of procurement of new fighter aircraft will lag far behind the 200 aircraft or so per year needed to begin reducing the average age of the current fleet.

There was a time when the Air Force showed a willingness to sacrifice force structure if required to finance essential modernization. However, that was before the peacetime operations tempo of much of the Air

Force was kept close to its sustainable maximum in the 1990s.[17] With the prospect of continued high demand for deployments of USAF combat and support units abroad in peacetime, cutting personnel from deployable units or eliminating entire units could place unacceptable burdens on those that remain, with consequent losses of trained personnel.

Treatises on "transformation," extensive operations research and analysis, and related musings by defense intellectuals sometimes can obscure rather than illuminate the art and science of conducting and preparing for military operations. The heart of the matter is not very complicated. What commanders want most is the ability to strike enemy forces and infrastructure where they want and when they want, without allowing the enemy to strike their forces or their nation in return. Dominant air forces today offer a means for doing just that under many circumstances. Modern military aircraft, in conjunction with support from space-based assets, can deploy rapidly over long distances, protect rear areas against air attacks, provide the primary means for observing enemy activities, and conduct precise and effective attacks against a wide range of assets valued by enemy leaders and commanders, all while minimizing the exposure of friendly personnel to enemy fires.

For these reasons, the viability of future U.S. strategy for power projection will remain closely tied to the ability of the Air Force, and the air arms of other services, to innovate. The degree to which the Air Force is able to field new capabilities appropriate to emerging threats will have more to do with the overall level of resources available to it than with developments in any particular areas of technology. The basic elements of new operational concepts relevant to many of the needs of future commanders are already in place or are close to being demonstrated. What is needed is a commitment to sustained investments in the hardware, people, training, and support assets needed to make these new capabilities a reality. Absent such resources, some stark choices will be unavoidable, and the Nation may find itself short of critically important capabilities in future conflicts.

## Notes

[1] Of course, there are limits in the extent to which superior quality can offset numerical inferiority. Lanchester suggests that under many circumstances, the capability of a force can be expressed by the equation $B^2b$, where B is the number of weapons or units available and b is an expression of their quality relative to an opponent's forces. Because the variable for quantity is squared, a force that is outnumbered 2 to 1 must have 4 times the quality of its opponent in order to be equal in capability. A force outnumbered 4 to 1 must be 16 times better in quality. This "Lanchester square equation" is a formal statement of what most commanders know instinctively, namely, that "quantity has a quality all its own."

[2] The pilots of the two U.S. aircraft that were shot down over Yugoslavia were rescued by U.S. combat search and rescue operations. Thus, the fatality/capture rate was zero.

[3] Air attacks on infrastructure targets can sometimes prompt a temporary rise in support for enemy leaders as people "rally round the flag," but air attacks that are sustained, intense, accurate, and one-sided can be devastatingly effective in reducing enemy morale. See Stephen T. Hosmer, *Psychological Effects of U.S. Air Operations in Four Wars, 1946–1991*, MR–576–AF (Santa Monica, CA: RAND, 1996).

[4] These levels of effectiveness apply to interdiction of armored units that are moving but not in contact with other ground forces. When friendly and enemy ground forces are in close proximity, concerns about fratricide constrain weapons, tactics, and rules of engagement in ways that can reduce the effectiveness of air attacks.

[5] To have 90 percent confidence of dropping a bridge span took, in 1944, 240 tons of bombs (B–17 with unguided bombs); in 1965, 200 tons (F4–D with unguided bombs); in 1972, 12.5 tons (F4–D with precision guided munitions [PGMs]); and in 1990, just 4 tons of PGMs (F–117). See Benjamin S. Lambeth, *The Transformation of American Airpower* (Ithaca, NY: Cornell University Press, 2000),160; and C.R. Anderegg, *Sierra Hotel: Flying Air Force Fighters in the Decade after Vietnam* (Washington, DC: U.S. Air Force, 2001),122–124.

[6] For example, an estimated 40 percent of the Iraqi soldiers in the Kuwait theater of operations deserted prior to the coalition's ground attack in late February 1991. Many of those who remained offered only token resistance once the ground invasion began, as evinced by the surrender of more than 85,000 additional Iraqi officers and enlisted men during the 100-hour ground operation. Less than 20 percent of Iraqi tanks and 10 percent of their armored personnel carriers showed evidence of attempts to resist during the ground attack. See Hosmer, 152–170.

[7] For an analysis of the factors bearing on the outcome of Operation *Allied Force*, see Stephen T. Hosmer, *Why Milosevic Decided to Settle When He Did*, MR–1351–AF (Santa Monica, CA: RAND, 2001). See also Benjamin S. Lambeth, *NATO's Air War for Kosovo: A Strategic and Operational Assessment* (Santa Monica, CA: RAND, forthcoming).

[8] Centered on a set of instrumental ranges outside of Nellis Air Force Base, Nevada, Red Flag exposes aircrews to a realistic simulated combat environment. Units are required to conduct air defense, sweep, defense suppression, interdiction, strategic attack, and other combat missions in the presence of air-to-air and surface-to-air defenses much like those they would encounter in a conflict involving a capable regional adversary. All missions are "scored" and critiqued daily.

[9] See *America's Air Force, Vision 2020*, U.S. Air Force (undated), available at <www.af.mil/vision>.

[10] Beyond addressing the ballistic missile threat, the airborne laser will provide an operational testbed for other potential applications of directed energy, perhaps to include defense against surface-to-air missiles, air-to-air missiles, and other aircraft. It might even prove useful in the antisatellite role.

[11] Combat-coded aircraft are those in operational fighter or bomber units. These do not include aircraft in training units or in long-term maintenance status.

[12] The terms *long range* and *short range* are, of course, relative. With help from the large USAF fleet of aerial refueling aircraft, fighter aircraft can operate routinely from bases 1,000 miles or more from their targets, as was demonstrated by the F–117 in Operation *Desert Storm* and the F–15E in Operation *Allied Force*.

[13] See John Stillion and David T. Orletsky, *Airbase Vulnerability to Conventional Cruise-Missile and Ballistic-Missile Attacks* (Santa Monica, CA: RAND, 1999).

[14] This project is called the low-cost autonomous attack system.

[15] Some Predator UAVs have been modified to carry and deliver Hellfire guided missiles. The Predator/Hellfire combination has been reportedly used successfully in Afghanistan.

[16] For example, it has been estimated that a constellation of SAR/MTI satellites capable of reliably tracking individual vehicles would have to consist of between 40 and 100 satellites, at $300 million to $500 million per satellite (including launch costs).

[17] For an assessment of the implications of ongoing deployments for USAF operations tempo and individual personnel, and the effects of potential force structure reductions on both, see David E. Thaler and Daniel M. Norton, *Air Force Operations Overseas in Peacetime: Optempo and Force Structure Implications*, DB–237–AF (Santa Monica, CA: RAND, 1998).

# Part III

# Coordinating Transformed Military Operations

**Chapter 7**

# Integrating Transformation Programs

Paul K. Davis

T his chapter describes an approach to transforming the Armed Forces that attempts to bridge the gap between high-level expressions of policy and the management of transformation through programs and other initiatives. I do not discuss specific activities because those are reviewed elsewhere in this volume. Instead, the focus is on principles for transformation that take into account the progress already made, the new Quadrennial Defense Review (QDR), and the events of September 11.[1] The principles are based on historical transformations in military affairs and the business world and draw from my own earlier work. The structure of the chapter is as follows. First, I describe a two-era framework for discussing transformation. I then review lessons from past transformations, suggest principles, and ask related questions about current challenges. Next, I suggest a strategy for managing transformation that is motivated by these principles. The suggestions may prove useful in assessing and integrating transformation plans as they develop.

## A Model and Terminology for Thinking about Transformation

It is helpful to distinguish between two roughly defined eras when discussing transformation. As shown in figure 7–1, Era A is the near- to mid-term and Era B is the longer term. Somewhat arbitrarily, the figure suggests a 30-year transition from about 1995 (just before concerns about "asymmetric strategies" began to emerge) to 2025. As indicated by shading, the seriousness of various "new dangers" will continue to increase throughout the 30 years. They are already with us, but they will grow substantially.

*Author's Note:* This paper draws on Paul K. Davis, "Analytic Architecture for Capabilities-Based Planning, Mission-System Analysis, and Transformation" (MR–1513–OSD) (Santa Monica, CA: RAND, forthcoming) and unpublished work on transformation developed under the RAND program of Internal Research and Development.

Figure 7–1. **Planning Eras and the Buildup of New Dangers**

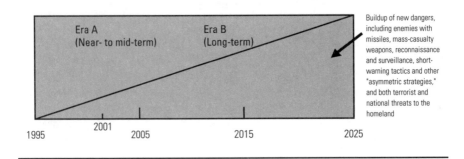

Preparing for them will require more than incremental modernization; it will indeed require transformation.[2]

Distinguishing between the two eras is useful because they require different instruments of control, as indicated in table 7–1. By and large, an Era A (near- to mid-term) transformation can be guided by a relatively well defined concept of where one is going, why, and how. It can be "managed," with clear assignment of responsibilities, authorities, and timelines. In contrast, tight management for Era B transformation would be counterproductive. What is needed is more diffuse and tentative, with exploratory experiments, rather than rigorous tests of the sort found in development programs.

Table 7–1 also makes the point that mainstream organizations within the services should play *primary* roles in Era A, whereas we might expect the same organizations to short-change or be actively hostile to many of the activities being explored for Era B. This is organizationally natural.

Although the Era A/Era B distinction is useful, it is only an approximation. For one thing, there is no end point. Figure 7–1 might apply equally well in the future if we merely slide the time scale to the right. Further, Eras A and B are connected in that success in Era B depends on laying the groundwork in Era A.

Because the term *transformation* makes no distinctions between eras, table 7–1 also introduces some additional terms. Era A transformation can reasonably be regarded as *pragmatic reengineering*, which can be defined as the fundamental rethinking and redesign of an organization's building block units and processes to achieve dramatic improvements in the ability to accomplish the organization's missions, including new ones. A distinguishing feature is that it is accomplished through relatively "managed"

## Table 7–1. Differences between Planning for Era A and Era B

| Planning for Era A and the Start of Era B | Planning for the Long Term in Era B |
|---|---|
| **Though surprises are likely, *pragmatic reengineering* is possible:** | **The nature of long-term changes is such that *exploratory experiments* are necessary:** |
| ■ Outcomes and outputs can be reasonably visualized<br>■ Operational challenges can be posed and decomposed<br>■ Responsibilities can be assigned and success assessed<br>■ Valuable mid-term measures can set the stage for the longer term<br>■ Mainstream organizations can and should make them work | ■ Fresh, out-of-the-box thinking is essential<br>■ Much "discovery" is needed<br>■ Outcomes are at best dimly understood<br>■ Highly structured management is counter-productive<br>■ Major surprises and changes of technology and concept are likely<br>■ Mainstream organizations are likely to actively oppose the changes |
| **Pragmatic reengineering may be:** | **Work now on Era-B transformation should include:** |
| ■ either highly designed (system-engineering character) or accomplished with iterative experimentation, operational analysis, and spiral development<br>■ comprehensive or focused on a small subset of the total force (with expansion possible if warranted) | ■ Relatively wide open research and development<br>■ Some rather well defined long-lead-time development<br>■ Some early "spiral prototyping," perhaps in rapid-exploration laboratories with forces set aside for experimentation |

*Source:* Table adapted from Paul K. Davis, "Transforming U.S. Forces," in Frank Carlucci, Robert Hunter, and Zalmay Khalilzad, eds., *Taking Charge: A Bipartisan Report to the President Elect on Foreign Policy and National Security* (Santa Monica, CA: RAND, 2001).

processes undertaken with a relatively strong sense of what is needed and how to get there, and on a relatively fast time scale. This definition does not require reengineering to be massively disruptive.

Pragmatic reengineering highlights the concept of building blocks (modular design) because a major goal is that future forces will be flexible, adaptive, and robust in the world in which they must operate. This implies a building-block approach to operations. Success then depends on the suitability of the building blocks and the organization's prowess in quickly assembling and controlling their integrated application to missions.

Usual discussions of reengineering tend to emphasize studies, detailed design, and testing. Indeed, reengineering often has a system engineering aspect. However, it may also occur in a very different way: more as the result

Figure 7–2. **A Spectrum of Approaches to Reengineering**

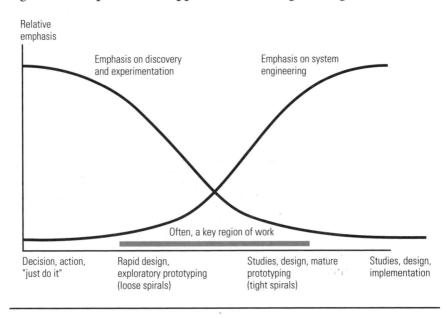

Relative emphasis

Emphasis on discovery and experimentation

Emphasis on system engineering

Often, a key region of work

| Decision, action, "just do it" | Rapid design, exploratory prototyping (loose spirals) | Studies, design, mature prototyping (tight spirals) | Studies, design, implementation |

of experimentation and iteration than of precise design. This is significant because organizations should be conscious of alternatives. Figure 7–2 characterizes the spectrum of possibilities schematically (along the x-axis). The two curves illustrate alternative approaches of mixed character.

Many reengineering efforts have been the result of determined individuals and teams who decide to "just do it" (emphasis on the left side of figure 7–2), which includes recognizing fundamental problems, identifying principles, having general notions of how to proceed, and proceeding without niceties such as studies. Sometimes such an approach is effective, in part because it harnesses the enthusiasm of problemsolving operators and in part because, as a matter of course, errors are discovered and changes of direction made without much agonizing. This avoids the pitfalls of studies, which can take on a life of their own and drag the process of change out interminably, resulting in too little, too late. U.S. business schools encourage the aggressive just-do-it approach, which is often said to be part of what the world sees as American pragmatism. By and large, this is also the approach of impatient and effective military leaders. Often, such just-do-it folks welcome new technology but see engineering as mere technician work to be done by industry.

Unfortunately, the just-do-it approach can sometimes be disastrous. If the needed reengineering involves large, complex systems that are to operate quickly together, the approach should have a strong system-engineering flavor. When major banks, for example, have muddled system engineering, their transitions to electronic operations have failed, and they have lost billions. One might expect the same need for high-quality system engineering when attempting to develop a capability for joint military operations comparable to *Desert Storm* or Panama in effectiveness that could be brought to bear within days, rather than months. Further, one would expect system engineering to be crucial in development of systems of systems.[3] In such cases, it is crucial to have top-notch system architects at the core of decisionmaking. Admiral Hyman G. Rickover's nuclear submarine program comes to mind.

The two curves in figure 7–2 represent two broadly different approaches, but neither is extreme. As indicated by the shaded region, it is usually wise to include thinking and serious initial design even in just-do-it work and rapid prototyping; "rapid" need not mean "mindless." Similarly, even work characterized by meticulous studies and design should plan for mature prototyping (prototypes expected to be almost right) and iteration. The result in either case can be called spiral development, but the first involves a more explorational spiraling, whereas the second starts with a mature design and then refines it iteratively.[4]

Fortunately, the United States is good at both approaches. We may be known for American pragmatism, but we also boast the world's finest capabilities for designing and implementing large and complex systems. The question for the Department of Defense (DOD) is which style should apply to specific aspects of transformation.

Having defined a framework for discussing transformation, let me turn to lessons about past transformations. These tend to corroborate and add to suggestions for transformation that have been made over the last several years.[5] They are drawn from a set of unpublished RAND papers developed as background in recent projects for U.S. Joint Forces Command (U.S. JFCOM) and the Office of the Secretary of Defense.[6]

## Learning from Business Experience

In a recent manuscript, Paul Bracken reviews lessons learned in the last decade about the connections between information technology and reengineering in the business world.[7] Instead of repeating the claims made a decade ago in the heyday of reengineering and transformation, which was then associated with radical restructuring, Bracken begins by noting that many efforts undertaken according to those faddish concepts have failed. He then discusses current business-theory understanding of how to view reengineering and how to accomplish it through deft exploitation of information technology (IT). Bracken's analysis supports the view that DOD should see the reengineering component of transformation more as a vigorous and interactive evolution than as an epochal revolution. Bracken's discussion in no way encourages incrementalism, but the most effective strategy for bringing about major changes appears to be one in which technology and operational concepts associated with information technology are disseminated and nurtured, and in which challenges are established to which organizations respond in ways that they themselves discover, rather than having solutions imposed from a central office at the top. This lesson should ring true to military officers who believe in distributed problemsolving.[8]

Bracken also provides a framework within which to recognize that, in addressing challenges of information and uncertainty, organizations attempting to apply IT solutions have alternatives of which they may be unaware.[9] One approach seeks to reduce the requirement for information by providing enough resources so that the organization has slack with which to deal with uncertainty or by creation of self-contained tasks that require little information from outside the unit conducting the task. The other approach focuses on improving the organization's ability to process ever-increasing quantities of information. It may emphasize vertical integration, horizontal integration, or a combination of the two. Organizations need to be conscious of the choices and tradeoffs, lest they chase expensive fads.

One example of this problem is the common tendency in discussions of command and control to focus unduly on technology issues, such as bandwidth, rather than development of the "commander concepts" that are often critical in wars.[10]

## Learning from Military Experience

Brett Steele has offered a fresh look at some of the military reengineerings attempted during the interwar period, drawing on experiences in Italy, France, Germany, Britain, the Soviet Union, Japan, and the United States.[11] Even familiar episodes, such as the development of German blitzkrieg, offer new insights when viewed through the lens of reengineering. Steele describes cases in which nations adopted new technology but did not really reengineer; nations adopted new technology and reengineered, but bet on the wrong vision; and nations reengineered successfully. Some of his examples represented attempts at planned transformation using within-reach technology, whereas others reveal a mix of the carefully planned approach and the experiment-driven emergent-discovery approach.[12]

A point that emerges from Steele's review was that the French, who are typically characterized as developing a simple-minded Maginot Line, had in fact studied the lessons from World War I intensively and approached their military planning with diligence and prowess. They accomplished a reengineering, but they got things wrong. The Maginot Line was fine, so far as it went, but the French concluded that the offense would, in the future, be accomplished "deliberately," with firepower amassed for incremental advances. There was no concept of fast large-scale maneuver, which had seemed to them discredited by World War I. As for defense, they recognized that they had an exposed flank that the Maginot Line could not cover, but they were dilatory in developing maneuver forces to provide that coverage. More generally, the French focus on the Maginot Line exhausted much of the available attention, energy, and funding.

The British, during the interwar period, were world leaders in studying and experimenting with tank warfare. Their work was enormously influential. However, much of this came to naught for Britain itself because traditional army thinking prevailed and limited the work's impact. Indeed, the top leaders of the British military establishment actively suppressed dissent once they had tilted toward the view that tanks were merely support for infantry. Despite their groundbreaking experiments, the British were ill-prepared for the kind of armored warfare that World War II entailed.

The United States was also woefully unprepared for World War II in many respects; along with most nations, it misunderstood the role of armored units. However, it learned, adapted, and could point to many developments by the end of the war. The Department of the Navy, for example, had not planned to have aircraft carrier battlegroups emerge supreme, but it had laid the groundwork, and it was wise enough—after Pearl Harbor—to recognize that the carriers that had been seen officially as support forces were now the appropriate core. The Marine Corps also had something of which to be proud. It had developed and honed the concepts and capabilities for amphibious landing operations long before they were needed.

Conventional wisdom holds that the Germans got things right, notably blitzkrieg and the use of tanks. Ironically, one can argue that the Germans got things precisely *wrong*; they focused all of their planning around what were intended to be rapid and decisive operations but did not prepare for what eventually transpired—a long, hard war of attrition won by dint of numbers, industrial production, and broad, deliberate offensives. Germany's loss, then, was not merely a matter of bad luck and overextension, but of profound strategic error. In contrast, the Soviet Union—despite suffering an initial catastrophe—was prepared conceptually and doctrinally to mobilize for and fight a long war. It mobilized and supported a huge army, which it then employed with great strategic and operational-level skill to doom Hitler's ambitions. The success of Soviet reengineering was made possible by the work of Marshal Mikhail Tukhachevsky, before Stalin executed him in one of his many paranoid rages.

One lesson to draw from these and other examples should probably be one of humility: serious nations working diligently and in ways that they regarded as scientific made profound mistakes during the interwar period. Is the United States so much smarter today? Or will we focus our transformation efforts on a vision of war that satisfies American predilections but proves wrong?

Other lessons from successful military transformations have been drawn by Richard Hundley, who focuses on processes that I associate with longer-term (Era B) work.[13] For this longer term, everything is even more uncertain than over the near term. Indeed, some of the integrated technologies that will be important in 20 years do not yet exist, much less the concepts for how to use them militarily. The premium, then, is on discovery-oriented research and development influenced by military professionals. Drawing on the experience of the Navy during the 1920s and 1930s, Hundley suggests an approach to joint transformation that would partner U.S. JFCOM with the Defense Advanced Research Projects Agency and centers of expertise. Such a partnership could serve as a halfway house in which technology developments are drawn upon by military innovators who have new operational concepts but need experiments and prototypes. This would not be about big-event demonstration-type experimentation, but rather a period of continuous discovery and of trying ideas out. Rough analogues might be the famous Skunk Works that produced the U–2, SR–71 Blackbird, and stealth aircraft.[14] However, some of the most important future developments are likely to involve not platforms but instead networked command and control and systems of systems.

## Principles for Transformation

From these historical lessons and the earlier work cited above, it is possible to sketch a theory of how transformation should be pursued—or, at least, to identify 10 important principles in 5 groups relating to technology, strategy, military art and science, the political front, and a strategy for management.

### Keeping Up with Technology

1. *Exploit fully the fruits of technological development.* With weak enemies, this is a matter of opportunity; with more capable competition, it is a necessity.

2. *When attempting to exploit information technology, pay close attention to the variety of strategies available.* Some strategies involve reducing dependence on information, while some focus on improving information flow by emphasizing vertical integration, horizontal integration, or both.

### Strategic Foresight

3. *Strategic anticipation is crucial.* One needs a broadly correct vision of the future of warfare; even better is to have a multifaceted vision that does not bet unduly on a particular type of war.

### Military Art and Science

4. *Get the new theory right.* It is important to understand the issues, systems, and phenomena correctly—not only in special cases but also more generally.[15] Consistent with that, the issues must be pursued deeply with a combination of rigorous experimentation and theory and with continuing debate rather than rigid adherence to particular concepts.[16]

### The Political Front

5. *Obtain sustained economic and political support.* The latter is at least as important as the former.

### Strategy for Management

6. *Pursue organizational and operational concepts that are consistent with deeply rooted cultural characteristics, or else take extraordinary efforts to overcome them.* An example of the first was the mission-order emphasis within the German officer corps; an example of the second was the U.S.

Navy creation of a special branch to develop nuclear submarines and associated doctrine.

7. *Organize requirements around outputs (that is, capability to accomplish important military operations), rather than inputs or open-ended functions, such as "strengthening logistics" or "improving communications."* As part of this, plan forces for flexibility, adaptiveness, and robustness; this requires new capabilities-based frameworks for analysis and metrics.[17]

8. *When all is said and done, get the new building blocks right.* Ultimately, an organization's building blocks are what dictate flexibility.

9. *Guide even some aspects of long-term development with concrete military challenges and an operational context.* This principle is discussed in detail below.

10. Despite efforts to get things right, *plan and lay the groundwork for later adaptations.* Even the best-laid programs and best-conceived capabilities will turn out to be not quite what is needed. Changes will be necessary. This occurred, for example, in the early days of what came to be carrier aviation and amphibious operations.

Many organizations have reengineered themselves successfully without meeting all of these criteria, but near-twins have failed through what might reasonably be seen as the roll of the dice. If DOD is more risk-averse than the world of business entrepreneurs, it might do well to consider these 10 principles as *necessary* conditions.

## Applying the Principles in the Current Era

The 10 principles suggest issues and questions for today, some of which are summarized in table 7–2. For brevity, I comment here on just some of the principles, starting with principle 3.

### Strategic Anticipation (Principle 3)

The U.S. military has chosen a concept-driven approach to transformation.[18] Doing so has many advantages. This choice has a potential shortcoming, however: attention and enthusiasm may be so focused on one or a few concepts that the foundation is not laid for eventual needed capabilities. The issues here relate both to concepts of future war and concepts of operations in those future wars. Reinforcing the point is the fact that we can see *multiple* trends. Consider that:

- Some adversaries in major theater wars will be able to use even second- or third-rate versions of modern technology effectively against current U.S. operations; examples include mines that are difficult to

Table 7–2. **Illustrative Questions and Concerns Raised by the List of Principles**

| Principle | Issues and Comments |
| --- | --- |
| 1. Commit to exploiting technological opportunity | Are the commitments currently there for initiatives such as network-centric warfare, *and* will they be sustained? |
| 2. Choose the right strategy for applying information technology | Is the enthusiasm for information superiority and related technology leading to information glut? Should planning also focus on *reducing* information needs? |
| 3. Strategic anticipation: plan for the right war(s) | Has transformation planning focused unduly on a particular class of war and class of operation? |
| 4. Understand the phenomenology of relevant wars | Are the experiment programs of U.S. JFCOM and the services designed to create a definitive knowledge base? |
| 5. Build the base for sustained political and economic support | Are influential service leaders buying in? Is Congress being informed and persuaded? |
| 6. Choose approaches that fit with existing organizational cultures *or* take extraordinary measures to overcome resistance | What changes need to be made to fix problems in item 4, which reflect the antipathy in much of U.S. military culture to the "science" part of "art and science"? |
| 7. For near- to mid-term initiatives, focus on *outputs*, notably capabilities to accomplish key operational missions in conflict | How does this relate to Quadrennial Defense Review operational goals for and pillars of transformation? |
| 8. Get the new mix of building blocks right | What changes in guidance and process are necessary for these matters to be discussed cogently in DOD Program, Planning, and Budgeting System? In this context, how do the global grid and other aspects of command and control fit in? |
| 9. For the longer term, develop special mechanisms to connect the worlds of military operators, technologists, and analysts | How does this relate to other initiatives undertaken over the years to speed up the research and development process? What, more specifically, would be useful now? |
| 10. Plan and lay groundwork for adaptations later | Can laying the groundwork for strategic adaptation and iteration of capabilities be an explicit part of defense planning? |

detect and precision-area weapons that would preclude prolonged massing within enemy range.

■ Other "modern wars" will be characterized by the special dangers and omnipresent constraints encountered in Kosovo.[19]

■ Some terrorist operations will involve enemies willing to commit suicide and to cause massive civilian casualties.

■ China is inexorably rising as a major regional power and will have at least some interests that conflict with those of the United States, most notably regarding Taiwan, but also broader issues of regional influence.

■ The U.S. homeland is now a target rather than a sanctuary.

This is not a complete list. Other entries, for example, might express concerns about drug wars and other causes of instability in the Western hemisphere, or about space becoming a theater of conflict.

It follows that many types of military operations will be important in the future, but the capabilities to accomplish them may not come along naturally if the military is overfocusing on a particular notion of war or particular operational concepts. Capabilities that might not come along without DOD intervention include those for the types of rapidly planned and executed dispersed, parallel, and quintessentially joint operations discussed in the *Joint Vision* documents.[20] They also include prompt anti-terrorist operations going beyond precision strikes and special operations forces. The prospect of inserting sizable ground forces deep into other countries without a good logistical base is always sobering, but that might happen in pursuing terrorists or in a war with Iraq. Even more unnatural but important to consider in the face of historical experience are capabilities such as those for fighting our way back onto the Arabian Peninsula or Korea after an initial debacle. Such possibilities have seldom been highlighted in the service or U.S. JFCOM experiment programs, nor even in strategy studies with a futures component.[21] Fortunately, the philosophy of capabilities-based planning, which is emphasized in QDR 2001, is consistent with broadening the scope of work.[22] I return to this in the last section.

## Military Art and Science (Principle 4)

Although there are many examples of fine military programs seeking to understand definitively one or another subject, there is no broad and systematic DOD effort to develop a definitive understanding of future warfare phenomenology as called for in principle 4, much less to develop the relevant theory and represent it intelligibly in models.[23] This has not always been so severe a problem.[24]

The causes of difficulty here are multiple. First, it is easier and arguably more natural to do experiments that are "merely illustrative" than to do something more comprehensive. Second, the U.S. military culture tends not to value definitive knowledge as much as it might. Indeed, "theory" often has the connotation of "unreal." Further, military models and simulations—which are a major de facto knowledge base—typically have the character of bottom-up procedural computer programs. They are not known for reflecting sound theories, clarifying issues, or facilitating adaptiveness in planning. Yet another cause appears to be a shortage at high levels of training in "system thinking," including the system engineering discussed earlier.[25] Finally, the experiment programs that are commissioned tend (some would say inexorably) to become "can't-fail" demonstration programs.

## Strategy for Management (Principles 6–10)

Principle 6 calls for either a match between initiatives and organizational culture or else extraordinary measures to overcome resistance. When the Navy created nuclear-powered ballistic missile submarines, doing so required creating a new culture. This would probably not have happened without DOD insistence, but—once given the assignment—the Navy proceeded with imagination and determination under the legendary Admiral Rickover. Many other examples can be found. The principle has special significance today when the Secretary of Defense wants to pursue capabilities-based planning but is saddled with organizations and processes that have evolved in ways antithetical to that style. Serious cultural changes are necessary.

I make relatively detailed recommendations about principle 7 (organize requirements around outputs) and principle 8 (get the building blocks right) in the next section, but the main issue is how to create an analytical architecture that assures good options are generated and that a rational process of analysis and comparison assists choice under massive uncertainty and economic constraints. If this sounds like capabilities-based planning, it is.

Principle 9 deals with the long-term component of transformation. Here the first question one might ask is, "What is broken?" Many observers believe that the DOD research and development (R&D) process has come to have several problems. First, the constant pressure to reduce costs has diminished the number of new ideas that are taken far enough to really taste and feel the possibilities. This sometimes requires at least prototypes, rather than rough conceptual studies. Second, it is notoriously difficult to move ideas from the early phases of research into development and notoriously difficult to move even very promising concepts through the entire acquisition system. One reason cited over the years is the lack of sufficient operator involvement. After all, it is the warfighters who ultimately head their military services and determine what developments go forward. Unless their imaginations have been captured, potentially good ideas can wither on the vine. Some examples of systems that have taken too long to acquire are laser-guided weapons, unmanned aerial vehicles, and aerial surveillance platforms with moving-target radar capability.

Planning for strategic adaptation (principle 10) sounds like a cliché, but it can be made concrete if DOD adjusts its planning framework and processes to make such matters explicit. The planning process often appears to embrace the myth that decisions are good forever. Much is made, for example, about a decision to buy a certain number of new aircraft, even though history tells us that the ultimate buy will likely be smaller or larger, depending on how the world develops. Making explicit the potential for such adaptations might improve the quality of programs by avoiding inappropriate optimizations based on faulty assumptions. More important strategically is the value of creating hedges against possible international developments. Most such developments, even those that appear at the time as shocks, can be anticipated. Their probability cannot usefully be estimated, but their nature can be.[26]

## Moving from Principles to Recommendations

Given this background, how might we move from principles to action? I next describe an approach that is intended to connect DOD planning efforts with the concepts and constructs of operations planning. As noted earlier, the focus should be on outputs. The ultimate outputs of capabilities-based planning are the capabilities of the U.S. Armed Forces to conduct important military operations: campaigns and their components as directed by a commander in chief (CINC) or Joint Task Force commander. Ultimately, it does not count for much that the United States has superb military space systems if it cannot use its projection forces effectively. Nor will it count for much that the United States has invested massively in information technology if the projection forces cannot conduct the important missions assigned to them. This is the difference between an input view and an output view. By focusing on output in the form of ability to conduct key operations (for example, to intervene to stop ethnic cleansing and preclude invasion), we automatically see issues as *system problems*. Functional capabilities, such as those for logistics and command, control, communications, computers, intelligence, surveillance, and reconnaissance, all appear as subordinate requirements because the mission cannot be accomplished without them.

### Operational Challenges

A key element of the approach is to identify an appropriate set of operational challenges for DOD to use as a focus. These operational challenges should:[27]

- correspond to military missions at the operational level of warfare, which is where national objectives and broad military strategy must be translated into war plans.
- be limited to particularly important future operations, the capability for which will not arise without DOD intervention.[28]
- as a set, cover all of the most important challenges of this type. As a corollary, they should neither be, nor be perceived to be, tilted toward a particular service.
- encompass and highlight the goals for and pillars of transformation identified in the most recent QDR.
- be such that developing the requisite capabilities will inevitably cause the innovative use of technology, new concepts of operation, and new organizational forms that are "in the right direction" for the transformation desired. Consistent with this, they should encompass and highlight the specific operational goals identified in QDR 2001.

The last item may seem strange. It assumes that a high-level concept of the "right direction" precedes the problemsolving to develop specific capabilities. This is in fact precisely what I mean. There are times in history when top leaders of an organization know what direction is appropriate—based on a combination of trends and possibilities—even though not everyone is yet convinced. Leadership then includes shoving the organization in the right direction. Of course, if the leaders are wrong, that will be a problem. Nonetheless, this is often an essential element of strategic leadership. To put the matters differently, the operational challenges should be chosen so as to force change along particular vectors.

A final consideration is that the operational challenges should be manifestly appropriate, rather than faddish. Americans are notoriously

---

Table 7–3. **Proposed Set of Operational Challenges for Projection Forces**

- early halt of a classic armored invasion
- quick destruction of critical mobile targets such as vehicles carrying missiles armed with mass-casualty weapons
- effective stop-the-killing intervention in a "next Bosnia"
- attack and destruction of mass-casualty weapons by inserting ground forces as well as conducting long-range strikes
- attack and destruction of terrorist strongholds
- early attacks or counteroffensives without massive buildup
- counteroffensives after a major defeat and loss of territory, into the teeth of an enemy able and willing to use mass-casualty weapons

---

fickle, and each new administration seeks opportunities to change names and concepts and thus to put its stamp on things. However, DOD needs objectives with legs—objectives in which officers, officials, scientists, and engineers can invest precious years of their professional careers. Whims have no place. A related matter is that creating the wrong subjects and categories can cause management problems for many years; it pays to start with a good framework.

With this background, I offer in table 7–3 a set of proposed operational challenges against which to measure transformation proposals. It addresses only projection-force issues.[29]

For each such challenge, it is possible to decompose the problem (figure 7–3 gives a top-level view of the first operational challenge); identify critical components; assign responsibilities, authorities, and resources; and monitor progress. These components, then, connect the operational challenge to specific programs and other initiatives. Further, metrics for followup work develop naturally from such an operational analysis.

### Generating Options

One role of the Secretary of Defense is to establish requirements (figure 7–4), including operational challenges. It is the role of the military departments and the Joint Chiefs of Staff to develop solutions, although sometimes the Secretary must weigh in personally. Secretary of Defense Donald Rumsfeld has indicated his intention to ask for options from which he will choose. Consistent with that, it should be part of transformation strategy for the Secretary to insist that the military departments

Figure 7–3. **Illustrative Components of an Operational Challenge**

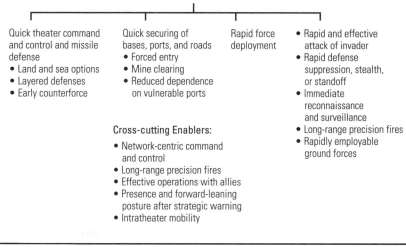

**Early Halt of Armored Invasion**

Quick theater command and control and missile defense
- Land and sea options
- Layered defenses
- Early counterforce

Quick securing of bases, ports, and roads
- Forced entry
- Mine clearing
- Reduced dependence on vulnerable ports

Rapid force deployment

- Rapid and effective attack of invader
- Rapid defense suppression, stealth, or standoff
- Immediate reconnaissance and surveillance
- Long-range precision fires
- Rapidly employable ground forces

Cross-cutting Enablers:

- Network-centric command and control
- Long-range precision fires
- Effective operations with allies
- Presence and forward-leaning posture after strategic warning
- Intratheater mobility

develop *alternative* programs and related initiatives that address the operational challenges effectively. One reason for doing so is to increase the likelihood that the Secretary will be presented with options that represent a range of views within the services about how to proceed. A traditional role of the Office of the Secretary of Defense has been to champion ideas generated by officers who are unable to convince their service leaders.[30] By demanding alternatives, the Secretary may bring further good ideas to the surface.

The Secretary should also insist that the costs of the various optional programs be calculated realistically. The idea of life-cycle costing goes back 40 years or more, but the discipline to enforce it has often been absent. If the programs presented are amply budgeted, the economic imperative for transformation will be visible, and the arguments for reengineering (substituting capital for labor) will be stronger.[31] Thus, an element of transformation strategy should be to insist on candor in costing.

## Support Issues

One important and subtle component of this issue involves support forces and infrastructure. The true capability of the total force cannot be understood without understanding that elements of the forces are

Figure 7–4. **Secretary of Defense Role in the Program Process**

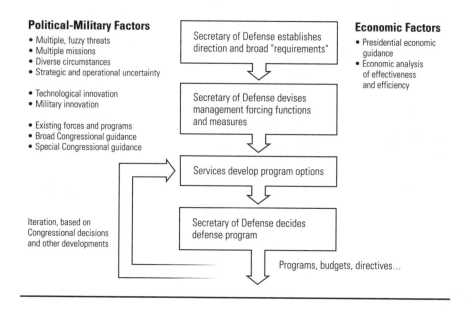

independently usable without gutting other elements of the force structure. Brigade-sized units are sometimes appropriate for small-scale contingencies, but a deploying brigade must take with it more than its "fair
share" of division and corps support structure because of optimizations
made long ago during the Cold War. If the Army now wants to move to
a more brigade-focused posture, it will not have the capability suggested
by the number of brigades unless it pays the bill to provide the extra support structure that would make the brigades independent. The Air Force
has analogous issues.

## Revising DOD Analytical Architecture

Given a set of operational challenges—and many other considerations, such as maintaining worldwide presence and being prepared for
near-term wars against rogues or terrorist supporters—the Department of
Defense must evaluate alternative plans for force posture. Unfortunately,
the DOD approach to analysis has for some years been antithetical to capabilities-based planning. Defense needs a new architecture for defining

Figure 7–5. **Process of Mission-System Analysis**

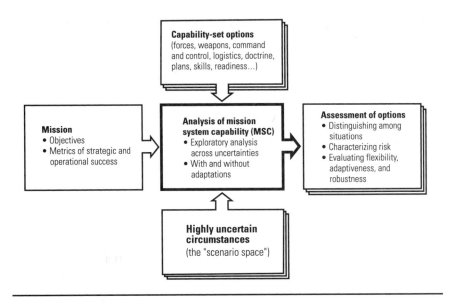

and conducting analysis.[32] Among the elements of that architecture should be the paradigm of mission-system analysis (MSA), sketched in figure 7–5.

The first principle of MSA is to organize thinking around output as discussed above. Doing so means organizing around mission capabilities. Although one can refer to aircraft, ships, and tanks as "capabilities," the capabilities of most interest in defense planning are the capabilities to accomplish key missions (that is, to conduct successful operations such as to defeat an armored invasion, achieve control of the seas in a region, defend against a missile attack on the United States, or capture a terrorist enclave, perhaps where weapons of mass destruction are hidden in mountain caves). Having platforms, weapons, and infrastructure is not enough. Of most importance is whether the missions could be confidently accomplished in a wide range of operational circumstances. This is a system problem.

Mission-system analysis has much in common with other methods, such as strategies to tasks, the idea of mission capability packages,[33] or the approach described in chapter 6 of the present volume. However, even though the underlying philosophy is similar, the MSA character appears rather different in practice. Mission-system analysis construes the system broadly; it emphasizes exploratory analysis under massive uncertainty;[34] and it can handle soft issues such as effects-based operations, analysis of which requires qualitative modeling (including cognitive modeling).[35]

Overall, the purpose of mission-system analysis is to achieve flexible, adaptive, and robust capabilities for the missions at issue. This means no-excuse, real-world capabilities, not just paper capabilities. Suppose that we want to develop requirements and capabilities for a particular mission (left side of figure 7–5). We consider a variety of capability-set options (top). For each option, we assess strengths and weaknesses across a wide range of operating conditions or scenario space, where "scenario" includes not only the political-military setting but also all of the key assumptions, such as warning times; force sizes; coalitions; enemy strategies (such as short warning or antiaccess strategies); and effectiveness. This concept of exploratory analysis across a scenario space enables planning for adaptiveness, flexibility, and robustness.[36]

Revising the analytical architecture also means addressing models. Unfortunately, models and simulation have distinct limitations when assessing some of the most important operations being considered for future warfare. These limitations will not go away with mere tweaks to current models or with the emergence of the Joint Warfare System.[37] What is needed is a modern family of models and games, with varied resolution and perspective. Part of this would be a capability for a rigorous version of war gaming that would provide the Secretary of Defense and Chairman of the Joint Chiefs of Staff with analytically structured assessments of capability by professional officers who "think joint" and act in behalf of future CINCs when war gaming. This capability could, for example, reside in the Joint Staff, Joint Forces Command, or some combination of one of these and federally funded research and development centers, which would provide structuring, continuity, and followup. Such war gaming is not new, but much more could be accomplished analytically to structure gaming and to refine and extrapolate its results.

### Monitoring Progress and Sustaining Pressure

It is one thing to do special transformation studies and to get ideas into the program; it is another to assure their sustained nourishment. Institutionalizing mission-system analysis and related metrics could be a big help. Another mechanism would be to establish yearly Secretary of Defense contingency games as a device for estimating the real-world capabilities that would exist as a result of planned near- and mid-term actions. These would combine features of the "Dynamic Commitment" games introduced in the Joint Staff in 1996, the sorts of force-employment gaming described above, and followup experimentation and analysis to assess the validity of planning assumptions. There would be multiple test cases, which would not be known to gamers beforehand and which would be designed to test flexibility, operational adaptiveness, and robustness. They might, for example, start with the assumption of a successful enemy strike on forward-deployed or allied forces, bases, or information systems.

### Explicitly Reviewing Suitability of the New Building Blocks

Since building blocks are so fundamental, DOD should dwell less on numbers of current major formations, such as carrier battlegroups and the like, worrying about whether to cut back their number to save money or increase their number because of worldwide commitments. Instead, it should focus on asking whether the future major formations arising from modernization and transformation are the *right* building blocks.[38] Assessing this will not be trivial in a networked world or when the full implications for support structure and infrastructure are considered.

### Addressing the Longer-Term Components of Force Transformation

Given the problems cited in the previous sections regarding longer-term transformation, several approaches suggest themselves:[39]

- Encourage diversity of concept exploration in R&D; dissuade continuing efforts by cost-cutters to stamp out as "redundant" what may actually be healthy and valuable competition of approaches.
- For some concepts, establish rapid-exploration laboratories bringing together operators, technologists, and analysts to pursue mission-oriented concepts through rapid prototyping, spiral exploration, and enrichment of the knowledge base. This could be accomplished by partnering relationships between JFCOM and the services, federally funded research and development centers or national laboratories, and industry.[40]
- Continue DOD efforts begun over the last decade, such as advanced concept development programs, to move certain promising concepts quickly from the world of R&D into the actual force, rather than bogging down in the normal acquisition system.

### Rethink Experimentation

There are chronic problems in the way that the American military pursues experimentation. A manifestation of the problem is the focus on "experiments." Although being against experiments would be heretical (and contrary to my beliefs), it seems that what is needed is to substitute the concept of studying the "Military Art and Science" of future warfare, rather than "conducting experiments." Obviously, conducting experiments should be a crucial component, but by embedding experiments in the larger endeavor, it might prove easier to generate efforts that more typically get short shrift. These include, for example, theorizing and studying.[41] It also includes research-level prototyping, small-scale controlled experiments to tighten knowledge of phenomenology, and larger-scale exercises and experiments. With this in mind, a proposal that is much less modest than it might at first seem is for the Secretary of Defense to establish a number of programs to study definitively the military art and science of selected warfare areas.

Taken as a whole, these recommendations would go far in applying the lessons of past experience and research. They should also be consistent with the new QDR and may be practical measures for moving from QDR-level expressions of policy to actionable measures related to warfighting capability.

## Notes

[1] Department of Defense, Quadrennial Defense Review Report (Washington, DC: Department of Defense, 2001).

[2] *Transformation* can be interpreted in many ways, as discussed by Richard L. Kugler and Hans Binnendijk in the present volume, as well as by Paul K. Davis, "Transforming U.S. Forces," in Frank Carlucci, Robert Hunter, and Zalmay Khalilzad, eds., *Taking Charge: A Bipartisan Report to the President Elect on Foreign Policy and National Security* (Santa Monica, CA: RAND, 2001). For a discussion of the difficulties in moving promptly toward revolutionary transformation, see Michael O'Hanlon, "Modernizing and Transforming U.S. Forces: Alternative Paths to the Force of Tomorrow," in Michèle Flournoy, ed., *QDR 2001: Strategy-Driven Choices for America's Security* (Washington, DC: Institute for National Strategic Studies, National Defense University Press, 2001).

[3] William Owens, with Edward Offley, *Lifting the Fog of War* (New York: Farrar, Straus, and Giroux, 2000).

[4] The author's views on this subject are based in part on having observed or directed large model-building efforts. Even in creative, exploratory work, it has proven invaluable to have significant design work up-front—even if rapidly accomplished and tentative. Similarly, even the development of allegedly understood models benefits greatly from spiraling and iteration.

[5] Davis et al., *Transforming U.S. Forces*; Irving Lachow and David C. Gompert, *Transforming the Force: Lessons from the Wider Revolution*, Issue Paper 193 (Santa Monica, CA: RAND, 2000); and Davis, "Transforming U.S. Forces."

[6] The papers are being collected in Paul K. Davis and Paul Bracken, eds., *Managing Military Transformation*, MR–714 (Santa Monica, CA: RAND, forthcoming).

[7] Paul Bracken, "Reengineering and Information Technology: Relationships and Lessons Learned," unpublished paper (Santa Monica, CA: RAND, September 30, 2001), to appear in Davis and Bracken, *Managing Military Transformation*.

[8] See related discussions in Paul K. Davis, David C. Gompert, Richard Hillestad, and Stuart Johnson, *Transforming U.S. Forces: Suggestions for DOD Strategy*, Issue Paper 179 (Santa Monica, CA: RAND, 1998); and Lachow and Gompert, *Transforming the Force*. These works emphasize the strong and positive role of the military services and recommend increased and specific efforts at the joint level, particularly with regard to joint adaptive command and control. The approach suggested may be described as one of "vigorous evolution" rather than complacent incrementalism or revolution. See also chapter 8 in the current volume by Douglas A. Macgregor and chapter 3 by Kugler and Binnendijk.

[9] Paul Bracken, "A Structure for Discussing the Application of Information Technology to Transformation," unpublished paper (Santa Monica, CA: RAND, September 2001), to appear in Davis and Bracken, *Managing Military Transformation*.

[10] Carl Builder, Stephen C. Bankes, and Richard Nordin, *Command Concepts: A Theory Derived from the Practice of Command and Control* (Santa Monica, CA: RAND, 1999).

[11] Brett Steele, "Military Reengineering in the Interwar Era: Responding to the Internal Combustion Engine," unpublished paper (Santa Monica, CA: RAND, July 2001), to appear in Davis and Bracken, *Managing Military Transformation*.

[12] See also Williamson Murray and Alan Millet, eds., *Military Innovation in the Interwar Period* (New York: Cambridge University Press, 1996).

[13] Richard Hundley, *Past Revolutions, Future Transformations: What Can the History of Revolutions in Military Affairs Tell Us About Transforming the U.S. Military?* (Santa Monica, CA: RAND, 1999); Richard Hundley, "A Proposal to Strengthen and Enhance the 'Third Axis' of U.S. JFCOM's Joint Experimentation Program," unpublished paper (Santa Monica, CA: RAND, 2001), to appear in Davis and Bracken, *Managing Military Transformation*.

[14] Ben R. Rich and Leo Janos, *Skunk Works: A Personal Memoir from the U–2 to the Stealth Fighter: The Inside Story of America's Most Secret Aerospace Company, the Airplanes They Built, and the Dangerous Missions That Won the Cold War* (Boston: Little Brown, 1994).

[15] To illustrate the significance of this, consider that most armies in the interwar period misunderstood the role of the tank because they focused too much on particular types of battles in which tanks could be destroyed by antitank guns. In contrast, the Marine Corps largely mastered amphibious operations.

[16] The Soviets were arguably successful at doing both in the interwar period. Marshal Tukhachevsky left behind rich materials on subjects, such as maneuver warfare. He also left a legacy of military science. Some of his legacy can be seen in later studies, such as Vasilii Savkin, *The Basic Principles of Operational Art and Tactics (A Soviet View)*, translated and published under the auspices of the U.S. Air Force (Washington, DC: Government Printing Office, 1974).

[17] See Davis et al., *Transforming the Force*; and Paul K. Davis, ed., *New Challenges in Defense Planning: Rethinking How Much Is Enough* (Santa Monica, CA: RAND, 1994), chapter 4.

[18] As one example, see U.S. Joint Forces Command, *Rapid Decisive Operations* (Norfolk, VA: U.S. JFCOM, 2001).

[19] Wesley K. Clark, *Waging Modern War: Bosnia, Kosovo and the Future of Conflict* (New York: Public Affairs, 2001).

[20] Joint Chiefs of Staff, *Joint Vision 2010* (Washington, DC: Department of Defense, 1996), and *Joint Vision 2020* (Washington, DC: Department of Defense, 2000). The issue of rapid employment is discussed in James McCarthy, Executive Summary to *Transforming Military Operational Capabilities*, accessed online at <http://www.defenselink.mil/news/Jun2001/d20010621transexec.pdf>; and in Eugene Gritton, Paul K. Davis, Randall Steeb, and John Matsumura, *Ground Forces for Rapidly Employable Joint Task Forces* (Santa Monica, CA: RAND, 2001).

[21] Michèle Flournoy, ed., *QDR 2001: Strategy-Driven Choices for America's Security* (Washington, DC: Institute for National Strategic Studies, National Defense University Press, 2001).

[22] Davis, *Analytic Architecture*. The term *capabilities-based planning* refers to planning for a diversity of conflicts in a diversity of circumstances, rather than focusing on a particular threat scenario.

[23] See also National Research Council, Naval Studies Board, *Modeling and Simulation*, vol. 9, *Technology for the United States Navy and Marine Corps: 2000–2035* (Washington, DC: National Academy Press, 1998).

[24] In the 1950s and 1960s, DOD and the Air Force comprehensively studied atmospheric and space phenomena related to rockets, missiles, and satellites. In the 1970s and 1980s, the Navy supported deep research to understand phenomena related to submarine observability. In earlier years, the Navy mastered the phenomena involved in operating nuclear-powered SSBNs and SSNs. In more recent times, one might think of the research base underlying stealth technology (Air Force) or the considerable Army research on how to increase the capability of light ground forces. See, for example, John Matsumura et al., *Lightning Over Water: Sharpening U.S. Light Forces for Rapid Reaction Missions* (Santa Monica, CA: RAND, 2001). The Marine Corps has done extensive work exploring the feasibility of different operational concepts in desert and urban settings.

[25] This issue was a matter of considerable concern in a recent study conducted for the Chief of Naval Operations. The study recommended increased emphasis on operational analysis, system engineering, and rigorously systematic experimentation in connection with network-centric operations. See National Research Council, Naval Studies Board, Committee on Network-Centric Naval Forces, *Network-Centric Naval Operations: A Transition Strategy for Enhancing Operational Capabilities* (Washington, DC: National Academy Press, 2000).

[26] See Paul K. Davis, "Protecting the Great Transition," in Davis, *New Challenges in Defense Analysis*.

[27] Davis et al., *Transforming the Force*.

[28] It would be foolish to "waste" Secretary of Defense guidance by directing the Air Force and Navy to develop capabilities to assure the ability to achieve air and maritime superiority in war.

[29] Most of the QDR operational goals for transformation relate well to these. Accomplishing the operational challenges requires being able to protect relevant bases, to deal with antiaccess strategies, and so on. Thus, the goals appear in a context that provides motivation.

[30] Such championing by the Office of the Secretary of Defense played a major role in procurement of both the A–10 and F–16.

[31] The effects will vary with service and may be less than some individuals hope for. See chapter 5 in the present volume by William D. O'Neil.

[32] Davis, *Analytic Architecture*.

[33] See David S. Alberts, John J. Garstka, and Frederick P. Stein, *Network Centric Warfare: Developing and Leveraging Information Superiority* (Washington, DC: C⁴ISR Cooperative Research Program, 2000).

[34] Exploratory analysis is a recently developed approach that examines capabilities for a broad operating space, rather than studying only a few point scenarios in detail. Thus, it considers simultaneous variations in warning time, real-world weapon effectiveness, real-world allied effectiveness, enemy strategy, and many other factors. The theoretical and technological base for such work has been described elsewhere. See, for example, Paul K. Davis, "Exploratory Analysis Enabled by Multiresolution, Multiperspective Modeling," *Proceedings of the 2000 Winter Simulation Conference,* available from RAND as RP–925. A recent application is described in Paul K. Davis, Jimmie McEver, and Barry Wilson, *Measuring Interdiction Capabilities in the Presence of Anti-Access Strategies*, MR–1471–AF (Santa Monica, CA: RAND, 2002).

[35] For definition and discussion, see Paul K. Davis, *Effects-Based Operations (EBO): A Grand Challenge for the Analytic Community* (Santa Monica, CA: RAND, 2002).

[36] See, for example, Davis et al., *Measuring Interdiction*.

[37] The Joint Warfare System (JWARS) is a large and controversial campaign-level model of military operations developed to support operational planning and execution, force assessment studies, system trade analyses, and concept and doctrine development. It will not be appropriate for exploratory analysis of the sort emphasized here but may permit selective analysis with a great deal of joint richness.

[38] This has been one of the author's themes from some years (see Davis, *New Challenges in Defense Planning*). It is much more fundamental than the greatly overdone and ill-defined issue of whether U.S. forces should be sized for two simultaneous major theater wars.

[39] A positive step recently taken was the DOD appointment of a special Director for Transformation, Arthur K. Cebrowski, who championed transformation in the Navy.

[40] Hundley, "A Proposal to Strengthen."

[41] Lest this seem like scholarly poppycock, consider the value that theorizing and studying had to Soviet military developments or that it has had in the United States in special domains, such as nonacoustic antisubmarine warfare or strategic command and control.

# Chapter 8

# Transforming Jointly

Douglas A. Macgregor

T he Bush administration took office amid high hopes for the fundamental transformation of the Armed Forces. Yet within months, the problem that transformation was designed to solve—changing a large, expensive industrial age structure into a leaner, more strategically agile information age force—receded as more pressing issues arose. Instead of being transformed, Cold War military structures will remain unchanged for the time being, while morale and quality of life are shored up. Into this policy vacuum, military leaders have tossed an expensive collection of wish lists that tend to one of two extremes: a bigger, faster, better version of some platform already in use, or something out of science fiction with delivery timelines that stretch all the way to 2032.[1] Although these modernization programs are billed as promoting transformation, they are business as usual.

Fortunately, this is not the whole story. The current Quadrennial Defense Review (QDR) anticipates the emergence of new ground, naval, and air forces reorganized for "more rapidly responsive, scalable, modular task-organized units, capable of independent combat action as well as integration into larger joint and combined operations" sometime after 2006.[2]

*Transformation*—defined as change in the structure of command, control, training, readiness, doctrine, and organization for combat—can produce short-term economies and increased capability well before 2006. Transformation can be phased in now through continuous adaptation, using today's forces and technology along with reform and reorganization to produce significant improvements in the quality of life and morale, as well as the fighting power, of soldiers, sailors, airmen, and marines.

A unifying strategic vision for transformation involves, first, recognizing that a strategy based on known threats, doctrines, and orders of battle no longer applies. The second step requires developing a new strategic formula for the use of American military power that is neither scenario-dependent nor based on service-centric concepts and structures designed to deploy masses of troops and matériel. Instead, the focus must be on critical warfighting capabilities. This has been described as a shift from *threat-based* to *capabilities-based* planning.

Technology and the experiences of the 1990s point the way to a paradigm shift that can reshape the structure of American military power through the integration of ground, naval, and air forces within a joint, network-centric system of warfare. To cope with the new strategic environment, a new operational paradigm based on air, space, missile, and information power must emerge to support military operations scaled to meet the requirements of any given contingency. At the same time, a fresh approach to American military strategy and the employment of its military power is needed to buttress the stability of key states around the world, preserve U.S. access to critical bases and infrastructure, and operate to prevent regional crises and conflict rather than reacting to them.

Transformation, strategy, jointness, and even readiness are inextricably intertwined. Reducing transformation to a service-centric, industrial age quest for a new armored vehicle, ship, or plane that can transform warfare, as the rifled musket and the machine gun are thought to have done, would miss the real promise of the information age. The potential for revolutionary change and transformation arises from the integration of critical military capabilities across service lines.

## Jointness Is Critical to Transformation

In his speech at The Citadel on September 23, 1999, Presidential candidate George W. Bush promised to begin an immediate, comprehensive review of the American military—the structure of its forces, the state of its strategy, the priorities of its procurement—conducted by a leadership team under the Secretary of Defense. Bush noted that he wanted to move beyond marginal improvements, to replace existing programs with new technologies and strategies, and to exploit the opportunity to skip a generation of technology. Shortly after being appointed Secretary of Defense in early 2001, Donald Rumsfeld used this guidance to create dozens of panels to study a range of security issues. The reviews ended in June 2001, and the Bush administration's recognition of the criticality of jointness to transformation is discernible from the results that were released.

General James McCarthy, USAF (Ret.), who led a panel on transformation, presented recommendations on June 12, 2001, that highlighted the concept of multiservice early-entry "Global Joint Response Forces." These forces would combine units from different services as tailorable force modules that train and exercise together and would use common building blocks: command and control ($C^2$) systems; intelligence, surveillance, and reconnaissance capabilities; space-based assets; and joint logistics capabilities. McCarthy stressed that "We are not talking about a new force... [but rather] how to organize, exercise, and train the existing forces and what capabilities to give them."[3]

RAND analyst David Gompert led the panel on America's conventional forces. He echoed McCarthy's recommendations in stating that all joint units must be "ready, rapidly deployable, and employable; tailorable for [a] range of operations; easily integrated and networked; [and] supportable despite distance and dispersion."[4] When asked about transformation initiatives during testimony in Congress in June, Secretary Rumsfeld also mentioned "rapidly deployable standing joint forces" as part of a new approach to handling military operations in both the near and long term.[5]

Thus, for the first time in recent history, a top-level defense review did not focus on what used to be the outputs of defense planning: carrier battlegroups, fighter wings, army divisions, and marine expeditionary forces. Instead, the defense review asked what capabilities a joint force commander will need today and in the future. The results of defense planning are, thus, the capabilities provided to a joint task force (JTF) pursuing an operational mission. In theory, this overturns the unstated World War II-era assumption (which survived the 1986 Goldwater-Nichols Act) that the process of developing tactical capabilities and conducting operations should be left to the individual services. The implications are profound for American defense policy.

If implemented as outlined by the panel in its public recommendations, JTFs would become the order of the day. Command at the three-star level and above would become joint. Service Title 10 functions would be modified to focus exclusively on organizing, training, and equipping for specific joint roles and missions versus current service missions. Each service would provide JTF building blocks or force modules based on its core competencies.

The recommendations set the stage for abolition of the World War II mode of relatively independent, sequential missions accomplished by service components under a regional warfighting commander in chief (CINC). This change implies the elimination of single-service three- and four-star headquarters that would no longer be required for the command and control of joint forces. If forces were converted to building-block formations for JTFs, the reshaped Armed Forces could adopt a joint rotational readiness base that would make deployments more predictable and that would identify the ground, naval, and air forces available at any given time for contingencies. If carried through to its logical end, the Bush administration brand of joint transformation could result in savings: it could end the practice of pouring billions into the services to build sufficient capability to compensate for an inefficient single-service mode of employment under an inadequate joint command and control structure. All of these measures could reduce unneeded bureaucratic layers and yield efficiencies that promise significant resource, dollar, and personnel savings.

Regardless of the national military strategy, however, the services will oppose change that does not give their core competencies due weight in defense planning and spending.[6] Although the Goldwater-Nichols Act was supposed to address this problem, so many single-service headquarters and control structures survived the process—on the grounds that joint organizations had yet to demonstrate their merit—that enormous and expensive redundancies remain.

Given this conceptual groundwork, the issue is how to maintain the current readiness of the Armed Forces to conduct operations while transformation is implemented through changes in organization, doctrine, and technology.

## From Implications to Implementation

The new national military strategy establishes four objectives: to assure friends and allies, dissuade future adversaries, deter threats and counter coercion, and defeat adversaries if deterrence fails.[7] The scenario-based, two-major theater war requirement that has driven U.S. military strategy since the end of the Cold War has been replaced.

However, these statements provide neither a formula that translates theoretical goals into attainable strategic military objectives nor guidelines for sizing or employing the force. The United States no longer faces an identifiable enemy: no Soviet tank armies are poised to invade allied territory on short notice. Only North Korea fields a force designed to attack on short notice, and even this force is rapidly declining in capability and strength. Instead, a complex range of threats to American and allied interests is emerging that no single service can address. State and nonstate actors eventually are likely to acquire some form of weapon of mass destruction as well as precision-guided munitions, modern air defense technology, and access to electronic intelligence and satellite imagery provided by third powers. A broader range of enemies armed with new mixes of technologies—some industrial age and some information age capabilities—will confront the Armed Forces. Moreover, these adversaries do not require the ability to defeat U.S. forces, only to frustrate their employment in some way.

Thus, the Armed Forces must maintain an overseas military presence on land, at sea, and in the air in pivotal states or regions to ensure that the United States and its allies can either influence or become involved in crises or fight in conflicts that directly impinge on strategic interests. They also must be able to intervene militarily and fight in areas where America and its allies have no presence but have either declared strategic interests or a real political stake in the outcome.

These forces must be organized into specialized modules of combat power on rotational readiness so that they can rapidly assemble into joint task forces. JTFs will be needed both in war and in peace to buttress the stability of key states and to prevent regional crises and conflicts rather than reacting to them. This has several implications for force design and employment. First, JTFs will need highly mobile, rapidly deployable forces-in-being. These forces must be structured for interoperability within an evolving joint framework to incorporate and exploit new technology on a continuous basis. Second, some portion of the ground, naval, and air forces is likely to be forward deployed in key states to preserve U.S. access to critical infrastructure so that the United States can project military power inland. Forward-deployed forces provide tangible evidence of American commitment and a link to the larger strategic power of the United States. In the absence of large forces poised to attack our allies, fewer forces will be needed in a forward-deployed posture than previously, which presents the opportunity to reduce, although not eliminate, expensive overseas garrisons. Third, what military power remains—the bulk of American military forces—must be capable of moving rapidly from widely dispersed staging areas overseas and within the continental United States, deploying into crisis or conflict and initiating offensive operations.

The 1999 Kosovo crisis illustrates the need for rapidly deployable, ready ground forces that can integrate seamlessly into the global strike capabilities that American air, missile, information, and space power make possible, both to exploit their potential and to guarantee the safety of the deployed American and allied ground forces. Technology can be exploited to create the conditions for an Inchon-style operation wherever strikes are concentrated, but this requires the development of a new structure for readiness and training that is inherently joint.

One proposal is to treat the forces under service control as a pool of capability packages and place them into a joint rotational readiness structure. This would be substantially different from the notion of having standing JTFs that would permanently control large numbers of forces nominally under service command and control. The military organization chart that evolved during the Cold War is no longer suitable because the same number of higher echelon headquarters must share fewer forces.[8]

The echelons clearly need to be reduced, but replacing them with standing JTFs that permanently control the shrunken forces at the bottom may not be the answer. For example, the two JTFs or global joint response forces suggested by Gompert would have to be designed for the full range of missions, from an Operation *Desert Storm* to an Operation *Sea Angel*. This seems unworkable and would limit flexibility.

Instead, reconfiguring existing single service three- and four-star headquarters to U.S. Joint Force Command modules and assigning them to joint command and control in the regional warfighting commands could provide the assets from which the CINCs can establish operational JTF command structures to command these forces. The JTFs could be established on the basis of specific mission requirements much more rapidly and effectively than is the case today. This arrangement also avoids the complicated and unrewarding interservice squabbling associated with the establishment of any one-size-fits-all JTF headquarters.

This approach would preserve today's forces that deploy and fight by creating a larger, predictable pool of ready and available ground, naval, and air forces on rotational readiness. These forces could be rapidly deployed to regional commands with a combination of strategic air and fast sealift to arrive in strategically pivotal regions "before the peace is lost." This approach would preserve the vital readiness of today's forces while routine joint experimentation and modernization are conducted. It also could reduce personnel tempo and make deployments and costs more predictable. A possible structure could resemble the following:

- Training cycle (6 months): Unit and individual training is conducted under service control.
- Deployment cycle (6 months): Units are ready for deployment to joint command and control and become part of the pool that responds to major theater of war missions, crises, peace support operations, or whatever mission the Secretary of Defense assigns.
- Reconstitution cycle (6 months): Unit returns to home station for refitting, modernization (if required), and leave.

This structure also facilitates regular joint training of the forces that are likely to be committed and makes the commitment of the Armed Forces more comprehensible to the Secretary of Defense. It allows more humane treatment of the soldiers, sailors, airmen, and marines who must deploy on a routine basis.

## Transforming Concepts and Organization for Improved Joint Operations

Secretary Rumsfeld has declared that new joint operational concepts are the keys to both transformation and rationalizing defense. A joint operational concept involves the integration of service core tactical capabilities on the operational level to achieve unity of purpose and action in the conduct of military operations. This has precedent: U.S. naval aviators in the interwar period experimented with carrier-based aviation and ultimately reversed the striking and supporting roles of battleships and aircraft carriers. American naval tactics evolved throughout World War II, and by 1945 no category of warship except minesweepers was employed for the purpose for which it originally had been built.

History suggests the required components of transformation:

- a new operational concept
- a new doctrine and organization to execute the concept that increases fighting power
- a new joint operational architecture to integrate the technologies of ground, naval, and air warfare
- a new approach to modernization, education, training, and readiness.

Information processes are also sources of combat power and should drive organizational design for combat. Warfighting systems, too, must evolve along with concepts and organizations.

The current pace of technological development is so fast that static organizational thinking is not possible. Adaptive structures for the continuous incorporation of new technologies to provide new capabilities are essential. Such a structure would integrate strike and maneuver assets through a nodal architecture empowered by advanced terrestrial and space-based communications. This structure would be the foundation for a new joint operational concept with enormous potential, but few people are sure how it would work in a purely joint setting.

Effects-based operations, which originated in the air and naval forces, present an opportunity to demonstrate the integrative nature of joint network-centric warfare in action. Effects-based operations would be inherently joint and network-centric; the ground, naval, and air forces involved must be interconnected or netted to be effective. All parts of the joint force must see the same scenario; what one part perceives and plans must be available to the whole force.[9] The United States will be able to exploit its airborne ground surveillance and precision-targeting capabilities by detecting, tracking, and targeting a moving or dispersed enemy with speed and precision throughout a large area. This creates an immensely powerful joint warfighting synergy by enabling a joint commander to orchestrate ground, naval, and air forces to achieve effects that complement each other dynamically at the operational and tactical levels of war.

New joint operational concepts and structures that integrate diverse service capabilities require a new joint operational architecture to be effective. A new set of command relationships different from today's single-service warfighting C[2] structure would provide the C[2] elements for joint task forces. This requires change on the operational level to supplant the multitude of single-service component commands at home and overseas with joint command and control elements from which JTFs can be constituted. The services also must organize their core capabilities into specialized modules of mission-focused combat power that can be integrated as required into JTFs. This requires change on the tactical level to achieve the interoperability essential to joint operations.

Scaling and equipping air and naval forces for integration into a plug-and-play joint operational architecture might entail modifications in communications and procedures to facilitate joint interoperability, but this would not necessitate dramatic organizational change. For the Army, however, the challenge of integration for joint interoperability has proved thus far insurmountable.

### Air and Naval Forces

For the air and naval services, grouping forces to become mission-focused capability packages within a joint network-centric framework is easier than it sounds. Operational thinking in the air and naval forces is converging on ways to exploit jointly the global reconnaissance-strike complex. The Air Force plan to establish 10 air expeditionary forces is a critical step in this direction. Air Force strike packages can be modified in response to the required mission and target set. The Navy is accustomed to assembling ships into task forces for specific missions. While new naval platforms are designed and built for strike and maneuver operations in the littoral, existing platforms can be equipped and employed differently to provide the specific capabilities that JTF commanders require.

In recent months, the concept of the Marine expeditionary brigade (MEB) has also received attention. The MEB is capable of deploying a force of 5,000 or more marines quickly and sustaining combat over a wider area than the 2,000-person Marine expeditionary unit can. The MEB is scalable in size and can execute independent missions within JTFs but cannot sustain the long deployment timelines that a larger Marine expeditionary force (the Marine equivalent of an Army corps) can handle.[10]

## Army

Army adaptation to joint operations has been less promising. U.S. Army ground forces in the Gulf War were deployed slowly and deliberately against Iraq's strength, the Republican Guard Corps. The opportunity to exploit the paralysis achieved in the opening days of the air campaign was lost, and as a result the strategic realities of Baghdad's regional influence remained unchanged. During the Kosovo crisis in 1999, the Army and Air Force were unable to overcome the single-service nature of American warfare. Yugoslav forces never faced a robust allied combat force on the ground capable of decisive maneuver operations, and thus they were never compelled to mass and present the target array allied air forces sought.

In the middle of the 20th century, General George Marshall's structure and vision for efficiently expanding an army of 200,000 to one of more than 6 million drew upon Henry Ford's assembly-line concepts. These are now outdated. Present-day organization for combat and concepts of warfare were developed when theater missile defense, deep strike operations, JTFs, and real-time information-sharing did not exist, and when new missions for today's ground forces were unknown or unanticipated. Without fundamental reorganization and reform of the Army's warfighting structure, the Army cannot integrate its ground formations. They must be able to maneuver around and through massed precision strikes from joint ground, naval, and air forces to seize the positional advantage in future war.

Victories are not achieved by the most blood lost or by the crushing weight of numbers, but by surprise, joint strike, and maneuver to paralyze the enemy. These capabilities cannot be attained if the Army attempts transformation in isolation from the other services, nor can it transform by reequipping the old division-based World War II force with new platforms, whether they are wheeled or tracked.

When applied to land warfare, joint network-centric warfare demands a "dispersed mobile warfare" design that differs radically from the traditional army, corps, division, and brigade formations of linear warfare.

It requires fewer echelons of $C^2$ and a faster decision cycle that employs joint sensors forward with maneuver elements to provide the coverage needed to exploit the joint potential in the Army's strike formations, as well as the advanced aviation and ground combat platforms in the Army's close combat formations. Maneuver and strike formations must be transformed into nodes of joint combat power—deep, close, or sustaining—that have the capacity for joint operations on land similar to the operation of ships at sea.

To do this, Army forces must be reorganized into mission-focused force packages that provide the building blocks for the integration of critical army capabilities into JTFs. These capabilities range from theater missile defense assets and rocket artillery to combat maneuver forces and modern attack helicopters.

## Integrating Critical Military Capabilities across Service Lines

In the information age, national military strategy, operational concepts, and force designs must lead to the creation of new interdisciplinary teams of armed forces capable of both adaptation and rapid joint employment. Developing forces to operate jointly within a new joint network-centric warfighting structure takes more than simply recapitalizing old warfighting structures. Old structures and old thinking are linked. There is a widening gulf between service transformation programs and transformation at the operational level, which must be joint. The various service transformation programs, if pursued separately, mostly tinker on the margins of America's military status quo. They seek, in effect, to electrify the horse cavalry. Without structural and organizational change, thinking is unlikely to change. Until the Armed Forces begin to operate differently with existing assets, the parameters of modernization will not change, unneeded equipment sets cannot be eliminated, and new requirements will not be identified. The Armed Forces must emulate successful businesses by incorporating some new technologies, rejecting others, adapting practices and structures, narrowing or broadening activities—all in response to changing conditions.

The task ahead is nothing less than the conversion of today's disjointed armed services into a truly joint force that can guarantee American security and influence for the remainder of this century.

# Notes

[1] Fred E. Saalfeld and John F. Petrik, "Disruptive Technologies: A Concept for Moving Innovative Military Technologies Rapidly to Warfighters," *Armed Forces Journal International*, May 2001, 48.

[2] Bill Gertz and Rowan Scarborough, "Inside The Ring," *The Washington Times*, August 17, 2001, 7.

[3] John T. Correll, "Rumsfeld's Review: The Closed-Door Approach Led to Problems, and They Are Not Over Yet," *Air Force Magazine*, July 2001, 2.

[4] Nicholas Lemann, "Letter from Washington: Dreaming about War," *The New Yorker*, July 16, 2001, 32.

[5] "Joint Operations Reality," *Defense News*, July 9–15, 2001, 10.

[6] These core competencies include the Navy and Marine Corps forward presence around the globe, the Air Force global precision strike forces, and the Army capacity to seize and hold strategic territory. Elaine M. Grossman, "DOD Is Shaping Major Review Outcomes Prior to Releasing Strategy," *Inside the Pentagon*, June 14, 2001, 1.

[7] Thom Shanker, "Defense Chief Will Propose Military Change in Course," *The New York Times*, June 15, 2001, 2.

[8] At the top was the Secretary of Defense; below that came the CINCs, the service component four-star headquarters, the three-star numbered fleets, air forces, Army corps, and marine expeditionary force headquarters. Below these were the "above-the-line" forces such as Army divisions and Air Force fighter wings. Today, nothing has changed at the top, but the bottom layer has contracted.

[9] Kenneth Watman, "Global 2000," *Naval War College Review* 54, no. 2 (Spring 2001), 76.

[10] Christian Lowe, "Marine Corps Resurrects Medium-Weight Force," *Defense Week*, August 20, 2001, 1.

# Chapter 9

# Coordinating with NATO

Charles L. Barry

resident George W. Bush's September 2001 call to arms against terrorism and the unprecedented North Atlantic Treaty Organization (NATO) Article 5 declaration injected new urgency into efforts to field robust, interoperable Alliance forces that can respond effectively in austere areas far beyond NATO territory. More than ever before, allies may now find themselves in a sudden, come-as-you-are war in which only the most capable, interoperable forces are able to contribute. This is inescapable confirmation that a real and significant gap in transatlantic military capabilities persists. However, the gap is in key functional areas and is not universal. Even the most critical gaps—deployment, broad network-centricity, better sensors and shooters, and logistics—are areas where allies have begun to invest in programs that will fix their shortfalls. Although closing the gap will take time, it is not so wide that it cannot be closed by 2010 with concerted effort and adequate resources.

Most allies came late to the revolution in military affairs and are just beginning to transform their forces to meet rapidly changing operational requirements. The goals of the NATO Defense Capabilities Initiative (DCI) helped focus their efforts in the right areas.[1] Perhaps more significant, Europe's commitment to create its own rapid reaction force has spurred real progress in building European capabilities. However, recent events have raised the bar by posing the far more demanding realities of an Article 5 declaration and U.S.-led operations in Afghanistan. Europe may be in danger of falling further behind as the United States moves to add at least $40 billion to its 2003 defense budget, with more certain to follow. That puts pressure on all allies to reexamine their defense resources and programs. NATO itself needs to take another look at its strategic guidelines. Instead of a mere progress report on DCI at its next summit in late 2002, NATO now must propose a new initiative, one that defines far more in terms of modern military forces and capabilities. Unless NATO creates the wherewithal to respond in the future, it will be greatly diminished as a military alliance.

This chapter looks at the factors behind the persistent gap in defense investments across the Atlantic and how U.S. and European attitudes are evolving. It examines the real technology gap today in land, air, and naval forces as well as in the functional areas of deployability; command, control, communications, computers, and information (C4I); and logistics.[2] We will see that for the forces themselves, the gaps in most areas are manageable, and closing them is within reach. The gaps in functional capabilities such as deployability, C4I, and logistics management are far more worrisome given the speed and extent of U.S. transformation. We then turn to trends in modernization and transformation and, considering the impacts of September 11, argue that the trends on either side of the Atlantic are not so much in conflict as in need of harmonization of their respective levels of effort, and that they also lack collaborative, open management. The chapter concludes with a look at initiatives, both planned and under way, aimed at closing the gap, and at how these initiatives are being redefined by the attacks on the United States and by NATO invocation of Article 5.

## Persistent Capabilities Gap

The United States and its allies around the world have pursued interoperability since World War II by invoking common standards and procedures, sharing technologies and joint or combined exercises, and exchanging a broad spectrum of military information on topics ranging from doctrine and training to joint planning, operational concepts, and lessons learned. Direct sale of U.S. military hardware abroad and purchase of foreign equipment for American use also have buttressed interoperability. Nowhere have allies pushed harder for interoperability and realized more progress than in NATO, the only alliance in the world that maintains a standing military structure.

However, in the decade following the Cold War, the United States and its NATO allies have followed ever more divergent attitudes toward the maintenance of military power, especially in the application of emerging information technology that in the United States is called the *revolution in military affairs* (RMA). Most allies were unable to contribute sophisticated capabilities—precision all-weather target engagement, secure communications, technical intelligence, or robust logistics—during either the 1991 Gulf War or the 1999 Operation *Allied Force* over Kosovo because they had chosen to forego investment in modern technologies and systems in favor of reduced spending and continued reliance on aging legacy systems. Allied defense budgets declined steadily as leaders and legislators were unable to identify a raison d'etre—either missions or threats—for new investment that could engender public support. A broad tendency to wring greater peace dividends from defense budgets persisted throughout Europe long after the United States began reinvesting. The result of these factors has been a growing transatlantic capabilities gap, with the United States all but alone in keeping pace with rapid changes in military technologies. The common underpinning of interoperable forces throughout the Cold War— the maintenance of similar capabilities—no longer figures in the defense budgets and military strategies of many allies. In order to close the gap, NATO will need a deeper sense of common purpose, and of common risks, for the use of military force, and it will need stronger, clearer agreement on the types of response options its forces must be equipped to undertake.

The NATO 1999 Strategic Concept declares that it will respond to crises beyond its borders whenever its members' collective interests are at risk.[3] Since 1995, the allies have been demonstrating that commitment in the Balkans. Yet the readiness and capabilities of NATO forces vary widely, from vintage systems to experimental technologies, because nations assess force requirements through different prisms. The main fault line in military capabilities lies between, on one hand, the United States and the United Kingdom (and to a lesser degree France) and, on the other, the rest of the allies. Closing the technology gap will require that Alliance members share the conviction that modern, information age capabilities are essential to accomplishing new NATO missions. Expressing that conviction openly, collectively, and often at NATO will give national parliaments and military programmers the solid, essential rationale to make the case for greater investments in research, development, and procurement.

## Defense Investments

European defense investments have, with few exceptions, trailed U.S. spending since the Cold War (see table 9–1). Although the gap between U.S. and allied spending is slightly smaller today than it was at the peak of U.S. spending in the mid-1980s, most Europeans started from a far lower basis as of 1990 and have declined to a point that provides few resources for investment in research and development (R&D) or new procurement. Even 2 years after Operation *Allied Force* over Kosovo, aggregate defense investment across NATO-Europe remains essentially flat. Many allies seek ways to wring more capability out of what they already spend. Seeking to get more out of current defense outlays before making the case for increased spending is a start, but real defense increases are unavoidable in the near term if we intend to preserve transatlantic interoperability.

Anemic economic conditions throughout the 1990s are partly to blame for Europe's decline in defense spending. Europe also faces competing investment imperatives: European Union (EU) restructuring and enlargement, adoption of the euro single currency (accompanied by the European Monetary Union [EMU] restrictions on deficit spending); the lingering costs of German unification; and the need to help EU industries make the transition to meet the forces of global competition. However, even at the present dramatically low ebb shown in table 9–1, defense budget considerations in Europe are not generating the level of legislative attention and public concern that mark U.S. defense debates. One reason for public apathy is the absence of an overt security threat to Europe. Another is the Continent's long reliance on U.S. military power and political leadership.

Analysts have described an even deeper divide. They argue that Europeans quietly perceive that there is utility and reduced risk in needing time to mount a military response when crises arise. They take a less idealistic approach than the United States when it comes to confronting regional troublemakers, such as Iraq, and are more accepting of the potential for casualties should they ultimately be forced to slug it out by less sophisticated means than the United States favors. One American ambassador described the difference as an attitude dating to events of 1914, when the easy availability of potent forces in Europe proved too tempting, and political tensions quickly escalated into a world war.[4] Conversely, U.S. views of military power were marked by the lesson of Pearl Harbor—and seared again by the devastating terrorist assault on U.S. soil on September 11, 2001—never again to be caught unprepared to respond. If these hypotheses are accurate, Europe may continue to lag in the readiness and modernization that are basic tenets of U.S. warmaking.

There are, however, also hopeful signs to the contrary, in EU policy statements such as those at Helsinki in December 1999 and Nice in November 2000; in the substance of a number of allied national strategic reviews in France, Germany, Greece, the Netherlands, the United Kingdom, and elsewhere; and in terms of recent, if limited, defense procurement. There are in these statements indications that European attitudes are moving, albeit slowly, toward favoring the fruits of the RMA. That bodes well for reconciling a sense of common purpose in the application of military

## Table 9–1. Defense Spending as a Percentage of Gross Domestic Product

| NATO allies | 1990 | 1995 | 1996 | 1997 | 1998 | 1999 | 2000 |
|---|---|---|---|---|---|---|---|
| Belgium | 2.4 | 1.7 | 1.6 | 1.5 | 1.5 | 1.5 | 1.4 |
| Canada | 2.0 | 1.5 | 1.4 | 1.2 | 1.3 | 1.3 | 1.2 |
| Czech Republic | 5.1 | 2.0 | 1.9 | 1.8 | 2.0 | 2.2 | 2.2 |
| Denmark | 2.1 | 1.8 | 1.7 | 1.7 | 1.6 | 1.6 | 1.5 |
| France | 3.5 | 3.1 | 3.0 | 2.9 | 2.8 | 2.7 | 2.6 |
| Germany | 2.8 | 1.7 | 1.6 | 1.6 | 1.5 | 1.5 | 1.5 |
| Greece | 4.6 | 4.3 | 4.5 | 4.6 | 4.8 | 4.9 | 4.9 |
| Hungary | 2.4 | 1.4 | 1.6 | 1.5 | 1.4 | 1.6 | 1.7 |
| Italy | 2.5 | 2.0 | 2.0 | 2.0 | 2.0 | 2.0 | 1.9 |
| Luxembourg | 0.9 | 0.8 | 0.8 | 0.8 | 0.8 | 0.8 | 0.7 |
| The Netherlands | 2.6 | 2.0 | 1.9 | 1.9 | 1.8 | 1.8 | 1.6 |
| Norway | 2.7 | 2.1 | 2.0 | 1.9 | 2.0 | 2.0 | 1.9 |
| Poland | 2.7 | 2.2 | 2.5 | 2.1 | 2.2 | 2.1 | 2.0 |
| Portugal | 2.7 | 2.6 | 2.4 | 2.4 | 2.2 | 2.2 | 2.2 |
| Spain | 1.8 | 1.5 | 1.4 | 1.4 | 1.3 | 1.2 | 1.3 |
| Turkey | 5.1 | 4.8 | 4.8 | 4.7 | 4.8 | 5.3 | 5.7 |
| United Kingdom | 4.2 | 3.0 | 2.9 | 2.6 | 2.6 | 2.5 | 2.4 |
| United States | 5.5 | 3.8 | 3.5 | 3.4 | 3.1 | 3.0 | 3.0 |
| Non-U.S. Average | 3.0 | 2.3 | 2.2 | 2.1 | 2.1 | 2.1 | 2.0 |
| NATO Average | 4.3 | 3.1 | 2.9 | 2.8 | 2.6 | 2.6 | 2.5 |

Source: DOD Report to Congress on Allied Burdensharing, 2001.

power and for narrowing the military-technology gap between the United States and its allies.

## The Role of Interoperability in U.S. Military Doctrine

Interoperability between U.S. and allied military forces anywhere in the world depends on a combination of systems connectivity and technological comparability. Multinational forces and platforms, no less than U.S. forces performing joint operations, must have comparable capabilities to execute a common operational concept such as standoff precision engagement or all-weather operations. Comparability requires more than plug-and-play technology for systems integration. It demands compatible doctrines, similar readiness levels, and sustaining resources sufficient to stay in the game. Transmitting secure, real-time targeting data is worthless if the receiving node or force element has no precision strike systems, doctrine for their employment, training for the engagement, or means to bring its systems to the fight. However, comparability can be achieved without having to buy identical hardware such as missiles or aircraft.

Communications connectivity among forces—voice and data networking—is the essential element: systems not linked to a common information grid cannot share information with other systems, sensors-to-shooters, commanders-to-subelements, or suppliers-to-consumers, in a multinational force. Organizations as well as individual systems must be linked for connectivity of command and control ($C^2$) as well as intelligence, reconnaissance, and surveillance, logistics, and all other essential combat functions. Reliable, secure, and real-time connectivity is required for every manner of communications and data exchange. With such a grid in place, every system will have access to what amounts to a common operational picture. The result will be true interoperability, collective functionality that provides for rapid decisionmaking and operational follow-through by a single cohesive force.

In U.S. national security strategy and military doctrine, as reflected in *Joint Vision 2020*, operating with other national militaries is considered the norm, not the exception.[5] Coalitions are valued for both political and military purposes, to share risks and burdens and to broaden international support and access. However, an inescapable reality is that the value of a coalition depends on the degree that interoperability has been contemplated and assured in advance, through investment in similar capabilities, development of common doctrine, combined joint planning, and multinational exercises.

The capabilities of each nation's forces determine what forces can participate and in what missions. Having several nations able to contribute to the most decisive combat roles is crucial to perceptions of a true combined operation rather than merely a coalition façade draped over a U.S. operation. Allies must have some capabilities similar to U.S. forces and, more important, not have to rely too much on U.S. support to sustain them in forward areas. Forces with outdated technology, incomplete contingency doctrines, limited sustainment, frail $C^2$, or weak intelligence capacity could dilute military power more by participating than if they stayed home.

NATO is unique in that Alliance forces already integrate more closely with U.S. forces than do any other forces in the world. NATO has invested a half-century in developing a common doctrine and common operating procedures (NATO Standardization Agreements, of which more than 1,300 have been published), and in urging its members to meet objectives for force modernization, technological capabilities, and other force goals such as readiness, supportability, and deployability.

Yet NATO interoperability has always fallen short of military leaders' desires, and prodding members (including the United States) to do more has been a constant theme of NATO declarations. In the future, agreements on operational and procedural standards alone will not be enough to achieve the kind of interoperability the United States sees as essential. Future operational success will demand far more data connectivity among forces than ever before. Nations will need forces equipped with fast, reliable, secure communications and high-speed data accessibility. Modern networked communications links and data systems will be essential at lower levels. Networks will be required between ships, aircraft, and small unit ground force elements, across all components and among allies.

Allied forces that the United States will seek for partners in the future must have systems with comparable capabilities, mixing leading-edge systems with older yet still potent systems. Legacy systems will still make important contributions for many years, even if their size, logistics requirements, or vulnerabilities preclude using them in first-response missions. However, to be effective, even legacy systems must be retrofitted with modern sensors and secure voice/data communications.

Newer technologies, some just being developed and some commercial off-the-shelf, will lead the way. Initial response forces, most notably air systems and special operations forces, must have a credible capability for rapid deployment and employment, effective engagement and sustainment, and force protection, and they must have these from day one of an operation. That means refocusing procurement priorities and adjusting approaches to multinational defense planning, doctrine, and operational concepts. Acquiring these capabilities, in years rather than decades, means focusing on commercially available technologies on both sides of the Atlantic, especially in the information technology sector.

The bad news about interoperability is that NATO militaries, although working more closely together than ever before in Bosnia, Kosovo, and Macedonia, are growing less compatible and less connected at the high end of technology. The United States places high priority on improving the ability of NATO militaries to cooperate across a growing array of missions related to crisis management, even as it transforms to embrace the potential of the RMA. The United States is irreversibly committed to the pursuit of the most advanced technology in order to preserve its military edge. If that pursuit slackens, the United States risks reduced military effectiveness and perhaps eventually the loss of its technological leadership. Pursuing these two strategic goals—allied participation in the full array of coalition operations and operationalizing the latest technologies as early as possible—is the right path for America. However, the two will work at cross-purposes unless ways are found to close the widening technological gap between the United States and its allies, especially in NATO. One remedy for bringing these two essential elements of U.S. military strategy into harmony, especially in the field of information technologies, is achieving the objectives of the NATO Defense Capabilities Initiative, and that goal should be the focus of greatest allied effort for the near term.

## Defining the Current Gap

Force capabilities result from many factors, including force size, planning, readiness, sustainability, and deployability. Yet even if all those factors are positive, a force will still not be interoperable with others if it cannot keep pace with other units, talk to other operators, or engage targets at the ranges and under the conditions of the operational concept for the mission at hand. Interoperability is linked to force modernization: keeping at least a portion of the force equipped with the latest military systems and technologies. That calls for continuous investment in R&D to find and refine new technologies. Without such programs, a nation will be incapable of taking part in the most crucial operations; it would be relegated to peripheral roles during a crisis while other allies picked up the slack.

Tables 9–2 through 9–6 indicate some of the most modern systems of each ally—their best capabilities—portraying primary features, their numbers, and their legacy age. This information gives a sense of how compatible these systems are, but what it cannot show is the systems' readiness to participate in combined crisis-response operations, or the "true interoperability quotient." That depends on a broader profile that would include personnel training, maintenance, supply, and spare equipment (such as operationally ready "floats" that can be quickly forwarded to replace losses) that are essential to sustain the force in the field. Also not apparent is the connectivity of these systems with other NATO systems as defined by a common NATO voice and data communications standard. The tables do make clear the notable trend that nations are investing, if meagerly, in new capabilities; this gives hope that, with reasonable effort, NATO can become far more compatible in the years just ahead.

## NATO Land Systems Technology

The major legacy land systems (see tables 9–2 and 9–3) are never foremost in RMA debates, yet heavy as well as light forces and special operations forces will remain essential to the future inventories of land forces. Technologies related to transformed land forces center on C⁴I, deployability, sustainability, target engagement solutions, and force protection. Most European land forces are in the process of restructuring into smaller, more deployable units in order to meet both NATO guidance and the EU commitment to field a deployable land force by 2003. France, Germany, Italy, the Netherlands, and the United Kingdom, among other European NATO members, have completed force restructuring plans and are executing them. On the U.S. side, land forces already were being task-organized routinely; actual restructuring to lighter forces only got started in the wake of the 1999 mission in Kosovo, where the need for a new mix of firepower, force protection, and speed hit home. (See chapter 4 in this volume on U.S. Army transformation.)

In fact, an impressive amount of NATO legacy systems such as tanks, indirect fire systems (artillery, rockets, and missiles), helicopters, and air defense systems have been upgraded throughout the 1990s to incorporate modern capabilities for fire control, communications, and self-protection. Other essential but less glamorous upgrades include protective gear for nuclear, chemical, and biological weapons, land mine protection, night vision sights, and individual soldier equipment. Another reality is that European militaries have long had light armored vehicles similar to those now being tested by the United States.

Table 9–2 indicates the primary tanks and table 9–3 the first-line indirect fire systems of each ally. Countries that have no equipment in a category are omitted. Note the prevalence of Germany's Leopard tank and the U.S. multiple launch rocket system (MLRS) among allied forces. Both these systems are relatively modern in their latest versions, though they would be regarded as legacy systems by age. The weight of the MLRS makes it a candidate for lighter armored forces. The latest version of the MLRS, the M270–A1, is essentially a new system and is capable of launching the Army tactical missile system (ATACMS)–A1, a long-range, GPS-aided missile. Only the United States has this system today; however, France, Germany, Italy, and the United Kingdom have it on order.

Table 9–2. **Most Capable NATO Armor**

| Country | Number and System | Main gun (mm) | Speed (kph) | Range (km) | Weight (tons) | Latest Upgrade |
|---------|-------------------|---------------|-------------|------------|---------------|----------------|
| Belgium | 132 Leopard 1A5 | 120 | 65 | 600 | 46 | 1990 |
| Canada | 114 Leopard C–2 | 120 | 65 | 600 | 46 | 1996 |
| Czech Republic | 250 T–72CZ M4 | 125 | 60 | 480 | 51 | 1996 |
| Denmark | 51 Leopard 2A5 | 120 | 72 | 550 | 61 | 1998 |
| France | 310 LeClerc | 120 | 70 | 545 | 56 | 1992 |
| Germany | 250 Leopard 2A6 | 120 | 72 | 500 | 66 | 2001 |
| Greece | 245 Leopard 1A5 | 120 | 60 | 600 | 47 | 1998 |
| Hungary | 238 T–72 | 125 | 60 | 480 | 51 | 1998 |
| Italy | 200 Ariete | 120 | 65 | 550 | 59 | 1995 |
| The Netherlands | 180 Leopard 2A6 | 120 | 72 | 500 | 66 | 1995 |
| Norway | 52 Leopard 2A4 | 120 | 65 | 600 | 66 | 2001 |
| Poland | 186 PT 91 | 125 | 60 | 650 | 50 | 1992 |
| Portugal | 86 M60A3 | 105 | 48 | 480 | 58 | 1978 |
| Spain | 219 Leopard 2A6 | 120 | 72 | 500 | 66 | 2002 |
| Turkey | 150 Leopard 1A5 | 120 | 60 | 600 | 47 | 1991 |
| United Kingdom | 192 Challenger 2 | 120 | 56 | 450 | 68 | 1994 |
| United States | 7700 M1A1/A2 | 120 | 65 | 390 | 62 | 2001 |

*Note:* All have night/infrared capability. All except Hungary can fire on the move.

These systems will no doubt be retained in transformed force structures, which the United States will want to be interoperable with its own transformed forces.

Another legacy system that will likely be retained in transformed force structures is the attack helicopter. European allies field almost 800 attack helicopters, although most are old, lacking all-weather target engagement and adequate self-protection. Still, at least France, the Netherlands, Turkey, and the United Kingdom (in addition to the United States) will be procuring new attack helicopters over the next few years.

### Modern NATO Air and Space Systems

The most serious gap between the United States and its allies is in air combat capabilities (tables 9–4 and 9–5). Key concerns are the lack of precision weapons, secure communications, aerial refueling, and strategic lift.

## Table 9–3. Most Capable NATO Indirect Fire Systems

| Country | Number and System | Range (km) | Primary Munition | Latest Upgrade |
|---|---|---|---|---|
| Belgium | 114 M109A2 SP | 14.6 | 155 | 1979 |
| Canada | 58 M109A4 | 14.6 | 155 | 1985 |
| Czech Republic | 135 RM–70 MRL | 20.3 | 122 | 1972 |
| Denmark | 8 M270 MLRS | 31.6 | M26 DPICM | 2002 |
| France | 55 M270 MLRS | 165 | DPICM/ATACMS | 2002 |
| Germany | 154 M270 MLRS | 165 | DPICM/ATACMS | 2002 |
| Greece | 27 M270 MLRS | 165 | DPICM/ATACMS | 1989 |
| Hungary | 56 BM–21 MRL | 22.5 | 122 | 1970 |
| Italy | 24 M270 MLRS | 165 | DPICM/ATACMS | 2002 |
| The Netherlands | 22 M270 MLRS | 31.6 | DPICM | 1989 |
| Norway | 12 M270 MLRS | 31.6 | DPICM | 1989 |
| Poland | 228 BM–21 MRL | 22.5 | 122 | 1970 |
| Portugal | 6 M109A2 | 14.6 | 155 | 1979 |
| Spain | 14 Teruel MRL | 28 | 140 | 1980 |
| Turkey | 15 M270 MLRS | 31.6 | DPICM | 1989 |
| United Kingdom | 63 M270 MLRS | 165 | DPICM/ATACMS | 2002 |
| United States | 19 M270A1 MLRS (of 800 total MLRS systems) | 300 | ATACMS–1A | 2002 |

*Note:* None have precision-guided munitions at present except United States. SP = self propelled; MRL = multiple rocket launcher; MLRS = multiple launch rocket system; DPICM = dual purpose/improved conventional munitions; ATACMS = army tactical missile system.

The paucity of specialized aircraft—for airborne early warning such as the airborne warning and control system (AWACS), airborne ground surveillance such as the joint surveillance target attack radar system (JSTARS), suppression of enemy air defenses (SEAD), or electronic warfare—is a major gap in a new era of sophisticated air campaigns. If these systems cannot be acquired at the national level, members should move quickly to fund them at the NATO level. In table 9–4, the column indicating the number of most capable combat aircraft also shows, for some countries, the overall combat aircraft inventory in parentheses: these are allies that have sizable inventories of legacy (in some cases obsolete) aircraft. Paring

Table 9–4. **Most Capable NATO Aircraft**

| Country | Number and System (selected totals in type)* | Year of Construction/ Latest Upgrade | Precision Weapons | Night/All-Weather Targeting | Secure C³/Data Links | Aerial Refuel |
|---|---|---|---|---|---|---|
| Belgium | 129 F–16 AM/BM | 1979/1997 | Yes | Yes | Yes | Yes |
| Canada | 122 CF/A–18A/B | 1988/1999 | — | — | Yes | Yes |
| Czech Republic | 47 L–159 (140) | 2000/— | — | — | — | — |
| Denmark | 69 F–16 AM/BM | 1980/1997 | — | — | Yes | Yes |
| France | 60 Mirage 2000D (517) | 1994/2000 | Yes | Yes | Yes | Yes |
| Germany | 189 Tornado (457) | 1991/1999 | Yes | Yes | Yes | Yes |
| Greece | 75 F–16CG (458) | 1988/1999 | Yes | Yes | Yes | Yes |
| Hungary | 12 MiG–29 | 1993/— | — | — | — | — |
| Italy | 116 Tornado (336) | 1989/1999 | Yes | Yes | Yes | Yes |
| The Netherlands | 157 F–16 AM/BM | 1979/1998 | Yes | Yes | Yes | Yes |
| Norway | 58 F–16 AM/BM | 1980/1998 | — | — | Yes | Yes |
| Poland | 121 MiG–29 (267) | 1989/1999 | — | — | — | — |
| Portugal | 20 F–16 AM/BM (51) | 1994/2000 | Yes | Yes | Yes | Yes |
| Spain | 90 EF/A–18 A/B (211) | 1999/1999 | Yes | — | Yes | Yes |
| Turkey | 240 F–16 C/D (505) | 1996/1999 | Yes | Yes | Yes | Yes |
| United Kingdom | 214 Tornado (429) | 1992/1999 | Yes | Yes | Yes | Yes |
| United States | 210 F–15E / 184 F16D | 1990/1998 / 1996/1999 | Yes | Yes | Yes | Yes |

* Numbers in parentheses denote overall total combat aircraft inventory.

these inventories would free considerable resources to invest in a smaller, more capable fleet.

The top operational U.S. air combat systems include the F–16D, F–15E, F–14D, and F/A–18D tactical fighters, as well as highly capable strategic fleets of B–52H and B–2A bombers. The top operational allied systems are early models of the F–16 and F–18, plus the British and German Tornado, the British Jaguar and Harrier, and the French Mirage 2000D. The latest model Mirage is the only European system that is in a class with the best U.S. systems. The Europeans do not field bombers comparable to U.S. aircraft; they use variants of ground attack fighter bombers instead. No European system includes stealth technology.

Many allied systems are capable of aerial refueling; as table 9–5 shows, seven allies of the United States together maintain a mix of over 70 tanker or tanker/transport aircraft, although these add up to a much smaller capability than the U.S. fleet of over 600 large tankers. Major European shortcomings are the lack of secure aircraft communications to link attack aircraft to key sensor systems such as JSTARS or AWACS and a very limited all-weather precision target engagement capability. In addition to NATO communication satellites, France and the United Kingdom operate communication and photoreconnaissance space systems, with several other states joining France as investment partners.

## Major NATO Naval Systems

For future operations, the most important major naval systems will be aircraft carriers, submarines, destroyers, and frigates (see table 9–6). Submarines are expanding their roles into special operations and cruise missile platforms. Destroyers and frigates serve several roles, including theater air defense, naval gunfire support of ground forces, and enforcing embargos at sea, as occurred during the 1992–1995 NATO/Western European Union SHARP GUARD operation that effectively embargoed the flow of arms to warring factions in Bosnia. Amphibious capabilities are also important for crisis management. As table 9–6 shows, four European NATO allies operate six small aircraft carriers, two of which are new or recently upgraded. Besides the United States, 14 NATO members have navies that together operate 102 submarines and 195 destroyers and frigates. Of the 14 members, 11 also have some amphibious capability.

## C⁴I Interoperability

C$^4$I is the central nervous system of interoperability, and it continues to be the area of greatest incompatibility. This is a rising concern as the U.S. focus turns to network-centric operations and warfighting. The United States and its allies, in seeking to modernize their command, control, and communications (C$^3$) capabilities, must of necessity look first for new systems that link to existing systems, yet that perpetuates systems that cannot link to each other, sometimes even within the same national force.

European C$^4$I modernization is a struggle to update cumbersome, outdated systems designed for forces operating along a fixed defensive front. Secure, advanced communications along with networks for acquiring, integrating, and exploiting real-time intelligence are still scarce, found mainly at major headquarters. Modernization trudges forward with acquisition of some mobile systems, such as France's RITA 2000 update and

## Table 9–5. Key NATO Support Aircraft and Satellites

| | Aerial Refueling | AWACS and AGS | EW Aircraft | SEAD Aircraft | Airlift | Communications/ Intelligence Satellites | UAVs |
|---|---|---|---|---|---|---|---|
| NATO | — | 18 E–3 | — | — | — | NATO 4 | — |
| Belgium | — | — | — | — | — | — | Yes |
| Canada | 5 C–130 | — | 5 helo | — | — | — | Yes |
| Czech Republic | — | — | — | — | — | — | Yes |
| Denmark | — | — | — | — | — | — | Yes |
| France | 14 C–135, 14 C–160 | 3 E–3 | 1 DC–8, 4 C–160 | — | 60 C–160 | Syracuse, II Helios 1A/1B | Yes |
| Germany | — | — | — | 35 Tornado | 84 C–160 | — | Yes |
| Greece | — | — | — | — | 15 C–130 | — | — |
| Italy | 4 B707 | — | 1 PD–808 | — | 15 C–130 | — | Yes |
| The Netherlands | 2 DC–10 | — | — | — | 2 C–130 | — | Yes |
| Norway | — | — | — | — | 6 C–130 | — | — |
| Poland | — | — | — | — | 2 Tu–154 | — | — |
| Portugal | — | — | — | — | 6 C–130 | — | — |
| Spain | 5 KC–130 | — | 2 Falcon 20 | — | 7 C–130 | — | — |
| Turkey | 7 KC–135 | — | 2 CN–235 | 20 F–16D | 13 C–130, 19 C–160 | — | Yes |
| United Kingdom | 4 Tristar, 21 VC–10 | 7 E–3D | 26 Nimrod 1 | — | 4 C–17, 51 C–130 | Skynet 4 | Yes |
| United States | 546 KC–135, 59 KC–10 | 33 E–3 AWACS, 8 JSTARS AGS | 2 squadrons EC–130 | Many | 126 C–5, 59 C–17, 125 C–141 | Many | Yes |

*Notes:* AWACS = airborne warning and control system; JSTARS = joint surveillance target attack radar system; AGS = airborne ground surveillance; EW = electronic warfare; SEAD = suppression of enemy air defenses; UAV = unmanned aerial vehicle

Table 9–6. **Most Modern NATO Naval Capabilities**

| Country | Aircraft Carriers (recent upgrades)/ number of associated aircraft | Submarines | Destroyers | Frigates |
|---|---|---|---|---|
| Belgium | — | — | — | 3 |
| Canada | — | 1 | 4 | 12 |
| Denmark | — | 3 | — | — |
| France | 1 (2000)/40 | 11 | 4 | 29 |
| Germany | — | 14 | 2 | 12 |
| Greece | — | 8 | 4 | 12 |
| Italy | 1/16 | 7 | 4 | 24 |
| The Netherlands | — | 4 | 3 | 12 |
| Norway | — | 10 | — | 4 |
| Poland | — | 3 | 1 | 2 |
| Portugal | — | 3 | — | 6 |
| Spain | 1/6–10 | 8 | — | 15 |
| Turkey | — | 14 | — | 11 |
| United Kingdom | 3 (2001)/8–16 | 16 | 11 | 20 |
| United States | 12 (2001)/66 | 74 | 52 | 35 |

the UK Falcon and Cormorant systems, both supporting land force operations. More modernization is in the pipeline. Since 1990, many allies have invested in upgrades to tactical communications, acquiring digital radios and networks that carry voice, data, and video. Operational programs include the German AUTOKO 90, used effectively in Bosnia; the Italian Mobile Integrated Digital Automatic System (MIDAS); the British MRS 2000 scalable tactical communications grid; and the French Tactical LAS, a secure multimedia, digital local area network, which Belgium also uses and Denmark will soon use. These systems do not connect all forces at all levels, nor are they linked to the forces of allies. Secure systems for high-volume voice and data sharing are far less common than in U.S. forces. The primary C⁴I conduit for allied interoperability remains the liaison team.

On the personnel side of C², Balkans missions have provided significant experience for European officers, which bodes well for success in future crises. European flag officers from the United Kingdom, France,

Germany, Spain, and Italy have served as operational commanders of combined and joint task forces in the Balkans theater of operations for almost 10 years, beginning in 1992 with the United Nations Protection Force and extending through the Implementation Force/Stabilization Force in Bosnia, the Kosovo Force, and now in Macedonia. European commanders and staffs at all levels have honed their decisionmaking skills in difficult, often combat-like environments. Perhaps more important for the long term, they have seen the value of secure, high-speed communications and information as effective C⁴I decision support and task execution tools. The growing cohort of Balkans-seasoned European commanders will eventually rise to lead European militaries and to influence the design and posture of future European C⁴I in a positive way.

Structurally, Europe has adjusted to the tasks of C⁴I in crisis management, from the political-military level to the operational and tactical levels. National and multinational (EU and NATO) military staffs have refocused their strategies, concepts, plans, and doctrines away from Cold War scenarios and toward peace operations. Institutional resistance to change is diminishing as a new generation of military leaders comes into positions of increasing authority. For example, Germany activated a new central command headquarters in 2001 to oversee the planning and execution of all contingency operations. France and the United Kingdom already have such headquarters. Below this level, the EU identifies force headquarters from among a list of national headquarters offered by member states as deployable C⁴I capability for EU-led operations. These are still, by and large, single-service commands with only limited experience controlling joint and combined task forces.

Intelligence gathering enhancements by European militaries remain focused on "stovepipe" reporting and analysis for immediate commands, and still produce either dated information or, if real time, only limited local reporting. Belgium, Canada, the Czech Republic, Denmark, France, Germany, Italy, the Netherlands, Turkey, and the United Kingdom have operational unmanned aerial vehicle reconnaissance fleets, although these are not networked. The use of automated information processing systems and networked sensors is sparse.

Strategic C⁴I systems in Europe are few compared to the United States. France operates the photoreconnaissance satellites Helios 1A and 1B. The French utilize the telecommunication satellite Syracuse II and the British use the Skynet 4, both commercially operated systems. However, these European telecommunications satellites have long been linked to the

United States via the NATO Defense Satellite Communications Systems. The French reconnaissance satellite program includes Italy and Spain as minority partners.

### In-Place Logistics Technologies

Deployable logistics capability and automated logistics management architectures are major shortfalls across Europe. Throughout the Cold War, nations bore sole responsibility for force sustainment, and they still do today. As a defensive alliance, NATO focused on fixed, interior lines of supply rather than long-range sustainment. Logistics is both a systemic and a resource problem. It is unlikely that European allies can generate solutions to either problem at the national or EU level anytime soon. Most nations are simply too small, while the EU has far to go before a consensus is reached on policies, much less systems, for multinational logistics, though that is the long-term goal. The only near- to mid-term solution is the NATO hybrid concept of pooling national logistics into a common multinational center, supported by strategic assets of larger members, as a way to support a deployed combined joint task force (described in more detail later in this chapter).

Regardless of how supplies are organized and automated, investment is lacking in on-hand stocks, especially of critical supplies such as spare engines, radios, medical items, and optimal munitions for an austere operating environment. The potential of a hostile operating environment involving nuclear, biological, or chemical weapons raises other logistics challenges that must be addressed. European nations will have to invest in sufficient supplies to sustain the proposed European Rapid Reaction Force (ERRF) for its initial deployment phase and ultimately for its declared goal of being able to deploy for one year. These shortfalls have no definitive solutions as yet.

## The Future Gap: Converging or Diverging?

While the current gap is narrower than many would suspect, the future gap is uncertain and could be more prone to widening than contracting. The allies already had a daunting task in catching up to the United States before the events of September 11 triggered acceleration in U.S. defense spending. Some European powers have responded to the terrorist attacks with major spending increases, but such funds will be spent piecemeal by individual members without either a centralized or sustained investment strategy. Some national programs, such as that of the United Kingdom, are focused and productive, but others are hampered by weaker political consensus. Much energy is spent in the debate over whether to join with the EU or the United States, and in each case, how deep the relationship should be. Some try to straddle both venues, further reducing their own effectiveness. In any case, the irreducible minimum of 15 separate national defense organizations means many duplicative programs and will continue to be a drag on Europe's ability to close the gap.

The state of the future gap will depend on both force modernization investments and force transformation strategies. Managing and eventually closing the capabilities gap is possible, provided diligence and high-level emphasis are sustained through the end of the decade. Serious efforts are now under way in both of these areas in several capitals. France has even emphasized the importance of coordinating defense plans by inviting comment from other European powers.

**Modernization Investments**

Figure 9–1 indicates that all European NATO allies except Turkey and the United Kingdom invest a lesser share of their defense budgets than does the United States on R&D and procurement, the two traditional measures of force modernization. Moreover, lower European percentages are exacerbated because national defense budgets are much smaller. Figures for 2000 are representative of the steady trend in significantly lower defense investments in Europe since the Cold War.

Although Figure 9–1 presents a bleak trend, the September 11 terrorist attack has triggered reassessments in spending priorities in several EU capitals. Time will tell what significance the attacks have on increasing European defense investment. Strategic defense reviews by France, Germany, Greece, the Netherlands, and the United Kingdom, among others, had already signaled that force realignments and new priorities were in the offing. New programs being supported aim at forces better optimized for crisis response. In fact, there is no shortage of modernization programs under way in Europe, though most only nip at the edges of real transformation. Many announced investment decisions would become operational (if they remain on track) in the 2008 to 2015 timeframe. In other words, Europe could have some transformed forces ready about the same time as U.S. transformation initiatives are forecast to reach operational capability, if our own momentum can be sustained.

The United Kingdom has emerged as a leader, not only in terms of its real defense capabilities and robust role in the Balkans, but also by imparting a sense of urgency to other European allies to do more on defense. That is helping create public support across Europe for defense. For instance,

Figure 9–1. **Modernization Spending as Percentage of Defense Spending, 2000**

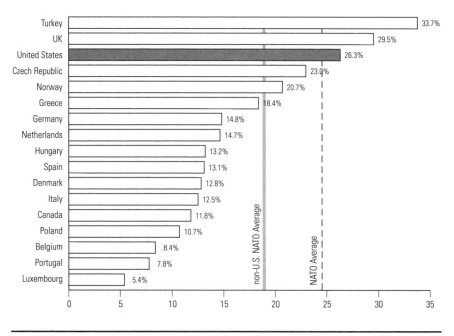

*Note:* The solid line represents non-U.S. NATO average of 19.4 percent. The dashed line represents overall NATO average for modernization spending as a percent of total defense spending (24.1%). Comparable data for France was not available. Modernization includes major equipment procurement and research and development, but excludes ammunition, for consistency with NATO reporting criteria.

Germany and France may follow the British lead in leasing strategic airlift assets (for example, C–17 or An–70) while awaiting the EU A400M airlifter in 2007. Another impetus for action comes from the EU commitment to field the ERRF by 2003. Operations in the Balkans have provided a first-hand look at how EU legacy capabilities stack up to the demands of new missions and have also crystalized new requirements. The programs shown in table 9–7 illustrate how Europe is responding to these catalysts and is beginning to answer the challenge of the RMA.

## European Transformation

The long, peripheral process of defining a European identity in security and defense is testimony to the enduring core of national sovereignty among EU members. Only major crises seem to catalyze progress. Such was the case when the Union declared its intention in Cologne in June

## Table 9–7. Select Major Defense Investment Programs in Europe: Program, Participating Powers, Forecast Operational Date, Remarks

### Land Systems

FELIN (France) Fielding date unknown: Clothing-integrated soldier communications system for one-third of ground force

VBCI, GTK, MRAV (France, Germany, the Netherlands, and United Kingdom respectively) 2006: Deployable infantry fighting vehicles (France, 700; others, 200 each)

Attack Helo (France, United Kingdom) 2002: France: Tiger (numbers undetermined); United Kingdom: Apache (16)

Transport Helo (France, United Kingdom) 2001: France, Italy: NH–90 (27), United Kingdom: Merlin

Air defense (Germany, Italy) Germany: LeFlaSys missile defense for air mobile forces 2002; Germany, Italy: MEADS 2007

### Air Systems

Eurofighter (Germany, Italy, United Kingdom) Late 2002: 620 planned. Not stealth, otherwise advanced. Brimstone (AT), Meteor (ATA) and Storm Shadow (cruise) missiles, all-weather, standoff capable

A–400M (Belgium, France, Germany, Luxembourg, Portugal, Spain, Turkey, United Kingdom) 2007: Transport aircraft critical to EU deployment capabilities. Approximately 190 aircraft

Rafale (France) ongoing: 76 for air force/navy. Deep strike, with Scalp/EG cruise missile and AASM air-to-ground missile

Meteor (France, Germany, Italy) 2008: Active radar, beyond visual range air-to-air missile

JSF (United States) (Denmark, Canada, Italy, the Netherlands, Norway, Turkey, United Kingdom) 2008: Ground attack fighter. United Kingdom full partner with United States. Replacement for U.S. F–16s and British AV–8 Harrier

### Naval Systems

Frigates (France, Italy, Germany, Spain): France: 2 Horizon Frigates (2006–08) + 8 multimission frigates, first in 2008; Germany: 3 Type 124 frigates (first in 2002); Italy: 3 Horizons (first in 2007); Spain: 4 Aegis F–100 frigates 2002–07

Destroyers (United Kingdom): 12 Type 45 destroyers beginning in 2007

Submarines (France, Germany, United Kingdom): France: 2 ballistic missile 2004/2010; and 2 attack subs 2012+; Germany: 4 U–212 diesel subs; United Kingdom: 3 cruise missile attack subs beginning in 2005

Aircraft Carriers (United Kingdom) 2012 and 2015: 2 larger carriers (CVF) replace 3 current Invincible class carriers

Destroyers (United Kingdom) beginning in 2007: 12 Type 45 destroyers

Strategic Lift (United Kingdom): two landing platform docks; two new landing ships (dates not determined)

Table 9–7. **Select Major Defense Investment Programs in Europe: Program, Participating Powers, Forecast Operational Date, Remarks**—*continued*

---

### C⁴ISR Systems

Satellites (France, United Kingdom) France: Syracuse III COMSAT 2003, Helios II INTELSAT 2004; United Kingdom: Skynet 5 COMSAT 2003; Helios II Recon Sat (all-weather)

UAV (France) 2009: 12 high-altitude, long-endurance reconnaissance UAVs

National C⁴I Systems (Turkey) Date unknown: command and control information system for C⁴I

Battlefield Communications (United Kingdom) Date unknown: Bowman land force digital communications/data system—48,000; Personal Role Radio—37,000

---

### Logistics Systems

Amphibious (France) 2004–06: Marine assault amphibious transports

FSTA (United Kingdom) 2007–09: Future Strategic Tanker Aircraft (number undetermined)

Landing Ships (United Kingdom) date unknown: Two landing platforms and two landing ships (under construction)

Joint Logistics HQ (United Kingdom) Present: Two headquarters set up to support two separate operations of the new multiservice JRRF

---

1999 to create what would become the European Rapid Reaction Force for acting within NATO, or autonomously (under the EU, for example) if NATO chose not to act. That watershed event may mark the beginning of a European structural transformation toward more effectively coordinated national programs and a more cohesive, capable European whole.

The immediate goal is creation of the ERRF by 2003. The ERRF, informally called the headline goal force,[6] is intended to be able to deploy 50,000 to 60,000 troops and associated air and naval capabilities within 60 days and to operate for up to 1 year across the full range of Petersberg Tasks, which are humanitarian and rescue, peacekeeping, and crisis management (including peacemaking).[7]

EU members have displayed resolve on the ERRF, and they probably will be close enough to their target to announce success by their deadline. Force commitments of over 100,000 troops, 400 aircraft, and 100 ships have been made, and gaps are being identified and filled. Exercises are planned, and permanent staffs have been formed to provide political and military advice to EU leaders.

The United States has concerns that the ERRF will be tailored only for low-intensity or peacekeeping operations, although the EU has neither qualified nor quantified the Petersberg Tasks. EU members are reported to have committed their best troops, front-line aircraft, and major combatant ships. If the Union designed its best forces for low-intensity operations only, NATO interoperability and cohesion would be undermined, and a modern, RMA-like EU force capable of operating alongside the United States in high-intensity scenarios would not emerge. The logical approach is for the EU to gain experience as it fields forces for the first time; however, it should declare and demonstrate that the ERRF will be capable of operating across the full range of military tasks. If so, then the ERRF should be a full partner for the United States by the end of the decade, when the U.S. transformation is expected to be complete.

### Germany's Future Defense Posture: The Critical Question

Germany, the most populous EU member and the one with the largest EU economy, is critical to the future strength or weakness of the Union in the domains of security and defense. How Germany invests in defense in the future will have a major impact on the capabilities gap and interoperability. Germany is the last major country to begin restructuring its armed forces, and it continues to have one of the lowest defense budgets in Europe, at 1.5 percent of gross domestic product (GDP), in spite of the Bundeswehr's long list of unmet requirements for future missions. Modernization investment is so low that German defense industries probably will have to merge with international partners to survive. Germany's domestic industrial base has shrunk by two-thirds since the end of the Cold War, and few contracts with the Bundeswehr are on the horizon. Although the Bundeswehr is larger than the forces of France and the United Kingdom, Germany's defense budget is but two-thirds that of either country.

Despite post-Cold War reassessments in 1994 and 2000, some German defense experts still point to the future—after the 2002 elections—as the period in which real reform is likely.[8] Future mission requirements for Germany's military forces are still uncertain. Germany reluctantly sent fighter aircraft to Turkey in 1991 as a Gulf War contingency, and it was hesitant to deploy forces 10 years later to the EU mission in Macedonia. However, following the September 11 terrorist attacks, Chancellor Gerhard Schroeder declared Germany's post-World War II timidity in international security to be "irrevocably" over. Subsequently, Germany has supported the U.S. operation in Afghanistan (Operation *Enduring Freedom*) with air transport, medical units, chemical defense, maritime, and special operations forces. That experience may speed the Bundeswehr's transformation and help clarify what Germany expects of its armed forces, beyond national self-defense, within a NATO or EU context. Germany's future direction is a major concern of the United States as it looks to see how strong a force the EU will provide.

## The EU Strategic Direction

Will Europe's strategic direction converge with that of the United States in the wake of the September 11 attacks? Estimating how much the Union collectively may move toward convergence with the United States on security matters, and thereby encourage interoperability, would be premature. Factors already in play—including concerns about export controls and competition and divergent views on arms control and missile defense—have not disappeared, although they will be overshadowed in the near term by close collaboration on countering terrorism. By November, two months after the attack, no European power had indicated an increase in defense spending. To the contrary, France indicated that September 11 and its aftermath would have no impact on its recently approved 2002 budget, although previously proposed increases to 1.9 percent of GDP (in procurement and R&D, as well as overall) were sustained. Germany and the United Kingdom have not acted, and analysts in both countries discount the potential for increases in the near term at least. Counterterrorism is not new in Europe, and it is seen as mainly a matter for police and interior ministry forces, not militaries.

## The NATO C³ Network Modernization

The many initiatives of the NATO Command, Control, and Communications Agency (NC³A) to adopt leading-edge information technology, define standards, and develop networking concepts are a positive indication of convergence in assembling NATO C³ networks. The shift in emphasis from platforms to networks, or network-centric warfare, makes NC³A a key agency in interoperability. The speed, security, and reliability with which NATO forces can communicate and exchange data will be ever more critical in determining what forces can operate together. NC³A is making progress toward a number of common standards, and it plans to have ready-made architectures for when nations look to plug their own C³ networks into a multinational framework. Several testbed initiatives are under way for both communications and Internet technologies, including next-generation Internet protocols, local and wide area network standards, and communications system protocols for deploying combined joint task forces. Nations are engaged in setting standards and have access to NATO testing and development, ensuring that national systems can interface with NATO. The U.S. and NATO standards are said to be approximately 80 percent congruent.[9] Work is under way to seek a single common standard for communications and data exchange. Success in this area will be a large factor in deciding which nations are able to participate in modern coalition operations.

## Closing the Gap

Closing the technology and capabilities gaps between the United States and its NATO allies will required greater emphasis on redoubling efforts to fulfill DCI objectives, increasing U.S. openness in technology transfer, making progress in consolidating European defense industries, and deciding at the next NATO summit to rekindle transatlantic resolve under a new capabilities initiative.

### Fulfilling the NATO Defense Capabilities Initiative

The initiative was launched at the 1999 NATO summit to provide "the forces and capabilities the Alliance requires to meet the security challenges of the twenty-first century, across the full spectrum of Alliance missions." The DCI concentrates on five areas for improved capability: deployability and mobility of forces; sustainability and logistics; survivability; effective engagement; and command, control, and information systems. These same areas of operational competency form the central focus of *Joint Vision 2020*. A temporary high-level steering group is overseeing DCI implementation with the intent of improving capabilities in each of the five areas as much as possible by the next NATO summit in November 2002. The DCI has received steady top-level emphasis at NATO and has benefited from the comparable ERRF initiative that identifies many of the same capability gaps. Still, NATO reported in mid-2001 that allies expect to meet only one-third to one-half of the 58 designated objectives by the end of 2002.

Although the outlook has been less than encouraging for DCI, NATO leaders continue to press for progress, especially on crucial subcategory capabilities such as SEAD, airborne ground surveillance, strategic lift, and $C^4I$. The main drag on allied modernization is low procurement spending by European allies. The five DCI categories are the right priority areas for NATO to meet its responsibility to be prepared for future conflict. An all-out press by members to increase defense investment across key programs in 2002 and beyond is warranted in the wake of September 11. The success the DCI has in closing the gap will be determined by their response.

## U.S. Technology Transfer Considerations and Options

Both U.S. and European defense industries have long viewed laws and regulations governing foreign investment in U.S. defense industries and the export of military technologies as a brake on developing transatlantic defense markets and interoperability. That outlook should change if recent U.S. initiatives are fully implemented.

In response to growing pressure from European and U.S. industries, the United States implemented the Defense Trade Security Initiative (DTSI) in 2000 with the aim of streamlining controls over sensitive military technology. It provides, among other things, for regular review of the U.S. Munitions List, which identifies technologies and weapons restricted from export, either completely or with few exceptions under tight controls. DTSI will create provisions for greater access to U.S. technology by allies. The aim is a better balance between legitimate national security concerns and the cooperative and interoperability values of sharing information, technologies, and systems with the industries of close allies. The Bush administration is implementing DTSI and is ahead of schedule in reducing the list. Congress also maintains a keen interest in DTSI with regard both to national security and to trade issues, either of which can affect the speed with which allies acquire U.S. technology. The United Kingdom and Australia are negotiating agreements to be afforded the same status as Canada, whose arms industry enjoys treatment as part of the U.S. domestic industrial base for unclassified information and selected technologies. If successful, these agreements would be a useful model for other NATO allies.

Other initiatives may affect allies' access to technology. The Department of Defense is working to speed processing times of foreign military sales through paperless transactions. Meanwhile, Congress is deliberating a new Export Administration Act. The outcome is uncertain, however, because opposition to loosening of controls, even for trusted allies, remains strong. As a signal of continuing concern, Congress shifted a number of critical space-hardware items from the Commerce to the State Department to provide for more rigorous oversight of export authorization.

The growing number of transatlantic joint ventures and arms industry mergers make technology restrictions an important factor in sourcing components and subsystems, and in determining the strength of the transatlantic arms trade.

## Attempts to Consolidate European Defense Capabilities

The defense establishments of the 15 European NATO states have renewed attempts to harmonize their industries as well as their strategic contribution to regional defense via the ERRF headline goal initiative; however, much remains to be done. Issues of sovereignty and domestic interests must be overcome. Italy's abrupt withdrawal, following a change of government, from the A400M transport aircraft (a slow-moving joint project involving Belgium, France, Germany, Luxembourg, Portugal, Spain, Turkey, and the United Kingdom) came just as the decision to move to production was at hand in December 2001. Germany's participation in the project has been marked by constant threats to critical funding. Such events are not uncommon in European attempts at collaborative defense projects and lead to more failures than successes. Still, Europe doggedly pursues a vision of a consolidated defense industrial base that can compete on a par with U.S. industry.

The goal is a worthy one. If Europe took an undivided approach toward its contributions to NATO as well as to EU tasks, it would enjoy greater influence, and member states would have stronger rationale for defense investments when speaking to their parliaments and public. Holding on to legacy forces optimized for attacks against NATO territory (Article 5 scenarios) only suggests to the public that these capabilities meet future needs and can be kept at relatively low levels of readiness.

The European Security and Defense Policy should elaborate credible EU policies on the employment of military force under the Union.[10] By making its intent and requirements more definitive, the EU indicates to its member governments and their national industries where investment is needed over the long term. That in turn encourages consolidation as companies gain confidence with regard to where business opportunities will emerge. A "coalition of the willing" strategy, dependent on ad hoc structures and come-as-you-are forces, is insufficient to guide long-term investment commitments by industry; coalitions materialize on short notice, and nations offer whatever forces are available, subject to political consensus. Industry sorely needs clearer EU-wide policies: only the aerospace industry has achieved noticeable consolidation; land and naval systems manufacturers await a better sense of what capabilities will be sought in the future. In this regard, the headline goal force is only a first step. Recently conducted defense reviews by France, Germany, the United Kingdom, and others in the wake of September 11 should be raised to the EU and NATO level.

### The Next Summit: Building on DCI Momentum

If NATO is to be relevant in future conflicts, the Defense Capabilities Initiative must be declared a beginning, not an end. A new initiative is needed to direct future investment and avoid the risk of losing momentum well short of operational requirements and the full potential of RMA capabilities. The United States and its allies should not let the limited gains of DCI languish. Instead, the EU should match the U.S. transformation force with a robust, highly capable force of its own. This suggests three possible initiatives for the next NATO summit meeting in Prague in 2002.

First, NATO leaders should agree on a more definitive strategic vision of the purpose and posture of NATO military forces, especially for non-Article 5 missions such as crisis response and peace enforcement. A common vision of the purpose of equipping the most ready NATO forces with modern technology will provide the essential justification for greater defense investment.

Second, NATO should define more focused force goals beyond DCI that will realize a fully transformed transatlantic force by 2010. Force contributions from the United States and Europe should have equivalent RMA capabilities and strength, have full interoperability, and be capable of the full spectrum of NATO missions, including combat operations. Force elements should be network-centric for all C$^4$ISR functions, equipped with similar sensor technologies and engagement capabilities, and should be rapidly deployable, highly mobile, and readily sustainable over even very extended logistics structures. Transformed European and U.S. forces should train and exercise together to generate common doctrine for employment, and they should be kept ready to deploy together on short notice for the full range of NATO missions. Meeting the force goals thus specified should be incorporated into the regular NATO force planning process.

Finally, NATO should agree at its next summit on new standards of interoperability for RMA-capable forces. Common system protocols for a "NATO information grid" should be defined, and each new system should be evaluated on "NATO network readiness" as part of each nation's engineering design and procurement processes.

If these initiatives are realized at the next NATO summit, real progress toward interoperability will be possible. Without them, the transatlantic technology gap will widen, U.S. and European forces will be employed more and more discretely from each other, and doctrines and operational concepts will diverge. All that would bode ill for the future of NATO as a military alliance.

### Notes

[1] The goal of the Defense Capabilities Initiative (DCI) is to raise the capabilities of NATO member forces in specific functional areas. DCI is aimed primarily at NATO Europe where forces are particularly deficient in the indicated areas. By giving a specified list of 58 (classified) capabilities to be

achieved in a particular time frame, NATO hoped to make significant progress by offering members sound rationales to increase modernization spending. Non-defense issues have dampened that effect as parliaments have resisted defense increases. See NATO April 1999 summit declaration on Defense Capability Initiative and all subsequent defense ministerial communiqués at <www.nato.int>.

[2] The collective functions of command, control, communications, computers, and intelligence ($C^4I$) guide all military organizations and operations. Command and control are "people" functions and are sometimes referred to simply as $C^2$. Adding the third "C" for communications ($C^3$) is another variant; however, with new emphasis on data connectivity as well as voice, $C^4$ is the dominant representation in current use. $C^4I$ is also used as the root of another alphanumeric, $C^4ISR$, where the additional functions of surveillance and reconnaissance are included, though their relationship to command is principally as sources of intelligence.

[3] NATO has always had an agreed strategic concept to guide its political and military policy-making, planning, and resource allocation. The most recent two concepts (1991 and 1999) have been unclassified and are available to the public. For the current (1999) version, see the Alliance Strategic Concept approved April 24, 1999, at <www.nato.int>.

[4] From the Honorable James Swihart, former U.S. Ambassador to Lithuania, in a conversation with the author in the mid-1990s, while both served as fellows at the Institute for National Strategic Studies at the National Defense University, Washington, DC.

[5] *Joint Vision 2020* is the current vision of the Chairman of the Joint Chiefs of Staff and the guiding concept for U.S. military capabilities. See the Department of Defense Web site at <www.defenselink.mil>.

[6] At their semiannual summit in late 1999 at Helsinki, EU leaders agreed to create, by 2003, a military force of 50,000 to 60,000 land forces and associated air and naval forces, deployable within 60 days and sustainable for up to one year. This became known as the "Helsinki Headline Goal Force," now called the European Rapid Reaction Force. See Annex IV of the Presidency Conclusions, Helsinki European Council, December 10–11, 1999, accessed at <www.eurunion.org>.

[7] The Petersberg Tasks were specified at a June 1992 meeting of the Western European Union (WEU) in Petersberg, Germany; the European Union signed on at the 1997 Amsterdam summit, and the Tasks are now part of the Treaty of the European Union. The Petersberg Declaration of the WEU Council of Ministers stated that "Apart from contributing to the common defence in accordance with Article 5 of the Washington Treaty and Article V of the modified Brussels Treaty respectively, military units of WEU member states, acting under the authority of WEU, could be employed for: humanitarian and rescue tasks; peacekeeping tasks; tasks of combat forces in crisis management, including peacemaking." Accessed at <www.weu.int/eng/comm/92-petersberg.htm>.

[8] The Bundeswehr produced the first post-Cold War defense study, *Der Weiss Buch* (The White Book) in 1994. The second study was conducted by the von Weizsaecker Commission for the federal government in May 2000.

[9] From a briefing by Ed Woollen, Vice President, Information Systems, Raytheon Corporation, to the European Institute, October 2001.

[10] The European Security and Defense Policy (ESDP) was first espoused at the EU summit at Cologne, Germany, in June 1999 and further defined in Helsinki in December 1999. ESDP is managed under the EU Common Foreign and Security Policy (CFSP, the so-called second pillar of the EU), and as such is not on a par with CFSP but a subordinate policy. The term *policy* is misleading. The salient feature of ESDP is not a policy but a military capability—the headline goal force described above.

# Part IV

# Broader Aspects
# of Transformation

# Chapter 10

# Strengthening Homeland Security

Michèle A. Flournoy

September 11, 2001, pierced the sense of invulnerability that most Americans had come to enjoy in the post-Cold War security environment. Although the sense of security at home waxed and waned with the dynamics of the Cold War—from the "duck-and-cover" drills of the 1950s to the détente in the 1970s—our sense of invulnerability became fairly entrenched after the collapse of the Soviet Union. Russia was no longer our enemy, we were the world's sole superpower, our military was unsurpassed—we were a nation at peace. If the 1991 Persian Gulf War reminded us that we still faced threats to our national interests, it also reinforced the sense that America's wars would be fought far from its borders. As one Pentagon strategist noted in the early 1990s, "The American military only plays 'away games.'"

In the decade following the Gulf War, U.S. national security experts began to worry openly and write about asymmetric threats, including potential threats to the American homeland.[1] Over the same period, the Clinton administration launched a number of initiatives to help Federal, state, and local governments enhance their respective capabilities to defend against and respond to potential attacks on U.S. soil and to coordinate their efforts better. But the American people remained largely unaware or unconvinced of the threat, even after the first terrorist attack on the World Trade Center in 1993. For many Americans, part of the shock of September 11 was that such attacks had seemed so inconceivable.

In the wake of the worst terrorist attacks in history, homeland security has soared to the top of the U.S. priority list. Before September 11, there was a growing commitment among many in government to take

---

*Author's Note:* This chapter has been adapted, with permission, from chapter 9 of Kurt M. Campbell and Michèle A. Flournoy, *To Prevail: An American Strategy for the Campaign Against Terrorism* (Washington, DC: Center for Strategic and International Studies, 2001).

prudent steps to guard against potential threats to the United States; after September 11, there is an urgent public demand and an unprecedented degree of political will to do and spend whatever is necessary, as quickly as possible, to enhance homeland security to the greatest extent we can. Congressional willingness shortly after the September 11 attacks to give President George W. Bush $40 billion in an emergency supplemental—fully twice what he had requested—was indicative of the country's new mood. The "day after," everything looks different.

Protecting the U.S. homeland from threats, such as terrorism, cyber-attack, and weapons of mass destruction, will be an extremely challenging task, one rendered more difficult by the open nature of American society, the economy's reliance on international commerce and trade, and the civil liberties that we hold dear. Each day, approximately 1.3 million people cross U.S. borders. Among them may be terrorists who have already demonstrated their ability to enter the United States, often legally, and live among us undetected for a period of years. More than 340,000 vehicles and 58,000 cargo shipments enter the United States daily, and only 1 to 2 percent of these are inspected by customs agents. Each year, there are more than 250,000 attempts to hack into Department of Defense (DOD) computers, which represents only a fraction of the attempted intrusions experienced by the Federal Government and the private sector as a whole.

Enhancing homeland security will be further complicated by the fact that responsibility for dealing with different aspects of these threats cuts across the jurisdictions of more than 40 Federal agencies and 14 Congressional committees, not to mention countless state and local offices, as well as the private sector. As one homeland security expert noted, "We've got great athletes. . . . But we don't have a coach, we don't have a game plan, and we're not practicing. How do you think we're going to do in the big game?"[2] Organizing for success will be critical—and also exceedingly difficult.

## A Three-Pronged Strategy

*Homeland security* can be usefully defined as the prevention, deterrence, preemption of, and defense against attacks on the United States and the management of the consequences should one occur. Inherent in this definition are three broad and enduring objectives that should provide the foundation for a new national strategy for homeland security: prevention, protection, and response.[3]

## Prevention

The first objective is to prevent future attacks on the United States. This objective is preeminent, as it is central to the survival of the open, democratic, market-based way of life that distinguishes American society.

Prevention involves stopping threats to the United States before they become manifest, preferably as far away from American shores and borders as possible. Prevention efforts overseas might include working with allies to roll up terrorist networks abroad, preventing the proliferation of weapons of mass destruction and long-range delivery systems, or shutting down hackers conspiring to launch attacks against American computer networks. It might also include more immediate actions inside the United States to stop a terrorist from crossing into the country, boarding a flight, or renting a crop duster or commercial truck. Prevention is by its very nature proactive and often requires taking offensive action to destroy or neutralize a threat before an attack occurs. The Federal Government and leaders must be prepared to act proactively in concert with established coalitions or alliances—and unilaterally, if necessary—to strike against defined, imminent threats to the homeland far from American shores.

Prevention also involves "shaping the security environment to avoid or retard the emergence of threats to the United States," which can only be achieved through American activities overseas.[4] In this regard, the Department of State, Department of Defense, U.S. allies, and foreign law enforcement agencies all play a significant role in defending the American homeland. Thus, prevention may be greatly aided by U.S. engagement abroad. But in the final analysis, the most important element of prevention is the ability to detect threats before they become manifest, with enough specificity and forewarning to permit preventive action.

Indeed, improving U.S. intelligence is the most crucial element of transformation for homeland security; as amplified below, it is the "long pole in the tent." To prevent attacks on the American homeland, decisionmakers must have not only a general sense of the kinds of attacks that various actors might be willing and able to conduct against the United States but also specific warning as to the nature, location, and timing of anticipated attacks. This requires superior intelligence collection and analysis and, in most cases, substantial sharing of intelligence across agency lines. Given the importance of surveillance and tracking of suspected terrorists within America's borders, one of the greatest challenges becomes enhancing our situational awareness without becoming a police state. Striking the right balance between intelligence collection within the

United States by law enforcement agencies and the protection of the civil liberties that define and distinguish our society is critical.

Because it may not be possible to prevent every attack, the goal in practice should be to minimize the likelihood that the most serious attacks on the United States could be mounted successfully. As Secretary of Defense Donald Rumsfeld has said, "Our victory will come with Americans living their lives day by day, going to work, raising their children and building their dreams as they always have—a free and great people."[5] The fact that Federal law enforcement and intelligence agencies have averted numerous such attacks in the past by acting rapidly on specific indications and warnings is proof that a degree of prevention *is* possible.

## Protection

The second objective is to enhance the ability of the United States to protect itself against attacks. This includes strengthening America's defenses against a variety of threats to the U.S. homeland that might come from a wide range of directions against any number of targets.

Essential to the protection of American citizens is an effective capability to defeat or neutralize enemy action once an attack is launched. Whether an immediate, responsive defense against an air or missile attack, a rapidly instigated manhunt to find and foil a terrorist cell, or day-to-day security measures to protect borders and critical infrastructure, a broad range of capabilities, including domestic law enforcement, intelligence, military, and public health, will be needed to mount effective barriers to such attacks. This aspect of homeland security is made particularly complex by the wide variety of acknowledged threats, the increasing sophistication displayed by known terrorists, and their ability to adapt concepts of operations to take advantage of new technologies and to exploit weaknesses in whatever security measures are in place.

As a result, U.S. efforts to enhance homeland security should not focus only or even primarily on ensuring that terrorists can never again hijack American commercial airliners and fly them into buildings. The United States must anticipate and be able to protect itself against a much broader range of possible threats—for example, terrorist attacks involving airplanes, missiles, trucks, cars, or ships; attacks involving the release of chemical or biological agents or nuclear materials in major U.S. cities; and both cyber and physical attacks on critical infrastructure. Both lethal, destructive threats and nonlethal, disruptive threats demonstrate the complexity of the problem and the broad range of participants, in public and private sectors, that must be involved in protecting the United States.

This multiplicity and diversity of threats highlight the need for prioritization. The United States cannot afford to give equal weight to strengthening its defenses against every conceivable threat scenario. One of the most important challenges that must be addressed early on is an assessment of the range of potential threats to the American homeland, based on both the likelihood of occurrence and severity of consequences were they to occur, to set priorities for allocation of resources.

### Response

The third objective is to improve our ability to respond to and manage the consequences of any attack. First, the United States must have a robust capability to ensure public safety; continuity of government; command, control, and communications; and the provision of essential services. Effective consequence management is also central to maintaining public confidence and reducing the physical and psychological impacts of terrorism. As we witnessed on September 11, state and local "first responders," such as local firefighters, police officers, and emergency medical teams, are often the most important element of effective consequence management. They must be given the resources, equipment, and training needed to do their jobs and coordinate their efforts well, even under extraordinary conditions such as those following the use of a nuclear, biological, or chemical weapon.

Second, the United States must be able to minimize disruption and restore the functioning of critical infrastructure rapidly in the immediate aftermath of an attack. This might involve restoring telecommunications service, repairing energy production and distribution systems, or providing alternative routes and means of communication and transportation. "Hardening" potential targets, developing contingency plans, and building a degree of redundancy into key systems will be critical to rapid restoration.

Third, the Federal Government must be prepared to take rapid steps to stabilize American financial markets and manage the immediate economic and financial consequences of an attack. This must involve relevant agencies, such as the Department of the Treasury and the Federal Reserve System, but should be done in partnership with major players in the private sector.

Fourth, Federal, state, and local agencies, as well as nongovernmental organizations (NGOs), must be prepared to provide immediate assistance to the victims of an attack, their families, and affected communities.

Central to success in both protection and response are advance planning, exercises, and simulations to identify problems and refine plans, as well as coordination across the Federal Government with state, local, private sector, and NGO representatives to prepare for future attacks.

## Intelligence

As we consider the long campaign against terrorism before us and the prospect of additional attacks against the United States, intelligence will be the indispensable element of the campaign on which the success of all others will depend.

Intelligence enables all other components of the campaign against terrorism to be effective: homeland security, law enforcement, military and covert operations, and coalition building. Decisionmakers in each of these areas must rely on information that is gathered, analyzed, and provided by the intelligence community. Meeting the multifaceted challenges associated with intelligence collection, analysis, and dissemination will be daunting, as each element of the campaign against terrorism poses unique intelligence requirements.

Given the nature of potential adversaries, there are no guarantees that the quality of our intelligence on terrorist organizations such as Osama bin Laden's Al Qaeda network will substantially improve without significant operational changes and sustained effort by the intelligence community. As a flat organization comprising small cells of individuals in more than 60 countries, Al Qaeda has demonstrated its ability to use a wide range of communications, from low-tech means such as face-to-face meetings to high-tech means such as encrypted messages. When its communications have been intercepted, it has been extremely agile in changing its modus operandi to evade Western intelligence collection.

Terrorist organizations like Al Qaeda do not rely on the kind of infrastructure that makes other intelligence targets such as governments easier to penetrate. Under these circumstances, national technical means of collection (for example, satellites, electronic eavesdropping, surveillance aircraft, and the like) are less effective. Furthermore, the extremist ideology that motivates recruits and cements an otherwise loose network together makes it extremely difficult—indeed, almost impossible—for Western agents to infiltrate. Due to the strength of their convictions, members are unlikely to defect, even if offered substantial incentives. Given these factors, the campaign against terrorism may pose the biggest intelligence challenge for the United States and its allies since the Cold War.

Homeland security presents a particular set of intelligence requirements. Those responsible for homeland security need to have a general understanding of the types of attacks that various terrorist organizations are interested in and capable of launching against America. If indicators suggest that such an attack is imminent, authorities also need specific warning information about the proposed location and type of attack so as to enhance law enforcement, security, and consequence management efforts. Such warning information is unlikely to emerge unless there is extensive information sharing and fusion across bureaucratic lines to facilitate synthesis of relevant information from the overwhelming amount of data collected by a variety of agencies and means into a coherent, timely picture of what is likely to happen.

One of the greatest challenges that we face in the homeland security arena is enhancing our situational awareness (that is, the ability to know what terrorists are doing inside our borders) without becoming a police state. Consider the fact that the planners and perpetrators of the September attacks lived, prepared, and hid among American citizens for several years, yet we were largely unaware of their activities. One of the things that stands out about that terrorist episode is how little actionable intelligence was available prior to that date and how much various intelligence and law enforcement agencies have gathered since then. How could this have happened?

One answer is that the system was not "tuned" to collect the right data and evaluate it properly. This suggests the need to redesign data collection and analysis priorities and strategies for the intelligence and law enforcement communities. Another answer is that relevant bits of information were available within various agency files but remained stray needles in the enormous haystack of intelligence data. This suggests the need for new technologies to organize, store, and retrieve information that the Federal Government already collects. A third answer is that individual agencies may have identified key pieces of information but failed to share and correlate this data in a way that enabled anyone to put all the pieces together and see the larger picture. This suggests the need to enhance data sharing and correlation across agency lines. But this inevitably raises the specter of intelligence agencies collecting information within U.S. borders, something that has long been seen as a threat to the basic privacy and political rights of Americans.

Being effective in the campaign against terrorism will require coming to terms with this difficult issue. Creating the situational awareness now deemed essential will require developing new methods for lawful surveillance of American citizens and foreigners living in America, while creating adequate oversight mechanisms to ensure that new methods are not used inappropriately. In short, we must do more to find and track terrorists on American soil while also protecting the civil liberties that are essential in our society.

Because better intelligence is the indispensable element of the campaign against terrorism, it is imperative that the United States act quickly and wisely to identify and address the most serious intelligence problems in the counterterrorism campaign. For starters, the President should call for a comprehensive assessment to identify shortfalls in intelligence policy, capabilities, practices, and resources that could hamper the future effectiveness of the campaign against terrorism. Based on these assessments, the administration should then develop a multiyear action plan to address priority issues and shortfalls.

Second, the President should give high priority to strengthening bilateral intelligence-sharing and cooperation with countries that have the most to offer the United States on the terrorist organizations of greatest concern. Since September 11, such intelligence arrangements have become defining political issues in American relations with many other countries. One of our central diplomatic goals in the months and years to come should be to broaden and deepen these arrangements as a cornerstone of bilateral relations with key countries. This should include seeking greater international cooperation in surveillance and tracking of the financial transactions of various terrorist organizations.

Third, Congress should substantially increase the resources devoted to the intelligence community in general and to the campaign against terrorism in particular. This will be essential to address critical shortfalls in a timely manner in areas such as human intelligence, covert operations, analysts, linguists and area specialists, and the integration of new technologies.

Fourth, the guidelines and processes for intelligence sharing within the United States need to be overhauled to enable more rapid and effective intelligence fusion and to ensure adequate situational awareness. This needs to occur not only at the Federal level but also between Federal, state, and local agencies. American lives are on the line, and there is simply no excuse for bureaucratic infighting that compromises our ability to exploit the intelligence we have.

This will be no small challenge. It will require a shift in focus from a case file approach to more fundamental and proactive data analysis. Where are the terrorists likely to be hiding among us, and how will we find them? How can we distinguish suspicious activities in our complex and dynamic society? It will also require substantial investment in data correlation and analysis capabilities, as well as a new willingness to share data across bureaucratic lines. Improving our ability to correlate data will inevitably require us to reevaluate the rules and procedures governing the gathering of intelligence on American citizens and others living in the United States. Specifically, the United States should create new combined-agency investigation centers that are supervised on an ongoing basis by an officer appointed by the court authorized by the Federal Intelligence Surveillance Act, who would essentially serve as a real-time privacy ombudsman to ensure that there is no inappropriate use of new investigative techniques.

Fifth, the intelligence and law enforcement communities need to undertake more simulations—for example, "red-teaming" and "If I were a terrorist . . ." exercises—to develop a better understanding of the types of attacks terrorist groups might be willing to contemplate and how they might respond in various situations. Though imperfect, at best, such exercises can be very useful in exposing gaps in thinking and shortcomings in preparation.

Finally, the intelligence community cannot and should not be expected to solve all its problems on its own. It should pursue new public-private partnerships to engage the best technologists in the country to help it surmount its most substantial technological hurdles. Particular emphasis should be placed on investment in new technologies to organize, store, and retrieve information. After September 11, it should not be difficult to find private-sector partners. More broadly, the intelligence community should seek to leverage America's diversity and openness at every opportunity, engaging experts and linguists outside the narrow confines of the Federal Government through a combination of outreach and outsourcing.

Since September 11, the intelligence and law enforcement communities have been recognized as both crucial and in need of additional resources and reform. Nothing will be more important to the success of the campaign against terrorism and to U.S. homeland security than meaningfully improving the capabilities and performance of these two communities.

## Bioterrorism and Attacks on Critical Infrastructure

As the United States develops a national strategy for homeland security, particular attention should be paid to two threats that pose the greatest danger to our basic way of life: bioterrorism and attacks on critical infrastructure.

Whereas an effective terrorist attack involving chemical agents could produce tens or hundreds of thousands of casualties, an effective attack using biological pathogens could result in millions. It is well established that members of Al Qaeda have sought to obtain biological means of attack and have contacts with states that have biological weapons programs. The anthrax attacks that followed the September 11 attacks effectively ended the debate about whether individual or small groups of terrorists could obtain and use biological agents. They have and they will.

The good news is that biological pathogens are generally difficult to weaponize; it is difficult to take them from a laboratory petri dish or vial, produce them in large quantities, and put them in a form that can be effectively dispersed to cause mass casualties. The bad news is that terrorists would need only a small quantity of a highly contagious pathogen such as smallpox to infect enough people to create a mass-casualty event. Each infected individual would become, in effect, a walking biological weapon. This is a danger whose dimensions are magnified in our mobile society. A local bio-attack could quickly become a national crisis with the potential to cripple the country. The United States should therefore give highest priority to keeping pathogens that could be used in such attacks out of the hands of terrorists and to enhancing our ability to deal with such attacks should they occur.

Today, security measures at American and foreign facilities are not adequate to prohibit theft of dangerous pathogens. In the United States, samples of some pathogens such as smallpox are kept under very tight security, but samples of others, such as anthrax, are found in research laboratories across the country that have only minimal security. Across the former Soviet Union, literally tons of Cold War-era biological weapons agents remain housed in nonsecure facilities.

In addition, we are ill prepared to prevent the dire consequences of a large-scale bioterrorism attack. The United States currently lacks the stockpiles of vaccines and antibiotics, as well as the means of rapid distribution, that would be required for an effective response. We lack an adequate cadre of first responders who are trained and equipped to deal with such a crisis.

The Federal Government also lacks adequate management strategies, plans, and information systems to cope with a bioterrorism assault. Today, senior leaders would simply not receive the intelligence and expert advice that they need to make informed decisions. As a result of these shortfalls, Federal and state officials could find themselves in the untenable position of having to impose forcible constraints on citizens because they lack other viable tools to contain a crisis. This would pose enormous challenges to civil liberties and horrific choices for decision-makers. Indeed, the less prepared we are for a bioterrorism event, the greater the panic that is likely to ensue, and the more threats there will be to the civil liberties of average Americans.

To address this situation, the President, working with Congress and with state and local governments, should launch a major public-private initiative on the scale of the Apollo Program to enhance the Nation's capabilities to prevent and respond to biological terrorism. The focus of this project should be fortifying and equipping the public health system to limit the potentially catastrophic effects of bioterrorism.

Substantial investments are needed to strengthen public health expertise, infrastructure, and early warning systems. New approaches must be developed to deal with the diseases that might be used as weapons of terror, especially stockpiling vaccines and antibiotics, strengthening regional and national distribution mechanisms, and researching and developing other means of facilitating rapid, effective disease control, such as funding the development of easily deployed diagnostic tools using new biotechnologies. The Bush administration's decision to create a stockpile of 300 million smallpox vaccines was a step in the right direction, but much more needs to be done. Particularly important will be developing an appropriate regulatory process to ensure the safety of new vaccines and antibiotics, as well as providing the medical and pharmaceutical industries with the necessary incentives, such as liability protection, to rise to this national challenge.

This modern-day Apollo Program also should include:

- development and implementation of an effective security protocol for all U.S. laboratories that store pathogens that could be used effectively in a terrorist attack
- extensive analysis, simulation, and exercise programs to improve understanding of the challenges that we would encounter in the event of such an attack
- identification and prioritization of shortfalls that need to be addressed
- development of detailed plans and decisionmaking protocols for dealing with a bioterrorism event, including clarification of jurisdictional issues between Federal and state entities
- development at all levels of government of the information systems that would be needed to manage such a crisis.

In addition, the United States must make reducing the biological weapons legacy of the former Soviet Union through cooperative threat reduction programs an even higher priority on the foreign policy agenda. It also should seek to reinvigorate and reorient the Biological Weapons Convention process to take the new bioterrorism threats into account. Only in preparing for this worst-case scenario can we hope to limit its consequences.

Enhancing the security of America's critical infrastructure—those physical and cyber-based systems essential to the minimum operations of the economy and government—is another central challenge in reducing the risks and consequences of future terrorist attacks. Vast disruption and panic would ensue if an aircraft breached the containment structure of a nuclear power plant, a major city's power supply was shut down, or the New York Stock Exchange's computer system was sabotaged.

Critical infrastructure includes telecommunications, electrical power systems, gas and oil infrastructure, banking and finance, transportation, water systems, and emergency services, 80 to 90 percent of which is owned or operated by private firms. With the advent of new information technologies, much of the Nation's critical infrastructure has become increasingly automated in recent years, bringing not only new efficiencies but also new vulnerabilities, including vulnerability to cyber attacks. As in the case of biodefense, an active and sustained partnership between the government and the private sector will be essential to address these problems.

Significant progress has been made in recent years, including the establishment of Information Sharing and Analysis Centers by the Federal Government, in partnership with the private sector, to address electronic threats, vulnerabilities, incidents, and solutions for a number of sectors. To date, however, these efforts have focused primarily on cyber rather than physical threats. Given that terrorist organizations such as Al Qaeda have demonstrated their interest in producing highly visible mass-casualty events, cyber strikes may not be their preferred mode of attack. The Bush administration would be wise to broaden its work on critical infrastructure protection to include a greater emphasis on physical vulnerabilities and threats in various sectors.

This will require not only new threat and vulnerability assessments but also a clearer delineation of who has the responsibility and who has the authority to enhance security measures against physical attacks on various elements of critical infrastructure. For example, who is responsible for providing adequate security at the 103 nuclear power plants operating in the United States? Is it the private utility companies who operate the plants, local law enforcement, or perhaps National Guard units under the control of the state governors? These issues urgently need to be addressed in a coordinated manner through consultations between Federal, state, local, and industry officials.

Private sector firms will have a particularly important role to play in this regard, in activities ranging from designing new facilities to better withstand attack, to enhancing physical security systems at existing facilities.

## Organizing for Success

How should the U.S. Government be organized for homeland security? This question—at the heart of virtually every policy discussion since September 11—was debated in depth for months and even years before.

Three basic options were discussed most frequently: give the entire homeland security mission to one existing agency or another, such as the Federal Emergency Management Agency (FEMA) or the Department of Defense; create a new agency by merging together elements of existing organizations and missions;[6] or create a strong coordinator in the White House.[7] President Bush seems to have settled the debate, at least for his tenure, by appointing Tom Ridge to be Assistant to the President for Homeland Security. In essence, the President chose the third option, a national coordinator in the White House charged with bringing together the assembled resources of the entire government. Yet within hours of the announcement, debate resumed over whether Director Ridge had been given the legal and budgetary authorities and institutional standing that he needs to be effective in his new post.

President Bush's decision was the right decision for now, but it is inadequate for the longer term. The precise structure of the long-term organizational solution is probably unknowable at this point, but changes will surely be needed.

Designing a long-term, integrated, effective response to the complicated problem of international terrorism waged on American soil requires understanding three fault lines that fracture the U.S. Government.[8] The first is divided Federal Government: the system of checks and balances that the founders put in place to preclude abuses of power and that is the very essence of American constitutional democracy. Over time, the U.S. Government has evolved to become enormously complex and redundant; nearly every major department and bureau has some relevant role in homeland security. The second constitutionally grounded fault line is

American federalism: the way in which authority is divided between the national level and the state and local levels of government. Coordinating a nationwide response to terrorism requires vertical coordination between various levels and agencies of government to bridge these gaps. The third fault line is more cultural than constitutional: the separation between our foreign and domestic security apparatus. American political culture has always been wary of excessive government power, and this has limited the role of military and intelligence agencies inside the borders of the United States. The military's role within the United States is highly circumscribed by the doctrine known as *posse comitatus*; the U.S. intelligence community cannot spy on American citizens, and the domestic surveillance activities of Federal law enforcement bodies are constrained by fairly strict operational restrictions and judicial oversight. When it comes to fighting terrorism, however, this division between foreign security and domestic security creates dangerous vulnerabilities. For example, in the past, the terrorist use of modern communications networks to leap across political jurisdictions allowed them to operate within the United States in ways that forced intelligence agencies to abandon the chase at the border. This foreign-domestic security fault line creates operational barriers to cooperation between military forces, intelligence, and law enforcement that must constantly be surmounted.

As if this picture were not sufficiently bleak, it should be noted that many other democracies are equally fractured in their government structures. The discontinuities on the American scene are also found among our partner states, complicating the problem of international information sharing and coordination.

## A National Coordinator for Homeland Security

In light of the deep divisions that mark American culture and constitutional governance, a national coordinator is currently the best and only solution to the problem of homeland security. However, Director Ridge has been assigned the most difficult job imaginable: to coordinate a vast and complex government and to instill the focus and agility required to stay ahead of small bands of ruthless terrorists. His task is further complicated by the inherent advantage that the terrorists have of hiding inside an America that values its diversity and its openness and that embraces transnational business practices and social interactions.

Given these challenges, Director Ridge should approach his mission at a strategic level. Virtually every major department of the Federal Government, and certainly the law enforcement and emergency response elements of the state and local governments, all have crucial roles to play in the homeland security mission. The national coordinator cannot run the daily operations of such a vast and disparate array of agencies and bureaus. Instead, he should use his power and influence to shape the priorities, plans, and future competencies of the government to deal with terrorism.[9] This requires establishing an overall strategy.

First, as mentioned above, the United States must resist the trap of preparing to fight the last war. It is unlikely that terrorists will attempt a strike that resembles the events of September 11, and if they do, we undoubtedly will be better prepared to foil their plans. Instead, terrorists are more likely to attack in unanticipated ways: airplanes one day, anthrax the next, and something else on the following. Therefore, the first task of the national coordinator is to think like a terrorist. He should establish a terrorism assessment unit that is specifically designed to strategize as a terrorist would and to research ways in which American security could be breached. This should not be an unbounded exercise of human imagination, but rather a disciplined review of intelligence assessments, more systematic and thorough analysis of terrorist doctrine and techniques, and a deliberate reasoning about the goals and effects intended by various terrorist organizations. The terrorist assessment unit should draw widely on the research community in the United States and in other countries as well as less conventional sources, such as Hollywood and the broader creative community. Its aim should be to challenge and shape the planning and programming priorities of the various departments and bureaus that share the homeland security task.

Second, the national coordinator should institute an extensive program of wargaming and simulation. For years, DOD has conducted so-called tabletop exercises to test assumptions and plans. Other elements of the government also have some forms of assessment, but most do not have the same degree of discipline or sophistication. Wargames serve five primary purposes: to uncover discontinuities in planning for unexpected events; reveal insights into the complexity of problems that cannot be developed by reading reports; establish operational working relationships among participants in peacetime that become crucial for communication and trust in crisis situations; help suspend the typical turf battles when organizations confront just what they can and cannot do, as well as what other organizations bring to the table in a time of crisis; and reveal critical shortfalls in processes and capabilities that need to be addressed.

A comprehensive antiterrorism wargaming program should include periodic training sessions for the President and his Cabinet. The wargaming program must contemplate different scenarios and spontaneous developments. The terrorism assessment unit described above would be instrumental in designing the scenarios and identifying the key learning points for each exercise.

Third, the national coordinator should establish an advanced concepts office for homeland security. This office would be chartered to develop new approaches to government operations that would bridge the discontinuities and address the shortfalls identified in the wargaming process. It would utilize current operations research techniques to identify alternative concepts of operations and help the national coordinator provide guidance to the Nation's various departments and bureaus to develop new capabilities.

Fourth, Director Ridge should conduct a homeland security strategy review—on the scale of a national security strategy review or the recent Quadrennial Defense Review—to define and prioritize objectives, develop a strategy to meet those objectives, and develop a concept of operations that clearly assigns responsibilities to specific agencies and actors for various aspects of the strategy. This planning process should include a comprehensive assessment of current U.S. capabilities to deal with the full range of threats to the American homeland. The objective should be to identify and prioritize shortfalls in national capabilities that should be addressed, based on a combination of the likelihood of the threat and seriousness of potential consequences.

Informed by this strategy review, the national coordinator, on behalf of the President, should develop a multiyear interagency action plan. The plan should specify short-term actions to be taken on a priority basis, long-term investments to be made to enhance capabilities in critical areas, and a clear division of labor, including lead agency responsibility for specific areas and actions. This plan should be issued over the President's signature to guide resource allocation for homeland security across the Federal Government. It should be a living document that is reviewed and revised on an annual basis. The process of developing this plan should include every Federal agency that will be assigned responsibility for an element of homeland security, as well as close consultations with key state and local agencies and actors. Both the assessment and the development of an integrated action plan will be important to ensure that the United States gets the highest possible returns on what is likely to be tens of billions of dollars invested in homeland security over the next several years.

Once this plan is in place, the national coordinator should establish a program and budget review process, whereby the activities and expenditures of relevant Federal agencies are reviewed annually in light of the requirements defined in the multiyear plan. This review process would provide a mechanism for ensuring that agency actions accord with the President's guidance and would provide the national coordinator with a critical mechanism for enforcing the President's priorities. Here, consistent and unwavering Presidential backing will be essential to the national coordinator's success. The President must effectively communicate to the various agencies that Director Ridge's decisions are his decisions and that there will be no appeals.

The national coordinator must also take steps to integrate Federal programs and plans more fully with those of state and local governments and to aid state and local authorities in enhancing their homeland security capabilities. Because state and local governments are likely to be the first to respond to an attack, they will bear the lion's share of responsibility in implementing decisions made in Washington. They also will feel the immediate impacts of any attack most acutely. These constituencies will have to be included in discussions and decisions if the United States is to succeed in strengthening security at home. The same is true of key parts of the private sector, particularly firms involved in operating or securing the Nation's critical infrastructure.

In the short run, a strong national coordinator for homeland security is the right answer. In the long run, however, we must develop new approaches to government that will bridge these fault lines more effectively. At this stage, it is not possible to determine with precision what new structures are required. This should logically emerge after insights are gained from the study-exercise-innovate-review process described above.

In the interim, Congress should refrain from passing legislation that would make the new Office of Homeland Security a Cabinet-level department or fundamentally reorganize the U.S. Government for homeland security. If history is any guide, such organizational change would be, at this time, both unnecessary and premature. Lessons from World War II and since suggest that the keys to success in organizing the Federal Government for any prolonged and complex campaign or effort—in this case, sustained homeland security operations—are full Presidential empowerment of one person under the Chief Executive to "drive the train";

institutional flexibility to adapt and change as the operations unfold; and ensuring that the empowered individual is focused on setting priorities, on determining who should be responsible for what, and on applying pressure where necessary to ensure that the President's priorities are actually implemented, rather than on conducting day-to-day operations. President Bush's conception of Ridge's role as Director of the Office of Homeland Security appears to be consistent with this model; establishing a new Cabinet-level Homeland Security Agency would not be.

In addition, major institutional change at this stage would risk diverting the attention and energy of both leaders and operators from the task at hand, away from taking concrete steps to improve our immediate capacity to deal with further terrorist attacks at home, to fighting rearguard actions to protect agency turf from encroachment by a new department. A time of crisis is not the best time to undertake a fundamental reorganization. Furthermore, we should not commit ourselves to legislated institutional change before we have enough experience to know what we really need to meet new challenges.

In time, a reorganization may be necessary; if so, Congress and the executive branch would need to work in partnership to define the best course of action. But it is simply too early to know what form such change should take. For now, Congress should give the President the time and discretion to try organizational and process innovations within the White House and departments. As the results come in, Congress and the executive branch should open a dialogue on whether and how the Federal Government should be fundamentally reorganized for homeland security missions over the long haul.

## Other Organizational Innovations

Given both the importance and the likely longevity of homeland security as an issue, Congressional leadership should convene a panel of members to evaluate and recommend options for reorganizing Congressional committees to enable more effective oversight of cross-cutting issues such as homeland security. Some 14 Congressional committees currently claim jurisdiction over some aspect of homeland security. In practice, this means that Congress is essentially trying to provide oversight by looking at the problem vertically through 14 different soda straws. Given that it has the power of the purse as well as the last word on how the Federal Government actually expends resources, Congress can have an enormous impact—positive or negative—on the coherence of an activity.

Within DOD, at least two proposals should be considered. The first proposal is for the Secretary of Defense to establish a new Commander in Chief (CINC) for Homeland Defense. The U.S. military must be better organized to support homeland defense. Historically, assigning responsibility for an area or function to a CINC has been the most effective way to ensure that it receives priority attention in military planning, training, and resource allocation. Creating a new CINC for Homeland Defense would put all or most of the military assets required to support homeland security under the command of a single four-star general or admiral. It would create a senior "go-to" person within the military whose sole job, day and night, is to prepare the military for operations to protect against or respond to threats to the American homeland. Currently, no such person or focal point exists, although a proposal to create a new Northern Command is being actively considered. The challenge in creating a new homeland defense CINC will be to balance the desire to put all military homeland defense missions under the control of one CINC against the need to ensure that the resulting CINC has a manageable set of missions and span of control.

The second proposal is for DOD to make homeland defense the primary mission of the Army and Air National Guard and for elements of the Guard to be reorganized, properly trained, and fully equipped to undertake this mission. Specifically, the Air National Guard should be given air and missile defense of the United States as its primary mission and should be restructured accordingly. The Army National Guard should be reoriented, reorganized, trained, and equipped to focus on consequence management in the event of a major terrorist attack, especially one involving chemical or biological agents. This includes maintaining civil order and augmenting civilian capabilities for protecting critical infrastructure. Geographically dispersed, with deep ties to local communities and well-established relationships with state governments, the National Guard is ideally suited to be the military's primary contributor to these missions. Reorienting the Army National Guard in this way would reorder its current priorities, making its role as a strategic reserve in the event of a long or difficult major war overseas a secondary rather than a primary mission. Over the longer term, the strategic reserve mission might be assigned to a restructured Army Reserve.

The administration should also give priority to strengthening the Federal Emergency Management Agency to be the permanent connection between the Federal Government and state and local governments for dealing with the consequences of terrorism on American soil. FEMA has an excellent track record of coordinating the national response to natural disasters, such as hurricanes and floods; however, prior to September 11, it was extremely reluctant to take on post-terrorism consequence management. As a result, it currently lacks personnel with the requisite skills for this mission. Rather than assign the Federal coordination role to another agency, the President, working with Congress, should strengthen FEMA to undertake this task, with considerable investment in new staff and training activities.

Finally, the government should create opportunities for national service in the area of homeland security. The attacks on the World Trade Center and the Pentagon led to an outpouring of national volunteering and participation in the recovery effort. Across the Nation, Americans are looking for ways to help. This offers an opportunity that should not be wasted. The President should create a task force to explore the creation of a Homeland Security Service Corps for Americans, young and old alike, who are prepared to give 2 years to help protect the Nation. Volunteers would be trained to serve in a variety of fields, including the Public Health Service, airport security, and the National Guard and Reserve. Modeled after the Peace Corps and AmeriCorps, this Corps could make suitable educational and financial benefits available to volunteers. The program would be likely to have strong bipartisan commitment from the President and Congress. The task force could also explore the merits of mandatory national service.

## The Imperative to Prevail

Homeland security is now front and center in America's consciousness, and it is likely to stay there for quite some time, especially if further attacks occur. Unlike the 100-hour Gulf War or even the Cold War, the war against terrorism will not have a clear end point. Rather, it will be more like the wars on crime or drugs or poverty. Because the problem can never be entirely eliminated, victory becomes defined in terms of managing the level of risk down to acceptable levels. In short, the need to strengthen homeland security will present not only a multifaceted set of requirements but also an enduring one.

The Federal Government, in partnership with state and local agencies and the private sector, must do everything in its power to enhance our homeland security capabilities if we are to prevail in this long war on terrorism. It should start by identifying critical shortfalls in capability, prioritizing those shortfalls, and then addressing them, starting with the most important items and working its way down the list. It also must establish new ways of doing business to better integrate policies, programs, and budgets across bureaucratic divides. This will require enormous political will and leadership on the part of America's elected officials and perhaps historic levels of resolve on the part of our Nation. But transforming on the home front is not just an option; it is an imperative if we are to prevail.

## Notes

[1] Most notable are the U.S. Commission on National Strategy in the 21st Century (the Hart-Rudman Commission), *Road Map for National Security: Imperative for Change* (Wilkes-Barre, PA: Kallisti Publishing, 2002), and the Advisory Panel to Assess Domestic Response Capabilities for Terrorism Involving Weapons of Mass Destruction (the Gilmore Panel), Second Annual Report, *Toward a National Strategy for Combating Terrorism*, accessed online at <http://www.rand.org/nsrd/terrpanel/>. These, among others, reflect detailed consideration of homeland security and made numerous recommendations in this area.

[2] Randall Larsen as quoted in Sydney J. Freedberg, Jr., "Shoring Up America," *National Journal*, October 19, 2001.

[3] These objectives were inspired by the three-part framework of prevention, protection, and response that was originally laid out by the Hart-Rudman Commission in *Road Map for National Security*, Phase III Report, January 31, 2001, 12–14.

[4] Michael Dobbs, "Homeland Security: New Challenges for an Old Responsibility," *Journal of Homeland Security*, March 2001.

[5] Donald H. Rumsfeld, "A New Kind of War," *The New York Times*, September 27, 2001.

[6] The Hart-Rudman Commission recommended the creation of a new Homeland Security Agency that would include the Federal Emergency Management Agency, Coast Guard, Border Patrol, and Customs. See *Road Map for National Security*, 15–16 and 21.

[7] See, for example, the Gilmore Panel, *Toward a National Strategy for Combating Terrorism*, 7; Joseph J. Collins and Michael Horowitz, *Homeland Defense: A Strategic Approach* (Washington, DC: Center for Strategic and International Studies, December 2000), 42.

[8] Much of this discussion is drawn from unpublished work by John Hamre, president and chief executive officer of the Center for Strategic and International Studies, in Washington, DC.

[9] Ibid.

# Chapter 11

# Changing the Strategic Equation

Peter A. Wilson and Richard D. Sokolsky

T he Bush administration has articulated a new paradigm for transforming U.S. strategic offensive and defensive forces to meet the demands of the 21$^{st}$ century security environment. It has also set out strategic principles to guide this transformation. In the spring of 2001, President George W. Bush stated, "We need new concepts of deterrence that rely on both offensive and defensive forces. Deterrence can no longer be based solely on the threat of nuclear retaliation."[1] On other occasions over the past 2 years, President Bush has emphasized that the United States needs a new strategic framework because Russia itself is no longer the enemy and the Cold War logic that led to the creation of massive stockpiles on both sides is now outdated. The President has stated that our mutual security need no longer depend on a nuclear balance of terror and that America should rethink the requirements for nuclear deterrence in a new security environment. The premises of Cold War nuclear targeting should no longer dictate the size of the U.S. nuclear arsenal.

In early January 2002, the Bush administration issued the results of its Nuclear Posture Review (NPR), which laid out the direction for American nuclear forces over the next decade. One of the key features in this blueprint for transforming the U.S. strategic posture is the shift to a new triad of capabilities that includes strategic offensive capabilities, both nuclear and non-nuclear, defensive capabilities, and a robust nuclear weapons infrastructure. The NPR concludes that the addition of defenses, as well as non-nuclear strike forces, will allow the United States to reduce its dependence on offensive nuclear forces to maintain deterrence in the evolving strategic environment.

Making the transition to a world in which deterrence depends less on maintaining a "nuclear balance of terror" and more on some as-yet-undetermined mix of offensive and defensive deployments is a major geostrategic and technological challenge. Indeed, the profound changes in the character of the U.S.-Russian relationship and the broader geostrategic environment, as well as changes in military technologies, cast the issue of strategic force reductions and the deployment of missile defenses in an entirely new conceptual framework.

A further, perhaps even more profound, question is that of the evolution of our nuclear relationship with China, which, unlike Russia, is an emerging great power. What meaning and relevance do the concepts of nuclear deterrence, strategic stability, and mutual assured destruction have in this changing strategic landscape? What is the appropriate doctrine that should guide plans for the employment of nuclear weapons? What new standard or metric should guide decisions on the size and composition of U.S. strategic forces and missile defenses?[2]

The purpose of this chapter is to illuminate the relationship between these broader strategic policy challenges and the emerging issues of strategic defense and offense technologies. The first section sets these issues in the context of recent developments that have profoundly altered the strategic landscape, including the terrorist attacks of September 11, the U.S. response to these attacks, and the Bush administration decision to withdraw from the Anti-Ballistic Missile (ABM) Treaty. The second section addresses the main technological issues and challenges associated with American plans to deploy missile defenses. The third section discusses U.S. strategic force planning in the new security environment. The fourth section looks at the impact of changes in American strategic policy on other key countries. The chapter ends with some observations about future directions for U.S. strategic policy.[3]

## Strategic Shocks of Fall 2001

Since the Bush administration's articulation of the very broad contours of this "new strategic framework," the geostrategic environment has undergone several shocks during the late summer and fall of 2001. The well-conceived and -executed slow-motion strategic attack on the World Trade Center and the Pentagon on September 11, 2001, was the first shock. As a result, our terminology about strategic warfare has changed. Now the United States is engaged in a global war against militant Islam with a revolutionary ideology, in the form of Osama bin Laden's Al Qaeda ("The Base") terrorist organization. This international terrorist organization has demonstrated a sophisticated capacity to prepare a battlefield inside the United States. With the rapid collapse of both World Trade Center towers and other deaths in Pennsylvania and at the Pentagon, the United States suffered the second-highest number of fatalities in a single day in its entire history—some 3,000 in 2 hours. Our vast nuclear deterrent posture stood mute and irrelevant to this form of strategic warfare, perpetrated by a globally diffuse opponent with unlimited war aims—the destruction of Western civilization—and undeterred by the threat of nuclear retaliation.

The United States then launched Operation *Enduring Freedom,* a global operation designed to "roll up" the Al Qaeda terrorist network and its primary nation-state host, an Afghanistan ruled by the Taliban, along with its religious and political allies. Although the Taliban regime was destroyed by late fall 2001, the Bush administration has acknowledged that the global war against Al Qaeda will be a long campaign, much of it fought in the shadows. A key feature of this protracted operation is the building of a wide global coalition that includes the Russian Federation and China. The former is absolutely vital; it has allowed the United States overflight rights and the basing of significant military assets in Uzbekistan, Kyrgyzstan, and Tajikistan, former states of the Soviet Union, to conduct operations inside Afghanistan. China also appears to be cooperating in the form of diplomatic support in the United Nations, economic assistance to Pakistan, and the sharing of information about Islamic terrorist organizations.

This act of hyperterrorism was followed by several additional major geostrategic events during the fall of 2001. Reflecting new political warmth between Washington and Moscow, Presidents Bush and Putin agreed during the November 2001 summit meeting in Crawford, Texas, to press ahead with major reductions of their countries' strategic nuclear offensive forces. However, the two countries were unable to reach a mutually satisfactory agreement on the fate of the ABM Treaty, leading to the U.S. official withdrawal from the treaty on June 13, 2002.[4]

## Review of Missile Defense Technologies

Unlike the Clinton administration, the Bush administration has decided to accelerate research and development (R&D) and to procure during this decade a full spectrum of active ballistic and cruise missile defenses without the constraints of the ABM Treaty. At the present time, the administration has not chosen the architecture of its deployment plans for ballistic missile defense (BMD), other than to acknowledge that the near-term requirement is to provide a missile defense against a small number of intercontinental ballistic missile (ICBM) warheads. This is the so-called rogue state threat, a handful of first-generation ICBMs equipped with very primitive reentry vehicles and penetration aid technology. The possible elements of any "layered" BMD architecture are reviewed in this section. However, several ongoing programs recently have been canceled due to development and cost overrun problems, a reflection of the technological challenge of developing effective BMD.

### Ballistic Missile Defense

The fundamental goal of the planned BMD system is to defend the forces and territories of the United States and of its allies and friends as soon as practicable. The integrated program under development is intended to counter the full spectrum of ballistic missile threats in all phases of flight using kinetic and directed energy kill mechanisms and a variety of land-, sea-, air-, and space-based deployment options.

*Terminal (endo-atmospheric) or lower-tier systems*

The first terminal BMD to become operational is the PAC–3 hit-to-kill (HTK) missile. The interceptor uses a microwave seeker and side-firing jets to maneuver to kill, by kinetic impact, short-range ballistic missiles and cruise missiles. The sea-based counterpart was the Naval Area Defense (NAD) system, which consists of a standard missile with an upgraded fuse and warhead to destroy incoming short-range ballistic missiles (SRBMs) with a fragmentation effect. Due to cost overruns and significant schedule delays, this program was recently canceled.

*Theater-wide (exo-atmospheric) or upper-tier systems*

Theater-wide or upper-tier systems are the high-performance HTK systems, such as the Army Theater High-Altitude Area Defense (THAAD) and the Navy Mid-Course (formerly Navy Theater Wide) system. In late January 2002, the Navy reached an important milestone with the first successful test of the Navy Mid-Course HTK interceptor. Operating off the coast of a hostile state armed with very long-range, perhaps transoceanic-range, ballistic missiles, Navy Mid-Course may have marginal boost-phase intercept capability against slow rising liquid propellant multistage rockets.

*Boost-phase BMD systems*

The near-term boost-phase theater missile defense system is the airborne laser (ABL) being developed by the Air Force. Current plans are to arm a 747–400 series freighter aircraft with a carbon dioxide-iodine laser that can intercept SRBMs out to a range of several hundred nautical miles. This weapon is not a viable boost-phase weapon against any missile that is launched beyond the slant range of the laser. It may be possible to use the

ABL against Pyongyang's long-range missiles off the North Korean coast, but the Air Force will have to be able to suppress the threat that both long-range surface-to-air missiles and manned interceptors pose to the very vulnerable wide-body aircraft carrying the laser.

### Land-based Midcourse

The Clinton administration proposed a land-based BMD designed to intercept a small number of ICBMs launched by a rogue state (North Korea is the state of most immediate concern). To conform as closely as possible to the ABM Treaty, the Clinton plan called for the deployment of only one site in Alaska equipped with 100 interceptors to deal with an emerging North Korean ICBM threat with an option to deploy an additional 100 interceptors in the continental United States.

### Sea-based Midcourse

The Bush administration hopes that major progress beyond the Navy Mid-Course system is feasible. With a new interceptor rather than the lower performance standard missile, the midcourse BMD could provide an additional layer of defense if ships are placed in the North Pacific and Atlantic to intercept oncoming ICBMs from North Korea, Iraq, or Iran. Similar to the Navy Mid-Course system, the sea-based BMD would be equipped with an HTK capability and might have a boost-phase role as well.

### Sea- and Land-based Boost-phase

A proposal has been made to base a very high-acceleration and long-range booster and HTK interceptor on board a new generation of BMD-capable warships. Such a system will be much more effective against long-range ballistic missiles that are based relatively near an oceanic coastline. To provide a defense against a very large country such as Iran, such a system would most likely have to be land-based in a neighboring country, which is no small diplomatic challenge.

### Space-based Boost-phase

The Bush administration desires to test two variants of a space-based interceptor. The first is a space-based HTK system, a variant of the old "Brilliant Pebbles" concept. The second is a space-based laser system. Under the most optimistic circumstances, in particular a substantial increase in funding, the testing of both the space-based HTK and chemical laser systems is unlikely until later in the decade. The strategic consequence of this type of BMD architecture could be much more profound than the array of HTK systems described above (this point is discussed below).

**Air Defense**

The PAC (Patriot Advanced Capability)–3 lower-tier HTK system has some capability against cruise missiles. Additional air defense (AD) improvements are being explored, including the development of lower-frequency radars held aloft by aerostats (tethered, streamlined balloons), the joint land-attack cruise missile defense elevated netted sensor program, and the medium extended air defense system (MEADS). Upgrades to the various airborne warning and control systems (AWACS) are under way. The Navy's E–2C and the Air Force E–3D are being reequipped with lower-frequency radars that are optimized to detect low-observable air targets, such as Tomahawk class cruise missiles. The Air Force is giving serious consideration to acquiring a next-generation AWACS using a larger B–767 class aircraft. The fleet of antiaircraft capable cruisers and destroyers equipped with the Aegis system are being upgraded with an antiballistic missile defense capability. Finally, the Navy and Air Force continue to modernize their fighter fleets with increasingly capable air-to-air missiles, such as the upgraded AIM–120 AMRAAM and AIM–9X. All these air defense capabilities are likely to be given much greater emphasis after the September 2001 aerial attacks on the World Trade Center and the Pentagon.

**Space Surveillance**

Critical to the success of any wide-area or layered BMD is the deployment of a new generation of space-based sensors that can perform multiple functions, including missile tracking and the discrimination of warheads from space debris and decoys and other countermeasures. The most significant of this decade is the deployment of the space-based infrared sensor system (SBIRS)-High, operating at geosynchronous earth orbit to replace the Defense Support Program early-warning satellites. There were also plans to deploy a SBIRS-Low constellation, operating at a low Earth orbit, by the end of the decade. SBIRS-Low or its equivalent will be vitally important to provide early-track and warhead discrimination data on medium- and transoceanic-range missiles as they rise out of the atmosphere, so they can be intercepted by a wide array of aerospace defense systems. At the present time, SBIRS-High is suffering from a major cost overrun; its initial operational capability date is slipping by several years to the end of the decade. SBIRS-Low is in even in greater disarray: Congress has canceled this program, although funds remain to resurrect the program or to begin development of a replacement array of sensors. Without the equivalent of SBIRS-Low to provide post-launch tracking data, the effectiveness of the full array of terrestrially based BMD will be seriously compromised. One option is to deploy a fleet of high-altitude unmanned aerial vehicles (UAVs), such as the Global Hawk, to carry infrared sensors to track missile payloads during their midcourse phase of flight.

## Some Missile Defense Technology/Operational Issues

To achieve very high performance levels against small low-technology threats, several technologies will have to be mastered and several milestones met by mid-decade.

### *Hit-to-Kill Interceptors*

A central feature of the U.S.-designed BMD systems is their heavy reliance on the development of HTK interceptors. Major advances in computer processing power, coupled with improved infrared sensors, appear plausible. However, the test experience of HTK is mixed. Development of the PAC–3 terminal defense interceptor has led to a success rate of better than 80 percent, while the more ambitious THAAD interceptor has had only two limited successes in four tries. Attempts to develop a high-performance HTK interceptor beyond THAAD have been troubled by recent test failures of a new-generation booster.

### *Countermeasure Resistance*

The current generation of BMD interceptor tests involves the least demanding countermeasure threats, since the focus of these early tests was on the development of the basic weapon capability. An extensive testing program will have to be sustained over a number of years to develop both electro-optical sensors and high-frequency radars to allow BMD systems to defeat a wide array of exo-atmospheric decoys that rogue states might develop by the end of the decade. A critical variable that will influence the severity of the threat to U.S. aerospace defense systems will be the willingness of the Russian Federation and China to limit the transfer of countermeasure technology to states such as North Korea, Iran, and Iraq.

### *Resilience in a Nuclear-Disturbed Environment*

Future opponents, especially the economically weaker rogues, may conclude that U.S. missile defenses can be defeated only by the use of nuclear weapons. A future opponent might choose to use a warhead that is "salvage fused" to detonate during collision with an HTK interceptor; the resultant high-altitude nuclear detonation could blind the terrestrially based BMD fire control radar. Depending upon the altitude of the nuclear detonation, effects could appear as scintillation in the ionosphere ("blackout") or wide-area electromagnetic pulse (EMP) effects. If unprotected from the latter phenomenon, the electronics of terrestrially based BMD systems could fail catastrophically. To build BMD systems hardened against these effects will require a significant R&D and system design investment prior to production.

### Dealing with Low Observable Cruise Missiles

By the end of the decade, Tomahawk class cruise missiles may be widely available to future U.S. opponents. Most worrisome is the prospect that one or more of these opponents will master the indigenous production of a modern V–1. This might be a cruise missile with a range of 1,000 kilometers and inherently low observable features, mass-produced in the hundreds or even thousands. The challenge to American and allied air defenses is to defeat a massed cruise missile attack that might be part of a structured attack involving the simultaneous use of theater ballistic missiles (TBMs). There are a variety of air defense programs designed to deal with that threat, but they may have to be hardened to nuclear weapon effects, especially the threat of high-altitude detonations that cause wide-area EMP effects.

With the American termination of the ABM Treaty, the Chinese are likely to become much more interested in cruise missiles. This interest will be further reinforced if the United States decides to deploy a space-based weapon segment of its BMD architecture. For example, China might make a major investment in a fleet of nuclear-powered cruise missile submarines (SSGNs) and conventionally powered submarines with air independent propulsion (AIP) to carry long-range submarine-launched cruise missiles (SLCMs). It might be much cheaper for the Chinese to develop such a fleet than to invest in a next generation of submarine-launched (intercontinental) ballistic missiles (SLBMs). The Chinese might be prepared to maintain a small number of SLCM-armed SSGNs in the eastern Pacific, especially during times of severe tension with the United States, such as a political-military crisis involving Taiwan. This stratagem would be intended to divert substantial American naval assets to monitor this fleet, which, though small, could menace the West Coast of the United States. Further, there is the prospect that rogue states or possibly transnational terrorist organizations might be prepared to deploy civilian freighters as cruise-missile-armed "Q ships" to bypass the BMD deployed by 2010.

## Would Space-Based BMD Disturb the Emerging Strategic Equilibrium?

Without the constraints of the ABM Treaty, the most significant future decision by the Bush administration on a future BMD architecture will be whether it has a space-based weapon component.[5] An effort to accelerate development and deployment of a space-based interceptor array may cause Moscow to view this as a powerful sign that the United States has decided to deploy a BMD that is capable of defeating threats far more capable than those that might be possessed by rogue states. In contrast, a U.S. missile defense architecture that is terrestrially based and relies on HTK interceptor technology cannot credibly threaten the assured retaliation capabilities of a Russian ICBM force based deep inside Russia. After further buildup of its centrally based next-generation ICBMs, with or without multiple independently targetable reentry vehicles (MIRVs), China may hold to a similar view.

On the other hand, the Bush administration may press ahead with a very robust space-based interceptor development program, with the intent of deploying either a version of the HTK-based Brilliant Pebbles concept or an array of very high-powered orbiting laser weapons by 2020. The Russians and Chinese may decide to tolerate the U.S. deployment of boost-phase systems that can intercept short- and medium-range ballistic missiles. However, a space-based BMD with a boost-phase capability will have the potential of negating ICBMs based deep inside Russia or China, thereby putting their assured retaliation capability at far greater risk. Both Moscow and Beijing are likely to press for some sort of regime of restraints on space-weapon testing and deployment. It is unclear at this time whether the Bush administration will accept any limits on space-weapon testing during the next decade or so.

Although an American decision to deploy a space-based BMD array might not trigger a classic Cold War-type arms race, it could encourage Russia and China to develop a far closer political and military strategic relationship. For example, Russia might be prepared to transfer advanced strategic offensive and defensive weapon technology to China just to maintain the overall strategic equilibrium with the United States. On the other hand, the Russian or Chinese response to a U.S. move to deploy space-based weapons might be muted if relations between Washington, Moscow, and Beijing are on a cooperative track.

These concerns suggest that there will be some major technological challenges for the American developers of aerospace defenses. As for the future of U.S. strategic nuclear offensive forces, the changes may be more profound doctrinally rather than technologically.

### Future Direction of the U.S. Strategic Force Posture

The Bush administration deserves credit for articulating the intellectual rationale for fundamental changes in U.S. nuclear weapons policy. Both the doctrine and force structure that it inherited from its predecessor were anachronistic and thus in need of transformation. Reflecting this view, the new Nuclear Posture Review (NPR) holds the promise of ending Cold War practices related to American strategic force planning and the prospect of a fundamental change in deterrence strategy. These changes include significant revisions to U.S. nuclear warfighting plans and the development of a new triad of strategic forces that would include non-nuclear as well as nuclear forces.[6] The NPR also breaks some important new ground, particularly in broadening the definition of *strategic* capabilities and focusing on capabilities-based planning.

Nonetheless, the results of the NPR to date reveal a gap between the rhetoric of strategic transformation and reality. Indeed, rather than making a clear break with the past, as was foreshadowed at the outset of the administration, what is striking about the changes in strategy and force structure announced in the NPR is their apparent perpetuation of the status quo. However, the NPR remains a work in progress, and DOD officials claim that no final decisions have been made on the important issues of the overall size of the active stockpile, the reserve of ready strategic warheads (called the hedge force by the Clinton administration but relabeled in NPR as the responsive force), or the inactive stockpile of weapons that are slated for destruction or in some disassembled form. Decisions on these issues could have significant implications for U.S.-Russian relations and for strategic force modernization, especially the need to develop new warheads with new capabilities.

The decision of the Bush administration to unilaterally reduce American strategic force levels to between 1,700 and 2,200 operationally deployed warheads broke the deadlock in the strategic arms control process, accomplishing in one bold stroke what years of arms control negotiations had failed to deliver. But these reductions are less sweeping than they appear. The force levels that are envisioned at the end of this decade are virtually the same as those agreed to by President William Clinton and President Boris Yeltsin in 1997. Moreover, only minimal changes are contemplated in the composition of U.S. strategic forces. In fact, at the end of this decade, the mix of strategic missiles, bombers, and submarines comprising the American nuclear triad will not differ significantly from the force structure established by the Clinton administration's 1994 Nuclear Posture Review.

A key issue raised in the NPR, and the one that has drawn considerable public attention and criticism, is the decision to store rather than destroy thousands of warheads that will be removed from strategic systems. The Bush administration, like its predecessor, has no plans to eliminate the capability of these platforms to be rapidly "uploaded" with these reserve warheads. This reconstitution capability of over 6,000 warheads is comparable to the one planned by the Clinton administration.

There is, to be sure, a legitimate argument for maintaining some type of reserve stockpile to sustain the active force, given worries about the mobilization capacity of the U.S. nuclear infrastructure, especially in production of plutonium pits and tritium. Still, if Russia is no longer our strategic enemy and the warhead requirements (as argued below) for dealing with China and rogue states are much more modest, there is no justification for maintaining thousands of warheads available for rapid uploading, particularly in light of the NPR acknowledgment that the new "responsive force capacity" is designed to deal with distant threats that may arise in the future but cannot be predicted.

Indeed, given the size and character of projected threats, the timelines in which they are likely to emerge, and the deterrent capabilities that the United States would need, the administration should be able to establish a new readiness system for strategic nuclear warheads (analogous to the readiness categories for Soviet and Warsaw Pact divisions during the Cold War) and to downsize significantly the number of warheads in the active (category one), responsive force (category two), and inactive (category three) stockpiles. If this approach were adopted, the category one force of warheads available for immediate use (or operationally deployed) would likely be far less than the planned 1,700–2,200 level; the category two stockpile of warheads (the hedge or responsive capacity) that could be uploaded within days or weeks would contain roughly the same number; and the category three stockpile of weapons that are in some disassembled form, designed to sustain the other stockpiles, may not need to exceed 1,000.

A valuable feature of the new NPR is the shift in nuclear planning from a threat-based approach, which sized and structured strategic forces to deal with the Soviet Union, to a capabilities-based approach, which relies on a broader mix of nuclear and non-nuclear capabilities to respond to a broader range of circumstances. In theory, this shift in emphasis in strategic force planning could be potentially significant if it leads to less dependence on nuclear weapons in national security policy. Whether it leads, in practice, to this outcome remains an open question in the NPR.

Administration officials have said that this new standard for sizing the nuclear posture takes into account multiple potential opponents over the next decade. However, it is hard to see how these possible opponents, which are projected to have a total of fewer than 200 nuclear weapons over the next decade, justify U.S. retention of 1,700 to 2,200 operationally deployed warheads and the much larger force being held in reserve for rapid uploading. Indeed, in its January 11 report to the Congress on the missile threat to the United States, the National Intelligence Council projected that China will deploy 75 to 100 strategic nuclear warheads by 2015; rogue states, such as North Korea, Iran, and Iraq, are unlikely to field no more than several dozen strategic nuclear weapons over the next decade.[7] Even if one were to postulate American absorption of a limited first strike by one of these powers alone or in combination, they would not justify the NPR bottom line. After all, the survivability of the U.S. nuclear forces does not depend upon raw numbers; rather, it relies on secure forces such as SSBNs at sea, ICBMs in silos, and a robust command, control, communications, and intelligence ($C^3I$) system.

It is even more difficult to justify NPR proposed force levels if one takes into account, as the NPR claims to have done, U.S. plans to build antimissile defenses and to develop long-range non-nuclear strike forces, such as those that were used successfully in the Balkans and Afghanistan, to perform missions previously associated with the use of nuclear weapons. Indeed, with the possible exception of hardened, deeply buried targets in rogue states, or other countries, there are very few key military, economic/industrial, or leadership targets that cannot be destroyed with non-nuclear capabilities. These other elements of American strategic power, if fully integrated into U.S. operational planning, should lead to substantial downsizing of our strategic nuclear forces beyond the reductions contemplated in the NPR.

The Bush administration may thus be missing an opportunity to adapt its nuclear strategy and forces to the new geopolitical and military/technological realities of the post-Cold War era. Put simply, it is hard to reconcile the NPR nuclear force posture with administration rhetoric that Russia is no longer our enemy and that we seek to build a partnership with Moscow. It is equally difficult to square NPR force levels with the administration view that the United States cannot rely solely on the threat of massive nuclear retaliation to deter rogue states. If this is the case, for example, it should hardly matter whether America maintains the capability to attack these countries quickly with 500 or 1,700 nuclear warheads; an attack of either magnitude would be sufficient to destroy any of these countries as functioning societies. After all, the Al Qaeda strategic attack on the United States was not deterred by the presence of the current nuclear arsenal.

The need to retain the capability to execute massive, preplanned, damage-limiting first strikes against Russia should no longer be the benchmark for determining American strategic force requirements. Instead, strategic forces should be sized and structured primarily to deter or defend against the use of weapons of mass destruction by smaller powers. The role and utility of nuclear weapons in confronting these types of threats, while important, is limited. A low number of nuclear weapons are needed to meet the requirements of deterrence and defense. Strategically and operationally, the number of targets that the United States would need to hold at risk in any conceivable combination of rogue countries (in military parlance, the target set) is relatively small by Cold War standards and can probably be met with approximately 1,000–1,500 deployed warheads at the most.

If the United States is to move to a strategic posture of 1,700 operationally deployed warheads or to consider further reductions, it will need to make a major revision of its nuclear force posture planning process. A key test will be whether the stylized Single Integrated Operation Plan (SIOP) process, controlled by the United States Strategic Command (U.S. STRATCOM), is drastically overhauled or abolished. Currently, the assured retaliation requirements of the strategic forces are dominated by the need to hold several thousand targets in the Russian Federation at risk. To go to an operational posture of 1,700 strategic warheads suggests that a new set of force planning requirements is needed.

For example, a new type of assured retaliation capability could emerge from a new set of strategic nuclear planning requirements. The assured retaliation requirements of the United States might be formulated according to the following principles: First, the United States needs only to be able to hold several hundred targets, say 500, at risk anywhere on the planet with 100 percent certainty. The location and character of these targets would not be specified before the fact. In essence, a limited nuclear operation would be planned on a contingency basis, similar to that of a theater-wide air tasking order. Unlike the rigid definition of an *assured destruction* requirement for Russia or China, the assured retaliation requirement might become more flexible and more contingent on the state of the geostrategic environment. Second, the U.S. assured retaliation requirement could drop substantially against the Russian Federation, while it might remain much higher vis-à-vis China.

Instead of preserving the SIOP, U.S. STRATCOM would be charged to develop the capacity to provide dynamic and near-real-time nuclear weapon targeting. A nuclear weapon contingency planning capability could be created. The United States could declare that it has an "all-azimuth nuclear assured retaliation capability." Within that broad guidance, there are a number of important planning issues. For example, should every component of the smaller inventory of weapons be able to attack the full range of possible targets, or should the nuclear arsenal instead include a range of weapon capabilities? This is the issue of the inherent targeting flexibility of a significantly smaller nuclear offensive posture. Second, should the 1,700 remaining nuclear weapons have a "dial-a-yield" capability to give the Secretary of Defense and U.S. STRATCOM planners the maximum flexibility in designing a near-real-time nuclear targeting capability? An additional deterrence or counterforce requirement is that some or all of the nuclear weapons should have earth-penetrating warheads. Should a selected subset of the arsenal be so designed, or is there a requirement for a universal bomb design?

If the answer to either question calls for new types of bombs, then a more convincing case can be made that the United States should seriously reconsider its commitment to a moratorium on underground testing (agreed in 1993), while the fate of the Comprehensive Test Ban Treaty (CTBT) or any other nuclear test restraint regime is decided. The development of lower-yield weapons with simpler and more rugged designs would reduce both collateral damage and the burdens of maintaining the current nuclear weapons infrastructure. Whether the United States would have to resume nuclear testing to obtain these benefits is a matter of debate and disagreement among nuclear weapons experts and will depend to some degree on whether the planned nuclear stockpile is scaled back beyond the current NPR plan. A resumption of nuclear testing, however, would carry significant diplomatic and political costs as well as undermine the global nonproliferation regime. In response to new U.S. nuclear testing, for example, Russia and China would probably end their testing moratoria to develop more advanced nuclear warheads;

India and Pakistan might also follow suit under the cover provided by an end to the global testing moratorium. These costs would have to be weighed against the military, operational, and technical benefits of nuclear testing.

Finally, there is the requirement that the smaller nuclear forces be able to penetrate emerging aerospace defenses without reliance on a brute force strategy that depends on the continued deployment of very high numbers of operational nuclear weapons and the maintenance of a very large responsive force. Given its high cost and demanding military technological requirements, it is unlikely that either the Russian Federation or China will deploy any significant ballistic missile defense based upon hit-to-kill interceptor technology. More plausible is the prospect that the Russian Federation will maintain a BMD focused on the defense of the Moscow region with nuclear-armed interceptors. It is conceivable that China may acquire a limited BMD capability through the upgrade of its S–300/400 class high-altitude surface-to-air missile systems. China might attempt to upgrade these assets with the development of nuclear-armed interceptors.

One critical problem for any nuclear-armed exo-atmospheric BMD is that the first use of nuclear-armed interceptors can blind the defender's battle management radars, due to a phenomenon known as blackout. The defensive interceptor's nuclear detonation does the work of the offensive by blinding ground-based radars. One alternative is to develop an infrared telescope onboard a large aircraft to look through the nuclear-disturbed high-altitude environment and to provide fire control solutions to follow-on nuclear-armed interceptors. If Russia or China developed such a capability, this would raise concern that the smaller U.S. nuclear offensive forces' assured retaliation capability could be compromised. Without the MIRV option on U.S. land-based ICBMs, an alternative might be considered, such as developing a transoceanic-range maneuvering reentry vehicle. Small nuclear-armed variants of the X–37 winged reentry vehicle could be used as an anti-BMD weapon.

## Defense Budget Implications

For the United States to deploy, by 2010, a robust, terrestrially based missile defense architecture designed to stop a small rogue ICBM threat will likely cost more than $5 billion per year in procurement costs alone after fiscal year 2003 (FY03). Apart from PAC–3 procurement, the bulk of the approximately $8 billion allocated for the BMD programs in FY03 is for research, development, and testing. Costs to deploy a space-based

BMD will be much higher, but that bill would not emerge until after 2010. In light of the September 11 strategic attack and the U.S. response, the budgetary implications of building a more robust missile defense posture, beyond the "anti-rogue" requirement, are unclear.

Prior to September 11, defense spending was not likely to rise more than 3 percent a year during the decade. Thus, to fund a robust BMD/AD program would have required that other investment accounts in the defense budgets would have to be cut back. Now there is likely to be a substantial increase in defense spending for the next few years. After that, sustained defense budget increases will face severe pressure as the Federal Government slides back into a period of fiscal deficits for much of this decade.

Certainly, much more will be spent on broad homeland defense requirements and a new generation of reconnaissance-strike systems associated with the "transformation" of non-nuclear forces. Operation *Enduring Freedom* has the potential of generating far greater costs than the campaign in Afghanistan, especially if a decision is made to destroy the regime of Saddam Husayn in Iraq by a major military campaign. How the costs of these emerging theater warfighting demands, expanded homeland defense requirements, and the non-nuclear transformation will affect the pace and scale of any BMD deployment during this decade remains uncertain at this time.

## Possible Chinese Responses

A critical variable is how China will react to the emergence of the American BMD program without the constraints of the ABM Treaty. If reassured by Washington that the U.S. aerospace defense architecture is not aimed at China, Beijing may take a more relaxed attitude, especially if cooperation with Washington in support of Operation *Enduring Freedom* is substantial, and U.S. and Chinese trade ties greatly expand after China's entry into the World Trade Organization. Nevertheless, Beijing might conclude that it will have to develop and deploy a robust assured retaliation capability against planned and future U.S. aerospace defense capabilities. A U.S. decision to press ahead with a space-based weapon segment of a BMD architecture is likely to prompt China to undertake a more vigorous and diversified nuclear offensive modernization program.

A key geostrategic driver for the American-Chinese relationship is whether the fate of Taiwan is moving in a direction satisfactory to Beijing. Left unresolved, the Taiwan problem is likely to remain the premier source of tension between Beijing and Washington throughout this decade. If the Taiwan problem is not resolved and is a serious source of tension between Washington and Beijing, China has an array of potential nuclear force posture responses.

China's strategic response to the emerging U.S. BMD capability will be tempered by the desire of the Chinese leadership not to ignite an offensive-defensive strategic arms competition with the United States. However, the political-military leadership in Beijing is likely to sustain a sizeable transoceanic-range missile program to ensure that China maintains a robust assured retaliation capability. This strategic offensive force modernization program is likely to include the deployment of several tens of the DF–31 and DF–41 class ICBMs. They will probably be based on mobile launchers that operate from dispersed, hidden, and heavily hardened main operating bases. Whether MIRV technology is developed and deployed likely will depend upon the assured retaliation requirement that emerges in Beijing, as well as the Chinese desire to minimize the economic cost of any nuclear arms competition with the United States. China may invest heavily in long-range cruise missile systems as a credible "by-pass option" to defeat the emergence of substantial BMD capabilities in East Asia or a more robust American BMD program. The Chinese may conclude that investment in a fleet of submarines armed with long-range cruise missiles is better than deploying a small number of very expensive SSBNs. They might conclude that it is in their military interest to deploy a nuclear-armed BMD system.

## Other Nuclear-Armed States, Major Powers, and NPT

A critical aspect of the Bush administration's new strategic framework is its approach to other nuclear-armed states, its major non-nuclear-armed allies, and the fate of the Nuclear Non-Proliferation Treaty (NPT). A central strategic objective of Operation *Enduring Freedom* was the destruction of Al Qaeda and the Taliban regime without destabilizing a nuclear-armed Pakistan. Other nuclear-armed states and other major powers are likely to react to the U.S.-Russian Strategic Offensive Reductions Treaty (SORT) and the U.S. withdrawal from the ABM Treaty in various ways.

### France and the United Kingdom

The French and British governments will likely take a positive public stance toward the new U.S.-Russian agreement to reduce nuclear arsenals. On the other hand, both will be concerned that without the restraint of the ABM Treaty, Russia might deploy a robust nuclear-armed BMD architecture. In response to this possible contingency, both might jointly explore the development of a nuclear-armed variant of the Scalp/Storm Shadow air-launched cruise missile as a low-cost means of diversifying their nuclear arsenal to hedge against an emerging Russian high-performance BMD capability.

The geostrategic relationship between the North Atlantic Treaty Organization (NATO) and the Russian Federation is likely to be transformed in a positive way as a result of several factors, including the establishment of the new NATO-Russian Council, rapprochement between Moscow and Washington prompted by the war on terrorism, and Russia's emergence as a major oil and gas producer, which acts as a brake on the ability of the Organization of Petroleum Exporting Countries to prop up oil prices.

Thus, the political, economic, and strategic demands of supporting the United States during Operation *Enduring Freedom* and other military campaigns during the war on terrorism are likely to overshadow nuclear-related issues for much of the decade.

## Other NATO Europe

The rest of NATO Europe will react to the U.S.-Russian SORT and U.S. termination of the ABM Treaty in a fashion similar to that of France and Britain. Most will be loath to make a major investment in BMD, even with American technological assistance, if only because of the high cost of any significant program. Some NATO countries, notably France, the United Kingdom, and possibly Germany, may be prepared to increase defense spending to deal with the emergent international terrorist threat. They could fund a moderate degree of military modernization to transform their armed forces from having a continental defense capability to that of theater power projection during this decade.[8]

## Israel

The Israeli government will be very interested in gaining American resources to fund its indigenous Arrow theater ballistic missile defense program. In the strategic environment that has developed since last September, the United States is likely to encourage the deployment of a wide range of systems for defense against theater ballistic missiles by its key Arab allies and by Turkey, especially if Iran makes major progress with its SRBM and medium-range ballistic missile (MRBM) programs. Israel will be intent on deepening its strategic relationships with Turkey and India, a process likely to be encouraged by the United States, especially in the context of the war on terrorism.

Israel will maintain and modernize its nuclear arsenal while resisting engagement in any formal negotiations that link its program to other emergent nuclear, biological, and chemical weapons programs in the Greater Middle East.

### India and Pakistan

With the launching of Operation *Enduring Freedom*, the Bush administration radically altered the U.S. geostrategic approach to South Asia. Pakistan has become a vital but very fragile ally in the war against Al Qaeda and the Taliban in Afghanistan. To improve relations with both countries, the Bush administration promptly dropped in September 2001 nearly all economic and arms transfer sanctions imposed upon Pakistan and India after their 1998 nuclear tests. De facto rather than de jure, both countries have now been grandfathered into the NPT regime.

The nightmare scenario of the next few years is that American and allied military operations in South or Southwest Asia end up severely destabilizing the Pakistani regime. Whether due to a coup by a more pro-radical Islamic faction within the military—or something close to outright civil war—the reliability of central control of the Pakistani nuclear arsenal could be diminished. In these circumstances, there would be the distinct prospect of Indian military intervention (with possible Israeli assistance), and the prospect of a major regional war in which the use of nuclear weapons could not be precluded.

India has become an important nuclear-armed ally of the United States, providing diplomatic and material support for Operation *Enduring Freedom*. U.S. rapprochement with India is consistent with the U.S. low-profile long-term containment or hedging strategy aimed at China. The Indian government has already warmly endorsed the elements of the New Strategic Framework, with its emphasis on ballistic missile defenses. India will tend to size its nuclear program to the evolution of the Chinese arsenal and not that of Pakistan. A robust Chinese missile modernization program would give advocates of a major Indian intermediate-range ballistic missile (IRBM) buildup good political ammunition. However, it is likely that any buildup of India's nuclear capability will be severely restrained by budget limitations.

### Iran, Iraq, and Saudi Arabia

Iran's chances of acquiring a small nuclear arsenal by the end of the decade will be strongly influenced by relations between Washington and Moscow. In the context of their improved relations, Iran's progress in this regard may be slowed considerably. In particular, if Russian direct and indirect support dries up, this will slow the Iranian long-range missile program. Unfortunately, Iran has useful alternative sources of missile technology. Obvious candidates include China, North Korea, and possibly Pakistan. Conversely, Moscow may continue to expand its military supply relationship with Tehran to solidify an enduring geostrategic and geo-economic relationship, and this is likely to be a source of ongoing tension with the United States.

A very important new geostrategic possibility is whether one of the objectives of Operation *Enduring Freedom*—that of destroying the Taliban regime in Afghanistan and stabilizing its successor regime—will facilitate a rapprochement between Tehran and Washington. A significant improvement in U.S. and Iranian relations might radically reduce Tehran's interest in a costly ICBM program, thus reducing the rationale for any American deployment of an antirogue BMD before 2010. On the other hand, even a significantly improved relationship between Washington and Tehran is unlikely to slow down Iran's regionally oriented SRBM and MRBM programs that are aimed at Israel and the possible reemergence of Iraq's missile capability. At present, the prospect of improved U.S.-Iranian relations has all but disappeared after the administration labeled Iran a member of the "axis of evil." Iran's involvement in transferring weapons to Palestinian terrorist groups and its support for regional warlords in Afghanistan who oppose the central government has put a further chill in the relationship.

Although the current and future Iraqi leadership will have great ambitions to acquire a nuclear arsenal, it is unclear whether they will be successful in this decade without outside assistance. Further, an Iraqi nuclear weapon program could, if detected, prompt a military response by the United States, Iran, Turkey or Israel.

The chances that the United States will launch a major military campaign to overthrow the current Iraqi leadership will remain high in light of the long-term goal of Operation *Enduring Freedom* to neutralize all states that support international terrorist activities and are developing weapons of mass destruction.

Saudi Arabia will remain a major geostrategic challenge for the United States. The Saudi regime appears to be more fragile as domestic sympathy for the ideology of Al Qaeda has emerged. The success and conduct of Operation *Enduring Freedom* may have a profound influence on the emerging geostrategic consensus within the Saudi elite. A major issue will be whether the elite is reassured by U.S. military action against Al

Qaeda and the Taliban or believes that it is instead highly destabilizing, both domestically and regionally. A major future source of strain between Riyadh and Washington is whether the United States will make a major military effort to overthrow the regime of Saddam Husayn, with or without Saudi support. Finally, U.S. and Saudi strategic relations will be profoundly affected by the outcome of the dramatic escalation of violence of the Israeli-Palestinian conflict. The success or failure of the Bush administration's effort to gain a durable peace agreement will likely color U.S. and Arab relations writ large for the foreseeable future.

Riyadh may seek to acquire a robust theater ballistic missile capability or a nuclear-armed follow-on to its long-range missile deterrent force of obsolete Chinese CSS–2 IRBMs. If it has a geostrategic falling out with the United States, if Iran or Iraq makes progress toward acquiring an operational nuclear arsenal, or, especially, if either Iran or Iraq succeeds in acquiring one, the Saudi elite might choose a French-style, go-it-alone nuclear strategy. Pakistan is a likely source of supply for such a strategic nuclear capability.

### Japan and the Koreas

The evolution of the Japanese "virtual arsenal"—its capacity for rapid development and deployment of nuclear weapons—is likely to depend upon the evolution of Japan's relations with the two Koreas and China and Tokyo's continued confidence in the credibility of the U.S. security commitment to Japan. The fate of North Korea's nuclear weapon and long-range missile programs will have a major impact on U.S.-North Korean relations. If the Bush administration cannot negotiate a termination of the North's long-range missile program and a ban on missile technology exports, then it is unlikely that Washington will take it off the list of potentially nuclear-armed rogue states. Indeed, the prospect that Washington and Pyongyang will successfully resolve these issues has dimmed after the North Korean regime was branded as a member of the "axis of evil" and the Bush administration decided not to certify that North Korea is in compliance with its obligations under the 1994 Nuclear Framework Agreement. A deep-freeze in U.S.-North Korean relations, a resumption of the North Korean nuclear weapons program, and a collapse in the South Korean "Sunshine Policy" of reconciliation with the North would all encourage Japan to hedge its bets by maintaining its "virtual nuclear arsenal" option and to acquire a substantial theater missile defense capability, even in the face of Chinese protests.

If, instead, Pyongyang decides to give up its missile program, as it has partially given up its nuclear weapon program for the right price, Moscow and China are likely to argue that this greatly reduces the need for Washington to rush ahead with an early BMD deployment, even without the restraints of the ABM Treaty. Certainly success in this regard might drastically cool any Japanese government support for a robust BMD program, especially as such a program would elicit strong Chinese opposition.

### Impact on NPT and Nuclear Testing

The new U.S.-Russian agreement on strategic force reductions will allow the United States and the Russian Federation to take the diplomatic high ground on the subject of nuclear weapons. Washington will make the argument that it strongly supports the objectives of the NPT, while hedging for its possible erosion through the worldwide deployment of robust missile defense systems. The actual effect on the durability of the NPT regime of the geostrategic earthquake caused by the events of last September is unclear.

The United States and its key allies now have accepted the fact that both Pakistan and India have become and will remain overt nuclear-armed states. Perhaps the NPT regime as a global non-nuclear norm will be strained but not broken. The consequences of Operation *Enduring Freedom*, especially the wider war against terrorism (including a possible major military campaign against Iraq), could have a profound effect on the viability of the NPT regime.

The fate of the Comprehensive Test Ban Treaty will be decided in the near future. With or without the treaty in force, several nuclear-armed states will have strong military and technical incentives to resume testing; these states include China, India, and Pakistan. China may desire further tests to improve its option to deploy small warheads on MIRVs on its next-generation long-range ballistic missiles. India and Pakistan may desire further tests to assure the effectiveness of their nuclear forces since public evidence suggests that both had technical difficulties during their 1998 test series. On the other hand, both Pakistan and India will have a much closer political-military relationship with the United States, reducing incentives for resumed nuclear testing. Finally, there is the remote prospect that Iran might choose to conduct a test series to announce its acquisition of a nuclear arsenal.

The United States may have a strong incentive to resume nuclear weapon testing if the Bush administration believes it necessary to develop a new generation of nuclear weapons to support its goal of a smaller, more flexible nuclear arsenal. Conversely, a geostrategic and geo-economic rapprochement with the Russian Federation and improved relations with China may preclude that option, whether or not Washington returns to the nuclear test ban negotiating table. It is important to note, however, that the NPR decision to maintain thousands of warheads in reserve, partly as a hedge against a declining nuclear infrastructure, undermines the rationale for the resumption of nuclear testing to maintain the safety and reliability of nuclear weapons in the active stockpile. Should such problems arise that cannot be fixed by the Department of Energy's Stockpile Stewardship Program, warheads in the inactive stockpile would be available for such a purpose.

## Concluding Observations

In the context of the new security environment, the relevance of the old Cold War-era concepts of strategic and arms race stability, which reflected the intense bipolar geopolitical and nuclear competition between two rival superpowers, should be reexamined, along with the implications of alternative offense-defense force mixes for both types of stability. In considering what form of stability is appropriate for the new security environment, or whether the Cold War concepts remain relevant, the number of strategic warheads deployed by America and Russia should not be the only or even the primary consideration. More important is the posture of rapid response forces—in particular, how they are deployed and whether they are survivable in all types of situations, from normal peacetime (day-to-day status) to periods of heightened tension, when a nation may put more of its forces on alert (generated status). Such factors, along with early warning and command and control capabilities, have a far greater impact than force levels on crisis or first-strike stability, particularly whether they encourage escalation in a crisis situation. While lower numbers may be justified on the basis of changes in the strategic landscape, they are not intrinsically better and should not be the primary measure to evaluate alternative offense-defense mixes or options for lower strategic levels.

Translating the broad concepts of the new strategic framework into a coherent strategic doctrine to guide specific policies, plans, and programs will prove challenging. If the nuclear theology of the Cold War is anachronistic, disagreements remain over the paradigm that should replace it. If the process of defining U.S. nuclear force requirements and nuclear weapons employment policy is outdated, the new standard for sizing and structuring strategic forces is by no means transparent. Moreover, if the traditional concept of deterrence based on the threat of nuclear retaliation is to be supplemented and strengthened by measures of defense, denial, and dissuasion, a new metric for judging the success of this effort has yet to be articulated. Put simply, major intellectual, doctrinal, and technological challenges confront the transformation of the American strategic posture.

To its credit, the Bush administration is seeking to redefine the concepts of deterrence and strategic stability. In dealing with these doctrinal and conceptual challenges, the core assumption of the Bush administration is that the role of nuclear weapons in U.S. national security policy, and in international security affairs writ large, is to be reduced through a coordinated transition from a world dominated by the concept of nuclear assured retaliation to one of defense. To date, however, the policies, plans, and programs developed by the administration, for both strategic offensive forces and missile defenses, suggest that this transition has only just begun.

The Bush administration has embraced the anti-rogue-state rationale for its decision to withdraw unilaterally from the ABM Treaty and proceed with deployment of missile defenses. It has also maintained that the system which will be designed and deployed is intended to intercept limited missile strikes and will therefore not threaten Russia's or China's strategic deterrent. Nonetheless, the plans that have been articulated thus far—specifically the interest in developing a layered system consisting of ground-, sea-, air-, and space-based elements capable of intercepting intercontinental-range ballistic missiles during every phase of flight trajectory—promise deployments well in excess of the "limited" system of 200 ground-based interceptors envisaged by the Clinton administration. In particular, the Bush administration interest in developing space-based boost-phase weapons may prove to be a major indicator of perceived U.S. strategic hostility—a "red line"—for both Russia and China.

Similarly, the NPR raises questions about the depth of administration commitment to transforming strategic policy. Notwithstanding the rhetoric of making a clean and clear break with Cold War nuclear theology, the Bush administration's nuclear strategy, force structure, and targeting philosophy closely resemble, with one or two exceptions, the outdated Cold War policies and practices that it inherited from its predecessor.

In the future, nuclear strategic stability between the great nuclear-armed powers will not rely upon precise quantitative Cold War-era calculations of "how much is enough" to ensure a massive assured retaliation capability. Rather, the great powers, especially the United States, Russia, and China, have entered a complex geostrategic era in which important issues of state will generate cooperation or competition. The requirement for assured nuclear retaliation will increasingly depend upon more qualitative judgments about the complex state of relations between these three nuclear-armed states. "How much is enough" will be based primarily upon a qualitative geostrategic calculus rather than one of narrow nuclear weapon exchange numerology.

## Notes

[1] President George W. Bush made the most comprehensive public exposition of the administration's "new strategic framework" in his May 1, 2001, speech at the National Defense University, Washington, DC, accessed at <http://www.whitehouse.gov/news/releases/2001/05/20010501-10.html>.

[2] There is an extensive literature dealing with the issues of nuclear weapons and deterrence doctrine. The following list, which is by no means exhaustive, offers a broad philosophical, conceptual, and historical perspective on these issues and elucidates the scope of contemporary policy debates. John Baylis and Robert O'Neill, eds., *Alternative Nuclear Futures: The Role of Nuclear Weapons in the Post-Cold War World* (London: Oxford University Press, 2000); Harold A. Feiveson, ed., *The Nuclear Turning Point: A Blueprint for Deep Cuts and De-alerting of Nuclear Weapons* (Washington, DC: The Brookings Institution Press, 1999); Keith B. Payne, *The Fallacies of Cold War Deterrence and a New Direction* (Lexington: University of Kentucky Press, 2001); Janne E. Nolan, *An Elusive Consensus: Nuclear Weapons and American Security after the Cold War* (Washington, DC: The Brookings Institution Press, 1999); and Roger Molander, David Mosher, and Lowell Schwartz, *Nuclear Weapons and the Future of Strategic Warfare*, MR–1420 (Santa Monica, CA: RAND, 2002).

[3] This chapter does not cover other major homeland defense issues, such as the design of defenses against a repeat of September 11, including the clandestine delivery of nuclear, biological, and chemical weapons. It focuses only on the relationship between U.S. nuclear offensive weapon plans and programs and the Bush administration's shift toward a posture emphasizing missile defense capabilities against both ballistic and cruise missiles. The September attacks highlighted the requirement that any strategic missile defense architecture will have to include active counters to both ballistic and aerodynamic means of delivery of nuclear weapons. In part reflecting this new reality, the Ballistic Missile Defense Office was renamed the Missile Defense Agency in December 2001.

[4] On May 24, 2002, President George W. Bush and President Vladimir Putin signed the Moscow Treaty on Strategic Offensive Reductions. Under this Treaty, the United States and the Russian Federation will reduce their deployed strategic nuclear warheads to a level of 1,700–2,200 by December 31, 2012, a two-thirds reduction below current levels. The Treaty does not include any specific commitment by either side as to disposition of those warheads taken out of service, an issue that may be a subject of future negotiaions. This Treaty is part of the new strategic framework that the United States and Russia have established that also includes a commitment to strengthening confidence and increasing transparency in the area of missile defense. Among the steps both countries have agreed to implement are the exchange of information on missile defense programs and tests and reciprocal visits to observe missile defense tests. In addition, both countries have agreed to study possible areas for missile defense cooperation, including the expansion of joint exercises related to missile defense and the exploration of potential programs for the joint research and development of missile defense technologies.

[5] For other discussions of weaponizing space and related issues, see chapter 12 by Stephen P. Randolph in the present volume.

[6] See J.D. Couch, Special Briefing on the Nuclear Posture Review, January 9, 2002, accessed at <www.defenselink.mil/news>. For a more detailed discussion of U.S. strategic policy by outside experts that influenced the key directions of the NPR, see National Institute for Public Policy, *Rationale and Requirements for U.S. Nuclear Forces and Arms Control*, January, 2001, accessed at <www.nipp. org>; and Center for Counterproliferation Research, National Defense University, and Center for Global Security Research, Lawrence Livermore National Laboratory, *U.S. Nuclear Policy in the 21st Century: A Fresh Look at National Strategy and Requirements*, October 1998, accessed at <www.ndu.edu/ ndu/centercounter>.

[7] See National Intelligence Council, "Foreign Missile Developments and the Ballistic Missile Threat through 2015," January 11, 2002, accessed at <www.cia.gov/nic/pubs>.

[8] For a more complete discussion of American and European military technology cooperation, see chapter 9 by Charles Barry in the present volume.

# Chapter 12

# Controlling Space

Stephen P. Randolph

S pace forces have transformed the U.S. military over the past 40 years. The experiences of the past 10 years, from the Gulf War through the Balkan wars and now in the war against terrorism, have accelerated that transformation. As the war on terrorism goes on, it undoubtedly will affect the development and employment of space forces, as well as their relationship with other American forces, in ways now unforeseen.

The broad mission areas executed by space forces have remained remarkably stable over the span of the space age. Within a decade of Sputnik's first exploration of low Earth orbit, the United States fielded space forces to meet critical needs for global reconnaissance, missile warning, navigation, meteorology, and telecommunications. Over the subsequent 30 years, there has been a dramatic increase in on-orbit capability to meet those missions. Probably the more significant change, though, has been in the overall reorientation of America's space forces—from a near-exclusive focus on strategic users and preconflict intelligence through the Cold War, toward a gradually ripening integration with theater forces as part of the operational targeting sequence.

The stability in the mission areas occupied by space forces reflects the balance between the utility of operating in that medium and the tremendous demands that the space environment levies on those who would operate there. At the existing level of technology, those demands generally translate into high program costs and delays in fielding space systems, beyond those normally experienced in military acquisition programs. Over the past few months, to provide recent examples, the Advanced Extremely High Frequency communications satellite program has gone to a two-satellite buy at roughly the price of the original proposed five-satellite constellation. The Space-Based Infrared System has reported massive cost increases and delays in the high, low, and ground segments, to the point where Under Secretary of Defense for Acquisition, Technology, and

**309**

Logistics Peter Aldridge has directed the Air Force and National Reconnaissance Office to explore alternatives to the high segment.[1]

This history is relevant in surveying the future possibilities for national security space programs. Throughout the space age, there has existed a tension between the lure of space, the "final frontier," with its endless possibilities for human exploration, and the real obstacles that have prevented its broader exploitation. It is easy to find aggressive visions for broad-scale transformations in the missions executed from space.[2] It is more difficult to manage the relatively mundane issues of technology, funding, and doctrine that must be conquered to realize those visions. The history of space flight in all sectors is littered with the remains of programs and applications that appeared promising but could not be delivered at an affordable cost or effectively in competition with terrestrial systems.

Those issues will become more, not less, difficult in the near future, with the array of other requirements that have become evident in the ongoing war. Just within the Air Force, those include broadened employment of unmanned aerial vehicles (UAVs), a new generation of manned intelligence, surveillance, and reconnaissance (ISR) platforms, the Joint Strike Fighter and F–22, the small diameter bomb, increased airlift, and recapitalization of the tanker force. All these will be competing not only for a finite number of development and acquisition dollars but also more broadly with the demands of the other services, all with their own requirements for recapitalization and modernization. It is unlikely that defense budgets, even with the growth expected over the next few years, will easily accommodate all those requirements.[3]

The competition for resources will be more acute since the maturation of UAVs has seen these vehicles move into mission niches previously reserved for space forces and into others that space forces could feasibly assume in the next few years. U.S. Air Force (USAF) Chief of Staff John Jumper said in a recent speech to the Air Force Association:

> Rather than having ISR assets that are primarily space-based or manned, both of which tend to have limited loitering time over any given area of interest, the DOD [Department of Defense] is looking to increase its inventory of UAVs that have longer loiter times. The United States should eventually treat UAVs like low-orbiting satellites.[4]

UAVs have proven their tactical contributions in remote sensing and have clear potential as communications relays as well.

So while American space forces will continue playing a critical role in theater combat capabilities, it is unlikely that they will see a major expansion in mission areas over the next few years. Instead, progress will more likely come in the less visible, but equally important, areas of integration with other forces, in protecting U.S. space capabilities and in building the foundation for the follow-on generation of space-based capabilities.

## The Global Space Arena, 2002–2022

Since the collapse of the Soviet Union, the United States has enjoyed near-absolute dominance in military space capabilities.[5] Only the European space program has mounted any sort of technical challenge to the United States, and the Europeans have placed very little emphasis on developing military space capabilities. That period of dominance is likely nearing its end now, as three related movements speed the proliferation of space capabilities across the globe.

First, space is no longer the exclusive preserve of national programs. Commercial telecommunications have thrived since the 1960s and have long carried an important role in communications structures of the Armed Forces. More recently, the remote sensing industry has seen the advent of high-resolution systems and their spread to non-American firms. Both the capabilities of those commercial systems and their technologies are spreading around the world. The high barriers to entry overcome by the United States and the Soviet Union 40 years ago have diminished with the advent of the commercial space market. A senior officer from the United Arab Emirates (UAE) declared, "We are now in the era of high-resolution imagery. With high-resolution imagery we are now able not only to monitor strategic movement of troops and equipment that may threaten our borders, but also to actually pinpoint individual targets of interest from a safe stand-off distance."[6] More recently, frustrated by America's imposition during the Afghan campaign of a blackout of satellite data that had previously been available, the UAE has called for the Gulf Cooperation Council nations to study buying their own satellite to ensure access to space-derived imagery.[7] That would be entirely feasible, given the availability on the open market of such systems as Russia's Mashinostroyeniye Science and Production Association's 1- to 3-meter-resolution optical/radar system. The Russian firm's offer includes launch and ground segment services as part of the package. Although the space imagery business has been slow to take off, it seems clear that it is here to stay and that the United States is entering a new era of transparency that will affect areas ranging from military operations to public diplomacy.

A second, related trend is the proliferation of newly maturing technologies that will ease access to space. In particular, the growing utility of small satellites provides opportunities for nations to bypass the enormous launch costs and investments in infrastructure that previously characterized space operations and set high thresholds for their use.

As with other aspects of space operations, *smallsats* enjoyed waves of enthusiasm that have receded as their limitations have become evident. Those limitations, however, are diminishing rapidly with advances in microelectronics and miniaturization. Already, minisatellites have demonstrated useful capabilities in communications, remote sensing, electronic environment characterization, and precision navigation and timing, all at a fraction of the cost of the larger systems now employed in those roles. Although these small satellites are not as capable as the larger and more complex systems used by U.S. forces, they offer military potential at a fraction of the cost of larger systems, while using components widely available on the commercial market.

Moreover, their low cost creates the opportunity to field constellations of satellites providing persistent coverage of selected areas, thus moving beyond the relatively intermittent coverage of existing imagery systems. As one observer recently commented in the *People's Liberation Army Daily*:

> Each microsat has a large computational capability. Tens, or even hundreds, of these microsats can be networked to form a "skynet," which would provide a carpeted global coverage and thus realize high-altitude military reconnaissance with no "dead zones."... The advantages of such a system include rendering an enemy's space defense mode deficient, and providing a global coverage of information transmission which allows total area monitoring and more timely data management and dissemination of imagery.[8]

A recent analysis in *The Economist* extended that vision still further, projecting that "It is clear that small satellites will remain a niche market for some years, but it is equally clear that they are here to stay—and that their prospects can only improve."[9] That improvement will rest, to a large degree, on the maturation of microelectro-mechanical systems, fabricated using techniques developed in the semiconductor industry, which will multiply the efficiency and the effectiveness of small satellites. At that point, "prices of small satellites could be expected to tumble and performance to rise remorselessly as the market widened from government agencies to include companies and universities, and then wider still to include small communities and co-operatives, and finally to embrace even wealthy individuals."[10]

For any such systems, the challenge will lie more with handling data than with putting hardware into space and keeping it there. Anyone building such a constellation would face the same issues of tasking, processing, exploitation, and dissemination (TPED) that have thus far defined the utility of national imagery systems in U.S. theater operations. However, any military force now setting about this course would have the advantage of starting with a clean sheet of paper, not needing to manage this data flow with organizations, processes, and technologies constructed for different purposes, as would the United States. In a sense, the maturation of microsatellites to full functionality would create a situation analogous to the development of the *Dreadnought* by Great Britain at the dawn of the last century. It would create the opportunity, for a nation able to master the technology and willing to make the investment, to bypass huge investments in infrastructure and start afresh with a new approach.

The full maturation of the small satellite will also rest on improvements in launch costs and responsiveness, neither of which appears imminent. It hardly matters how cheaply one can operate in space, if the expense of getting there is prohibitive. Nor is it possible to take full advantage of the rapid and flexible development cycles theoretically available to smaller satellites, if launch cycles remain as expensive, cumbersome, and inflexible as present technology dictates. American efforts over the past decade to develop reusable, responsive launchers have proven acutely disappointing, but the work done on propulsion, structures, flight software, and thermal protection has moved the world closer to the day when reusable systems, either single- or two-stage, could reduce launch costs significantly. The National Aeronautics and Space Administration (NASA) Space Launch Initiative, if it survives the intense budget pressures now besetting that agency, will move us closer still to that critical goal.

This is certainly an area where existing policies and responsibilities should be reviewed. The division of labor between NASA and the Department of Defense (DOD) outlined in the 1994 National Space Transportation Policy yielded the successful Evolved Expendable Launch Vehicle program. This initiative has met the more acute needs of the Armed Forces and commercial sectors for launch vehicles competitive on the world market and significantly less expensive to operate than legacy systems. But the arrival of competing Boeing and Lockheed-Martin launch vehicles later this year will mark the end of the pathway outlined in that policy. As we look toward the next decades of space operations, the national importance of moving ahead toward responsive, less expensive launch systems is clear, as is the importance of an effective NASA–DOD relationship in moving toward those systems.

The third trend tending to reduce the U.S. margin of superiority in space operations reflects the fact that in the world of military technology, every action eventually brings a reaction. America's space forces have enabled the Nation to extend its military power to distant shores and to achieve information dominance even in operations on an adversary's home terrain. However, those remarkable capabilities have created vulnerabilities that others will inevitably seek to exploit. America's national strategy and style of warfare have necessitated a heavy reliance on space forces for connectivity, global capability, and real-time intelligence. Over the past decade, as the United States has proven increasingly successful at inserting space-derived data into theater decision and targeting chains, that reliance has grown. It is not a question of whether others will seek to exploit the vulnerabilities created by this movement; that has already begun. The questions are, rather, what form those challenges will assume and what responses are appropriate.

## American Advantages and Obstacles to Exploiting Them

Given the trends noted above, it is likely that America's margin of superiority will diminish over the coming decades. However, as we look toward that time, it is important to understand the strengths that America will bring to this competition in the world of space capabilities. First among these is the Nation's long experience in space operations, which has created a vast pool of expertise among the thousands of men and women who have made this a space-faring nation. That long experience has rested on massive investments in space technologies and has yielded a balanced set of space capabilities and a broad technological lead over all competitors, most pronounced in the areas focused on military capability. Finally, those capabilities feed into a highly developed communications infrastructure and world-class information architecture, with synergistic effects among these three components.

Those advantages have been dissipated in the past by the fragmentation of the American space effort.[11] The inefficiencies generated by the "stovepipes" separating the civil, intelligence, and military sectors, and further subdividing efforts within the sectors, have long been recognized.

This recognition finally led to the review by the Commission to Assess United States National Security Space Management and Organization, generally known as the Rumsfeld Space Commission.

The Commission, and the subsequent implementing actions taken by Donald Rumsfeld as Secretary of Defense, aimed at rationalizing the management of the national security space program and enabling stronger advocacy of space within the Air Force and DOD as a whole. The major organizational adjustments taken since then have reached from the departmental level into the unified command chain and down to the component level, redefining the relationship between the Air Force Space Command and Air Force Material Command.

Given the time required for organizational adjustments to take hold and for programs to reflect management reforms, it will be some years before these changes yield improvements to operational capabilities. However, the actions taken to this point will, in time, measurably strengthen the integration of space programs across DOD and within the Air Force. At this point, four adjustments appear to be the most significant.

First, the Under Secretary of the Air Force has been assigned to be the Director of the National Reconnaissance Organization (NRO) and the Air Force Acquisition Authority for Space. Milestone Decision Authority for defense space programs has been delegated to this position through the Secretary of the Air Force. These changes will strengthen the relationship between the National Reconnaissance Office and the military space program and will help align the services' space programs.

Secretary Rumsfeld directed the Secretary of the Air Force to assign a four-star officer separate from the Commander in Chief, U.S. Space Command (USCINCSPACE), as commander of Air Force Space Command (AFSPACECOM). He ended the requirement that USCINCSPACE be a flight-rated officer and opened the position to "an officer of any Service with an understanding of space and combat operations."[12] These changes will open the highest ranks of DOD space operations to career space experts, a development that will have both direct programmatic benefits and large payoffs in the morale of officers in the space career field. Equally important, these actions will enable an Air Force general to sit at the table as programmatic decisions are made within the service and will ensure that space capabilities and requirements are argued effectively.

The authority of the AFSPACECOM commander has been vastly strengthened by assigning to this position the responsibility for space research, development, and acquisition. Organizationally, this has required the realignment of the Space and Missile Center from the Air Force Material Command to the Air Force Space Command (a wrenching realignment for the career acquisition professionals affected by the move). Over time, if effectively executed, this move will establish the same powerful linkage of requirements definition-research with development-acquisition-operations that has characterized the NRO since its formation in 1961. The Commission also recognized the importance of strengthening the career tracks for space experts and so recommended that the commander of the Air Force Space Command assume responsibility for managing the space career field. In addition, a "soft Major Force Program (MFP)" has been created by directing the establishment of a tracking mechanism to "increase visibility into the resources allocated for space activities."[13]

It will be some time before any concrete results become evident from these reforms. It will also be some time before they can be fairly assessed. At this point, two major issues are worth watching. First, the Commission stopped short of recommending the reestablishment of a National Space Council to manage space policy at the national level. Given that almost all space technologies and applications are dual use, it may prove necessary to look at this issue again in the near future to ensure a proper balance among commercial, industrial, and national security concerns. The ongoing struggles to rationalize the export control regime provide a clear example of the difficulties that the Nation has had in managing the balance, as well as the damage that can be done when decisions in this area are made on an ad hoc basis. Beyond refereeing among the requirements of the various sectors, such an organization could provide a powerful means of integrating their efforts and ensuring, for example, that budgets and research and development (R&D) efforts across the agencies are coordinated effectively.[14]

On a more mundane level, the workload imposed on the Under Secretary of the Air Force by these reforms seems nearly impossible to manage. Certainly some of the more traditional service roles played by past under secretaries will fall to others, and these new responsibilities will demand much more staff support than has been available to previous occupants of this position.

These reforms may be considered as a necessary but not sufficient foundation for further progress in military space. However rationally organized the bureaucracy, space capabilities will advance only at the rate fed by resources and the vision shared by senior leaders for the role of space forces within DOD. At the end of the road, the real measure of success is not just the internal efficiency of the military space effort, but its contribution to the joint team and its integration with all the elements of the joint force. The effects of the recent reorganization have been to centralize and concentrate space expertise. In a few years, it will be time to assess whether that centralization has contributed effectively to meeting the broader requirements of the commanders in chief (CINCs) and the Secretary of Defense.

## Space: Things to Do Next

The importance of national security space forces from the first days of the space age through the Cold War can hardly be overstated. Bilateral strategic stability, crisis management, and finally arms control all rested on the capabilities created by space systems. While probably less critical, and certainly less well known, space forces also played a significant role in American theater capabilities as early as the Vietnam War. By the late 1960s, U.S. air commanders relied on satellite-based meteorological systems to plan their air operations and on geosynchronous communications satellites for connection with the national leadership.[15]

On the whole, though, strategic and national users were the primary customers of space forces through this period. This changed with the end of the Cold War and, more visibly, with the Gulf War in 1991. Suddenly, the contributions of space forces to theater operations became manifest to all, from the tank columns maneuvering across the desert, to the fighter pilots' reliance on space forces for mission planning and weather data, to special forces' use of space-based communications. But as this potential and this reliance became clear, so, too, did the distance remaining to be traveled before space capabilities could be considered truly integrated with U.S. theater forces.

As effective as space-based support to *Desert Storm* operations proved, this support was largely a result of heroic ad hoc adjustments, provided on the run as new requirements and opportunities appeared. Anecdotal examples of this adaptation include Army officers getting global positioning system (GPS) receivers from home for use in helicopters, the provision of missile warning data to theater forces, and the provision of overhead imagery outside established channels to meet theater timelines.[16] Overall, this was a classic and near-perfect trigger event, displaying for all the utility of these systems and the work that remained to take full advantage of what they could do. That recognition established the work program that has guided space forces over the past decade.

The process has proven to be much more difficult and time-consuming than first estimated. While progress has been steady, and improvements have been evident from operation to operation since 1991, every after action report throughout this period has identified issues with the integration of space and theater forces that still demand improvement. Even as results are still forthcoming from the current operations, early reports indicate that this will be the case once again. This pattern represents a combination of causes: the inherent challenges of the task, the continuing expansion in expectations of theater users, and the initial underestimation of the challenge being the most dominant.

From an operational perspective, the reorientation of space forces has demanded a series of collateral improvements in those forces. These include fusion, timeliness, coverage, integration, dissemination, command and control, and survivability.

### Fusion

In general terms, the space forces that went to war in 1991 operated through a series of discrete information conduits, with system-unique sensors and communications pathways feeding a well-defined set of users. With the vision of information dominance established in *Joint Vision 2010* and *Joint Vision 2020*, theater users now expect to operate within an "infosphere," taking advantage of fused, correlated information, tailored to their own needs.[17] Data derived and transmitted through space must be fused with that arriving from other sources to provide full utility to the users. The magnitude of this task will grow in the coming years as new space-based sensors entering the inventory create ever-larger quantities of sensor data.[18]

### Timeliness

Until 1991, space forces focused largely on preconflict planning and intelligence. Their integration into theater operations demands that they operate on the same timelines as other theater forces and that operational tempo has been increasing rapidly over the past decade. The criteria for acceptable timeliness are shortening still further under the pressure of ongoing operations, as the United States focuses attention on means for attacking fleeting targets.

### Coverage

In 1991, black-and-white photographs represented the height of the aspirations for theater users. As capabilities have expanded, so too have expectations for a range of complementary sensors, enabling real-time coverage of the battlefield across a range of wavelengths and sensor technologies.

### Integration

Space forces are just one of the array of capabilities available to the theater and must be integrated with other systems—manned, unmanned, aerial, and surface—to reach full potential. Through the first 30 years of the space age, little thought was given to the programmatic or operational integration of space systems with other elements of the Armed Forces. They were developed largely in isolation to meet specific needs. This is no longer feasible. Given the convergence in capabilities among UAVs, manned ISR systems, and space systems, these systems must be integrated in the program and in operations alike.

### Dissemination

The well-defined, relatively narrow pipelines of data once characteristic of space forces are no longer adequate. As the user community has grown, so have the complexities and costs of getting the data to the right users at the right time. To some extent, meeting this requirement is a technical issue of bandwidth and systems integration. More broadly, though, getting information to the proper set of users has organizational and cultural implications that have proven more significant than expected at the outset of this new era in space operations.

### Command and Control

As space capabilities have become more and more critical to an increasingly wide set of users, allocating and tasking space systems has become increasingly challenging. As space systems continue to advance—and the old lines dividing intelligence, surveillance, and targeting continue to blur—this competition for limited resources will continue and very likely intensify.

### Survivability

As space systems become an intrinsic part of the theater command and targeting architecture, they likewise become attractive targets for adversaries seeking not to be targeted. Past exercises have indicated that space forces may in fact prove an Achilles' heel for American forces. Unlike other theater forces, which are built to withstand attack and to degrade gracefully, space forces have not been—a situation that demands change.

## Areas for Future Progress

Given this range of adjustments, it is hardly surprising that work has continued for the past decade with no end in sight. Already the integration of GPS data into weapons guidance has transformed the U.S. military into an all-weather precision strike force, creating unparalleled capabilities that have proven themselves in Afghanistan. More broadly, reports indicate that in ongoing operations, imagery has been piped directly to special forces units for tactical decisionmaking in real time. If accurate, this report marks the progress that has occurred in a relatively short time in transcending old organizational, doctrinal, and technical barriers. As recently as 1999, informed observers estimated that space force contributions to theater operations reached only 10 to 15 percent of their potential.[19] It appears that space-based contributions across the range of theater operations have now gone far beyond that estimate.

The aim of integration is a transparent employment of space forces and manned and unmanned sensors, all feeding into a command system able to use the information for real-time decisionmaking and targeting. The Navy's Network Centric Warfare concept, originating in the late 1990s, represented the first sustained movement in that direction; the Air Force is now working toward a similar construct.[20] The role of space forces in that construct, in providing sensor data, connectivity, and precision navigation and timing, will be critical.

Further progress will be accelerated and guided by the specific lessons of current operations. One issue in defining further requirements will be extrapolating the lessons into more demanding environments. Not all future wars will feature a low-tech adversary, with no means to challenge U.S. control of the air or space, and with the operational tempo defined almost entirely by the Armed Forces. Too literal an extension of ongoing operations into future requirements would be a serious error.

Certainly, any more capable opponent would seek means of countering the information dominance that is central to U.S. combat capabilities. With America's reliance on space to provide that dominance, it is essential that the United States ensures that space forces are survivable enough to withstand such a challenge. Already, GPS jammers are available on the open market, designed to deny GPS-guided weapons their guidance signals. Various antisatellite (ASAT) programs are reportedly in progress in the People's Republic of China, fed both by old Soviet technology and indigenous developments. These reports have included everything from old co-orbital ASAT systems, to laser blinders, to parasitic microsatellites.

All of these are technically feasible, and they represent only a portion of the range of options open to an adversary seeking to cut the chain of data derived and transmitted through space. Given the importance of space systems to the national information infrastructure, their protection is far more than a strictly military requirement.

With a few exceptions, notably the Milstar communications satellite, the United States has historically paid little attention to the survivability of its space systems. The need to do so now reflects the growing importance within the theater command structure and the proliferation of technology around the world. At present, the United States does not meet even the most basic of requirements for military operations: the ability to maintain situation awareness in the arena. The space surveillance system now in place was structured during the 1960s, "developed and optimized to meet the needs of the Soviet threat," as noted by a recent Defense Science Board task force. Now, "the nation is faced with aging sensors, rapid growth in the number of nations with access to space, a loss of the intelligence information base, a declining space surveillance budget, and a growing U.S. dependence on space for national security."[21] This lack of situation awareness extends to the system level where "the nation currently has no means to determine whether national security space systems are under deliberate attack ('purposeful interference') or are experiencing some type of malfunction. Accurate knowledge of an attack is critical for developing appropriate and timely responses."[22]

A better understanding of the threat environment will strengthen America's ability to protect its space capabilities. While there is a broad range of theoretical modes of attack for those capabilities, the attention generally focused on the vulnerability of the space segments of U.S. systems is probably misdirected. From a mission perspective, the links and ground stations are more accessible to attack and probably an easier target than space systems. As with any military capability, there exists a broad menu of options that could be used to protect American space capabilities; these will be dependent on their role, orbital regime, and technological composition. Generalizations are impossible here, except to note that more attention must be given to survivability of these systems if they are to continue in their central role in U.S. theater capabilities. Too often in the past, survivability measures have been traded off for competing performance or cost considerations.

While looking toward protection of its capabilities, America must also build an effective denial capability. Already other nations are taking advantage of commercial space-based imagery systems for military purposes. All indications are that the use of space by other nations will broaden in the years immediately ahead.

Countermeasures will be complicated by factors unique to the space community. First, the problem will not be defined by hardware that can be counted but by the ability of others to gain access to space-derived information and then use it effectively within their forces. Traditional intelligence measures of merit will play a small role, and net assessments are almost meaningless in this context. Even if a clear understanding of the threats is possible, in many cases traditional means of countering them will be unavailable. The information will come from commercial systems, sometimes multinational, perhaps traveling via third parties—in short, difficult to track and difficult to counter. In many cases, as in the operation in Afghanistan, diplomatic and economic measures will be more effective than military counters. In this environment, realistic exercises exploring politico-military options will be important in defining American options for a crisis. Should nonmilitary measures prove unsuccessful, it will be important to have temporary, reversible attack options available to lower the threshold for employment. Over time, in any case, it will be necessary to have some kind of lethal option to protect the Armed Forces. The time to develop this option has arrived.

The critical challenge of building toward a space-denial capability probably is accounting for the complexity of the environment and planning for the range of options that will be necessary. It will be equally important for operators at all levels to understand the implications of this new global transparency and to account for it in doctrine, training programs, and contingency operations.

## Now Coming over the Horizon

The array of competing requirements is likely to delay space programs for the near future. Over the longer term, though, the new strategic environment creates operational requirements that may well demand space solutions.

The virtues of constant surveillance, or *persistence,* have become clear to all and are at the heart of the drive toward more responsive targeting. In the Afghanistan campaign, with a permissive air-defense environment, UAVs and manned aircraft have provided the persistent surveillance necessary to meet theater requirements. Over the long run, though, a space-based system would provide both global capabilities beyond the reach of any practical force of air-breathing systems and coverage in a denied-access situation. It is unlikely that any space-based system could fully replace air-breathing platforms, but a constellation of satellites might relieve some of the operational tempo burden now placed on manned ISR aircraft. A space-based surveillance force would provide full-time coverage of selected areas, through the spectrum of peacetime, crisis management, and operational employment. Among the lessons being repeated in Afghanistan is that preconflict preparation is the key to effective battlefield intelligence; a space-based system would provide exactly that capability. It would also avoid the complications of basing rights and overflight requests for ISR assets and provide surveillance unobtrusively for any region necessary to meet national or theater requirements. Naval forces would find a space-based radar (SBR) system especially valuable, extending their stand-off range and increasing targeting flexibility.[23]

DOD has explored SBR concepts over the past 5 years with a view toward providing this capability, most visibly in the Defense Advanced Research Projects Agency (DARPA)–NRO–Air Force Discoverer II program of the late 1990s. Discoverer II was designed to provide an advanced technology demonstration of space-based ground moving target indicator (GMTI) capability on the path to an affordable production system; the intent was to provide an operational capability for under $100 million per satellite and within a $10-billion program life cycle cost. The failure of the program to stay within its cost goals led to the demise of Discoverer II, but work on basic technologies has continued, and the Air Force has resurrected the program. The Air Force is exploring the tradeoffs among satellite capability, system architecture, and operational requirements, studying an array of low Earth orbit, medium Earth orbit, and mixed systems. The different constellation configurations raise different technology issues; electronically scanned antenna technology, onboard processing capabilities, and power generation are now considered the highest-risk elements. If the SBR concept is delayed, as seems likely due to budget pressures, the time made available for technology development in these areas could contribute to a lower-risk deployment later on.

It may be that the real challenges for SBR will lie more in TPED than in the space component of the system. The quantities of data available through this system will be staggering. They will make extremely heavy demands on bandwidth and on the terrestrial information infrastructure. The organizational issues may prove as difficult as the technical. As the system matures, it will be necessary to explore operational alternatives for tasking the system to satisfy the demands of the theater CINCs, SPACECOM, NRO, the National Imagery and Mapping Agency, and other mission partners. This movement toward a generation of low-flying, taskable systems will also move the world of military space to a whole new level of operational and technical complexity that will place heavy demands on planners and operators alike. Defining the operational and technical linkages among SBR, other sensors, and theater forces will also require careful thought.

The generation beyond this may see the operational advent of clustered systems: small satellites flying in formation, cooperating to perform the functions of a large "virtual satellite." In principle, these could provide a flexible mix of passive and active sensors, reconfigurable while on orbit to meet new operational demands. They could provide the opportunity to field sparse-aperture systems that could provide staring electro-optical surveillance from geosynchronous distances. Alternatively, clustered microsats could provide a GMTI capability comparable to SBR.[24]

Coordinating the interactions of clustered satellites will demand a focused development effort. The U.S. military is just beginning to address these capabilities with the TechSat 21 cluster of three satellites scheduled for launch in 2003. Both DOD and NASA are exploring these technologies for applications, such as surveillance, passive radiometry, terrain mapping, navigation, and communications; certainly this would be an opportunity for cooperative development between these two agencies. These technologies will demand government-led development since commercial applications lie far in the future.

## Weapons in Space?

Over this time horizon, the United States will face the longstanding question of whether it is strategically wise and militarily cost-effective to place weapons in space—a question that arose in the first days of the space age and has arisen recurrently since then. Despite all the various studies and development programs by the United States and Soviet Union, no nation has yet crossed that threshold, although the military has gotten successively closer to that line with weapons targeted by space systems and guided by GPS.[25]

Legal restrictions have played a role, but only a secondary one, in this outcome. The legal regime governing military space operations is permissive to a degree that surprises many new to the field, and the recent U.S. decision to abrogate the Anti-Ballistic Missile (ABM) Treaty has further opened legal possibilities for development of space-based weaponry. In a larger sense, the existing legal framework reflects the judgment of the major powers that it has not been in their national interest to pursue space-based weaponry; that, on balance, strategic risks, technical issues, and military cost-effectiveness considerations ruled against pursuing this option. However, as the strategic environment evolves, military requirements change, and technology advances, these considerations will inevitably be readdressed.

Planners envision three mission areas in which space-based weaponry might provide necessary capabilities: terrestrial attack, antisatellite missions, and missile defense. From a technical perspective, three broad approaches have undergone study: kinetic weapons, delivery of conventional precision weapons, and directed energy weapons (most often radio frequency or laser).[26]

Kinetic weapons are generally studied in the form of tungsten or titanium rods to be released from orbit in clusters and directed against large fixed targets or for missile defense. If used for terrestrial attack, these would be limited to a vertical attack profile and so would be most suited for use against tall buildings, missile silos, hardened aircraft shelters, and the like.

Conventional weapons would reenter the atmosphere from orbit or a suborbital flight into a "basket" around the target and then use GPS or other precision guidance. The Air Force has discussed a version of this system in its Common Aero Vehicle (CAV) and may be developing the technology in the X–41A program. Details of this program are classified, but the Air Force describes it as "an experimental maneuvering reentry vehicle which carries a variety of payloads through a suborbital trajectory, reenters the Earth's atmosphere, and safely dispenses its payload in the atmosphere."[27]

Directed energy weapons would be capable of light-speed attack for either destructive or disruptive effects. This category offers the greatest technical challenges, most urgently in the areas of generating and directing the power necessary to achieve required effects within a spacecraft weight budget low enough for launch. The Air Force's Space-Based Laser (SBL) program has continued work since the mid-1980s on these technologies and had been working toward a test mission launching in 2012. Recent reports indicate that the program is now undergoing a complete restructure and will return to component development with no plan for a flight test.[28]

The fate of the SBL program illustrates a long-term hurdle for the development of space-based weaponry. In the absence of a catastrophic trigger event, consensus behind the strategic utility and military requirement for space-based weapons will be very difficult to sustain through the extended development periods and the expense necessary to field these capabilities. In the absence of a triggering event, the standard incremental acquisition sequence leading to space weaponry is hardly conceivable.

Among these candidate technologies, it appears that the current balance of technical maturity and operational requirements most favors the development of conventional precision-guided weaponry. Depending on orbital geometry and the basing mode, these weapons could provide a very rapid response capability and an attack option that precludes effective defense. Against a highly capable adversary, these weapons might provide a leading-edge attack option to blunt the effectiveness of defending forces. They might provide the only effective counter to an opposing directed-energy weapon. Technology for reentry vehicles is now over 40 years old, and so the technical barriers to fielding this capability seem readily surmountable. Until launch costs fall dramatically, however, this will remain a prohibitively expensive way to attack surface targets.

The diplomatic and political costs of these capabilities would depend on the circumstances surrounding their deployment, and in particular whether they are viewed as a justifiable response to valid threats. From a narrower perspective, those issues will only become worth considering when standard measures of cost-effectiveness and mission requirements support the investments required. As this point nears, it will be necessary to consider the likelihood of an open arms race in space, as other nations look toward means of countering American systems.[29]

This range of options for exploitation of space 20 years hence changes fundamentally if there is a breakthrough in launch technology. If launch costs can be reduced and responsiveness improved, the possibilities for human exploitation of space expand beyond any horizon now envisioned.

## Key Enablers of Space Technology

Just a few years ago, knowledgeable observers looked forward to the day, expected to arrive soon, when U.S. military space capabilities would be fueled by developments in the commercial market. Military space was expected to ride a wave of commercial technology and capabilities in a partnership of equals with the commercial sector.

That bright future never arrived and is now on indefinite hold. The expectations for a vast increase in the commercial use of space led to an expansion of capacity for both launch and satellite systems that now leaves the industry with massive overcapacity in both sectors. The wave of industrial consolidation of the past decade has left the space industry with an unhealthy combination of few firms, limited profit margins, shrinking capabilities through the supply chain, and keen competition for the few contracts still open for bid.[30]

These conditions demand attention if the United States is to preserve its capabilities in this sector and to sustain its ability to meet future requirements. Three related components must be addressed: adequate R&D funding; people with the expertise and energy to move the bounds of the possible still further; and the overall structure and capability of the industrial base.

### Research and Development

Over the past decade, DOD cut space-related R&D funding, expecting that commercial pressures would drive developments that would then be available for national security purposes. Meanwhile, competitive pressures forced firms to focus R&D funding on near-term programs, choosing near-term survival over long-term possibilities. With everyone looking toward others to finance research, the technological lead enjoyed by the United States has eroded in launch, in remote sensing, in telecommunications satellites, and in systems integration. For the foreseeable future, DOD will get as much space technology as it is willing to fund. Capabilities will stagnate unless departmental funding permits programs to move beyond laboratory efforts to flight tests. There are also opportunities for close cooperation with NASA in developing next-generation sensors and launch technology. While the historical record of NASA–DOD cooperation is not very encouraging, neither agency has enough money to ignore opportunities for cooperation.

### Personnel

Sometimes termed the *quiet crisis* of the U.S. space program, workforce issues face the space community in every sector and every skill set. The community has evolved into a bimodal age distribution, with the wave of people who entered the space world during the glory days of the Apollo Program now on the verge of retirement. There is a serious demographic gap where their successors should be found. The problems range across the military, civil, and commercial space sectors, as more attractive opportunities open up in other industries. The acute pressures of a few years ago have been relieved, as people who had left the industry to seek their fortunes in the Internet startup world have drifted back. But over the long run, broader issues of job satisfaction and compensation will have to be faced to ensure that the right people remain in this community.

### Industrial Base

The U.S. industrial base, ultimately the source of America's national security space capabilities, has lost its global predominance, first in launch and later in satellite manufacture. Various factors have contributed to that result, including a decline in DOD procurement, the weak euro, and the export control regime that has been in place over the past few years. Despite frequent calls for a more rational approach to technology control, little practical improvement in licensing speed and flexibility is visible at this point. Improvements are pending; the question will be whether the damage done to American industry is reversible or whether the market shares forfeited by U.S. primes and subcontractors will remain overseas.

Despite the mixed results of earlier consolidations, it appears that this trend is nowhere near its end. The series of mergers of the past few years is credited with having improved productivity and honed the companies' focus on customer satisfaction. Those advantages have come at the cost of considerable turmoil to the people involved, feeding the problems in the personnel area cited above. As noted by one observer, "the industry's track record of integrating acquisitions has been abysmal and has failed to produce the synergies touted when transactions were announced."[31] These problems have been accentuated by the instability in government policies toward consolidation and trans-Atlantic cooperation. The Commission on the Future of the U.S. Aerospace Commission is now sorting through these issues, seeking to define the industrial capabilities needed to support U.S. national security needs and the policies required to secure those capabilities.[32]

### Summary

The competition for funding over the next 5 to 10 years will probably delay the advent of major new space-based systems. Over that period, however, DOD should continue its efforts to integrate space forces more broadly into its terrestrial forces; lessons from ongoing operations will accelerate and guide that process. DOD must also move aggressively to ensure that its space forces retain necessary levels of survivability and that American situation awareness for space operations is adequate to understand this increasingly busy environment.

The Department of Defense can make good use of this time to buy down the risk in developing next-generation systems. In particular, the space-based radar offers significant strategic and operational capabilities. Clustered "virtual satellites" offer considerable operational potential, and focused development of these systems should continue. Throughout this period, DOD should take a stronger role in the development of next-generation launch technology than it has to this point, working in cooperation with NASA.

The United States now rests its national military capability largely on the information dominance made possible by space systems. In that light, the health of the industrial base that provides those systems is a real concern.

## Notes

[1] *Inside the Air Force*, January 4, 2002, 1.

[2] See, for example, George Friedman and Meredith Friedman, *The Future of War: Power, Technology, and American World Dominance in the Twenty-first Century* (New York: St. Martin's Griffin, 1998).

[3] See "Pentagon Seeking a Large Increase in Its Next Budget," *The New York Times*, January 7, 2002, 1, for a partial list of service requirements for the 2003 budget.

[4] *Jane's Defence Weekly*, January 2, 2002. General Jumper outlined his thoughts on the integration of air and space forces in a speech to the Air Force Association in Los Angeles, CA, November 16, 2001, accessed at <www.af.mil/news/speech/current/sph2001_20.html>.

[5] For a fine summary of global space capabilities, see Steven Lambakis, *On the Edge of Earth: The Future of American Space Power* (Lexington: University of Kentucky Press, 2001), 142–174.

[6] Warren Ferster, "Persian Gulf Hot Market for Satellite Imagery," *Space News*, August 27, 2001, 1, 28.

[7] Warren Ferster and Gopal Ratnam, "Gulf States Consider Buying Spy Satellite," *Space News*, December 10, 2001, 1, 3.

[8] Quoted in Wei Long, "China to Launch Micro Imaging Birds," *Space Daily*, November 20, 2000, accessed at <www.spacedaily.com/news/china-00zzq.html>.

[9] "A Bigger Role for Small Satellites?" *The Economist* 360, no. 8240 (September 22, 2001), 20–22.

[10] Ibid.

[11] For a more comprehensive discussion of the development and organization of the U.S. space effort, see Joshua Boehm, with Craig Baker, Stanley Chan, and Mel Sakazaki, "A History of United States National Security Space Management and Organization," background paper supporting the Commission to Assess United States National Security Space Management and Organization.

[12] Secretary of Defense assessment of the Commission to Assess United States National Security Space Management and Organization, May 8, 2001, reprinted in *Space Daily*, May 8, 2001, accessed at <www.spacedaily.com/news/milspace-01p.html>.

[13] Ibid.

[14] See "Peters: Better Interagency Budget Work Needed for Aerospace," *Inside the Air Force*, January 4, 2002, 2, for recent comments by members of the Aerospace Commission on this issue.

[15] Curtis Peebles, *High Frontier: The U.S. Air Force and the Military Space Program* (Washington, DC: Government Printing Office, 1997), 44–57.

[16] David Spires, *Beyond Horizons: A Half Century of Air Force Space Leadership* (Washington, DC: Government Printing Office, 1998), 243–269.

[17] Mark H. Linderman and Paul T. Webster, "The Joint Battlespace Initiative," *Technology Horizons* 2, no. 2 (June 2001).

[18] Ibid.

[19] Barry Watts, *The Military Use of Space: A Diagnostic Assessment* (Washington, DC: Center for Strategic and Budgetary Analysis, February 2001).

[20] Arthur K. Cebrowski and John J. Garstka, "Network-Centric Warfare: Its Origin and Future," *U.S. Naval Institute Proceedings*, January 1998, accessed at <www.usni.org/Proceedings/Articles98/PROcebrowski.htm>. General Jumper's speech of November 16, 2001, offered a complementary vision from an Air Force perspective.

[21] Defense Science Board Task Force, "Space Superiority," February 2000, 12–13.

[22] Ibid., 16.

[23] Norman Friedman, *Seapower and Space: From the Dawn of the Missile Age to Net-Centric Warfare* (Annapolis, MD: Naval Institute Press, 2000), recounts the Soviet and U.S. navies' development of space-based solutions to their operational problems, focusing on over-the-horizon (OTH) detection and targeting. A space-based radar would further extend naval OTH capabilities, increasing the lethality of naval attack forces and decreasing their vulnerability to land based attack, continuing a trend that has shaped naval employment concepts since the 1960s. In pursuing those concepts, the U.S. Navy has played a remarkable role in developing the current range of space applications and technologies. Examples include the first signals intelligence (SIGINT) system (GRAB, orbited in 1960), the first navigation satellites (Transit, operational 1964), and the Clementine, used to prove the utility of small satellites in deep space exploration.

[24] Alok Das, "Choreographing Affordable, Next-Generation Space Missions Using Satellite Clusters," *Technology Horizons* 1, no. 3 (September 2000), 15–16.

[25] A minor exception is the 23-millimeter cannon mounted on Soviet space stations for self-defense purposes. The USSR's Polyus space station represented a far more significant attempt to field space-based weaponry as a counter to the Strategic Defense Initiative ("Star Wars"), but it failed to reach orbit during a launch attempt in 1987. See the *Encyclopedia Astronautica*, accessed at <www.astronautix.com/index.htm>, for details.

[26] See Bob Preston et al., "Space Weapons Earth Wars" (Santa Monica, CA: RAND, 2001), for a complete discussion of weapons effects, key technologies, basing considerations, and possible pathways toward U.S. or foreign deployment of these weapons. Watts also explored these issues in *Military Space*.

[27] Quoted in Ben Iannotta, "Explaining X-planes," *Aerospace America* 39, no. 11 (November 2001), 30.

[28] "Space Based Laser Activities Reduced Because Of Deep Funding Cut," *Aerospace Daily*, January 4, 2002. William Martel, ed., *The Technological Arsenal: Emerging Defense Capabilities* (Washington, DC: Smithsonian Institution, 2001), includes three chapters exploring different applications of space-based lasers and the technical challenges that must be overcome.

[29] For opposing views on the wisdom of proceeding with space-based weapons, see Howell Estes' speech, "National Security: The Space Dimension," at the Los Angeles Air Force Association National Symposium, November 14, 1997, accessed at <www.defenselink.mil/speeches/1997/s19971114-estes.html>; and John Logsdon, "Just Say Wait to Space Power," *Issues in Science and Technology*, Spring 2001, accessed at <www.nap.edu/issues/17.3/p_logsdon.htm>.

[30] For more detail, see the Defense Science Board (DSB) Task Force report, "Preserving a Healthy and Competitive U.S. Defense Industry to Ensure Our Future National Security," final briefing, November 2000; and J.R. Harbison, T.S. Moorman, Jr., M.W. Jones, and J. Kim, "U.S. Defense Industry Under Siege—An Agenda for Change," Booz-Allen Hamilton report, July 2000.

[31] Anthony L. Velocci, "Consolidation Juggernaut Yet to Run Its Course," *Aviation Week and Space Technology*, December 3, 2001, 48–49.

[32] John Deutch, "Consolidation of the U.S. Defense Industrial Base," *Acquisition Review Quarterly*, Fall 2001, 137–150.

# Chapter 13

# Protecting Cyberspace

Jacques S. Gansler

Information systems are the critical elements in the transformation of both military operations and the functioning of society, and they will be increasingly vital in the future. In the military area, the centrality of these systems varies from growing dependence on the real-time linking of distributed intelligence "sensors" and distributed "shooters" (through complex networked command, control, communications, and computers [C⁴] systems) to the rapid responsiveness provided by modern information-based logistics support systems. On the civil side, it includes the exponentially growing dependence on computer and communication networks for everything from government operations to the full infrastructure of the financial, medical, transportation, utilities, and other systems that determine the effective operation of modern society. The problem, of course, is that with this growing dependence on information systems, we expose ourselves to a rapidly growing and increasingly dangerous spectrum of information warfare (IW) operations. These might include direct military information system attacks aimed at prevention, disruption, intelligence gathering, or deception; cyberterrorism attacks on civil infrastructures, such as banks, water and power systems, air traffic, and hospitals; and even combined and simultaneous attacks on both military systems and their supporting civil infrastructures.

This vulnerability of modern military and civil society to information warfare must be addressed with appropriate defenses. Clearly, however, the potential benefits of offensive information warfare are also likely to be fully exploited by all sides. To better understand this cat-and-mouse game of offensive and defensive information warfare operations, consider the almost-ubiquitous Internet.

## Origins of the Internet

The Internet has evolved from its roots 30 years ago as an academic research tool to become a global resource serving millions of individuals as well as providing critical connectivity for national security, industrial, economic, and governmental functions. To understand the current issues of Internet security, it is important to understand its history and heritage. The Department of Defense (DOD) Advanced Research Projects Agency (ARPA), now DARPA, sponsored the initial research on packet-switching technology, the enabling technology for the Internet, and published a plan for a computer network called ARPANET in 1967. In October 1969, the first four nodes were established at the University of California at Los Angeles, the Stanford Research Institute, the University of California at Santa Barbara, and the University of Utah.

The potential utility of computer networking was not lost on other communities, and by the mid-1970s other computer networks began to spring up at the Department of Energy, the National Aeronautics and Space Administration (NASA), the National Science Foundation (NSF, which funded CS–NET), and throughout a variety of academic communities. These networks were still largely incompatible until 1986, when ARPA and the NSF made their networks interoperable using the ARPA-developed communication protocol known as TCP/IP. The high-speed national links developed by the National Science Foundation (NSFNET) became the national backbone for this combined network, but it was still restricted to research and education; commercial use was, in fact, prohibited. Security was not believed to be an issue, since access was restricted to trusted users.

By 1990, the Internet had grown from 4 hosts to 300,000. The ARPANET was formally shut down, and the NSF began to manage the Internet. In 1991, liberalized restrictions on commercial use coupled with the growing availability of personal computers fueled the explosive growth of the Internet. In 1995, the Internet was privatized, and by January 2001, it had grown almost twenty-fold to 109,574,429 hosts.[1] Based on the nature of the Internet's early evolution, however, security was not a primary consideration in the design. Partly for that reason, the Internet continues to provide many security challenges.

## Increasing Public-Private Activity

In the near future, the Internet will be ubiquitous, transparent, and integrated into everything we do. The benefits of this cheap, reliable communication have been enormous. As the public and private sectors continue to look for ways to take advantage of opportunities created by the Internet, the interaction and activity between the two sectors will continue to increase in ways that often obscure the ways in which we are becoming dependent on it.

As a result of advances in information technologies, it is possible for us to tie together infrastructure, data, and daily operations in ways not possible before. Today, computer networks control the Nation's powergrids, natural gas pipelines, and transportation systems. Both Federal Express and United Parcel Service, for example, depend upon computer networks to get packages where they are going on time. U.S. industries design and manufacture products on computer aided design/computer aided manufacturing (CAD/CAM) systems (for example, Boeing designed the Boeing 777 in "virtual space"). More than people realize, these systems and networks are all interconnected on the Internet. The business sector, early on, recognized the commercial potential of the information revolution and quickly made the Internet a commercial medium. Although there have been some setbacks, electronic commerce has a bright future; business-to-citizen revenues are estimated at $96 billion in 2001, and business-to-business online revenues at $448 billion, nearly double the previous year.

Most of the initial Internet-related efforts by Federal and state governments were aimed at making information available to internal users and to the citizens at large; the Federal Government, for example, maintains approximately 100 million Web pages at 25,000 Federal sites. DOD placed virtually all of its unclassified data online, including what was, in hindsight, sensitive data, such as the floor plan of the home of the Chairman of the Joint Chiefs of Staff; the operational status of Air Force wings; and unit personnel rosters. (DOD Web sites have since been "sanitized" and are continuously monitored for sensitive data.)

Government has absorbed lessons from private industry (for example, reengineering processes to reduce paperwork and delays can improve performance and efficiency). As government use of the Internet has broadened and become more sophisticated, so-called E-government is booming. Both Federal and state agencies are actively migrating many essential functions to the Internet. Agencies are now turning to the Internet to provide interactive electronic public services. For example, the Internal Revenue Service has a working presence online and is actively encouraging taxpayers to get help and to file their returns online. In 2001, 28 percent of U.S. returns were filed electronically. Federal employees are now able to access and manipulate their pension funds online, and some can monitor and manage their pay online. In the near future, we can expect that many other generally available services, such as Social Security, Medicare, and

Medicaid, will be conducted primarily online, offering citizens better service and improving agency performance.

Additionally, agencies are turning increasingly to the Internet for "paperless acquisition." Since Federal, state, and local governments spend approximately $550 billion annually on goods and services, there is significant incentive for process improvements and savings. The Department of Defense already has several mature electronic procurement sites, including the DOD "E–MALL," an initiative to provide a single entry-point for DOD customers to find and acquire off-the-shelf goods and services, such as information technology (IT) equipment, textiles, and training from both the commercial marketplace and government sources. The E–MALL target market is in excess of $4 billion annually. The Defense Medical Logistics Standard Support (DMLSS) program is an integrated system to accommodate the needs of the Armed Forces at the wholesale and retail levels for medical logistics support. It relies on electronic commerce and Web-based technology to speed delivery of pharmaceutical, medical, and surgical items to customers, negating the need to stock large inventory at depots and military treatment facilities. At the Great Lakes Naval Hospital, one of the first sites online, inventory was cut from $3 million to $3,000 using DMLSS.

These examples illustrate the kinds of programs that the government is migrating to the Internet to make available and integrate fully online as many functions as possible with private citizens and private industry. Not only as we expand our definition of national security interests, particularly since September 11, to include financial security, healthcare, education, and personal privacy but also as ownership of critical IT infrastructures moves increasingly into private hands, it is clear that the Internet will require a public-private partnership with a high degree of collaboration to develop effective policy, goals, objectives, and, especially, defenses against information warfare attacks.

## Growing Vulnerability

In the United States, we are blessed with wonderful geography from a national security perspective; we have friendly countries to the north and south and large oceans to the east and west. In the past, few enemies have ever had the means to threaten our homeland seriously. So, for most of our history, we have not had to worry about being attacked at home. There was a 40-year period during the Cold War when Soviet bombers and intercontinental ballistic missiles were poised to attack our cities, but with the demise of the Soviet Union, the successes of strategic arms reduction talks, and the warming of relations with Russia, we once again felt safe. Recent terrorist attacks, however, have reminded us of our physical vulnerability.

At the same time, we also are making the transition to the new borderless geography in cyberspace. As we grow more dependent on the Internet, its inherent vulnerabilities have put all of us—government, military, industry, and citizens—at risk. The Internet was originally designed to be open, based on the premise that users were known and trustworthy. Security was not designed in from the beginning, so as the Internet has evolved into the current global network of networks, we have found it difficult to provide security for our data and transactions. The rapid pace of technical innovation introduces unanticipated vulnerabilities with every advance, and commercial software suppliers are often more eager to get their new products out in the market than they are anxious to assure their invulnerability.[2] Our security planning, often based on the older models of mainframes or well-defined networks within a single organization, have proved inadequate for this new environment with its ever-increasing threat.

## Shared Threat

Cyberspace tends to level the playing field between the entities in that space and offers attackers many high-value, low-risk targets. The threats can come from a hacker, an insider, a criminal, a terrorist, a hostile nation-state, or even some combination of these. The motivations can be equally diverse—mischief, theft, data collection, disruption of operations, falsification of data. The threats, obviously, can be aimed equally well against military or civilian targets. The weapons, with innocuous-sounding names like worms, viruses, and even Trojan horses, are themselves readily available on the Internet. Most important, the Internet itself is a very attractive target.

Unlike physical break-ins, Internet attacks are easy. An attacker who gets access to a Web site can roam around freely and from a safe distance. Although in the past, a great deal of technical sophistication was required to penetrate a computer network, attacks are now possible even by much less well-informed adversaries; successful intruders share their programs—often with "hacking for dummies" type scripts—enabling anyone to duplicate their efforts.

Attackers can and do obfuscate who and where they are, making Internet intrusions and attacks difficult to trace. Additionally, because the Internet allows packets to flow easily across political, administrative, and geographic boundaries, cooperation from many different entities, many without a vested interest, may be required to trace an attack. Consequently, attackers often operate (or appear to operate) from other countries, and thus international cooperation is required to trace and investigate attacks.

Internet attacks are low-risk: since the attackers do not need to be physically present, the risk of identification is greatly reduced. Much of the activity is often masked by legitimate or unrelated activity, and because multiple jurisdictions may be involved, prosecution can be difficult and sometimes impossible.

As a result of these factors, and in spite of increased awareness and security measures, attempted penetrations of Internet sites are steadily increasing. The number of incidents reported worldwide grew from approximately 2,000 in 1997 to 21,756 in 2000. Fully 15,476 incidents had been reported in the first half of 2001.[3] Since this reporting is voluntary, these figures presumably understate the actual number considerably and reflect merely the trends in the numbers.

## The Department of Defense

Hundreds, and more likely thousands, of attacks are attempted against DOD systems and networks each week. DOD estimates that, in 2001 alone, it was likely to face around 40,000 attempted attacks.[4] Most of these are unsuccessful, but in 2000, 715 documented attacks were reported that achieved varying degrees of success. Of course, many others may have gone undetected.

Although the threat to and vulnerability of U.S. information systems has been the focus of much discussion, DOD perception of the information warfare threat has particularly been shaped by several real-world events. In 1997, recognizing that the American information infrastructure was at risk, DOD planned the first large-scale exercise to test Defense ability to respond to a cyber attack on the national infrastructure, nicknamed ELIGIBLE RECEIVER 97 (ER97).[5] It was planned and executed by a team of National Security Agency (NSA) computer specialists.[6] Their role in the exercise was to play the adversary making a concerted effort to hack into U.S. systems.[7]

The offensive team operated under many restrictions: they had to conduct their attacks without violating any U.S. law; they could not take advantage of any insider information or collateral intelligence; and they could only use tools that could be claimed to be in an adversary's hands (all tools and techniques were based on unclassified, open-source data).

During the exercise, NSA specialists scripted attacks that would have resulted in a series of rolling electricity blackouts and an overload of the 911 emergency telephone service in Washington, DC, and a handful of other cities. The potential for attack on the powergrid was demonstrated by simulated attacks on the computerized sensing and control devices that are commonly used in operating electrical, oil, gas, transportation, and water treatment systems.[8]

Even with restrictions and a tight 3-month schedule, the exercise demonstrated many weaknesses.[9] It was clear that a dedicated and moderately sophisticated adversary with modest resources could inflict considerable damage unless the target systems were more effectively protected.[10]

In 1998, the United States was involved in a serious weapons inspection crisis with Iraq, which was refusing to permit United Nations (UN) inspectors unrestricted access. The United States, in addition to being involved in the UN negotiations with Iraq, was preparing for possible military strikes.[11] Several cyberattacks—unauthorized intrusions into approximately six military networks around the country—were picked up in the U.S. Air Force's Information Warfare Center in San Antonio, Texas.[12] Five hundred domain name servers were compromised. The attacks used the same technique to exploit a vulnerability in the Sun Solaris operating system. The intrusions were initially tracked to Abu Dhabi in the United Arab Emirates.[13] Under the circumstances, there was considerable concern about a major asymmetric attack by Iraq or its sympathizers on logistics, medical, or resource systems during the crisis period.[14]

The newly established National Infrastructure Protection Center (NIPC) coordinated a multiagency investigation into the attacks (code-named SOLAR SUNRISE) that determined within a few more days that they were not the work of Iraqi agents operating from the Middle East but were in fact orchestrated by two California teenagers with the help of an Israeli citizen.[15]

The Department of Defense was still evaluating the implications of ER97 and the SOLAR SUNRISE investigation when, in January 1999, DOD, the Department of Energy, military contractors, and civilian university computer systems were attacked in the largest assault yet.[16] Congressman Curt Weldon (R–PA), quoting Deputy Secretary of Defense John Hamre, stated: "We are at war right now. We are in a cyberwar." Weldon characterized these attacks as being in a different class from the approximately 400 probes picked up each week: "These attacks are organized, very capable efforts that have very specific goals, based upon what we've seen."[17]

The attacks, which apparently originated in Russia, began at a low level in January and reportedly gained "root access" to certain systems. The penetrations were on unclassified but nonpublic systems; they apparently achieved no access to classified data. Nevertheless, the damage could be significant because these unclassified systems often contain useful and sensitive information.[18] After 3 years of investigations and thousands of files stolen, the evidence still points to Russia. James Adams, a consultant who serves on the NSA Advisory Board, wrote in May 2001:

> the assault has continued unabated. . . . Despite all the investigative effort, the United States still does not know who is behind the attacks, what additional information has been taken and why; to what extent the public and private sectors have been penetrated; and what else has been left behind that could still damage the vulnerable networks.[19]

A more recent example was a malicious denial-of-service attack that took place on July 19, 2001. According to the NIPC, Code Red, an Internet worm, infected more than 250,000 Internet systems in just 9 hours; Computer Economics, Inc., estimated over 1,000,000 infections worldwide.[20] Code Red damaged sites by defacing Web pages; it also denied access to certain Internet addresses by sending massive amounts of data, which effectively shut down the addresses. As a result of the attacks, DOD was forced to shut down its Web sites; the White House was forced to change its Internet address; the Department of the Treasury Financial Management System was infected and had to be disconnected from the Web; users of the Qwest high-speed Internet service experienced outages nationwide; and the Federal Express package-tracking system was infected, causing delivery delays. The initial economic cost was estimated at over $2.4 billion in costs associated with cleaning, inspecting, and patching servers, as well as damage to productivity.

## Shared Responsibilities

Public and private sectors are increasingly dependent on the Internet, even with its many systematic vulnerabilities to a broad range of threats. There is no question that defending against information warfare and assuring unhampered access to the Internet is a responsibility shared by both public and private sectors. The government has a clear responsibility in the protection of information systems, especially where national security is at stake. One of the Federal Government's fundamental responsibilities is to protect the Nation from all threats, foreign and domestic, and this, of course, includes protection from threats to the collective information systems that comprise the Internet. There are, additionally, law enforcement responsibilities for protecting these systems against terrorist threats and criminal activity. While attacks to date have not caused devastating disruption, the potential for catastrophic damage is significant. As the events of September 11 demonstrated, sometimes even the unimaginable is possible. Cyberterrorism is clearly a growing and very real probability.[21]

The private sector, on the other hand, owns most of the information infrastructure and develops most of the technology and software that enable it. As a result of these factors, the shared public-private responsibility of providing security to our information systems suffers from a misalignment of authority, responsibility, and capability: "those with authority to act often lack the capability, while those with the capability to act often do not have the responsibility."[22]

## Directions for Solutions

As the way in which we use information and information systems continues to evolve, it may be some time before the public and private elements are correctly aligned. In the interim, if we are to improve our capability against cyberattacks, we must do a much better job of sharing information between the public and private sectors. First, having information on threats and on actual incidents experienced by others can help an organization better understand the risks that it faces and determine what preventive measures should be implemented. Today's nuisance incidents may in fact be tests or probes for future attacks. Information attacks cannot be launched blindly but, like any other weapon, must be tested. In addition, urgent real-time warnings can help an organization take immediate steps to mitigate an imminent attack. Finally, information sharing and coordination after an attack are critical to facilitate criminal investigations, which may cross many jurisdictional boundaries. After-the-fact coordination will be essential to speed the recovery from a devastating attack, should one ever occur.

The government has recognized its central role in this information-sharing function and has several developing efforts. At the Federal level, for example, the National Infrastructure Protection Center, located at the Federal Bureau of Investigation (FBI), was established to serve as a focal point in the Federal Government for gathering information on threats, as well as to facilitate and coordinate responses to incidents affecting key infrastructures. It is also charged with issuing attack warnings to private-sector and government entities, as well as alerts about changes in threat conditions. The National Institute of Standards and Technology is building a database containing detailed information on computer attacks. The

Federal Government also sponsors the Computer Emergency Response Team Coordination Center at Carnegie Mellon University, which studies Internet security vulnerabilities, handles computer security incidents, publishes security alerts, researches long-term changes in networked systems, and develops information and training. Early in 2001, the Department of Commerce sponsored the formation of a private-sector nonprofit alliance, the Information Technology Information Sharing and Analysis Center (IT–ISAC). Its mission is to exchange information on potential and known threats and vulnerabilities for the information sector and sharing that information with Federal law enforcement. (It joins existing ISACs for the energy, financial services, transportation, and telecommunications sectors.) IT–ISAC has 19 members so far, including major corporations, such as AT&T, IBM, Cisco, and Microsoft. President George W. Bush has appointed Richard Clarke as a special adviser to work with Governor Tom Ridge in the Office of Homeland Security to coordinate the protection of the Nation's computer infrastructure.

One of the key elements to the success of information-sharing partnerships is developing trusted relationships among the broad range of stakeholders involved with providing information assurance, including the public and Internet community at large, law enforcement, government agencies, the intelligence community, providers of network and other key infrastructure services, technology and security product developers, incident response teams, and international standard-setting bodies. Information sharing must be seen as equitable, and it must provide value over and above the costs that it imposes. There are some real and perceived industry concerns that range from antitrust issues of sharing information with industry partners to subjecting information to Freedom of Information Act (FOIA) disclosures. Inadvertent releases of trade secrets or proprietary information are a concern because they could damage reputations, lower consumer confidence, and hurt competitiveness. Sharing information with law enforcement could result in costly compliance with strict rules for preserving the integrity of evidence. The government is reluctant to share classified information, even though it could be of value to the private sector in deterring or thwarting electronic intrusions and information attacks. This is particularly the case with any potential offensive tools and techniques, which are extremely sensitive from a national security perspective but are, of course, necessary for effective testing of defensive capabilities. The government clearly must work with industry to develop mechanisms to overcome each of these impediments.

## Specific Recommendations

Some useful actions to decrease U.S. vulnerability to information warfare include the following: First, we need to have meaningful information sharing, and for this, we must develop standard definitions and terminology for use throughout the government and industry. A clear understanding of what is meant by an *attack* and how to categorize an incident will be essential to enable faster and more efficient reporting, responding, and remediation. Distinguishing between an incident that is classified as criminal and one that is a national security threat will help determine the type and timeframe of the response. We may, for example, choose to let potential criminal activity proceed to gather evidence but may need to react immediately to a national security attack.

Second, we need to overcome information-sharing roadblocks. Information sharing between the government and private sector remains a vitally important yet elusive goal. Among the several Federal Government initiatives, its primary focus is with the NIPC, which is housed within the FBI and has a decided emphasis on criminal investigation. This creates a problem within the government since it puts the FBI in a position to decide what information other agencies need to see. Industry, to say nothing of any international partners, will also naturally be reluctant to report incidents to the FBI. Another source of private-sector reluctance to share information with the government is the requirements imposed on government by FOIA.[23] To facilitate uninhibited information exchange and protect competitive positions, sensitive industry data needs to be exempted from FOIA requirements. Other models for collection and dissemination of vulnerability and threat information—for example, a single nonprofit information clearinghouse—should be explored and developed.

Finally, government needs to develop mechanisms to share sensitive and perhaps even classified threat data about pending attacks with industry partners, both domestic and international. This will help ensure that all information is available to those entities that are best equipped to mitigate the impact. Government must be willing to share all appropriate information in response to industry concerns if it hopes to overcome the hurdles to achieving a mutually beneficial partnership.

Although improving organizational information sharing can significantly improve our ability to defend against an IW attack in the near term, there are still many technical challenges to providing security and assurance within a distributed information environment. Our goal should be to create an Internet infrastructure that is highly automated, adaptive, and resilient to all types of attacks. An obvious first step is to improve the overall quality of software security. Identifying products with easily exploitable vulnerabilities and preventing them from being widely used will reduce the more pedestrian attacks. Incentives should be created for firms to improve the attention and resources that they devote to enhancing their software and system protections; this suggests a useful role for government managers and buyers, and even more for senior industrial managers and buyers.[24]

In addition, there are technologies that could, if properly developed, be useful in resisting and responding to inevitable cyberattacks. Among those that merit increased attention are some in the area of intelligence gathering. We should be developing tools that allow us to take the initiative to gain insight into the capabilities and intentions of potential adversaries. For example, it would be quite useful to have an active software agent, using secure mobile code, that could monitor and collect information on hostile entities in order to provide early warning of attack. We currently have difficulty identifying novel attack patterns, especially against the Internet's widely distributed network. Insiders pose a particular threat to all information systems; therefore, developing systems to automate the processes of detecting, identifying, and analyzing novel attack patterns and anomalous behavior would improve our ability to provide warnings and reduce false alarms.

Opportunities for disruption will only increase as the complexity of the Internet networks increases. We need to continue research and development to guard against unknown attacks and to protect against systems with unknown flaws. We need to develop automated mechanisms to detect and nullify malicious codes that may be left behind in an undetected attack. We have designed many fault-tolerant systems to cope with naturally occurring faults and failures, and we need to extend these capabilities to develop networks that are resistant to insertion of intentional faults and to denial-of-service attacks conducted by adversaries. Present capabilities for detecting large-scale intrusions against multiple systems are limited. We need to accelerate the development of an advanced intrusion detection capability that can fuse and correlate information from distributed sensors.

Even with an adequate warning system and good defenses, some attacks will be successful. Thus, we need to have the technology in place to address the consequences of these attacks. We need to be able to assess systems quickly and answer important questions: Was something done to the system? If so, what was done? Is the system okay? What is the reliability of the data? When we understand the answers to these questions, we need to be able to move quickly to restore user trust in the system. If a system has been attacked successfully, we need to be able to recover quickly from the attack, bring the system back to full performance, and take corrective action so that it will not be susceptible to a similar attack.

This discussion has focused on information-sharing processes and technology, but we should also recognize that one of the most critical elements in any comprehensive defense against an information warfare attack is the people who use and operate our systems. Whatever else we do, we must develop a continuing program to promote understanding of security policies and controls and of the risks that prompted their adoption. Better understanding of the risks will allow executives to make more informed decisions regarding the resources required to protect their systems. The first line of defense is the system user, who must understand the importance of complying with policies and controls.

One of the most effective ways for both the private and public sector to assure secure systems is to conduct frequent red team attacks on their own systems. Skilled attackers can test the vulnerabilities of systems and fix them before someone else finds them. While many in the private and public sector have a reluctance to test their own systems, the return on investment here is extremely worthwhile.

## Conclusion

While this discussion has focused on the illustrative case of the Internet, its expansion to other systems—both military and civilian—is obvious. Today, we know that 20 foreign nations are developing information warfare doctrine, programs, and capabilities for use against U.S. military and private sector networks; numerous terrorist networks have similarly recognized the potential of these "weapons of mass disruption" and have begun to exploit them. Of course, the United States can also take full advantage of the offensive military potential of information warfare to broaden its military options and capabilities. However, as a military force and as a civil society, the United States is already the world's most dependent on information systems, and we are moving more and more in that direction. As we transform our forces and our society in the information age, we become ever more vulnerable. Thus, we have a very real requirement to address our information systems vulnerabilities before it is too late.

# Notes

[1] Based on data from the Internet Software Consortium. A *host* denotes a single machine on the Internet. However, the definition has changed in recent years due to "virtual hosting," in which a single machine acts like multiple systems (and has multiple domain names and IP addresses). Ideally, a virtual host will act and look exactly like a regular host, so they are counted equally. For the research above, and in many other areas of this chapter, the author is deeply indebted to the assistance of William Lucyshyn.

[2] Moreover, to lower costs, many software firms now go offshore for their programming, further raising the chance of vulnerability.

[3] Statistics are from the Computer Emergency Response Team (CERT) Coordination Center at Carnegie Mellon University.

[4] D.A. Fulghum and R. Wall, *Aviation Week and Space Technology*, November 5, 2001, 26.

[5] John J. Hamre, Congressional testimony, February 23, 1998.

[6] Bradley Graham, "Hackers, Simulation, Expose Vulnerability," *The Washington Post*, May 24, 1998, A1.

[7] Stephen Green, "Pentagon Giving Cyberwarfare High Priority," Copley News Service, December 21, 1999.

[8] Graham.

[9] Goss.

[10] Kenneth Minihan, Statement before the Senate Governmental Affairs Committee, Hearing on Vulnerabilities of the National Information Infrastructure, June 24, 1998.

[11] "Prospect against Iraq Prompts Demonstrations," *The Washington Post*, February 15, 1998, A31.

[12] Graham.

[13] Gregory L. Vistica and Evan Thomas, "The Secret Hacker Wars," *Newsweek*, June 1, 1998, 60.

[14] *Protecting the Homeland*, 2.

[15] Michael A. Vatis, Statement for the Record on the National Infrastructure Protection Center before the Senate Armed Forces Committee, Subcommittee on Emerging Threats and Capabilities, March 1, 2000.

[16] Gregory L. Vistica, "We're in the Middle of a Cyberwar," *Newsweek*, September 20, 1999, 52.

[17] John Donnelly and Vince Crawley, "Hamre to Hill: 'We're in a Cyberwar,'" *Defense Week*, March 1, 1999.

[18] Vistica.

[19] James Adams, "Virtual Defense," *Foreign Affairs* 80, no. 3 (May–June 2001), 98.

[20] A *worm* is an attack that propagates itself through networks without any user intervention or interaction.

[21] See Mike Toner, "Cyberterrorism Danger Lurking," *The Atlanta Journal-Constitution*, November 4, 2001, A4.

[22] Arnaud de Borchgrave, Frank J. Cillufo, Sharon L. Cardash, and Michele M. Ledgerwood, *Cyber Threats and Information Security: Meeting the 21ˢᵗ Century Challenge*, Center for Strategic and International Studies, December 2000, 4

[23] The Freedom of Information Act guarantees that the public has a right of access to Federal records and that these records must be made available to the public, unless specifically exempt from public release.

[24] In early 2002, the U.S. Air Force explicitly began to address this issue with suppliers. See Byron Acohido, "Air Force Seeks Better Security from Microsoft," *USA Today*, March 11, 2002, 3B.

# Chapter 14

# Maintaining the Technological Lead

Mark L. Montroll

*If, unhappily, there should be another war, there should be no need for another OSRD [Office of Scientific Research and Development]. It will be needed only if there is a large deficit of military research such as existed in 1940. With the experience of World War II behind them, our military leaders should not permit that to happen. But if it is not to happen, there should be more adequate research within the Services and a more adequate use made of civilian research by the Services in the years immediately ahead.*

—Irvin Stewart,
*Organizing Scientific Research for War,* 1948

Throughout World War II, Vannevar Bush directed the immensely successful Office of Scientific Research and Development (OSRD). The agency was winding down when, in fall 1946, Bush articulated his startling observation:

World War II was the first war in human history to be affected decisively by weapons unknown at the outbreak of hostilities. This is probably the most significant military fact of our decade: that upon the current evolution of the instrumentalities of war, the strategy and tactics of warfare must now be conditioned. In World War II this new situation demanded a closer linkage among military men, scientists, and industrialists than had ever before been required, primarily because the new weapons whose evolution determines the course of war are dominantly the products of science, as is natural in an essentially scientific and technological age.[1]

Throughout the Cold War, the linkages of which Dr. Bush spoke were nurtured and strengthened. Since the collapse of the Berlin Wall in 1989, which marked the end of the Cold War, these linkages and their supporting infrastructures have begun to fray. This breakdown is a cause for alarm

**345**

because today, just as in the 1940s, scientific advances and technological innovations are the foundation upon which the great military transformations of the 21$^{st}$ century will depend.

The world is again on the precipice of instability. During the 1990s, armies throughout most of the world were not posted on front lines engaging in mortal combat, nor were the inhabitants of great nations living in constant fear of immediate and deadly attack. Societies were stable, and people throughout most of the world went about their daily lives unfettered by external military threats. This did not mean, however, that humankind had eradicated armed conflict, nor that conflicting national vital interests would never again lead to global wars. One need only to look at the current situation in the Middle East, some parts of Africa, or some areas of the Balkans to see conflict brewing. Indeed, on September 11, 2001, a new episode of active conflict was begun. With the destruction of the World Trade Center in New York and the attacks on the Pentagon and aboard United Flight 93, a new wave of asymmetric violence was unleashed on the world.

The global security environment is ever changing, and all aspects of our military structure are undergoing dramatic transformations to remain at the vanguard of peace and security. Our forces again have been deployed to foreign shores to thwart a military adversary attempting to undermine the goals of the Nation.

If these transformations are to succeed, the processes used to acquire the new tools of war, as well as the research and development (R&D) infrastructure upon which they depend, must be transformed to meet the emerging requirements. Links between the military, the scientific communities, and the industrial communities are more vital now than they have ever been. The facilities, organizations, and acquisition processes that have begun to bend under the weight of scarce resource allocations, an aging workforce, and conflicting priorities threaten to undermine the current transformation processes described in the other chapters of this book. If the situation is not managed with care and diligence, it will fall prey to Irvin Stewart's warning of 1948: we will be faced with a large deficit of military research such as existed in 1940. The lessons of history will be lost, and our military forces will suffer the consequences as they engage on the battlefield.

The military transformation process will only be successful if defense R&D processes and rapid procurement processes are properly focused and tightly coupled. This chapter examines four R&D issues that enable rapid procurement and introduces a few policy options available to ensure that advanced technology development remains available to defense planners. We examine the role of the internal defense R&D infrastructure, the industrial R&D infrastructure, and the processes that have been established to link R&D outputs closely with rapid procurement, fielding of new technologies and systems, and the effect of major program acquisition strategies on research and development.

## Background

What was startling and revolutionary 55 years ago is ordinary and commonplace today. New instrumentalities of war are routinely introduced into each new conflict. Weapons, tactics, and strategies that were introduced into one conflict may be decisive factors in the next war and be mainstream tools by the following one. Concepts that are decisive in a target-rich environment require fundamentally different tools in a target-sparse environment. The rest of the world studies U.S. procedures and develops asymmetrical responses for the next conflict.

In short, although the arms race associated with the attrition-based strategy of the Cold War era may be over, the technological race associated with the information-based strategy of the current era is just beginning. If the technology gap is sufficiently large, information-based strategies may prove decisive in network-centric warfare environments. Should this gap close, with the adversary successfully utilizing symmetric information warfare strategies or asymmetric strategies, the network-centric environment collapses and becomes a classical attrition-warfare environment. Maintaining a U.S. advantage requires constant improvements, which depend in turn on research and development.

## Internal Research and Development Infrastructure

Since the earliest days of the Nation, the military services have owned and operated their own internal R&D facilities in conjunction with the old arsenal system. Today, all of the services have organizations that sponsor and facilities that perform science and technology (S&T) research. The Army Research Laboratory, the Naval Research Laboratory, and the Air Force Research Laboratory are the core internal S&T labs for their respective services. The Office of Naval Research and the Offices of Scientific Research for the Army and Air Force sponsor S&T research, utilizing universities to conduct most of the research. In addition to the primary S&T labs, all of the services also operate a number of research facilities tied to their system acquisition commands. For example, the Naval Sea Systems Command manages the labs associated with the Naval Surface Warfare Center and the Naval Undersea Warfare Center. The Army's Tank and Automotive Command manages a vehicle R&D lab; the Air Force manages aeronautics and avionics R&D labs throughout the country.

The daily activities at the in-house defense research laboratories are governed by three key forces: priorities and policies established by the chain-of-command authorities, program requirements established by paying sponsors, and external constraints such as environmental limitations imposed by other regulatory and policymaking organizations. By controlling or influencing any or all of these elements, the Army, Navy, and Air Force can influence their laboratories to serve their current and emerging priorities. However, even in a single service, no single person or institution controls all three of these forces. As a result, a dynamic mix of competing forces combines to form a swirl of ever-changing activity at each of the research labs.

It is precisely this high level of seemingly chaotic activity that, when properly managed, gives the labs an exceptional degree of agility and flexibility. These qualities allow the labs, quickly and efficiently, to create, analyze, and synthesize new ideas and concepts that become the bases of new and innovative military systems. This same behavior, if not skillfully administered, can also lead to inefficiencies, irrelevancies, and redundancies within the labs. Thus, the service laboratories' ability to perform their critical role—bonding military requirements, scientific knowledge, and technological innovation to create useful and achievable military system concepts—depends directly on their leaders' ability to balance the multiplicity of forces acting on their labs.

These internal R&D labs have traditionally focused their efforts on supporting the major acquisition programs within their parent commands. As military transformation progresses, all the services are generating radically new system requirements. To support the emerging military missions outlined in chapter 1, smaller, lighter, and more agile major systems are being demanded throughout the military. As discussed in more detail in chapter 2, the sensing, communication, and information processing subsystem requirements necessary to support the major systems are also being rapidly transformed, demanding the latest cutting-edge technologies to sustain them.

The rapid pace of technological advancement and of identifying emerging system and subsystem requirements to support the military transformation is redefining the role of internal defense research facilities.

Scientists are being called upon to examine new areas of study, to focus on extremely rapid transition from concept to fielded system, and to integrate modern high-tech concepts with legacy fleet systems.

This approach presents a dilemma analogous to issues faced in the procurement world. In the constrained resource environment of the defense laboratory system, spending funds on improving legacy systems leaves little money to fund leading-edge transformation-enabling technologies. If the funds are diverted to transformation-enabling technologies, legacy improvement research is curtailed. Since the source of funding for the labs is usually major system program offices, almost all of which are developing systems introduced before DOD embarked on its current military transformation process, the labs are often directed to focus their expertise on legacy and evolutionary improvement programs. To change this focus, new sources of funding must be identified, or funding from legacy-related systems must be redirected.

Both these cases present issues that are extremely complex but that must be overcome by the research facilities. For example, people, skills, and facilities may be mismatched as a laboratory changes its focus. The testing facilities important for the development of tracked vehicles may be a burden to maintain as the research shifts to developing wheeled vehicles. People with vast experience developing avionics for manned aircraft may be less capable of conducting leading-edge research in avionics for unmanned aircraft. In light of all these issues, attention must be paid to maintaining the true technological leadership needed to enable the ongoing military transformation.

### Technological Leadership

Maintaining a true technological lead, as a nation, is a very complex process. It requires continuous, careful orchestration of numerous enterprises, both public and private. Over 4,000 governmental organizations in the United States sponsor or conduct scientific research;[2] DOD alone accounts for over 700 of them. Almost 2,000 U.S. university facilities are involved in the conduct of scientific research.[3]

In 1947, DOD was spending around $3 billion for R&D activities. Today, it spends around $48 billion per year.[4] Although this level of spending should be sufficient to keep the military equipped and trained to use systems at the leading edge of technology, many disparate forces keep us from reaching that elusive goal. Because the $48 billion is spread across many organizations and is managed by many different constituencies, appropriating the level of funding necessary to carry out adequate and timely research for a specific project is often difficult. In addition, since Federal funding of research is an element of the political process, funding decisions are made on an annual basis, sometimes to the detriment of the long-term stability of the project's funding.

## Workforce Issues

Workforce issues of particular concern include the aging of a trained and expert workforce without replenishment; pay disparities at entry level, compared to the private sector; a less-than-optimal apprenticeship or mentoring system; and decaying infrastructure.

### Aging Workforce

Since World War II, government laboratories have hired scientists and engineers in waves. Major hiring occurred in the late 1940s and early 1950s as the defense establishments sought to capture the expertise developed during the war and to follow the guidance of research policy experts to strengthen the permanent research establishment lest the country face another deficit of science like that encountered before the war. Another significant hiring spell took place during the early 1960s as the Soviet launch of *Sputnik* led to a national focus on science and engineering as the solution to society's ills.

The government found a window of opportunity to hire another wave of researchers in the early 1970s as the commercial market for these professionals dried up and vast numbers were laid off as a result of the dramatic decline of the aerospace industry. When the Vietnam War was in full swing, the government had an immediate need for scientific and engineering talent but had a difficult time competing with the aerospace and burgeoning electronics industries for workers. When the commercial industries collapsed, the government took advantage of the situation and filled its labs with new talent. There was another small window of hiring during the early 1980s as President Ronald Reagan led a dramatic defense buildup. The early 1990s saw a small bulge in hiring to begin replacing retiring scientists and engineers who had been hired in the late 1950s, 1960s, and early 1970s. However, it did not begin to approach the necessary replenishment level.

### Entry-Level Pay Disparity

Since the first Bush administration, the wide pay disparity at the entry-level and early-career level between engineers and scientists employed in the Federal Government and those employed in the private sector has been recognized. This incongruity was particularly acute during the high-tech boom of the 1990s. Starting salaries for government employees were 20 to 40 percent lower than those offered by the high-tech industry, whose appetite for technical talent seemed insatiable.

This phenomenon was not limited to government employees; it affected the private-sector defense industry as well. Since many major defense contractors use pay scales closely associated with their counterpart government partners, they too had great difficulty attracting new entry-level technical talent for their research positions. Even universities found themselves losing the hiring competition for newly graduated scientists and engineers. The salaries and benefits that Internet startup companies offered were so great that new graduates naturally gravitated toward them.

In the year 2000, the high-tech boom began to turn to a high-tech bust. The marketplace was oversaturated with venture capital and other investment money. Companies could not always produce what they had promised, and even when they did, consumers did not buy their products. As a result, many high-tech companies went out of business, and thousands of engineers and scientists lost their jobs.

Thus, as in the early 1970s when the aerospace industry collapsed, employment with the government and the defense industry (with the long-term stability it has come to represent) once again began to look attractive to engineers and scientists. However, unlike the early 1970s, neither the government nor the defense industry in general was in a hiring mode. They were still responding to the reduced budgets and associated workloads associated with the post-Cold War drawdown.

### Low Turnover and Poor Apprenticeship Relationships

As in many other professions, the ability to conduct scientific research and technology development is fostered through a long apprenticeship program. The scientific method, the basis of scientific study and peer review, is a process that demands that new scientific discoveries build upon the old. Without a continuous flow of new people, knowledge of the art of science cannot be passed from one generation to the next. Since the early 1980s, there have been no significant hiring waves of scientists and engineers, other than the very small one of the early 1990s. Even this period came to an abrupt halt when programs began to be canceled and bases began to be closed as the Cold War came to an end. As a result, members of the scientific and engineering workforce today are on average in their late 40s. Many of these people are in their professional prime. This is the time they should be working with a new crop of apprentices to train the next generation of professionals. However, there are few apprentices on the payroll to work with. With nearly 60 percent of the current workforce eligible to retire within 5 years and very few new scientists entering the system, the defense research establishment is already facing severe problems in keeping up with the latest technologies and scientific discoveries.

## Decaying Infrastructure

Leading-edge enterprises get to the top and stay there by having leading-edge facilities, but scarcity of recapitalization funds and rapid advances in technology complicate the process of keeping the defense research infrastructure current.

The budget available to the defense research establishment for overhead, including infrastructure capitalization, is at best stable and is in many cases diminishing. At the same time, lab facilities and equipment are both aging and becoming obsolete. As new technologies are developed, new equipment and advanced facilities are required to pursue research. Advanced visualization tools—for example, those that allow scientists to see the effects of structural modifications on turbulence reductions—greatly enhance the research capability of the lab but cost an enormous amount of money. Such money is not normally budgeted into the research program, but without this equipment, the lab ceases to be a state-of-the-art facility capable of performing leading-edge research.

Like the debate in the healthcare industry over how many expensive pieces of equipment are needed in each city and where they should be placed, the defense research establishment is faced with the dilemma of where to situate its scarce infrastructure resources. When a new but very expensive investigative tool is developed that directly supports the defense research mission, where should it be located? The tool could be placed in a government laboratory, with access provided to both university researchers and defense contractor researchers. It could be placed at a university, with access available to government and contractor researchers. It could be placed at contractor facilities, with access granted to both university and government researchers.

This debate raises the question of research facility rationalization, part of a larger process: the whole defense establishment in the United States is currently working through the issues associated with infrastructure rationalization. How many military bases should we have to support the future defense force structure? What is the appropriate mix of public and private facilities necessary to support the defense mission? The research establishment is part of this debate. It is looking at issues such as what mix of university, private industry, and government research facilities is appropriate and necessary to support the defense research mission of the transforming force structures.

## Defense Research Industrial Base in Support of Transformation

The defense research industrial base is undergoing dramatic changes as rapidly as the internal research infrastructure is. Indeed, the whole defense industrial base is being consolidated and redefined as a result of the post-Cold War defense downsizing. In the early 1990s, the government reassessed its defense procurement requirements and acquisition budgets. As a result, the defense market power shrank relative to the overall economy, and industry reacted by significantly consolidating across many product lines. Only four major prime contractors remain of over 50 separate companies that supported aerospace defense requirements in 1990 (see figure 14–1).

Companies in the defense industry reacted to the post-Cold War drawdown by adopting one of three strategies: exiting the military-industrial sector; diversifying into nonmilitary production or services; or remaining in the defense industry and expanding military production.

The government reacted by relaxing antitrust rule interpretations, defining competitive markets on a global basis, encouraging global competition, promoting consolidations where economies of scale matter, and transferring system-integration function and expertise from the government to prime contractors.

The effect of these practices and policies was to reduce significantly the number of industrial facilities available to engage in defense research. In addition, the government no longer encouraged industrial companies to use their own funds to support research programs with the hope of being rewarded with large procurement contracts. The research and procurement of many systems were decoupled.

One other factor influenced industrial research: the consolidation of the industrial base left many of the largest companies with enormous debts that needed to be serviced from their current cash flow. This caused some companies to reduce their internal expenditures—in some cases, research expenditures—in many areas that did not directly contribute to near-term revenue.

Both the government and its industrial partners are developing processes to link research activities that support the military transformation

Figure 14–1. U.S. Defense Aerospace Industry Consolidation, 1980–1997

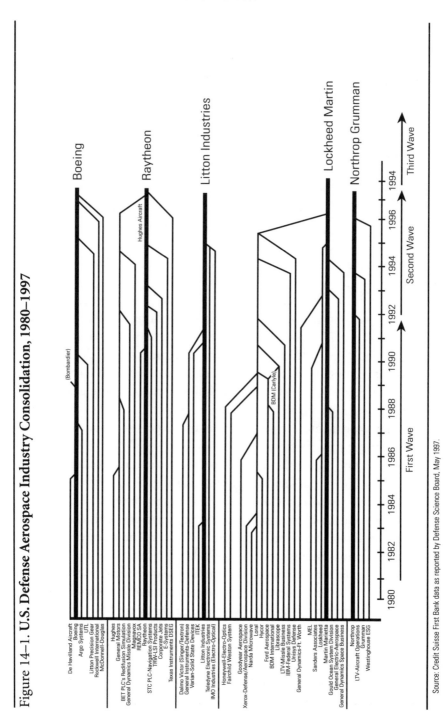

Source: Credit Suisse First Bank data as reported by Defense Science Board, May 1997.

process closely to the industrial base that will be required to manufacture the systems and provide them to the deployed forces.

## Rapid Fielding of New Technologies and Systems

During the 1990s, to provide a means for rapidly fielding new concepts, DOD and the services introduced several significant transition processes. In the early 1990s, Advanced Technology Demonstrations were introduced and managed by the individual services to identify and demonstrate technologies that showed great promise to serve urgent operational needs. In 1994, DOD introduced the Advanced Concept Technology Demonstrations (ACTD) program to "allow users to gain an understanding of proposed new capabilities for which there is no user experience base." The Joint Staff established Joint Experimentation Programs in 1998 to allow operational forces to experiment with novel technological advances to compress the time required to field advanced capabilities. This process provides a means of getting technological advances rapidly into the hands of the fighting forces, even before initiation of formal procurement actions. In addition, in the late 1990s, the Navy introduced the Future Naval Capabilities (FNC) program to link the research community and the operating forces. Both the Air Force and the Army are currently working on similar programs. At the policy level, the concepts of reconstitution, "develop and hold," and acquisition reform tended to dominate. Implementation and ramifications of some sort of reconstitution policy set the research agenda. How can the research infrastructure be shaped so that future military systems will retain an enduring technological edge even as the force structure and its supporting elements are being reduced? A proposed solution to this issue was a policy recommendation that the United States continue to develop advanced military systems, bringing them completely through the concept and development phase all the way up to the actual full-scale procurement phase. At this point, the program would be shelved and the system procurement package would await a future time when pressing operational requirements would necessitate actual procurement. This proposed develop-and-hold policy was the source of numerous debates. Neither the operational forces nor the research communities felt it was an optimum solution.

From these debates, a new policy issue emerged: How could the research infrastructure, needed as a foundation during some future reconstitution phase, be preserved if current requirements and budgets could not support its ongoing operations? The formal policy of encouraging and even mandating technology transfer to civilian uses emerged as the most promising solution to this issue. Under this scenario, government researchers would develop intellectual property that could be licensed to commercial enterprises in return for a stream of royalty payments made to the government research facility. The nonappropriated, privately secured royalties would be used to help maintain the research facility, supplementing the federally appropriated funds it normally receives for this purpose.

Over time, however, it appeared that depending on nondefense organizations to support the defense research infrastructure was not going to be a viable policy. Toward the end of the decade, acquisition reform took hold as the primary formal means of rapidly linking advanced research developments and emerging operational requirements. The acquisition process was to be transformed from a linear sequence—develop, procure, create operational doctrine, and train forces to use the system—to a nonlinear, concurrent process: develop system and doctrine together, procure, and train together. This was aimed at considerably compressing the time from concept identification to actual field operation.

## Acquisition Reform and Spiral Development

The private sector, driven by market forces, is arguably more efficient in the development, production, and sustainment of new products and systems. As such, the focus of early acquisition reform initiatives has been on the adoption of best commercial practices to reduce costs and improve the quality and sustainability of Department of Defense (DOD) weapons systems. For example, emphasis was placed on eliminating numerous unique military specifications and standards in favor of commercial specifications and standards. Other important commercially derived initiatives include the adoption of integrated process and product development, single process initiative, and performance-based specifications.

Each of these initiatives has reduced the costs of acquiring and sustaining weapons systems. However, lengthy cycle times—that is, the time from initiation of an acquisition program to initial operational capability—has continued to plague defense acquisition. Data taken on programs during the 1980s and 1990s indicate the average cycle time for large defense programs is slightly more than 11 years. Current programs such as the F–22 and Joint Strike Fighter are projected to exceed 15 years. Clearly, long cycle times are exacerbated by the highly complex nature of modern weapons systems such as the F–22. Cycle times are also negatively impacted by inefficient funding profiles that stretch development time. Largely, though, long cycle times are the result of the highly structured, risk-adverse DOD serial product development process of sequential developmental phases and milestones—the so-called DOD 5000 process. As such, a current focus of acquisition reform and the intent of the recent rewrite of the DOD 5000.1 and 5000.2 instructions is to establish a more flexible, streamlined process for the development of new weapons systems.

## Advanced Technology Demonstrations

In the early 1990s, the defense research community faced a difficult and unforeseen challenge. Basic and early applied research programs were being reduced in scope or eliminated just as they were reaching maturity. Many new research programs had been started or old ones enhanced during the strong defense buildup of the mid-1980s. By the early 1990s, many of these programs were at the point of fruition but had not yet fully matured when the programs they were meant to support were eliminated. The technology was still showing great promise, but program managers were hard-pressed to show how the fully developed technologies could transition into ongoing procurement programs. Without the ability to show a clear transition path, even very promising research programs were in danger of being canceled. To remedy this, the Advanced Technology Demonstration (ATD) process was established.

The purpose of the ATD process was to identify the most promising technological advancements being made in the ongoing research programs

The new product development process, known as spiral development or evolutionary acquisition, promises significantly shorter acquisition cycle times. The stated goal is to reduce cycle times by 50 percent or more. In a test of the new spiral development process, the Air Force has established an ambitious set of pilot programs with a stretch goal for a four to one reduction in cycle time. Assuming success in these pilot efforts, the warfighter will receive new weapons systems and capabilities in less than 3 years on average over the traditional 11-year cycle time average.

The key to the new spiral development process is the familiar 80–20 rule. That is, the user accomplishes 80 percent of the objective with 20 percent of the time and effort, the remaining 20 percent requiring the remaining 80 percent of the time and effort. In the context of product development, the acquisition community would strive to develop an 80-percent solution and field this new capability to the warfighter as rapidly as possible. As such, immature technologies are bypassed in favor of mature technologies, large software integration efforts are broken into core capabilities and advanced capability modules for later development, and growth is built into the initial design to accommodate subsequent or sequential product upgrades or production blocks. As the initial design or block is being refined and produced, parallel design and maturation efforts are begun for subsequent blocks. The riskier technologies are matured and advanced hardware and software are added in later production blocks. At the end of the full product development cycle, several related blocks of weapons systems might have been produced, each more advanced than the previous one—each advancing toward the ultimate user requirement first envisioned.

*—continued*

and to fund them fully (around $15 million) for 3 years in order to develop their potential on an extraordinary fast track. Each service allocated a percentage of its annual research budget to fund a few of the highest-priority ATDs. Each service also developed its own method for choosing which programs would be funded as ATDs, but all of them required a firm link between the researchers and potential users of the technology. Most programs funded under the ATD program had a program manager of an ongoing acquisition program who would commit both philosophically and fiscally to use the technology at the end of the ATD program if it lived up to its expectations.

Over the years, many successful transitions were made from ATDs to system procurements. For example, the Advanced Enclosed Mast/Sensor built by Ingalls Shipyard and installed on the Navy destroyer USS *Radford* at the Norfolk Naval Shipyard was developed as an ATD by the Naval Surface Warfare Center Carderock Division; it is currently specified for inclusion on all LPD–17 class ships.[5]

*—continued*

While the initial 80 percent product solution would not completely satisfy the full operational deficiency, it provides the warfighter a more immediate new capability closer to the desired solution than the current legacy equipment. This also allows the warfighter an opportunity to train and become familiar with employment, doctrine, support, and feedback lessons for incorporation in later blocks.

Spiral development allows production weapons systems to be fielded at more rapid and predictable intervals, each iteration more advanced than the previous spiral. One can clearly understand the notion of evolutionary acquisition as each successive iteration of the weapon system evolves from the initial product design to the final production block, which may require only two or many successive parasequential spirals.

Some may argue that this is merely a reapplication of the lessons of the 1970s and 1980s in which preplanned product improvement and F–16-style block production were common product development strategies. While there is some merit in these observations, the primary difference today in implementing spiral development is the clear motivation to reduce cycle time. In so doing, spiral development will also drive complementary changes in other segments of the product development process, such as a spiral requirements generation process and flexible training and support concepts to develop, field, and sustain new weapons systems more quickly.

—Lt Col Douglas Cook, USAF

Because of the instability of the overall defense procurement budgets, however, some ATDs that were successful as research programs were never fully integrated into procurement programs. Even in these cases, the ATD process proved useful. Researchers were encouraged to meet with acquisition program sponsors and operating forces to examine how advancements in technology could serve the needs of the operating forces. This alone went a long way to help reshape many research programs to be more responsive to emerging operational requirements, even if the proposed ATDs were not approved for funding.

Some limitations to the ATD process pointed to the need to reexamine its scope. Although the typical funding of $15 million was a large sum of money for some research programs, it became clear that the ATD process could not fully support advances in computer technology, communications, and data fusion and processing technologies as these grew during the 1990s. Meanwhile, commercial enterprises matured these technologies without defense sponsorship. DOD therefore began looking for ways to capture these new concepts and demonstrate their utility for defense-related requirements.

## Advanced Concept Technology Development

DOD introduced the ACTD program in early 1994 to help encourage and expedite the rapid transition of emerging matured technologies from researchers and developers to the operational users. Since the ACTD process focused on matured technologies, it emphasized technology assessment and integration over technology development. Nonetheless, it served as an interim step from the research lab to the operational field.

A typical ACTD lasts about 4 years and operates on a budget of approximately $100 million. Another significant feature of an ACTD is that, by definition, it has some level of jointness built into it. The concept that an ACTD is demonstrating must contribute to the mission of more than one service. Each of the participating services is required to partially fund the program with its own funds.

The goal of an ACTD is to provide operational commanders with actual prototypes of advanced systems that demonstrate unique military capabilities. Having prototypes gives the operational commanders a way to evaluate and indeed shape the potential system's ability to meet operational needs. It also allows commanders to develop and refine a concept of operations to exploit the capability under evaluation. As the operating forces gain experience and understanding of the capability through realistic military demonstrations of prototype systems, they are better able to assess the military efficacy of the proposed capability.

A number of successful capabilities have been evaluated and shaped through the ACTD process. The medium-altitude endurance unmanned aerial vehicle, Predator, was one of the earliest ACTDs to be funded. It was flown and operated in Bosnia even before the ACTD was over, and it has been used extensively in Afghanistan during Operation *Enduring Freedom*. It has since transitioned into a mainstream acquisition program.

The ACTD process has proven quite effective at identifying emerging technological capabilities with high potential operational application. It gives the services an opportunity to test an application before buying it. In the environment of very rapidly changing technology advancements, however, the process can seem slow; one must first build a prototype system, deploy it to the field, develop concepts of operation for its use, conduct operations with the system, and then evaluate its military effectiveness. By the time this process has been completed, it may be difficult and expensive to modify the system to take advantage of the knowledge gained during the demonstration phase.

## Joint Experimentation Program

Toward the end of the decade, the Joint Staff introduced the Joint Experimentation program. The purpose of joint experimentation is to examine new technologies, operational concepts, and force structure (organization) options together rather than in isolation from one another to discover and develop advances in warfighting capabilities. Joint experimentation allows warfighters access to new technologies before systems utilizing them are fully developed. In this way, operational commanders can assess the utility of emerging technologies and modify the technological developments early in the development process so that they will be more useful to the operating forces.

The Joint Experimentation Office (J–9) was established in Norfolk, Virginia, to manage the program. It gives the research community a new way to link closely with the operational forces. Concepts identified in the research lab can be introduced into the joint experimentation process even before they are fully developed. This allows the researcher to understand whether the concept is worth pursuing from a military perspective, and, if it is, which aspects should be emphasized. In addition, it allows the operating forces to see developments in the research lab long before they are available for field use. This gives forces the opportunity to begin developing doctrine and training programs while the concept is still being developed.

It also allows the operational forces to have more direct input into the direction that research programs will take.

All three of these technology transition processes have helped both the researchers and the operational forces link to focus their efforts and set priorities for the use of scarce research budgets. They are only really effective at advancing operational capabilities if they are closely linked to the acquisition and procurement process. If great new technologies and capabilities are identified and developed but not procured and fielded, the operational forces cannot take advantage of their capabilities.

## Acquisition Reform

Throughout the past decade, acquisition reform has changed the way DOD procures and fields new systems. Technology was improving so rapidly that the traditional acquisition process could not keep pace. New platforms and systems were being delivered with technology that was obsolete, expensive to operate, and difficult to maintain. Utilization of commercial off-the-shelf components made defense systems more dependent on commercial spare parts inventories, and when commercial companies changed their products, defense systems were no longer supportable. To compress the time from approval of an acquisition program to fielding of the operational system and thus speed the time for development, new initiatives were introduced into the acquisition process.

Under the traditional acquisition process, systems were procured in a sequence. First research was done, then the engineering completed, then the system went into production, and finally the system was evaluated by the operating forces and integrated into operational capabilities. This process was useful when the technology being integrated into new systems had not yet matured because it ensured that only fully developed technologies were embedded into new systems. However, as ATDs and ACTDs as well as commercial technological advancements began to yield new concepts faster than the traditional process could accommodate them, a new process of concurrent development had to be introduced.

Utilizing concurrent development, integrated engineering (supported by ongoing research) and production occurred simultaneously. Like the traditional process, the introduction into operational doctrine and training programs took place after the system was placed in the field. Although this speeded up the process, operational forces had few feedback loops to the developers to help shape the systems to the operators' needs. This process did, however, allow the efficient integration of ATDs and ACTDs into the acquisition process.

After the Joint Experimentation program was introduced, the acquisition process was modified to allow for direct transition from ATDs and ACTDs into production, coupled closely with user input throughout the process. Utilizing an experimentation-demonstration-acquisition process, integrated engineering (supported by ongoing research) and operational evaluation occur simultaneously. Only after the system is refined through the interaction of both the users and the developers is it put into production. Production runs are scheduled and the system is designed so that the latest technology can be integrated into the system during each succeeding run. This methodology links the researchers, developers, and users as never before.

### Future Naval Capabilities

In the late 1990s, the Navy introduced a new process for closely coupling its research activity with the requirements of its operating forces. Supporting all of the ongoing research activities at levels high enough to ensure that significant progress could be achieved in time to influence high-priority naval requirements was impossible with the limited research resources available. To direct its scarce resources, the Navy established the Future Naval Capabilities program.

Senior leadership of both the research and the operations communities meet to establish several specific research priorities. This priority-setting process enables the Navy to focus its resources and attention on significant projects. The close coupling of the research and operations community ensures that the research directly supports emerging operational requirements and the Navy transformation process.

The Army, through its Future Combat System focus, and the Air Force, through its Lightning Bolts and Agile Acquisition initiatives, are currently employing comparable priority-setting procedures within their research communities.

### Acquisition Strategy and Research and Development

Many platform acquisition programs are experimenting with practices derived from private industry, delegating the jobs of developing, identifying, and specifying advanced technological solutions to the prime contractor. Rather than specifying the details of platform procurement, the government sets the performance specification and asks the prime vendor to deliver a platform that performs as requested. Private industry uses this process as the primary means of acquisition, paying the vendor only after the product is tested and delivered. In contrast, the government usually pays the vendor progress payments, so that by the end of the procurement, the vendor has been paid 90 percent of the cost of the item. Under this practice, the government assumes the risk of, but does not have the same level of control over, the internal decisions.

An attribute of the new acquisition strategy is that the government assigns the role of product and process development, including the supporting research, to the prime vendor. Research funds that in the past were provided to in-house government research laboratories are now given directly to the prime vendors. This process has both positive and negative attributes.

Directly funding the prime vendors assures a very close coupling of the research with product development. It enables the prime vendor to have full control of the research priorities and ensures that the research is focused on current requirements. In contrast, when government labs perform research without prime vendor interaction, the coupling between the progress and results of the research and the needs of the prime vendor may be weak. Differences in management structures have meant that research and production schedules are not always synchronized as well as they could be.

Direct funding of research by vendors also produces a few areas of concern for defense research. Three issues include technology migration to other programs, strategic integration across services, and long-term technological stewardship.

When research is conducted in a government facility, the results of that research usually are available to any government program that can utilize them. In contrast, the results of research conducted in a private facility utilizing program-specific funding may not be available to competing programs or vendors. In fact, the results may not even be made public; complementing programs might not know they exist. This secrecy has the effect of limiting and constraining technology migration that might otherwise accrue to government-funded research.

In the same vein, funding vendors for program-specific research may complicate government efforts to rationalize and prioritize its research programs across all of the military services. Coordinating research programs among the Army, Navy, and Air Force enables all of the services to take advantage of advanced technologies developed by any one of them. To keep the close contact across the services that this type of coordination requires, new management processes will need to be established that recognize the vendors' role in research priority-setting.

DOD and the services' in-house research laboratories have traditionally been the long-term stewards of the technological disciplines associated with their missions. In between major acquisitions programs, in-house laboratories keep a workforce current with the latest techniques and processes so that when the next program begins, the research does not need to start again. Research is a continuous process, requiring continuity of knowledge, processes, and techniques—and of personnel and the mentor-apprenticeship relationship discussed above. If each new research program is placed at a different facility, based solely on the identity of the prime contractor of a major acquisition program, this continuity will be broken.

### Diminished Paths for Transition

The defense drawdown associated with the end of the Cold War decreased the number of platforms being developed. As a result, there are fewer sponsors of platform-associated research and fewer transition paths for research results to migrate. A typical measure of the effectiveness of a research establishment is how well it contributes to new products. If only one ship is being designed at any one time and a number of organizations are developing new technologies for ships, most of the new concepts will not be integrated into that new class of ship because of scheduling and cost constraints. Thus, utilizing traditional metrics, many of the research programs will be deemed failures due to their inability to transition to production in the near term, even if they have made great scientific or technological discoveries. This stigmatization is an artifact of the different timelines associated with research and acquisition.

Research operates in an extended timeframe. Discoveries made today may not be utilized for decades, until some other enabling development allows their potential to be fully exploited. But, when new findings are finally incorporated, they may enable profound advancements in the final products into which they are imbedded.

Acquisition programs, on the other hand, operate over relatively shorter time periods. A research program that cannot provide results in time to meet the acquisition program's tight development schedule will not be utilized in that program. Since, by definition, research discoveries cannot be guaranteed to meet a production schedule, most of the research must be accomplished before the acquisition program needs the results. Often, the basic research must be completed before the acquisition program begins so that the technology developed by the research program can be integrated into a new product.

The effect of these different timeframes, coupled with the policy of assigning the research role to the prime vendors, yields another area of concern in the ability of the research establishment to support the ongoing defense transformation. If prime vendors of major acquisition programs are also the primary performers of defense research, new processes will need to be established to ensure continuity of research during the period between acquisition programs. In addition, new processes will need to be established to ensure that the results of government-funded research are made available to all users, not just the single prime vendor who performs the research.

While some acquisition programs use direct-vendor funding of research, the practice is not ubiquitous. In many situations, both government in-house laboratories and prime-vendor facilities are performing complementary research. A mix of government, private, and university research is the result. Balancing these to support the transformation of the services is the major challenge of the near future.

### Business Model

While the defense acquisition community is working to ensure that its research establishment is shaped and focused to support the military transformation process, private nondefense high-technology companies are also reexamining their research processes. A primary focus is on rationalizing the "make-versus-buy" decision. Many of the largest and most successful industrial companies, such as RCA and Xerox, have begun divesting themselves of their in-house dedicated research laboratories, while others such as IBM and General Electric continue to support and depend on their world-renowned in-house research facilities.

In fast-growing industries, especially the electronics industry, large corporations are increasingly looking outside their walls for new products and processes to offer their customers. For example, other companies initially developed many of the products that are now in Microsoft's inventory. Like almost all high-tech companies, Microsoft has a staff whose mission is to search the outside world and identify products, processes, services, and companies that complement their product line. When they find something they like, they purchase the rights to use it in Microsoft's inventory; in some cases, Microsoft purchases the whole company to get access to the new technology. Many opportunities exist for DOD to use this practice to satisfy its technology requirements by looking to independent entrepreneurs and nondefense-related industries for already developed advanced technologies.

## Policy Options

Successful transformation of the military to a knowledge-based force structure requires new operational concepts, new equipment to support them, and new training processes to integrate the operational concepts and advanced equipment with the fighting forces. Maintaining the technological lead in the U.S. military means that all three factors—concepts, equipment, and training—must be on the forward edge of technology. Force planners and concept generators must understand what advanced technology solutions can offer, while technologists must comprehend the requirements of emerging operational concepts. Both force planners and technologists need to work with the force trainers to ensure that the fighting forces know how to carry out the advanced operational concepts using advanced equipment suites.

Continuously integrating advanced operational concepts supported by the most advanced technological equipment into U.S. fighting forces is key to sustaining their competitive advantage. Over the past 50 years, the United States has developed a research and technology infrastructure to nurture and sustain advanced technological development related to the military mission. Many processes were developed to enhance the efficiency of technological transition from the lab to the fighting forces. This is a continuous process that evolves with the changing environment.

The most important issue in the current environment, from the technological perspective, is ensuring that forces have operational concepts that enable them to perform their mission and that they have the equipment that most efficiently supports their needs. A fighting unit in the heat of battle does not care who invented the technology they are using or who perfected its integration into warfighting equipment—only that they have it, it works, and they know how to use it.

In light of all of the issues and obstacles described in this chapter, it is the responsibility of both the operating and the technology communities to develop processes and procedures aimed at supporting future operations efficiently. Technologists from all different environments must participate. In-house government research labs must identify and integrate advanced technological concepts into advanced fighting equipment to support advanced operational concepts. Universities and other private research organizations participate by conducting the basic-level scientific research from which advanced technological solutions to emerging problems could be developed. Defense contractors take part in developing and incorporating advanced technological concepts into the weapons and platform systems they design and build. Nondefense industrial enterprises have a role to play in inventing and developing advanced technological concepts that, even while supporting their own industries, can be carried over to serve defense requirements.

Although many of the policies and processes currently in place remain important and serve to manage the technological integration process, a few improvements should be considered, especially in the areas of workforce stability and integration, as well as technology identification and integration.

### Workforce Stability and Integration

The defense community is facing a crisis concerning its technological workforce as a result of the salary disparity with nondefense private industry and previous hiring patterns. Many senior technologists may leave defense service in the near future, and the mentor-apprentice chain will be broken. The government can do a few things about this.[6] Many initiatives related to pay levels and monetary incentives are under consideration already. Supporting these incentives alone is not sufficient.

In light of the new environment in which prime vendors are increasingly being assigned more responsibilities with respect to technological development and integration, the government should institute processes that foster mentor-apprenticeships across organizational boundaries. For example, junior engineers and scientists employed by government research labs should be assigned as apprentices to senior technologists and developers employed by prime vendors. Employees of prime vendors should be placed as interns and fellows at government or university facilities.

During periods of intense activity in an acquisition program, technologists from government laboratories should be routinely called upon to support the prime vendors. During periods of slack activity between acquisition programs, technologists from the defense industry should be asked to support research at the government laboratories. These processes will ensure that technologists on all sides of the partnership are current and that technology flows freely across organizational boundaries.

### Technology Identification and Integration

Although the existing research and technology infrastructure will remain an important element in the future, new processes must also be developed for rapid identification of technological advances taking place outside of the defense industry that could support advanced operational concepts being developed by the military. Better mechanisms are needed for acquiring and integrating these technological advances into operational concepts. For example, the advances in communications technologies and in power systems (batteries) are taking place rapidly, but U.S. troops sometimes miss the opportunity to use them because the acquisition process can be so cumbersome. Programs such as ACTD and the Joint Experimentation program were developed to help alleviate this problem, but neither of these is a direct acquisition process; both of them are "research" programs.

The government should create a direct acquisition process under which "technology spotters" identify products developed in the commercial marketplace, procure them, and integrate them directly into field use. The acquisition funds could continue to be managed by the individual services in accordance with Title 10 rules, but direct linkages would be established between the technology acquisition team and the operating units. This process would not work in every situation; for example, with major platform procurements, the full acquisition and testing processes will always be necessary. However, in a world of rapid technological advancement and standardization, many new products, especially at the subsystem level, could be simply purchased and used immediately in the field.

## Conclusions

In a December 11, 2001, speech to the students at The Citadel in Charleston, South Carolina, 3 months after the attacks on the World Trade Center and the Pentagon, President George W. Bush said:

> While the threats to America have changed, the need for victory has not. We are fighting shadowy, entrenched enemies—enemies using the tools of terror and guerrilla war—yet we are finding new tactics and new weapons to attack and defeat them. This revolution in our military is only beginning, and it promises to change the face of battle.... The Predator is a good example. This unmanned aerial vehicle is able to circle over enemy forces, gather intelligence, transmit information instantly back to commanders, then fire on targets with extreme accuracy. Before the war, the Predator had skeptics, because it did not fit the old ways. Now it is clear the military does not have enough unmanned vehicles.... What's different today is our sense of urgency—the need to build this future force while fighting a present war. It's like overhauling an engine while you're going at 80 miles an hour. Yet we have no other choice.

Advanced technological development by itself is clearly not sufficient to ensure a successful military transformation. Coupled with advances in doctrine, strategy, tactics, and training, however, advanced technology is a significant force multiplier.[7] Maintaining our technological lead in the future will be critical to the operations of our fighting forces. Technologists, operators, and acquisition specialists together can create and implement the policies so vital to ensuring this critical requirement.

## Notes

[1] Irvin Stewart, *Organizing Scientific Research for War* (Boston: Little, Brown and Company, 1948).

[2] Grant Eldridge, ed., *Government Research Center Directory* (Detroit: Gale Group, 2001).

[3] Peter D. Dresser, ed., *Scientific and Technical Organizations and Agencies Directory*, 3rd ed. (Detroit: Gale Group, 1994).

[4] Research, Development, Test, and Evaluation Budget; 2002 Defense Appropriations Bill.

[5] James D. Hessman et al., "Ingalls Delivers Navy's First AEM/S Composite Mast," *Sea Power* 40, no. 6 (June 1997).

[6] David S.C. Chu and John P. White, "Ensuring Quality People in Defense," in Ashton B. Carter and John P. White, *Keeping the Edge: Managing Defense for the Future* (Cambridge, MA: Massachusetts Institute of Technology Press, 2001).

[7] Edward Rhodes, Jonathan DiCicco, Sarah Milburn Moore, and Tom Walker, "Forward Presence and Engagement: Historical Insights into the Problem of 'Shaping,'" *Naval War College Review* (Winter 2000).

# Chapter 15

# Getting There: Focused Logistics

Paul M. Needham

T he search for new military strategies necessitates the transformation of the logistics processes and organizations that support the current military structure. We begin this chapter by examining the logistics transformation process, reviewing various definitions of logistics (especially those used by the Department of Defense and Joint Staff). Each definition places emphasis on a specific reason for logistics processes and organizations to exist.

Next, we look at *Joint Vision 2010* Focused Logistics and *Joint Vision 2020* Focused Logistics to examine the direction that the Joint Staff is pursuing in linking logistics and operational concepts. We look at the process of generating military power by considering logistics organizations in the Department of Defense (DOD), the services, the Defense Logistics Agency (DLA), and the Office of the Secretary of Defense (OSD) to identify the logistics initiatives that these organizations are pursuing and the potential impact on operational capability. We then analyze the two fundamental processes of projecting and sustaining military power. Finally, we briefly discuss some vulnerabilities related to focused logistics.

## Definitions

To define *logistics*, we focus first on the DOD dictionary:

The science of planning and carrying out the movement and maintenance of forces. In its most comprehensive sense, those aspects of military operations which deal with:

- design and development, acquisition, storage, movement, distribution, maintenance, evacuation, and disposition of material
- movement, evacuation, and hospitalization of personnel

- acquisition or construction, maintenance, operation, and disposition of facilities
- acquisition or furnishing of services.[1]

This definition both highlights the movement and maintenance of forces and identifies a comprehensive systems approach to logistics.

The Joint Staff defines logistics as "the process of planning and executing the movement and sustainment of operating forces in the execution of a military strategy and operations."[2] This definition directs our attention to a process approach to logistics.

A third definition comes from the civilian realm. The Council of Logistics Management (CLM) states that "logistics is that part of the supply chain process that plans, implements, and controls the efficient, effective flow and storage of goods, services, and related information from the point of origin to the point of consumption in order to meet customers' requirements."[3]

The range of DOD logistics responsibilities includes those identified by the CLM definition, planning and controlling the "efficient and effective" flow of goods, services, and related information to meet customers' requirements. In addition, DOD logistics operations concern the repair of capital assets, such as aircraft, tanks, vehicles, engines, and avionics boxes. DOD logistics also includes design, development, acquisition, inventory responsibilities of storage and distribution, reverse logistics (return of items), and disposal. DOD logistics responsibilities include building and obtaining infrastructure; obtaining services; and movement, evacuation, and hospitalization of personnel.

Thus, the range of DOD logistics responsibilities far exceeds the traditional logistics responsibilities in commercial firms. However, if we consider the CLM definition—planning, implementing, and controlling "efficient, effective" flow and storage of goods, services, and related information from point of origin to point of consumption based on the customers' needs—the military finds much in common with the civilian definition. Recognition of the similarities in the processes, and the need to support customers efficiently and effectively, has led DOD and the services to examine the military logistics processes and organization thoroughly. DOD has a strong incentive to adopt and adapt the best business logistics practices.

Logistics transformation is essential to the defense transformation efforts that have been labeled the revolution in military affairs (RMA). The RMA new operational concepts all demand improved logistics. These include joint response strike forces, enhanced information networking, accelerated deployment of missile defenses, realigned overseas presence and swifter power projection, interoperable allied forces, maritime littoral operations, standoff targeting, forcible entry, enhanced tactical deep strikes, and decisive close combat operations.[4] The logistical support processes and current logistics organizational structure must be transformed to support these new, flexible military operations.

### *Joint Vision 2020:* Focused Logistics

Transformation of military doctrine, strategic and operational concepts, and logistics processes began with the reviews that took place after Operations *Desert Shield* and *Desert Storm*. The Joint Staff, in 1996, published its vision of the direction the military should focus on for the future in *Joint Vision 2010* (*JV 2010*). The tenets of *JV 2010* were primarily directed toward the operational capability of forces and called for the capabilities of dominant maneuver, precision engagement, information superiority, and force protection, as well as focused logistics.[5]

*Joint Vision 2010* was followed by *Joint Vision 2020*, which takes the Focused Logistics goal of *JV 2010* and continues the implementation actions it began. Focused logistics is intended to refocus the services and the commanders in chief (CINCs) toward reducing forward inventories to a minimal amount ("reduced footprint") and relying instead on consistent resupply. The idea of reduced footprint is intended to apply not only to inventory but also to other support systems, such as hospitals. This reliance on transportation and throughput requires careful analysis, confidence on the part of the CINC, and continued access to ports.

Focused logistics is more, however, than a "reduced footprint." *JV 2020* identified six elements of the focused logistics program:

- Joint Deployment/Rapid Distribution
- Multinational Logistics
- Agile Infrastructure
- Force Health Protection
- Information Fusion
- Joint Theater Logistics Command and Control ($C^2$).

These six program initiatives are leading to significant transformation of logistics processes.

Improvements within the deployment and distribution arena are being pursued by the U.S. Transportation Command (USTRANSCOM), the Defense Logistics Agency, and the services. Under the Multinational Logistics program, planners must consider what is available in the location to which American forces will deploy. Agile Infrastructure is aimed at changing from a presumption that DOD must build and own the infrastructure to the expectation that it can lease infrastructure or use it temporarily. Force Health Protection is aimed at improving healthcare while reducing the support forces needed in a forward location. Information Fusion and Joint Theater Logistics $C^2$ are information programs aimed at providing visibility of the inventory, transportation, and material management. Two enabling programs, the Joint Total Asset Visibility program and the In-transit Visibility program, are aimed at providing reliable data to decisionmakers and reducing the total cost, while continuing to provide effective support. Focused logistics is transforming the way in which logisticians plan to support warfighters and provide them with flexible options for military operations.

Recognizing that it needed to streamline logistics processes and logistics systems, DOD looked to business for models. Businesses had begun close examination of logistics processes to decrease costs, increase profits, and improve customer service. In doing so, they found that these objectives were not mutually exclusive. Improving logistics systems—that is, inventory, order processing, transportation, warehousing, and distribution networks—improved their bottom line: profit.

Changes in the logistical processes of firms originate from the application of various theoretical constructs. These included the inventory-transportation paradigm, which makes tradeoffs between inventory and expedited transportation; the postponement principle, which delays the final form or assembly; the speculation principle, which attempts to anticipate demand; substitution, which allows the use of other components; adoption of "lean" manufacturing, which reduces work-in-progress; just-in-time and time-definite delivery; and application of information technology to logistics processes. Although these constructs fit in the category of logistics tradecraft, each construct affects the firm's entire strategy. These principles are now being applied to military transformation.

## Organization

DOD created various organizations to provide support for both combatant commands and administrative commands. The Unified Command Plan creates various geographical and unified combatant commands. The administrative lines are formed by the Title 10 responsibilities of the services—the Army, Navy, and Air Force—to organize, train, and equip their forces.[6] This requirement leads the services to create organizations that support the forces; both the forces and their supporting organizations are assigned to the warfighting CINCs.

The services follow a straightforward paradigm in creating combat forces. First, they identify the tasks that the forces must accomplish. Then, the services develop doctrine as to the best way of accomplishing tasks. The services train and experiment to test doctrine and strategy and make changes as needed. These changes can significantly affect logistics requirements.

External changes also can change logistics requirements significantly. For example, improvements in microcircuitry can result in an improvement in reliability of avionics systems. A ten-fold increase in reliability reduces the frequency of repair and calibration; this ripples through the logistics organization to result in fewer maintenance technicians, fewer sets of repair equipment, and less equipment, repair parts, and people to deploy.[7]

The need to repair parts and systems to balance operational use rate and investment in spare parts has decreased because of improved reliability. The impact of improved reliability on the organization is seen in the reduction and elimination of intermediate-repair capability at the unit level. The ripple effect of this is geographic centralization of repair, the reduction in manpower (for example, repair technicians and warehouse workers), and an increase in transportation (in the return logistics channel for repair and overhaul).

This cascading effect of technological change and the impact on logistics functions requires a continuing review of the organizational structure that provides logistical support to warfighters. The organizational change as a result of improving reliability has a secondary benefit of reducing the need for deploying large numbers of repair technicians and equipment. We will look at how each service has responded to these changes.

### Navy

The Navy, like the other services, has seen improvements in reliability of its weapon systems, with a cascading impact on its repair parts requirements and manpower reductions. However, the operational demands on logistics systems have changed little since the mission of the Navy—power projection and protection of sea lines of communication—has not changed.

Improvements in reliability and transportation have, however, allowed the Navy to focus on reducing its large inventory of spare parts and the large infrastructure of land- and sea-based repair facilities and ships. The Navy has seen organizational changes as repair and storage of parts have become more centralized. These changes in the shore environment have included the consolidation of fleet support centers, maintenance depots, and both shipbuilding and repair facilities. Under the DOD Strategic Logistics Plan 2001, the Navy has just one inventory control point (Naval Supply Systems Command) from which it is able to manage all unique or Navy-assigned items with the use of modern information technologies. The Navy Sea Systems Command manages three depot maintenance centers and two Trident submarine repair facilities. The Naval Air Systems Command manages three aviation repair depots. The overhead for the Navy's material management and repair capability is spread over three separate commands. In addition to this decentralized organizational structure for material management, the Navy has additional organizations for intermediate-level repair for the fleets.

The Navy's combat logistics system that supports ships and battlegroups at sea has also been changed as a result of improvements in reliability, the reduction in the total number of ships, and improvements in transportation. The Navy has reduced the number of logistics ships (ammunition and stores ships) and the number of tenders (repair ships). To provide the necessary support, the Navy has turned to refueling in various ports, taking on provisions during these port visits, and applying common business practices of buying commercial off-the-shelf instead of acquiring customized, purpose-built matériel for all its needs.

The Navy has implemented a program called High Yield Logistics. The goal of this program is to optimize available funds through best value, customer support and communication, process innovation, and workforce productivity.[8] The objectives of the program are to "provide extraordinary support to the warfighter, strategically source support inventory, infrastructure, maintenance, and service functions and to optimize the resources the Navy keeps to increase effectiveness and reduce redundancy within the remaining infrastructure." The Navy plans to create a one-touch system using the Internet for access to the Navy and DOD inventory control system at all customer service points. A Navy-Marine Corps intranet is being established to create a central information system that will eventually replace 200 separate Navy and Marine computer systems.

Reliability improvements are allowing some organizational realignment within the Navy, but the service is retaining much of the organizational overhead that was previously needed for a much larger support structure. Thus, there is a need to continue transforming the logistics structure.

## Marine Corps

The Marine Corps has begun several initiatives to improve and speed logistics processes. These initiatives center on the need for an integrated logistics system and a centralized organization to focus and manage the various logistics systems. A third initiative is aimed at creating a cadre of officers who are exposed to the best current logistics practices in industry and the best current applied logistics research. As with the Navy, the thrust of these initiatives is to improve the effectiveness of the combat forces and create the efficiencies found in the best-run commercial organizations.

The Corps' Integrated Logistics Capability initiative is aimed at examining a total program—from development to disposal—for the best total-cost solution to logistics. This initiative recognizes the inherent relationship among such qualities as reliability, maintainability, availability, and serviceability. In the acquisition logistics arena, for example, these relationships are expressed as mean-time-between-failures, which helps determine the number of anticipated replacement parts that must be acquired. The mean-time-to-repair is a measure of the degree of maintainability associated with a system. Balancing these product characteristics, along with transportation-inventory trade-offs, helps to define the logistics support structure required for different systems. The Marine Corps seeks to balance these characteristics to maximize effective operational support.

The Corps has created a single organization to focus on the life cycle of the product—its equipment and matériel—from design to production to support to disposal. The newly established Marine Corps Matériel Command will be the single point within the Corps to evaluate operational requirements, field solutions (systems) to satisfy the requirements, and (perhaps from a logistics viewpoint most important) to sustain the system through to disposal. This command will operate in a manner similar to the existing Air Force Materiel Command and the Army Materiel Command; it will be a single organization responsible for all materiel used by the operating force.

The Marine Corps has partnered with academia and industry to ensure that its officers are exposed to innovative commercial practices. The benefit will be seen in more effective and efficient Marine Corps support to the operational forces. As the Marine Corps develops new operational concepts, the logistics officers will be able to design optimal logistics systems to support the forces.

## Air Force

The current Air Force logistics organizational structure was defined by the Air Force to support its operations structure. Its centralized supply and maintenance concept centered on the Air Force's need for a main base with a runway. The fact that the runway is in a fixed location dictated the operational structure and allowed the logistics organization to be centralized. This allowed certain economies of scale.

The Air Force has now begun changing its organizational structure to decentralize maintenance and supply to individual operating squadrons. Air Force doctrine has changed to reflect the post-Cold War need for deployable units. The new Expeditionary Air Forces now have supply and maintenance personnel as integral parts of the squadrons. This new squadron structure with integrated maintenance and supply personnel is similar to the structure found in Navy units. The changes are intended to improve operational effectiveness and flexibility and create efficiencies based on reliability improvements.

The Air Force has initiated several programs to improve logistics support to operational units, known as Agile Logistics, Logistics Transformation, and Product Support Strategy. Although these programs are aimed at improving the efficiency and effectiveness of support, they also create opportunities to alter operational deployment and support strategies.

The Agile Logistics program is an adaptation of the lean logistics concept that reduces the amount of inventory maintained. This program intends to use time-definite transportation and real-time information to reduce inventory levels at centralized storage locations and to allow deployment and support of units with fewer parts. A goal is to reduce the forward support footprint by 50 percent.[9] Agile Logistics will allow operational concepts to be considered without the extensive "logistics tail" seen in the past. Reliability improvements, transportation enhancements, and support-organization changes are enablers of the Agile Logistics program.

The Air Force also is embarking on a Logistics Transformation program. The goal of the program is to transform the focus from providing massive support to large, forward-deployed units to, instead, mobile precision support for smaller deployable operational units. Several key concepts of the program are "time-definite delivery; time-definite resupply; effective command and control; theater 'reachback' to [the continental United States (CONUS)] logistics centers; and the use of integrated, state-of-the-art information systems to source, acquire, and transport items directly to the warfighter."[10] The desired effect of this logistics transformation program is to make logistics support more effective and efficient while capitalizing on technological and other changes in the transportation industry, the use of new information technologies, and improved reliability.

The third new Air Force logistics initiative is a new Product Support Strategy. This strategy is based on the need for comprehensive management of products (weapon systems) from design to production to support to disposal. The Air Force plans to have a single product manager who will be responsible for the product throughout its life cycle. This initiative aims at incorporating "best business practices" such as a prime (single) support integrator, long-term business relationships, use of commercial standards, partnering, developing service-oriented, performance-based agreements between suppliers and warfighters, and emphasizing long-term continuous improvements.

### Army

The Army has made similar organizational changes for almost the same reasons. Reliability of equipment has allowed the reduction of the intermediate-level logistics organizations required to repair equipment. Reliability improvements, increases in transportation availability, and improved speed of repair have contributed to the changes. The Army has initiated several logistics initiatives, identified in the DOD Strategic Logistics Plan 2001 as Velocity Management, the Single Stock Fund, and the Wholesale Logistics Modernization Program.[11]

The Wholesale Logistics Modernization Program is intended to develop an enterprise resource planning service for the Army to replace the legacy systems that it uses to manage maintenance and supply. The Army's Velocity Management program is one of its initiatives to improve processes and transform the logistics system.

Velocity Management is the Army program to examine the full range of product development and support in order to analyze and redesign the logistics system to leverage improvements in reliability, transportation, and information. It is based upon recognition that rapid material movement allows the commercial business sector to reduce inventory and improve customer service levels. Business logistics transformation resulted in applying rapid transportation and information rather than keeping large inventories (the information/inventory tradeoff). The reliability improvements now engineered into equipment result in fewer failures, longer periods between major repairs, and greater assurance that the equipment will function as expected. In the past, multiechelon maintenance organizations (unit, intermediate, and depot) were established to take advantage of

economies of scale and investments in inventory, maintenance technicians, repair equipment, and transportation. Improved reliability has reduced the need for intermediate-level maintenance. Tradeoffs in terms of
manpower, deployment requirements (people and equipment), and cost
(dollars) reduce deployment requirements while retaining required effectiveness. The new logistics structure incorporates a unit-level organizational structure that focuses on remove-and-replace forward maintenance;
intermediate and depot-level repairs are done at a centralized facility. To
reap all of the benefits of Velocity Management, the Army objective is to
substitute velocity of material movements for inventory investments.

The Velocity Management program also aims to "reduce processing
times for repairs, financial management, and determination of inventory
requirements, procurement, transportation, and financial management."
The Army's own internal management processes have been partially responsible for the large, bulky logistics systems that existed. Over the years,
each level of the organization developed to respond to various management directions that the Army or other agencies have imposed. The combinations of reliability improvements and process reengineering allow
significant organizational changes that should result in a leaner, lighter,
more mobile Army.

The Single Stock Fund is an initiative to improve the logistics and financial processes of the Army's Working Capital Fund. This initiative
merges the retail (local) and wholesale processes into a single, centrally
managed fund. The purpose of the initiative is to bring better financial accounting procedures and logistics functions together.

### Defense Logistics Agency

Another major organization within DOD also has logistics responsibility: the Defense Logistics Agency, which was established originally to
act as a wholesaler for DOD. Its purpose has changed over the years with
various defense management reform actions; it is now responsible for 94
percent of the consumable items managed within DOD, all of the distribution centers within DOD, and the processing of 88 percent of all
material requisitions. DLA is transforming itself through three initiatives: DLA 21, Strategic Sourcing, and Business Systems Modernization.

The DLA 21 transformation initiative is a broad, integrated plan for
DLA to provide "essential military logistics support for the 21st century
warfighter." This plan focuses on "organizational redesign, modernization
of automated business systems, employment of strategic partnerships with
industry, better knowledge and understanding of customer (warfighter)

needs, and replenishment and development of a world-class workforce."[12] Each segment of the plan creates a more flexible and responsive organization with a customer-focus orientation.

The organizational redesign has focused on streamlining DLA. The new Logistics Operations organization is intended to focus on supply-chain management, readiness, and contingency operations support. An Information Operations organization has been created to integrate information technology and electronic business practices. A Financial Operations organization has been created to centralize and streamline financial systems for DLA and the interfaces with the Defense Financial and Accounting Service. The Human Resources department has been created to develop and maintain the workforce. These organizational changes reflect a major effort to transform DLA from a large bulk provider to the "provider of choice."

The DLA Strategic Sourcing Initiative is aimed at creating and maintaining supply-chain relationships with key suppliers. DLA is attempting to create the types of partnerships with producers that are successful in business, such as sharing information in exchange for lower total price commitments. DOD is attempting to create a win-win situation for itself and the producers of materials. Within this initiative are several DLA initiatives—including Prime Vendor, Virtual Prime Vendor, and Direct Vendor Delivery—that seek to incorporate "best business practices" into DLA operations.

### Deployment Issues

U.S. military strategy calls for significant military power to be forward deployed. The operational side of DOD is currently organized into geographic regions and functional areas. The geographic regional commanders are assigned forces for daily operations and forces for contingency planning purposes. The functional commanders are assigned specific functional areas to operate in and provide support to the geographic commanders. These include space, transportation, strategic, and special operations. These functional commanders are assigned forces for daily operations and forces for various other levels of increased activity. Of specific interest in logistics transformation is the U.S. Transportation Command because of the service that it provides to the services and the CINCs.

USTRANSCOM is in the process of transforming itself to provide better, more integrated transportation service to the warfighters. Three transformation initiatives have been started: Reinvention CINC; Defense Transportation System Enterprise Architecture; and Strategic Distribution

Management Initiative. These initiatives are aimed at improving the deployment ability and sustainment ability for the geographic CINCs.

The Reinvention CINC initiative started when Secretary of Defense William Cohen tasked the Commander in Chief, U.S. Transportation Command (USCINCTRANS), to "emulate the best business practices of private industry."[13] The areas that the USCINCTRANS chose to focus on are financial controls, organizational controls, and process controls. USTRANSCOM operates with a revolving-fund financial system similar to that used by DLA. The system basically requires the command to charge its customers (warfighters) for their transportation. Customers request funds for transportation and then use their operating accounts to buy from and pay USTRANSCOM for the service. The method of financing the operations creates the need for change. This transformation effort is aimed at improving this process and having real-time financial data available to decisionmakers. This financial process focuses on peacetime activities, but the overall viability of the system is dependent on proper financial management in peace in order to be able to operate in war or a crisis.

Organizationally, USTRANSCOM consists of three major components: Air Mobility Command from the Air Force, Military Sealift Command from the Navy, and the Military Traffic Management Command from the Army. USTRANSCOM was created originally to operate in wartime or a crisis to coordinate and manage the deployment of forces and their equipment. In the early 1990s, the peacetime transportation responsibility was also given to USTRANSCOM. This move allowed it to organize better, operate for maximum performance, and integrate wartime training into peacetime support operations.

Change to the process controls is the other major initiative included under the Reinvention CINC umbrella. The DOD Strategic Logistics Plan states that "instituting business rules, information processes, and contracting decisions for optimal effectiveness and efficiency" are the objectives of this initiative.[14] Sound business practices and procedures are needed; the objective of these changes improved deployment and sustainment of warfighters—that is, customers.

The Defense Transportation System Enterprise Architecture is directed toward building the military transportation system of the future. The primary focus of this effort is to create an information system with a set of decision support tools (models) that will enable rapid analysis and decisions. New information technology will enable optimal use of transportation assets for deployment and sustainment.

USTRANSCOM and DLA, along with the services and DOD agencies, are improving the DOD distribution system. The Strategic Distribution Management Initiative is aimed at reducing friction between the elements of the distribution system.[15] Within the distribution system, USTRANSCOM has transportation responsibility between a designated port of embarkation and a port of debarkation ("port to port"). DLA, which has responsibility for the distribution centers, is working with USTRANSCOM to improve the flow of materials to warfighters. The CINC, representing the warfighter or customer, is currently responsible for the distribution system from a designated port of debarkation to the forward location of the warfighters ("from port to fort"). The current term for this segment of the distribution system is "reception, staging, onward movement, and integration." The CINC identifies where he or she wants forces and material delivered, where to assemble, how and by what means they will travel forward, and how the forces and material will be integrated into the existing operational structure. The Strategic Distribution Management Initiative is intended to create an integrated supply chain in which stockage decisions are integrated with storage locations, with distribution nodes such as ports and transshipment locations, and with transportation.

The above initiatives accomplish two tasks. The first is to make the daily operation of USTRANSCOM as efficient as possible so as to reduce the overall costs for the users of transportation services. Second, by examining the entire supply chain and making it more effective, USTRANSCOM, along with DLA, is improving provision of the essential sustainment support.

### Service Initiatives

Additional initiatives from the services are also aimed at enhancing the capability to deploy. The Army is fielding the Interim Armored Tactical Vehicle to be able to deploy more quickly. This vehicle provides several new enhancements related to deployability. First, the new armored vehicles are much lighter than the 30-ton Bradley or the 70-ton Abrams. Second, because they weigh less, the vehicles need less fuel to operate. Additionally, the lighter vehicles may be candidates for electric drives now being developed, which would reduce the fuel requirement further.

Research and development are coming up with new products all the time; the potential second- and third-order effects from adapting this new technology are being examined for potential further reductions in support requirements. The other services are also making changes to fielded equipment to take advantage of improved operating capability along with reduced logistical support requirements.

Several other research and development projects may have significant impact on the deployment of forces. One is the large, medium-speed dirigible that is currently being researched by several firms. If this effort is successful, then 1 million pounds could be airlifted on a single air ship traveling at 150 to 200 miles per hour. Another project is a high-speed cargo ship that would permit transportation of large military forces to be accomplished very quickly. These would be transformational changes to the deployment equation.

## Strategic Reach

Deployment considerations also raise questions of strategic reach, touching on the system of bases, departure ports, en-route support bases, arrival ports, and destination locations. These are not new issues. In a 1959 book, *Logistics in the National Defense*, Henry Eccles discussed these issues in the context of lessons learned from World War II.[16]

The deployment process begins at a home station: a base where forces are garrisoned. The deployment commences with the passing of information from the Joint Staff, to the services, to the commands, to the individual units. Information about the number of people, weight and size of equipment, support equipment, and the like is passed to USTRANSCOM and to the geographic CINC who will be relying on the forces. USTRANSCOM, in conjunction with the services and CINC, plans the movement of the forces to a port of debarkation. The first movement is thus "from the fort to the port." The USTRANSCOM Military Traffic Management Command arranges for movement via motor carrier or rail to airports or seaports; Air Mobility Command from airports; and Military Sealift Command from one seaport to another.

Several decisions must be made by USTRANSCOM and its components regarding the method of movement. Will DOD transportation equipment be used? Will equipment have to be leased or chartered? Since DOD does not own sufficient transport aircraft and ships to move forces for a major contingency, agreements have been made with the airlines and shipping firms to ensure the availability of aircraft and ships in time of crisis. This Civil Reserve Air Fleet (CRAF) has worked and enables the participating firms to receive various benefits, such as government business and operating subsidies based on added expenses to support DOD. The use of the commercial transportation system was a significant initiative in 1952, but it must now be reexamined. From a strategic standpoint, these agreements and the intent to use the commercial transportation system raise the importance of the system to a national security level. The issue related to deployment is what level of investment DOD should make in airlift and sealift assets and how to obtain the necessary lift in a crisis. A new program called VISA is modeled on the CRAF program; it ensures that space for containers will be available in crises. Both this program and CRAF must be examined continuously to ensure that they meet the deployment demands of the future. The recent relief package for the airlines is an example of the possible support that DOD must give to the airlines to keep them viable, healthy, and available for the CRAF program. Although some would question this government relief, most would agree with the decision to provide relief support to the airlines that contribute to national security.

### Strategic Bases

Another major logistical issue related to deployment is the need for strategic bases. Current aircraft technology requires that aircraft be refueled after 3,000 to 4,000 miles. Several options exist to fill this need. First, bases can be established to allow aircraft to land and be refueled. They can be military bases on U.S. territory, commercial bases on U.S. territory, or allied bases, military or commercial, that the ally has agreed to allow us to use. If the desire is not to land certain aircraft on an ally's homeland, then a tanker bridge could possibly be created using refueling aircraft. However, even tankers must be able to land and load fuel.

For sealift, the issues of concern include throughput, access, and resupply at sea. Throughput is a measure of the rate of arrival and servicing available at a port to bring materials forward to the warfighter. Access refers to the ability to use a port—that is, whether permission from some other government has been received and whether the draft of the port is adequate. Resupply at sea also presents challenges. The Navy has perfected the ability to perform underway replenishment, but the supply ships must obtain supplies (food, fuel, and repair parts) from some location in the area. Some sort of forward support base is needed to support the Navy. In *Operational Naval Logistics*, Eccles proposed an offshore, mobile, floating base that gives the Navy the capability to take its base with it anywhere the ocean allows.[17] This concept is currently reflected in the Navy with the use of aircraft carriers as landing fields for helicopters and the system of repair ships that accompany battlegroups. This concept needs further exploration.

Transformation in the area of deployment may require new technology to provide lift; new information systems to optimize deployment flow with available lift assets; and new thinking. Technology may provide the opportunity to bypass ports of debarkation and strategic bases en-route and go straight to a deployed location. New information systems can ensure optimal use of transportation assets and the tracking of forces at all times. New thinking is what will transform the deployment process and allow new operational concepts to be explored without current constraints.

## Sustainability

Sustaining deployed forces depends upon the distribution network that will transport sustainment stock along the supply chain.[18] The distribution network will in most cases be similar to the deployment network, although the nodes—ports of embarkation and debarkation—may be different. The supply chain is of critical importance since DOD split logistics responsibility requires careful coordination and cooperation. A separate but equally critical issue is that of maintaining the defense industrial base that provides critical support for sustaining the forces.

The distribution channel that leaves the factories to go to warehouses, then to the distribution centers, and onward to the forward support bases must be able to handle the requirements for the forces deployed. The capacity of the system depends on the ability of the nodes (ports) to support throughput levels sufficient to provide a constant flow of material or to build up a sufficient inventory. The current practices call for a just-in-time inventory approach, where minimal inventory levels are retained; this critically depends on assured, timely transportation. This idea is an extension of the classic inventory-transportation paradigm of building and maintaining a large inventory versus using expedited transportation to provide items when needed.

## Industry

A major area of concern for all logistics issues is the capability of industry to provide timely support to DOD. The economics of the reduction in the size of the military establishment has contributed to a real decline in the numbers of firms that manufacture defense products. The challenge for the future is how to ensure the viability of critical firms in a market that is DOD-controlled. This problem requires innovative approaches to ensuring that the American domestic defense industry remains capable of supporting the U.S. military.

The other problem area connected to industry is the globalization of world trade due to efforts of firms to find the most efficient manufacturing sources. The result is that many firms now locate manufacturing operations off shore. As more components for major systems are manufactured off shore, questions arise as to how reliable the source is and whether it can be counted on, especially in a crisis. As the transformation of our logistics operations continues, we need to ensure that efficiency does not become the sole criterion for decisions. Preservation of domestic defense industrial capability may thus require changes in acquisition regulations and laws to ensure that an adequate level of manufacturing capability is retained within the United States.

## Vulnerabilities

As the United States transforms its military logistics to focused logistics processes to support deployed forces, certain vulnerabilities may be created for those forces. The new focused logistics processes—lean logistics, velocity management, and the like—require rapid, dependable transportation; assured communications; and continuous throughput. When any of these elements are inadequate, support to the deployed forces could be jeopardized. Additionally, new operational concepts that rely on the assumption of focused logistics will be at risk when any of its enabling elements is not available.

An opponent could attack several of the enablers. Along the supply and communications chain, several weaknesses could reduce the logistics support for deployed forces. First, rapid, dependable strategic transportation must be available. This includes sealift, airlift, rail and road, pipelines for fuel distribution, and inland waterway transport. Along the first leg of the deployment—from the "fort to the port"—the communications channels and the command and control channels are vulnerable. Units and commands must have timely, accurate information for unit activation, preparation, and movement scheduling. Accurate, assured communications are essential to planning timely unit movements.

The next leg of the deployment—"from port to port"—requires use of en-route support bases for refueling, crew rest and changeout, and throughput considerations. Such bases have several vulnerable points: force protection, protection of communications, and assured availability of fuel for aircraft. Throughput considerations are critical to sealift, including the availability of ports for discharging forces, unit equipment, and sustainment stocks. There are vulnerabilities in force protection issues, assured communications, and the availability of suitable ports and facilities. Although most problem areas can be alleviated for some time period, this may not be enough: focused logistics requires the constant arrival of rapid forces and resupply to avoid a large buildup of sustainment stocks. Time is a major factor, especially when suitable infrastructure is not adequate.

The final leg of the deployment—"from the port to the fort"—is from the point of arrival to the forward location that needs support. Here there are several specific vulnerabilities, especially in transportation and communication. As units, equipment, and sustainment stocks are moved along, there is significant dependence on rails, roads, and inland waterways. The geographic CINCs, along with CINCTRANSCOM, design and develop the transportation network to ensure that CINC operational capabilities are integrated with the distribution systems.

*Joint Vision 2020* and focused logistics provide new capabilities to increase flexibility, but their vulnerabilities must be addressed. Two major areas of concern are the deployment and sustainment stages of support for deployed forces (Joint Deployment/Rapid Distribution). Other areas of focused logistics also create vulnerability, in particular the communications required in order to "trade information for inventory," maintain Joint Theater Logistics $C^2$, and provide Information Fusion. Multinational Logistics requires the support of host nations providing material, manpower, and infrastructure. Force Health Protection is required for medical regulation and care of troops. Stabilizing and evacuating injured troops can allow reductions in deployed hospital staff, support, and protection forces, but they require communications for diagnosis, rapid transportation to protected areas for treatment, and new technology to allow enhancement of treatment capabilities. Agile Infrastructure recognizes the need for ports, bases, transportation systems, and communication systems, yet vulnerabilities are created because the services or the CINC do not necessarily own and control the infrastructure.

An additional major concern is in the services' support to deployed forces. Several services, most notably the Air Force, have adopted a support concept called *reachback*. The concept recognizes the need to be able to deploy without very much support equipment or very many people, and instead to receive the necessary level of support from a secure area far away. The secure areas may be a unit's home station within the continental United States, a centralized facility within the United States, or a forward, secure main support base within or closer to a theater. This concept reduces the initial lift requirements but shifts the sustainment requirement to assured, time-definite transportation and communication links. Herein lies the vulnerability. For reachback to work, transportation must be guaranteed, and communication of logistics requirements from a forward theater to the support location must also be guaranteed. Transportation and communications are the vulnerabilities in a reachback support system.

## The Future

The fundamental logistical processes that contribute to flexibility in military strategy are those involved in generating military power, deploying military forces, and supporting military forces. Each of these three fundamental processes are subject to the frictions that arise because of organizational issues, relationships, and "seams" between organizations. We must also examine the secondary and tertiary effects of acquisition changes, engineering changes, and changes in the logistics "tradecraft." Organizational issues require the coordination and cooperation of the people involved, to ensure that the seams do not become barriers or rifts. Engineering changes provide new applications of science and manufacturing that result in products that require less support and maintenance.

Logistics will remain a comprehensive discipline in support of military operations. As DOD continues to transform its processes, it will find new ways to incorporate the best practices developed in civilian business contexts. DOD will continue to move its logistics processes closer to the Council of Logistics Management ideal: planning, implementing, controlling the efficient, effective flow of goods, services, and related information from origin to the point of consumption to meet the customer's requirement. *Joint Vision 2020* and focused logistics, along with the efforts of the services, will provide direction for transforming current logistics processes. Logistics transformation in conjunction with development of new military concepts or reassessment of old concepts must ensure that DOD has the flexibility to respond to any crisis.

## Notes

[1] Joint Publication 1–02, *Department of Defense Dictionary of Military and Associated Terms* (Washington, DC: U.S. Government Printing Office, April 2001).

[2] Ibid.

[3] Council of Logistics Management, accessed at <www.clm1.org>.

[4] See chapter 3 in this volume by Richard Kugler and Hans Binnendijk.

[5] Joint Chiefs of Staff, *Joint Vision 2020*, Focused Logistics, accessed at <www.dtic.mil/jcs/j4/projects/foclog>.

[6] 10 USC 3013, 5013, 8013.

[7] Eccles discussed the *snowball effect* that described the expansion of support forces. The concept described in the text is the inverse of the snowball effect. Henry Eccles, *Logistics in the National Defense* (Harrisburg, PA: Stackpole Company, 1959).

[8] Goals as stated in the *DOD Logistics Initiatives* of the 2001 DOD Logistics Strategic Plan, 2001, accessed at <www.acq.osd.mil/log/programs/logtransformation/log_transformation.pdf>.

[9] Ibid.

[10] Ibid.

[11] Army Strategic Logistics Plan, May 11, 2000.

[12] DLA 21 Strategic Plan 2000.

[13] DOD Logistics Strategic Plan, 2001.

[14] Ibid.

[15] USTRANSCOM Strategic Guidance FY 2002, accessed at <www.transcom.mil/J5/fy02sg.pdf>.

[16] Eccles, *Logistics in the National Defense.*

[17] Henry Eccles, *Operational Naval Logistics* (Washington, DC: U.S. Government Printing Office/Bureau of Naval Personnel, 1950).

[18] James Toth, *Military Strategy Note Theater Distribution Concepts,* ICAF Military Strategy and Logistics Note, 2001.

# About the Authors

Charles L. Barry is an independent defense consultant working in the Washington, DC, area. Among his recent publications is *Reforging the Transatlantic Relationship* (Washington, DC: National Defense University Press, 1995).

Hans Binnendijk is the Roosevelt Professor of National Security Policy at the National Defense University and director of the Center for Technology and National Security Policy. He was previously senior director of the National Security Council for defense policy and arms control and a special assistant to the President.

Paul K. Davis is a senior scientist and research leader at RAND and a professor in the RAND Graduate School. His research involves defense planning, military transformation, theories of deterrence, and advanced methods of analysis.

Michèle A. Flournoy is a senior adviser at the Center for Strategic and International Studies (CSIS). Her most recent book is *To Prevail: An American Strategy for the Campaign Against Terrorism* (Washington, DC: CSIS, 2001). She has served as a distinguished research professor at the National Defense University, and as Principal Deputy Assistant Secretary of Defense for Strategy and Threat Reduction and Deputy Assistant Secretary of Defense for Strategy in the Clinton administration.

Norman Friedman is an internationally known weapons design and development specialist. His most recent books are *Seapower and Space* (Annapolis, MD: Naval Institute Press, 2000) and *Seapower as Strategy* (Annapolis, MD: Naval Institute Press, 2001).

Jacques S. Gansler is professor and Roger C. Lipitz Chair at the Center for Public Policy and Private Enterprise, School of Public Affairs, University of Maryland. He served as Under Secretary of Defense (Acquisition, Technology, and Logistics) from 1997 to 2001.

Thomas C. Hone is the Principal Deputy Director, Program Analysis and Evaluation, Office of the Secretary of Defense.

Richard L. Kugler is distinguished research professor in the Institute for National Strategic Studies at the National Defense University. He is a defense planner and strategic analyst with over 30 years of experience in DOD and RAND. He has published 14 books and book-length reports, plus articles in *Foreign Affairs*, *Survival*, and other journals. Recently he co-edited (with Ellen Frost) *The Global Century: Globalization and National Security*, Vol. 1 and 2 (Washington, DC: National Defense University Press, 2001).

Douglas A. Macgregor is a colonel in the U.S. Army and a senior military fellow in the Institute for National Strategic Studies at the National Defense University.

Thomas L. McNaugher is vice president for the Army Research Division of the RAND Corporation, and Director of the RAND Arroyo Center, the Army's Federally funded research institute. He has also been a senior fellow in the foreign policy studies program at the Brookings Institution, specializing in U.S. military strategy and politics. Among his books are *New Weapons, Old Politics: America's Military Procurement Muddle* (Washington, DC: The Brookings Institution Press, 1989).

Mark L. Montroll is a professor of acquisition at the National Defense University's Industrial College of the Armed Forces. He teaches courses in defense acquisition and research and technology policy. In addition, he is the course director for the Shipbuilding Industry Study and manager for an annual international exchange program with the Center for Higher Education–Armaments (CHEAr) in Paris. Dr. Montroll has also served as the director of innovative technology initiatives for the Carderock Division of the Naval Surface Warfare Center.

Bruce R. Nardulli is a defense analyst at RAND, where he has worked on a variety of military studies for the U.S. Army and other services. Most recently he co-led a major study for the U.S. Army examining Operation *Allied Force,* published as *Disjointed War: Military Operations in Kosovo, 1999* (Santa Monica, CA: RAND, 2002). He also has taught at the Naval War College as a visiting professor.

Paul M. Needham is a member of the faculty of the Industrial College of the Armed Forces at the National Defense University. His publications include articles related to transportation and inventory tradeoff decisions along with examination of the Civil Reserve Air Fleet. His professional experience includes over 23 years of active duty service with the U.S. Air Force in a variety of logistics positions and as a logistics consultant working on DOD-related logistics studies.

David A. Ochmanek is a senior analyst at RAND. He has held several positions in the Federal Government, including service in the U.S. Air Force, the Department of State, and the Department of Defense. His most recent book is *The Real and the Ideal: Essays on International Relations in Honor of Richard H. Ullman* (Lanham, MD: Rowman and Littlefield, 2001).

William D. O'Neil is chief scientist of the CNA Corporation, a nonprofit research and analysis organization serving the U.S. Government. He has been a technical executive in the aerospace industry and in the Department of Defense.

Stephen P. Randolph is professor of military strategy at the National Defense University, where he directs the annual Space Industry Study conducted by the Industrial College of the Armed Forces and instructs courses in grand strategy, logistics/mobilization, and space policy.

Richard D. Sokolsky is a distinguished research fellow in the Institute for National Strategic Studies at the National Defense University and a former senior fellow at RAND. From 1990–1997 he served as the director of the Office of Strategic Policy and Negotiations in the Department of State. He is the co-author of three books, including *Persian Gulf Security: Improving Allied Military Contributions* (Santa Monica, CA: RAND, 2001), and has published numerous articles on foreign and national security policy in leading journals and newspapers. His most recent publication, "Imagining European Missile Defense," appeared in the Autumn 2001 issue of *Survival.*

Sam J. Tangredi is a captain in the U.S. Navy and a senior military fellow in the Institute for National Strategic Studies at the National Defense University, where he also served as a member of the NDU 2001 Quadrennial Defense Review Working Group. His previous assignment was as the head of the Strategy and Concepts Branch, Office of the Chief of Naval Operations. His most recent publications include *All Possible Wars? Toward a Consensus View of the Future Security Environment, 2001–2025* (Washington, DC: National Defense University Press, 2000).

F.J. ("Bing") West is the president of GAMA Corporation, a firm that conducts computer-based training for the Marine infantry. He served as Assistant Secretary of Defense in the first Reagan administration.

Peter A. Wilson is a senior political scientist at RAND who specializes in defense policy and planning research. To that end, he is the co-author of the RAND "Day After" strategic planning exercise methodology that has been used to explore major national security issues such as developing counter-proliferation investment strategies, dealing with asymmetric threats, and developing information operations plans and policies. Aside from co-authoring a variety of major RAND studies, he has authored essays on a wide range of national security issues that appeared in the Institute for National Strategic Studies *Strategic Assessment* series, the Strategic Studies Institute of the U.S. Army War College, *The Washington Quarterly*, the Progressive Policy Institute, and *Parameters.*